Essential Kanji

P. G. O'NEILL

Essential Kanji

2,000 Basic Japanese Characters
Systematically Arranged for
Learning and Reference

New York • WEATHERHILL • *Tokyo*

First edition, 1973
Eighth printing, 1983

Published by John Weatherhill, Inc., of New York and Tokyo, with editorial offices at 7–6–13 Roppongi, Minato-ku, Tokyo 106, Japan. Copyright © 1973 by P. G. O'Neill; all rights reserved. Printed in Japan.

Library of Congress Cataloging-in-Publication Data: *O'Neill, Patrick Geoffrey.* | *Essential Kanji, 2,000 basic Japanese characters systematically arranged for learning and reference.* | *1. Chinese characters—Study and teaching.* | *2. Japanese language—Study and teaching.* | *I. Title.* | *PL1171. 05* | *495.6'8'2421* | *73-2832* | *ISBN 0-8348-0082-9*

CONTENTS

PREFACE

Japanese has been described as a difficult language so often and so widely that what is meant by this is now seldom questioned. It is undeniable that such features as a large vocabulary, the constant coining of new words of all kinds, the complications of respectful forms of the language, and, to most Westerners at least, the peculiarities of idiom and sentence structure make Japanese appear a formidable opponent, particularly if, in the early stages of study, the material the student meets is not carefully controlled. Any language has its difficulties, however, and Japanese is no exception in this nor, conversely, in also having aspects, such as its pronunciation, which present very few problems to most foreign students. All in all, therefore, the Japanese language *as such* is only marginally more difficult than, say, a European language.

Where Japanese does present unique complications and difficulties is in its writing system, a combination of phonetic signs and the ideographic characters that the Japanese call *kanji* (literally, "Chinese characters"), which, as the word suggests, were originally derived from China. The learning of some hundred such phonetic signs and many hundred *kanji* constitutes a considerable barrier to the ready use of the written language, especially so since each character can have several different possible readings depending upon context, to say nothing of the quite separate problem of the characters and readings used in proper names.

Yet the spoken and written forms of Japanese are so inextricably linked that a good familiarity with characters is necessary for anything more than superficial conversation, and the practical problem therefore is how best to acquire and retain a knowledge of the written forms. This inevitably requires a great application of time and effort and there need be no end to the learning of characters, but it is important not to

7

exaggerate the difficulties of developing the ability to deal at least with the modern written language. The phonetic signs and their usage can be mastered in a couple of days and, as a result of the postwar attempts to simplify the written language, most popular publications now use no more than around two thousand *kanji*.

The core of the problem, then, is the memorization of some two thousand characters, and this is no light task, particularly if the characters are all learned as isolated items without understanding their structure, whenever and however they happen to be met in the reading of Japanese. On the other hand, the limitation of the number of characters in general use does mean that, once they and their main readings are learned, the understanding of most modern Japanese writing becomes comparable in difficulty to reading a language written in a phonetic script.

The present book therefore aims to ease the learning of the two thousand most essential characters and their main readings, and it seeks to do this in three main ways:

First, it introduces the characters systematically, in that the simpler and more common ones are given first, and the compounds illustrating the readings of a character use only the character itself and such others as have already appeared in the course. This arrangement reinforces the knowledge of characters already learned by their sporadic reappearance and makes it possible to know exactly how many characters have been covered fully at any particular time. In addition, the main-character entries have been arranged so that it is easy to test how well the characters and their readings have been remembered and how many of them can be written, by using a cut-out card to cover whichever part of the entry is to be tested. It is assumed that students will be reading Japanese material of various kinds and meeting characters in an uncontrolled fashion while using the course and that, as they progress through it, they will have the encouragement of seeing characters which they already know partially from their reading.

Second, the book makes use of the fact that the same phonetic element occurring in different characters often gives them all the same Sino-Japanese ON reading in modern Japanese. *Kanji* consisting of a radical (indicating the general area of meaning of a character) and a phonetic (indicating its sound or reading) form by far the largest group, more than three-quarters of the total number, and by showing on the introduction of a character that its phonetic has the same reading in other characters too and by grouping all these characters together under the same entry in the index of readings (Part II), the ON readings of a number of different characters can be learned at one and the same time.

Third, the index of ON and *kun* readings in Part II lists, after the main entries, characters which, because they contain similar elements, may be thought to have the same reading but which, in fact, are read differently in modern Japanese. These contrastive characters serve as warnings and, at the same time, provide reminders of what their different readings are.

Part I of the course gives both readings and vocabulary items for each character, but, of the two, the readings have been regarded as the more important. This means, for example, that where in giving words and phrases for a character a choice had to be made between a common word and a less common reading, the latter was generally chosen on the grounds that, while a common word may already be known or will be met soon anyway, a good knowledge of the varied readings of a character can save a great deal of time in looking up words in dictionaries. The basic aim of the course is to bring the student as quickly as possible to the stage where, in reading modern Japanese, he can largely dispense with the use of a character dictionary. The occasional use of such dictionaries may be unavoidable, but familiarity with the various readings of a character and increasing experience of the language will usually suggest the reading most likely in the particular context and, if the meaning is not then known, recourse can be had immediately to such dictionaries as the alphabetically arranged Kenkyūsha's *New Japanese-English Dictionary,* which gives full examples for each meaning, or to any of a number of good, phonetically arranged, Japanese-Japanese dictionaries, which give very precise definitions for each word. All too often the foreign student of Japanese confronted by a character of uncertain reading goes first to a Japanese-English character dictionary as a matter of course, and then has to decide whether to try to make do with a one-word meaning which may not seem to fit the context or, now that the reading is known, to go to another dictionary for more help; but the character dictionary is best regarded as a valuable aid during an intermediate stage which should be outgrown as quickly as possible.

The process of gradually dispensing with a character dictionary for reading modern Japanese can begin as soon as the first characters are learned and can be largely completed after two years' study of the language. In that time, it is perfectly reasonable for an average, conscientious university student to come to recognize (as distinct from write) two thousand characters and to learn their main readings, when studying them as part of a full-time Japanese course. Thereafter, this familiarity with the characters and readings used in ordinary modern Japanese can save him many hours of dictionary use and lead him to regard the written language not as an obstacle or an end in itself, but as the means by which to broaden and deepen his interest in Japan.

Finally, I should like to express my thanks for the exemplary calligraphy included in Part I, by two well-known Japanese teachers of the art. The main, brush-drawn characters are the work of the late Takatsuka Chikudō and are taken from his book *Kakikata Jiten* (How-to-Write Dictionary), published by Nobara-sha, Tokyo, 1959, and are reproduced by kind permission of Shimura Bunzō, President of Nobara-sha. The smaller, pendrawn characters have been done expressly for this book by Arayashiki Shunrai, who belongs to the same school of calligraphy as did Chikudō. I hope their fine work will be an inspiration to the users of this book, as the pleasure of writing characters well can greatly ease the task of learning them.

P. G. O'NEILL

EXPLANATORY NOTES

The main body of this book is a course in two parts. Part I contains 2,000 character entries and gives for each character three or more different forms (brush, pen, and printed forms, and where appropriate, old and variant forms also); the stroke order; the various Sino-Japanese, or ON, readings and the pure Japanese, or *kun*, readings; the modern Mandarin Chinese reading or readings, with tone markings; indications of how the character came to have its particular form, as an aid to memorization; and compound words or phrases, with meanings, to illustrate the readings of the character.

Part II lists all the ON and *kun* readings given in Part I, each followed by the character or characters having that reading and, where appropriate, by contrastive characters.

These two main parts are followed by two appendices: a list of radicals, given under the English names used for them in the course; and a list of all the characters in the course arranged according to their total stroke count, for use in finding a character when none of its readings is known.

1. CONCERNING PART I

Selection and Arrangement of Characters   The 2,000 characters treated in this book comprise six groups, all but the penultimate of which have, at one time or another, been designated as essential for everyday use by the National Language Commission organized by the Japanese Ministry of Education. The groups are given in the following order:

Nos. 1–881. The 881 basic "education characters" (*kyōiku kanji*)

Nos. 882–1822. The other 941 characters from the original list of "current-use characters" (*tōyō kanji*) remaining after the amendments proposed in 1954

Nos. 1823–50. The 28 characters proposed for addition to the *tōyō kanji* in that same year

Nos. 1851–78. The 28 characters recommended for deletion at the same time

Nos. 1879–1908. The 30 other characters which, though not in the *tōyō kanji,* are common enough to be important and have been added here to round out the total to 2,000 characters

Nos. 1909–2000. The 92 extra characters approved for use in names

The order of characters within each of these groups was decided on the basis of a number of often conflicting considerations, which varied in the importance attached to them at different stages of the course. In presenting the first two hundred characters, for example, every effort was made to introduce simple elements first, so that the student would be led gradually into the writing of the more complicated characters since, at that stage, the writing can be a problem in itself. (Virtually the only exception to this is character 14, 曜, which was introduced early so that the days of the week could be given.) From then on, generally the more common characters were introduced first, together with less common ones at times if they could be easily learned by being put into a sequence with other characters.

Readings, Compounds, and Meanings　The ON and *kun* readings given are the main ones for the characters concerned. In the case of the *tōyō kanji,* they cover those given in the official list, including those recommended by the National Language Commission in December, 1971; and the usage of the *kana* accompanying them (that is, the *okurigana*) follows the recommendations of the draft report published by the same commission in May, 1972. These readings, like the ON readings usable on their own as independent words and the compounds given for each character, are by their very nature derived from the written styles of the language and are the type of vocabulary used, for example, in newspapers and news broadcasts. Some of them are therefore not commonly heard in ordinary speech, and the English translations have been chosen to give some indication of the "feel" of the Japanese words (e.g., *Kara* has "Cathay" as its first meaning); but some care is always advisable before introducing written vocabulary into conversation.

2. KEYS TO ENTRIES IN PART I

1) BRUSH CHARACTER in stiff form (*kaisho*), with numbers showing stroke order.

2) PEN CHARACTER in stiff form.

3) OLD OR VARIANT FORM OF CHARACTER. There is no need to learn to write these forms, but since most of them were in standard use until 1947 and are still to be met from time to time, care should be taken to learn to recognize them. (These old or variant forms have been given only when they are significantly different from the main-entry forms; e.g., *tōyō kanji* containing the element ⻌ have not been shown also in their older forms in which this element has an extra stroke [辶] if this is the only difference.)

4) IDENTIFYING NUMBER for the character within the course.

5) RADICAL AND STROKE NUMBER according to *The Modern Reader's Japanese-English Character Dictionary* by Andrew N. Nelson.

6) ON READINGS, listed in descending order of importance. An asterisk against an ON reading means that it can be used as an independent word with the meaning or meanings which follow until a semicolon or the end of the entry is reached; e.g., "HON* book; . . . "

7) KUN READINGS, with the parts to be written in *kana* given in parentheses, followed by English meanings. In order to save space, wherever possible transitive and intransitive verbs and the verbal nouns derived from them are listed in the order vt./ vi./vb.n. without further identification, with an English meaning only for the transitive form. (Remember that, while a verb form will always end in *-u*, a verbal noun will end in either *-i* or *-e*.) Thus, "*yoroko(basu/bu/bi)* delight" means "*yoroko(basu)* (vt.) delight, *yoroko(bu)* (vi.) be delighted, *yoroko(bi)* (vb.n.) delight." Where only one verb form is found, the abbreviation "(vt.)" or "(vi.)" has been added when the English translation does not make clear which type it is.

The English translations have also been chosen to show whenever possible the particles normally used with the Japanese verbs: where the Japanese verb is not followed by "(vi.)" and the English has no preposition in parentheses, the particle normally used, if any, will be *o;* where the English translation ends in "(with)," the particle normally used with the Japanese verb will be *to;* where it ends in "(from)," the particle will normally be *kara;* and where the English has any other preposition in parentheses, the particle normally used in Japanese will be *ni.* If a Japanese verb is followed by "(vi.)" but the English has no word in parentheses, this means that the Japanese verb normally takes a particle other than *o* but it was not found possible to indicate this by a suitable English translation.

Thus, entries such as "*ka(u)* buy" and "*aru(ku)* walk" mean that if a particle is used with these verbs, it will normally be *o;* "*sōdan suru* consult (with)" means that *to* is the normal particle; "*na(ru)* be completed/formed (from)" means that *kara* is the normal particle in this meaning; "*nozo(mu)* face (onto), be faced (by), be present (at)" means that *ni* is the normal particle; and "*a(u)* (vi.) meet" means that a particle other than *o* is normally used but could not be indicated by a suitable translation.

Readings which are used in proper names but are not ordinary meaningful words have been put last with no following English equivalent (e.g., *yoshi* under character 1998).

8) MODERN CHINESE MANDARIN READING or readings, according to the Wade system of romanization, with superior numbers indicating the tones.

9) EXPLANATION OF CHARACTER TYPE. The usual system of divid-

ing characters into six categories (four according to the composition of the characters, and the last two according to their usage) has been followed, with an identifying letter or letters used for each category:

D = Diagrammatic or pictographic characters, which were originally simple pictures of whatever they represented; e.g., 木 tree, 月 moon, 山 mountain (showing three peaks), 川 river.

S = Symbolic characters; e.g., 一 one, 上 top, above.

I = Ideographic characters, in which two or more meaningful elements were combined to produce a derived meaning; e.g., 女 "woman" and 子 "child" were put together in the form 好 to give the meaning of "goodness, liking."

R&P = Radical-and-phonetic characters, in which a basic element known as a radical was used to indicate the general area of meaning of a character, and a phonetic element put with it to show its sound or reading; e.g., the radical 言 "words" was put with the phonetic element 丁 (read TEI in modern Japanese) to form the character 訂, and this was then used to write the word of identical pronunciation which meant "correction."

The letter R is always followed by the English meaning of the radical (see Appendix 1 for a complete list of these). The phonetic element too was usually chosen because its meaning was appropriate to that of the new character being formed and, where this helps in the learning of the character, this meaning also has been given. For example, the etymology of 糧 "RYŌ provisions" has been explained as "R rice & P* quantity."

An asterisk against the letter P means that the character has some similarity in appearance with at least one other character and that reference should therefore be made to Part II under the character's main reading (i.e., the one given first, immediately after the radical and stroke number). This Part II entry will show whether the other characters concerned also have the same reading in modern Japanese; whether they are contrastive characters which, although having some similarity in their written forms, are in fact read differently; or whether there are characters of both kinds to be noted. (Usually the similarity among the characters in question arises from a common element which is the phonetic of the characters referred to in the preceding paragraphs.)

The numbers given in some explanations of character type are either cross-references to other characters in the course (e.g., "13" under character 336) or, more often, are stroke numbers used to identify particular parts of the main character (e.g., "3–4," "1–2," and "5–8" under character 336).

E = Extended usage, in which a character was used in a meaning derived but different from its original one; e.g., 楽 musical instrument → music → pleasure.

B = Borrowed usage, in which a character was used for a meaning quite unconnected with its original one; e.g., 十, which is said to have originally represented a needle and to have been "borrowed" to write the numeral "ten."

Although these traditional categories have been used, it must be stressed that the primary aim here has been to provide aids to the memorization of the characters and their readings, not to give explanations of the etymologies of the characters for their own sakes. Authoritative explanations (most often those given in *Shinjigen,* by Ogawa et al., Kadokawa Shoten, Tokyo, 1971) have been followed as far as possible, but the presumed changes in the pronunciation and written forms of the characters over the centuries often make such explanations less than helpful in learning the readings and forms of the modern, often simplified, Japanese characters. The explanations given in the course, therefore, are based on these Japanese forms of the characters and are in many cases only mnemonics with no historical basis.

It should also be noted that the radicals indicated in the explanations of character type will not always correspond with those of the radical numbers given at the beginning of the entries, because the Nelson dictionary does not always follow the traditional system of classifying characters according to their etymology.

10) COMPOUND WORDS OR PHRASES, to illustrate the readings of the main character. These also show the printed forms of the characters.

11) READINGS AND MEANINGS of the compound words or phrases. Hyphens between parts of Japanese compound words and fairly literal English translations have been used as required to make clear the meaning of each part of a Japanese entry. For the first two hundred characters, readings of com-

pounds which are not obviously derived from those of the characters concerned and which may therefore puzzle the beginner have been marked "(ir.)" to show that they should just be accepted as irregular readings.

When the examples given are verbs, the Japanese particles normally used with them have been indicated as explained in paragraph number 7 above.

3. KEY TO ENTRIES IN PART II

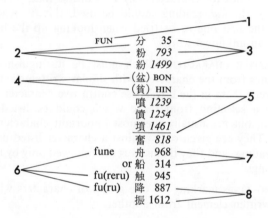

1) ON READINGS, given in small capitals.

2) CHARACTERS WITH A COMMON ELEMENT AND THE SAME READING, listed below each other without any dividing line. Characters having a common element have been grouped together only if the element is a true phonetic or if, from the point of view of learning characters, it is not misleading to regard it as such. Thus, 中, 仲, 忠, and 虫 are put together under CHŪ even though historically 中 is not a phonetic in 虫; but 頑, 顔, and 願 are kept separate even though they all have a common element and the same reading GAN, in order to avoid giving the impression that 頁 is a phonetic read GAN.

Occasionally, even within the *tōyō kanji*, identical elements have been simplified in some characters and not in others. Where these elements give the characters the same reading, they have been listed in the same group. In these few cases, therefore, characters with apparently different elements will be found put together; one reason for this is to provide reminders of the full forms of at least some of the simplified characters. Thus, 売 (formerly 賣) and 買 have been put together under BAI.

3) IDENTIFYING NUMBERS by which to find the main entries for the characters in Part I. An italic number indicates that the ON reading in question is the main reading of that character. (Above, for example, FUN is the main reading for characters 793 and 1499, but not for character 35.) This means that, unless it appears that the *kun* reading should be used, this ON reading should be the first one to be tried when looking up the likely reading of an unknown word.

4) CONTRASTIVE CHARACTERS which must be distinguished in their readings from the characters with similar written elements which precede them in the list. These contrastive characters are often only a selection from those which could be listed for comparison, but are usually the most important characters in each case. They are given only against a character listed under its main reading, and they themselves are followed only by their main readings.

5) DIVIDING LINES marking off one group of characters with a common written element from another.

6) KUN READINGS, given in lower-case roman, with the parts to be written in *kana* shown in parentheses. Related readings have been combined into single entries when the alphabetical order brings them together in the list, e.g., *kata(maru/meru)*. Note that, in the case of such pairs of verbs, the transitive form will not necessarily always appear first as it does in the Part I entries.

7) INTERCHANGEABLE CHARACTERS, i.e., characters which, having the same *kun* reading and much the same meaning, can for general purposes be used interchangeably in modern Japanese. Such characters are indicated by the use of the word "or" between them.

8) UNRELATED CHARACTERS, i.e., characters which have the same *kun* reading but differ in meaning. Such characters have been listed without any special indication.

4. How to Use This Book

This book can be used for three purposes: 1) as a course for learning characters; 2) as a means of testing one's knowledge of characters previously learned; and 3) as a reference work. The following notes are intended as a guide to the best way to use the book for each of these purposes.

As a Learning Course   If no *kanji* are known, start from the beginning of Part I; if some characters are already known, look through Part I until unknown characters begin to appear and start from there. Proceed as follows:

1)   Look carefully at each character and spend a few minutes learning its readings and meanings. See if the explanation of the character type helps in this by showing how the character came to have its particular form, readings, and meanings. If this explanation contains "P*," showing that a similar element is also found in other characters in the course, find the entry for the main reading of the character in Part II and briefly look over the related characters. By doing this, you will gradually become familiar with the readings associated with a particular phonetic element.
2)   Copy the character several times, reminding yourself the while of its readings and meanings.
3)   Learn the compound words or phrases given to illustrate the readings of the character.
4)   Continue in this way to the end of the page and then test your learning of the characters given on the *previous* page.
5)   About every ten pages or so, test your memory of the characters learned by picking pages at random and using any of the four testing methods given below.

For Testing Purposes   The arrangement of entries in Part I makes it possible to test one's knowledge of characters in any of the following ways, listed in ascending order of difficulty:

1)   Looking at the characters of a compound (3rd column, lower section), give its reading and meaning
2)   Looking at a main character and its other forms (1st and 2nd columns), give its readings and meanings

3) Looking at the readings and meanings of a main character (3rd column, top section), write the character

4) Looking at the reading and meaning of a compound (3rd column, lower section), write its characters

For convenience in testing, take a postcard measuring approximately 5 by 3 inches and cut away three areas—a CENTER SLOT, an OBLONG CORNER, and a SQUARISH CORNER—as shown in the following half-size diagram:

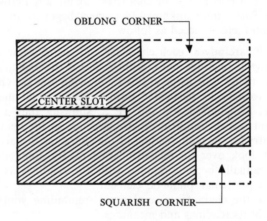

OBLONG CORNER

CENTER SLOT

SQUARISH CORNER

By turning this card as required, it can be used to cover whatever part of the character entry is being tested. When you have supplied an answer, you can verify its accuracy by moving the card down or across. The four tests listed above can be carried out as follows:

1) RECOGNITION OF COMPOUNDS. Turn the card so the center slot is at the left and place it over an entry in such a way that only the characters of a compound are visible. Supply the reading and meaning; then check by moving the card to the right.

2) READINGS AND MEANINGS OF A MAIN CHARACTER. Turn the card so the squarish corner is at the upper left and place it so that only the main character and its other forms (i.e., the two left-hand columns) are visible. Supply the various readings

and meanings of the character; then check by moving card downward.

3) WRITING A MAIN CHARACTER. Turn the card so that the oblong corner is at the upper right and place it so that only the readings and meanings of the main character are visible. Write the character; then check by moving card downward.

4) WRITING COMPOUNDS. Turn the card so that the center slot is at the right and place it so only the meaning and reading of a compound are visible. Write the characters; then check by moving card to the left.

For Reference Use If any recognized reading of the character is known, look this reading up in Part II and, using the reference number given there, find the appropriate entry in Part I.

If no reading for the character is known, look the character up in Appendix 2 according to its total stroke count and, using the reference number given there, find the entry in Part I.

5. ON THE WRITING OF CHARACTERS

Good calligraphy can normally be learned only from a good teacher, but in studying Japanese most people soon develop an eye for a well-written character and, with a little initial guidance and their own care and practice, are able to learn to write presentable characters on their own. The following suggestions will help in the early stages:

1) Use squared paper to help you keep the right proportions and spacing.
2) Follow the correct stroke order: this will make the writing easier, as the same elements reappear, and will also help you read cursive handwritten script later on.
3) Keep vertical strokes absolutely vertical.
4) Keep all "horizontal" strokes at the same angle. You will develop a natural slope with these lines and, within reason, it does not matter what this slope is, provided it is always kept the same.
5) Try using a sheet of thin paper to trace over good model characters when you are first learning to write or when you meet characters which seem particularly difficult.

6) Write each stroke slowly and deliberately, with firm control all the time. Speed and an individual style of writing will come gradually with practice.

6. ABBREVIATIONS AND SIGNS

ab.	abbreviation
adj.	adjective
B	borrowed-usage character, i.e., one used for a meaning quite unconnected with its original one
cf.	compare
D	diagrammatic or pictographic character
dep.	depreciatory
E	extended-use character, i.e., one used in a meaning derived but different from its original one
emp.	emphatic
fam.	familiar
fn.	female name
hon.	honorific
I	ideographic character, in which two or more meaningful elements are combined to produce a derived meaning
ir.	irregular
lit.	literary, literally
mn.	male name
n.	noun
neg.	negative
orig.	originally
P	phonetic element in a character
P*	a character with an element, usually its true phonetic, found in more than one character in the course, which should therefore be looked up in Part II
pn.	place name
psn.	place name and surname
pref.	prefix
q.v.	which see
R	radical of a character
S	symbolic character
sn.	surname
suf.	suffix
vb.n.	verbal noun

vi.	verb intransitive
vrt.	variant
vt.	verb transitive
*	1) used against an ON reading, indicates that the reading can be used in modern written Japanese as an independent word; 2) see P* above
( )	1) used at the end of Japanese words to show the parts to be written in *kana;* 2) encloses items which can be either included or omitted; thus, A(B) means A or AB
/	separates alternatives; thus, A/B means either A or B
→	leading to
←	derived/arising from

Part I

From Characters to Readings

一	一	1; 1/0. ICHI, ITSU, *hito(tsu)*, *hito-* one [I¹, YI¹ • S] 一 — *ichi* — one 一つ — *hitotsu* — one
二	二	2; 7/0. NI, *futa(tsu)*, *futa-* two [ERH⁴ • S] 二つ — *futatsu* — two 一つ二つ — *hitotsu futatsu* — one and/or two
三	三	3; 1/2. SAN, *mit(tsu)*, *mi(tsu)*, *mitsu-*, *mi-* three [SAN¹ • S] 三つ — *mittsu, mitsu* — three 一二三 — *ichi ni san* — one two three
人	人	4; 9/0. JIN, NIN, *hito* person [JEN² • D] 一人二人 — *hitori futari* (ir.) — one or two people 三人 — *sannin* — three people
日	日	5; 72/0. NICHI, JITSU, *hi* day, sun; *-ka* suf. for counting days [JIH⁴ • D] 一日 — *ichinichi, ichijitsu* — one day, 1st (of month); *tsuitachi* (ir.) — 1st (of month) 二日 — *futsuka* (ir.) — two days, 2nd (of month)
四	四	6; 31/2. SHI, *yot(tsu)*, *yo(tsu)*, *yo-*, *yon-* four [SSU⁴, SZU⁴ • D→B] 四人 — *yonin* — four people 四日 — *yokka (← yotsu + ka)* — four days, 4th (of month)
五	五	7; 1/3. GO, *itsu(tsu)*, *itsu-* five [WU³ • D → B] 五人 — *gonin* — five people 五日 — *itsuka* — five days, 5th (of month)
六	六	8; 8/2. ROKU, *mut(tsu)*, *mu(tsu)* six [LIU⁴ • D → B] 五六人 — *gorokunin* — five or six people 六日 — *muika* (ir.) — six days, 6th (of month)

七	七	9; 5/1. SHICHI, *nana(tsu)*, *nana-* seven [CH'I¹ • S→B] 六七日 — *rokushichinichi* — six or seven days, 6th or 7th (of month) ⌐month」 七日 — *nanoka, nanuka* (ir.) — seven days, 7th (of
八	八	10; 12/0. HACHI, HATSU, *yat(tsu)*, *ya(tsu)*, *ya-* eight [PA¹ • S→B] 七八人 — *shichihachinin* — seven or eight people 八日 — *yōka* (ir.) — eight days, 8th (of month)
九	九	11; 4/1. KYŪ, KU, *kokono(tsu)*, *kokono-* nine [CHIU³ • D→B; P*] 九人 — *kyūnin* — nine people 九日 — *kokonoka* — nine days, 9th (of month)
十	十	12; 24/0. JŪ, *tō* ten [SHIH² • D→B; P*] 十六人 — *jūrokunin* — sixteen people 十日 — *tōka* — ten days, 10th (of month)
月	月	13; 74/0. GETSU, *tsuki* moon, month; GATSU month [YÜEH⁴ • D] ⌐(of the year) 十二三カ月 — *jūnisankagetsu* — twelve or thirteen 四月 — *shigatsu* — April ⌐months
曜	曜 曜	14; 72/14. YŌ day of the week [YAO⁴ • R sun & P*] 日曜〔日〕 — *nichiyō* [*bi*] — Sunday 月曜〔日〕 — *getsuyō* [*bi*] — Monday
火	火	15; 86/0. KA, *hi* fire, flame [HUO³ • D; P*] 火曜〔日〕 — *kayō* [*bi*] — Tuesday 火と日 — *hi to hi* — fire & sun
水	水	16; 75/0. SUI, *mizu* water ⌐stream 1」 [SHUI³ • D: driblets 2–4 each side of a main 水曜〔日〕 — *suiyō* [*bi*] — Wednesday 火水 — *himizu* — fire & water, discord; *kasui* — Tuesday & Wednesday

木	木	17; 75/0. MOKU, BOKU, *ki* tree, wood [MU⁴ • D; P*] 木曜〔日〕— *mokuyō* [*bi*] — Thursday 木木 — *kigi* — every tree, many trees
金	金	18; 167/0. KIN*, KON gold; *kane* money [CHIN⁴ • R earth & P*] 月水金〔曜日〕— *gessuikin* [*yōbi*] — Monday, Wednesday & Friday 「money 金のある人 — *kane no aru hito* — a person with
土	土	19; 32/0. DO, TO, *tsuchi* earth, ground [TU³ • D: mound of earth] 火木土〔曜日〕— *kamokudo* [*yōbi*] (ir.) — Tuesday, Thursday & Saturday 「on the moon 月にある土 — *tsuki ni aru tsuchi* — the earth/soil
本	本	20; 2/4. HON* book; unit for counting cylindrical objects; *moto* source, origin [PEN³ • D & S: line at base of tree trunk; P*] 日本 — *Nihon / Nippon* (ir.) — Japan 六本木 — *Roppongi (← roku + hon + ki)* — pn.
山	山	21; 46/0. SAN, *yama* mountain [SHAN¹ • D: three peaks] 火山 — *kazan* — volcano 山水 — *yamamizu* — mountain water; *sansui* — mountains & water, landscape
目	目	22; 109/0. MOKU, BOKU, *me* eye; -*me* ordinal suf. [MU⁴ • D: an eye (originally drawn horizontally); 一目 — *hitome/ichimoku* — one look/glance ⌊P*] 人の目 — *hito no me* — a person's eye
見	見	23; 147/0. KEN, *mi(ru)* see; *mi(seru)* show [CHIEN⁴ • I: a man 6–7 surmounted by a big eye; 一見 — *ikken* — one look/glance ⌊P*] 月を見る人 — *tsuki o miru hito* — a person who looks at the moon
行	行	24; 144/0. KŌ, AN, *i(ku)*, *yu(ku)* go; *oko(nau)* carry out; GYŌ* line 「to & fro; P*] [HSING² • D: crossroads, where many people go 八九行 — *hachikugyō* — eight or nine lines 月見に行く — *tsukimi ni iku* — go moon-viewing

29

来	来	25; 4/6. RAI, *ku(ru)* come [LAI[2] • D→B] 来月 — *raigetsu* — next month 日本に来た人 — *Nihon ni kita hito* — a person who came to Japan
方	方	26; 70/0. HŌ* direction, side; *kata* side, way of [FANG[1] • D; P*] ⌐ — ing, person (hon.) 四方 — *shihō* — all [the 4] directions 見方 — *mikata* — way of looking, viewpoint
東	東	27; 4/7. TŌ, *higashi* east [TUNG[1] • I: the sun rising behind a tree; P*] 東方 — *tōhō* — [the] east 東の方 — *higashi no hō* — eastward 東山 — *Higashiyama* — psn.
西	西	28; 146/0. SEI, SAI, *nishi* west [HSI[1] • D B; P*] 西方 — *seihō* — [the] west 東西 — *tōzai* — east & west 西山 — *Nishiyama* — psn.
上	上	29; 25/1. JŌ, SHŌ, *ue* top; *a(geru/garu)* raise; *nobo-(ru)* go up to the capital; *kami* upper part [SHANG[4] • S] 水上で/に — *suijō de/ni* — on the water 上人 — *shōnin* — saint 目上の方 — *meue no kata* — a superior/senior
下	下	30; 1/2. KA, GE, *shita* bottom; *sa(geru/garu)* lower, move back; *ku(daru)* go down; *o(rosu)* lower, put down; *o(riru)* get down; *shimo* lower part [HSIA[4] • S] 目下 — *mokka* — at present 目下の人 — *meshita no hito* — an inferior/junior
中	中	31; 2/3. CHŪ, *naka* middle, inside; *-jū* throughout [CHUNG[1,4] • S: an object pierced dead center; P*] 日本中 — *Nihonjū* — throughout Japan ⌐tains 山中 — *Yamanaka* — psn.; *sanchū* — in the moun-
大	大	32; 37/0. DAI, TAI, *ō(kii)*, *ō(ki na)* big; *ō(i ni)* greatly ⌐P*] [TA[4] • D: a man with arms & legs spread wide; 大目に見る — *ōme ni miru* — overlook, let pass 大水 — *ōmizu* — flood

小	小	33; 42/0. SHŌ, *chii(sai)*, *ko-*, *o-* small [HSIAO³ • S: originally a triangle of three small 大小 — *daishō* — big & small, size ⌐marks; P*] 小山 — *koyama* — hill, psn.
刀	刀	34; 18/0. TŌ*, *katana* sword; knife [TAO¹ • D; P*] 日本刀 — *Nihontō* — the Japanese sword 小刀 — *kogatana* — (pocket) knife; *shōtō* — small sword
分	分	35; 12/2. BUN* share, lot; *wa(keru)* divide; *wa-* *(kareru)* be divided; *wa(karu)* be clear; BU* rate, part; FUN* minute (of time) [FEN¹,⁴ • I: a divided top and a knife; P*] 三分の一 — *sanbun no ichi* — one-third 二十五分 — *nijūgofun* — 25 minutes
切	切	36; 18/2. SETSU, SAI, *ki(ru)* cut [CH'IEH¹ • R knife & P*] 大切な — *taisetsu na* — important ⌐sword 刀で切る — *katana de kiru* — cut down/off with a
手	手	37; 64/0. SHU, *te* hand [SHOU³ • D; P*] 上手な — *jōzu na* (← *jō* + *shu*) — skillful 切手 — *kitte* (← *kiri* + *te*) — postage stamp
口	口	38; 30/0. KŌ, KU, *kuchi* mouth [K'OU³ • D; P*] 人口 — *jinkō* — population 人の口 — *hito no kuchi* — a person's mouth
入	入	39; 11/0. NYŪ, *hai(ru)* enter; *i(reru)* put/let in; *i(ri)* entering [JU⁴ • D: two roots going into the earth] 金入れ — *kaneire* — money-box, purse, wallet 入口 — *iriguchi* — entrance
出	出	40; 2/4. SHUTSU, SUI, *da(su)* put/bring/take out; [CH'U¹ • I; P*] ⌐*de(ru)* go/come out 出〔入〕口 — *de[iri]guchi* — exit [& entrance] 出来る — *dekiru* — be possible/completed

川	川	41; 47/0. SEN, *kawa* river 「P*] [CH'UAN[1] • D: river flowing between two banks; 川口 — *kawaguchi* — river mouth, psn. 川下り — *kawakudari* — river descent
外	外	42; 36/2. GAI foreign; GE, *soto* outside; *hoka* other; *hazu(su/reru)* remove, undo [WAI[4] • R divination & P] 外人 — *gaijin* — foreigner 外へ出る — *soto e deru* — go outside
言	言	43; 149/0. GEN*, GON, -*koto*- word; *i(u)/yu(u)* say [YEN[2] • D: words issuing from the mouth; P*] 方言 — *hōgen* — dialect 小言を言う — *kogoto o iu* — scold, complain
貝	貝	44; 154/0. *kai* (sea) shell [PEI[4] • D] 川の貝 — *kawa no kai* — river shell 「water 水の中の貝 — *mizu no naka no kai* — shells in the
寺	寺	45; 32/3. JI, *tera* temple [SSU[4], SZU[4] • I; P*] 東大寺 — *Tōdaiji* — pn. 山寺 — *yamadera* — mountain temple
時	時	46; 72/6. JI, *toki* time [SHIH[2] • R sun & P*] 七時 — *shichiji* — seven o'clock 時時 — *tokidoki* — sometimes
売	売 賣	47; 32/4. BAI, *u(ru)* sell [MAI[4] • I; P*] 売手 — *urite* — seller 売出し — *uridashi* — sale
買	買	48; 122/7. BAI, *ka(u)* buy [MAI[3] • I: shell/money 6–12 & net (= catch, obtain) 1–5 → buy; P*] 売買 — *baibai* — buying & selling 買手 — *kaite* — buyer

主	主	49; 8/3. SHU, SU, *nushi* master, owner; *omo (na)* main; *shu (to shite)* mainly [CHU³ · D→E: flame 1 of holy light 2–5 → its guardian → master; P*] 主人 — *shujin* — master, husband 買い主 — *kainushi* — buyer
持	持	50; 64/6. JI, *mo(tsu)* have, hold, last [CH'IH³ · R hand & P*] 持ち主 — *mochinushi* — owner 持って来る — *motte kuru* — bring
夫	夫	51; 4/3. FU, FŪ, *otto* husband [FU¹ · D & S: an adult 2–4 & a man's hatpin 1 = a fully grown man; P*] 人夫 — *ninpu* — laborer, coolie 夫人 — *fujin* — married lady, Mrs.
田	田	52; 102/0. DEN, *ta* rice field [T'IEN² · D: fields surrounded by footpaths; P*] 水田の水 — *suiden no mizu* — water in the rice field 本田 — *Honda* — sn.
力	力	53; 19/0. RYOKU, RIKI, *chikara* strength [LI⁴ · D: muscular arm; P*] 主力 — *shuryoku* — main strength/force 力を入れて — *chikara o irete* — vigorously
車	車	54; 159/0. SHA, *kuruma* vehicle, wheel [CH'E¹ · D: plan view of two-wheeled carriage with central axle; P*] 人力車 — *jinrikisha* — rickshaw 水車 — *mizuguruma/suisha* — water wheel
読	読 讀	55; 149/7. DOKU, TOKU, TŌ, *yo(mu)* read [TU² · R words & P*] 読本 — *tokuhon* — school reader 本を読む人 — *hon o yomu hito* — a person who reads a book
者	者 者	56; 125/4. SHA, *mono* (dep.) person [CHE³ · I→B; P*] 目下の者 — *meshita no mono* — an inferior/junior 読者 — *dokusha* — reader

林	林	57; 75/4. RIN, *hayashi* a wood [LIN² · I; P*] 山林 — *sanrin* — mountain [&] forest 林の外 — *hayashi no soto* — outside the forest
明	明	58; 72/4. MEI, MYŌ, *aka(rui)*, *aki(raka na)* bright; *a(keru)* to dawn; *a(kasu)* pass the night, divulge [MING² · I: sun & moon together; P*] 明日 — *myōnichi/asu, ashita* — tomorrow 明け方 — *akegata* — (early) dawn
士	士	59; 33/0. SHI man, samurai, retainer [SHIH⁴ · D→B; P*] 士分 — *shibun* — samurai status/class 力士 — *rikishi* — wrestler
自	自	60; 132/0. JI, SHI, *mizuka(ra)* oneself, in person [TZU⁴ · D: a nose → oneself; P*] 自分 — *jibun* — oneself 自力 — *jiriki* — one's own strength/efforts
子	子	61; 39/0. SHI, SU, *ko* child; -*shi* person [TZU³ · D: baby with big head & slender arms & legs; P*] 分子 — *bunshi* — molecule; element, group 売子 — *uriko* — salesman, salesgirl
女	女	62; 38/0. JO, NYO, *onna* woman; *me*- female [NÜ³ · D: a kneeling woman with arms crossed 女子 — *joshi* — woman ⌐over her knees; P*] 女主人 — *onna shujin* — proprietress
男	男	63; 102/2. DAN, NAN, *otoko* man [NAN² · I: field & strength = man; P*] 男子 — *danshi* — man 男の子 — *otoko no ko* — boy
年	年	64; 4/5. NEN, *toshi* year [NIEN² · R grain & P] 来年 — *rainen* — next year 年上の — *toshiue no* — older

先	先	65; 10/4. SEN, *saki* prior, previous, future, (pointed) ⌐tip [HSIEN[1,4] · I; P*] 先日 — *senjitsu* — the other day 行き先 — *yukisaki* — destination
学	学 學	66; 39/5. GAKU* learning, study; *mana(bu)* learn [HSIAO[2] · R child & P*] 入学する —*nyūgaku suru*—enter school/university 見学する — *kengaku suru* — watch & learn, make study visit
生	生	67; 100/0. SEI*, SHŌ life; *u(mu)* give birth to; *u(mareru)* be born; *i(kiru)* be alive; *ha(yasu/eru)*, *o(u)* (vi.) grow; *nama* raw; *ki-* pure, undiluted [SHENG[1] · D & S: plant growing above ground; P*] 先生 — *sensei* — teacher 学生 — *gakusei* — student
竹	竹	68; 118/0. CHIKU, *take* bamboo ⌐side; P*] [CHU[2] · D: two bamboo stems growing side by 竹林 — *chikurin/takebayashi* — bamboo forest 竹で出来た — *take de dekita* — made of bamboo
筆	筆	69; 118/6. HITSU, *fude* writing brush [PEI[3] · I: bamboo & writing 7–12 = bamboo-handled writing brush; P*] 筆者 — *hissha* — writer, calligrapher 筆先 — *fudesaki* — brush point
書	書	70; 129/4. SHO, *ka(ku)* write [SHU[4] · R writing & P] 読書する — *dokusho suru* — read (books) 書き方 — *kakikata* — way of writing
文	文	71; 67/0. BUN, MON writing, letters; *fumi* letter [WEN[2] · D: a robe crossed over the chest 3–4→ weave, pattern → mark, sign; P*] 文明 — *bunmei* — civilization 文学 — *bungaku* — literature
立	立	72; 117/0. RITSU, RYŪ, *ta(tsu/chi)* stand, depart; *ta(teru)* set up ⌐P*] [LI[4] · D: a man standing 1–4 on the ground 5; 中立者 — *chūritsusha* — a neutral 立ち上がる —*tachi-agaru* — stand up

事	事	73; 6/7. JI, *koto* matter, thing [SHIH⁴ · I]　　　　　　　　　　「the year, annual events 年中行事 — *nenjū gyōji* — ceremonies throughout 出来事 — *dekigoto* — event, happening
物	物	74; 93/4. BUTSU, MOTSU, *mono* thing, object [WU⁴ · I: cut/butcher 5–8 an ox 1–4 = sacrificial offering → thing, object] 見物 — *kenbutsu* — sight-seeing 買物 — *kaimono* — shopping
仕	仕	75; 9/3. SHI, *tsuka(eru)* serve　　　　　「man & P*] [SHIH⁴ · I: a man 1–2 & retainer = serve; also R 仕事 — *shigoto* — work 仕上げる — *shi-ageru* — finish
化	化	76; 9/2. KA, KE, *ba(keru)* change one's form; *ba-* *(kasu)* bewitch　　　　　　　　「change; P*] [HUA⁴ · I: a man 1–2 in deformed shape 3–4 = 化学 — *kagaku* — chemistry 文化 — *bunka* — culture
工	工	77; 48/0. KŌ, KU construction [KUNG¹ · D: ancient carpenter's square; P*] 工夫 — *kōfu* — workman; 　　　*kufū* — device, scheme　　「it-yourself man 日曜大工 — *nichiyō daiku* — Sunday carpenter, do-
天	天	78; 1/3. TEN, *ame* heavens, sky [T'IEN¹ · D: the heavens 1 over man 2–4; P*] 天火 — *tenpi* — oven; 　　　*tenka* — fire caused by lightning 天文学 — *tenmongaku* — astronomy
白	白	79; 106/0. HAKU, BYAKU, *shiro, shiro(i)* white [PAI² · D & S: the first small sign 1 of the sun 2–5 = the white of early dawn; P*] 白人 — *hakujin* — white man 白木 — *shiraki* (ir.) — white/plain wood
心	心	80; 61/0. SHIN, *kokoro* heart, spirit [HSIN¹ · D; P*] 中心 — *chūshin* — center 心が大きい — *kokoro ga ōkii* — big-hearted

史	史	81; 2/4. SHI history, annals [SHIH³ • I; P*] 文化史 — *bunkashi* — cultural history 文学史 — *bungakushi* — history of literature
百	百	82; 1/5. HYAKU* hundred [PAI³ • R one (= number) & P*] 百年先の事 — *hyakunen-saki no koto* — something 　　　　　　　　　　　　　　　100 years ahead 三百分の九 — *sanbyakubun no kyū* — 9/300
千	千	83; 4/2. SEN*, *chi* thousand [CH'IEN¹ • R ten (= number) & P*] 竹千三百本 — *take sensanbyakuhon* — 1,300 pieces 千切る — *chigiru* — cut up finely　　　⌊of bamboo
万	万 萬	84; 1/2. MAN* ten thousand; BAN many, all [WAN⁴ • D (of scorpion) → B] 万年筆 — *mannenhitsu* — fountain pen 万物 — *banbutsu* — all things/creation
代	代	85; 9/3. DAI* generation, price; TAI, *ka(waru/wari)* take the place (of); *yo* generation, age; *shiro* price, [TAI⁴ • R man & P*]　　　　　　　　　⌊substitute 代代 — *daidai/yoyo* — for generations, hereditary 代る代る — *kawarugawaru* — alternately
交	交	86; 8/4. KŌ, *ma(jiru)* become mixed (in among); *maji(eru)* mix; *maji(waru/wari)* associate (with); *kawa(su)* exchange (talk, etc.) [CHIAO¹ • D: man with legs crossed; P*] 交代で — *kōtai de* — by turns, alternately 外交 — *gaikō* — diplomacy
左	左	87; 48/2. SA, *hidari* left [TSO³ • I: the left hand 1–2 holding a tool 3–5; 左方 — *sahō* — the left　　　　　　　　　⌊P*] 左手 — *hidarite* — left hand, the left
右	右	88; 30/2. YŪ, U, *migi* right [YU⁴ • I: the hand 1–2 which goes to the mouth 3–5 in eating; P*]　　　　　　　　　　⌈dominate 左右 — *sayū* — left & right; *sayū suru* — control, 右手 — *migite* — right hand, the right

母	母	89; 80/0. BO, *haha* mother 「P*] [MU³ · D: a woman 1–2 & 5 with nipples 3–4; 母子 — *boshi* — mother & child; principal & interest お母さん — *okāsan* — (hon.) mother
父	父	90; 88/0. FU, *chichi* father [FU⁴ · I: a hand 2–4 holding a stick 1 = parental authority; P*] 父母 — *fubo, chichi-haha* — father & mother お父さん — *otōsan* — (hon.) father
校	校	91; 75/6. KŌ school, correction [HSIAO⁴, CHIAO⁴ · R tree & P*] 学校 — *gakkō* — school 小学校 — *shōgakkō* — primary school
毎	毎 每	92; 80/2. MAI every [MEI³ · D & S; P*] 毎日 — *mainichi* — every day 毎月 — *maigetsu/maitsuki* — every month
古	古	93; 24/3. KO, *furu(i)* old [KU³ · S: the sayings of ten 1–2 mouths (= generations) 3–5 = traditional, ancient; P*] 古代 — *kodai* — ancient times 古本 — *furuhon* — secondhand book
今	今	94; 9/2. KON, KIN, *ima* now [CHIN¹ · I; P*] 古今東西 — *kokon tōzai* — all ages & places 今日 — *kyō, konnichi* — today
思	思	95; 102/4. SHI, *omo(u)* think, feel [SSU¹, SZU¹ · I: head/brain 1–5 & heart 6–9; P*] 思いの外 — *omoi no hoka* — unexpectedly 思い出す — *omoi-dasu* — recall
当	当 當	96; 42/3. TŌ, *a(teru)* apply, guess; *a(taru)* hit the [TANG¹,⁴ · R field & P] ⌊mark 本当 — *hontō* — truth 日当りで — *hiatari de* — in the sun(shine)

	相	97; 75/5. sō* aspect, phase; shō government minister; *ai* mutual [HSIANG¹ · R eye & P*] 相当 — *sōtō na* — suitable, adequate, considerable 相手〔方〕— *aite[kata]* — opposite number, opponent
	安	98; 40/3. an peace, calm; *yasu(i)* cheap; *-yasu(i)* (vb. suf.) easy to [AN¹ · I: a woman under the home roof = peace; P*] 安心 — *anshin* — peace of mind 安売り — *yasuuri* — selling cheaply
	海	99; 85/6. kai, *umi* sea [HAI³ · R water & P*] 海水 — *kaisui* — sea water 海相 — *kaishō* — Navy Minister
	軍	100; 14/7. gun* army, military force [CHÜN¹ · I: military vehicles 3–9 within a compound 1–2; P*] 軍事 — *gunji* — military (affairs) 海軍 — *kaigun* — navy
	里	101; 166/0. ri* old linear unit [2.44 miles]; *sato* village, native place [LI³ · I: fields 1–5 & earth 5–7 = village; P*] 千里 — *senri* — 1,000 *ri*, a great distance 海里 — *kairi* — nautical mile
	石	102; 112/0. seki, shaku, *ishi* stone; *koku* unit of capacity [4.9629 bushels] [SHIH² · I: a rock 3–5 at the foot of a cliff 1–2; P*] 石化 — *sekka* — petrifaction 小石 — *koishi* — pebble
	玉	103; 96/0. gyoku, *tama* jewel [YÜ⁴ · D: jade jewels 1 & 3–4 on a thread 2, with an extra dot 5 (to distinguish from 310); P*] 玉子 — *tamago* — egg; budding expert 玉石 — *gyokuseki* — jewels & stones; *tamaishi* — pebble
	理	104; 96/7. ri* reason, principle [LI³ · R jewel & P*] 心理 — *shinri* — mental state, mentality 物理学 — *butsurigaku* — physics

門	門	105; 169/0. MON*, *kado* gate [MEN² • D; P*] 石門 — *sekimon* — stone gate 門出する — *kadode suru* — depart, leave home
元	元	106; 7/2. GEN* Yüan [China]; GAN, *moto* source, origin ⌈basis, source; P*] [YÜAN² • I: the top part 1–2 of a man 3–4 = 元年 — *gannen* — first year of a reign 元金 — *gankin/motokin* — capital, principal
耳	耳	107; 128/0. JI, *mimi* ear [ERH³ • D] 耳目 — *jimoku* — eyes & ears; one's attention 耳元で — *mimimoto de* — around the ears
取	取	108; 128/2. SHU, *to(ru)* take ⌈1–6; P*] [CHÜ³ • I: a hand 7–8 taking someone by the ear 書き取り — *kakitori* — writing down, dictation 取り交ぜる — *tori-mazeru* — mix together
聞	聞	109; 169/6. BUN, MON, *ki(ku)* hear, ask about, heed; *ki(koeru)* be audible [WEN² • I: an ear at the entrance 1–8 listening; 聞き手 — *kikite* — listener ⌊also R ear & P*] 聞き耳を立てる — *kikimimi o tateru* — prick up one's ears, listen attentively
用	用	110; 101/0. YŌ* business, errand; *mochi(iru)* use [YUNG⁴ • D: three-legged bronze vessel used for offerings; P*] 男子用 — *danshi-yō* — for use by men 火の用心 — *hi no yōjin* — precautions against fire, beware of fire
国	国 國	111; 31/5. KOKU, *kuni* country ⌈1–2 & 8; P*] [KUO² • I: a region 3–7 surrounded by borders 外国 — *gaikoku* — foreign country 国国 — *kuniguni* — countries, nations
米	米	112; 119/0. BEI America; MAI, *kome* uncooked rice [MI³ • D: an ear of rice, etc., with the stem 3 & three grains each side 1–2 & 4–6; P*] 米国 — *Beikoku* — America 外米 — *gaimai* — foreign rice

糸	糸 絲	113; 120/0. SHI, *ito* thread [SSU[1], SZU[1] • D: twisted silk threads 4–6 below the cocoons 1–3; P*] 糸口 — *itoguchi* — thread end; lead, clue 糸物 — *itomono* — haberdashery
雨	雨	114; 173/0. U, *ame* rain ⌈below the sky 1⌉ [YÜ[3] • D: raindrops 5–8 falling from clouds 2–4 雨天ならば — *uten naraba* — if it is rainy 小雨 — *kosame* (ir.) — light rain, drizzle
支	支	115; 65/0. SHI branch; *sasa(eru)* support [CHIH[1] • I: a hand 3–4 holding a branch 1–2 for 支出 — *shishutsu* — expenditure ⌊support; P*⌋ 支持する — *shiji suru* — support
会	会 會	116; 9/4. KAI* meeting, society; E, *a(u)* (vi.) meet [HUI[4] • I: a lid 1–3 & the pot 4–6 which it meets & joins; P*] 国会 — *Kokkai* — the Diet, National Assembly 出会う — *deau* — chance (upon), run (into)
早	早	117; 72/2. SŌ, SATSU-, *haya(i)* early, fast [TSAO[3] • I: the sun 1–4 just above the grass 5–6 in the early morning; P*] 来月早早 — *raigetsu sōsō* — early next month 早目に — *hayame ni* — ahead of/in good time
草	草	118; 140/6. SŌ, *kusa* grass [TS'AO[3] • R grass & P*] 草書 — *sōsho* — cursive/running hand 草取り — *kusatori* — weeding [tool]
市	市	119; 8/3. SHI* city; *ichi* market [SHIH[4] • I; P*] 市立大学 — *shiritsu daigaku* — municipal university 四日市 — *Yokkaichi* — pn.
姉	姉	120; 38/5. SHI, *ane* elder sister [TZU[3] • R woman & P*] 姉の主人 — *ane no shujin* — elder sister's husband 姉さん — *nēsan* — elder sister; waitress

字	字	121; 40/3. JI* character, letter; *aza* village sector [TZU⁴ · I: a child under a roof, i.e., indoors, studying characters; P*] 文字 — *moji* — character, letter 「characters 字が読める — *ji ga yomeru* — be able to read
位	位	122; 9/5. I, *kurai* grade, rank; *-kurai* or so, about [WEI⁴ · I: a man's 1–2 standing 3–7; P*] 学位 — *gakui* — academic degree 位取り — *kuraidori* — grade, class; unit
正	正	123; 1/4. SEI, SHŌ, *tada(shii)* correct; *masa (ni)* exactly, certainly 「right; P*] [CHENG⁴ · I: a foot 2–5 toeing the line 1, exactly 正月 — *shōgatsu* — the New Year, January 「ior 正しい行ない — *tadashii okonai* — correct behav-
政	政	124; 66/5. SEI, SHŌ, *matsurigoto* administration [CHENG⁴ · I: correction 1–5 by hand 7–9 wielding a rod 6; also R rap & P*] 行政 — *gyōsei* — administration 市政 — *shisei* — municipal administration
毛	毛	125; 82/0. MŌ, *ke* hair [MAO² · D: hair/fur growing; P*] 毛筆 — *mōhitsu* — [hair] writing/painting brush 毛糸 — *keito* — woolen thread
戸	戸	126; 63/0. KO, *to* door [HU⁴ · D: cf. left half of 105; P*] 戸外へ出る — *kogai e deru* — go out of doors 雨戸 — *amado* (ir.) — shutters
近	近	127; 162/4. KIN, *chika(i)* near [CHIN⁴ · R proceed & P*] 近代化する — *kindaika suru* — modernize 手近な — *tejika na* — nearby, handy
野	野	128; 166/4. YA, *no* moor, field [YEH³ · R village & P*] 野生 — *yasei* — wild, uncultivated 上野 — *Ueno* — psn.

少	少	129; 4/3. SHŌ, *suko(shi)* a little; *suku(nai)* few, little ⌜P*⌝ [SHAO³ • I: small 1–3 & one (= number) 4 = few; 少年文学 — *shōnen bungaku* — juvenile/children's literature 手が少ない — *te ga sukunai* — be shorthanded
不	不	130; 1/3. FU, BU (neg. pref.) [PU², ⁴ • S: bird flying up 2–4 but unable to reach ⌞the sky 1; P*⌟ 不安 — *fuan* — uneasiness 不当な — *futō na* — unjust, unreasonable
名	名	131; 36/3. MEI, MYŌ, *na* name, fame [MING² • I: in the evening darkness 1–3 one calls out 4–6 one's name; P*] 名物 — *meibutsu* — noted product, speciality 大名 — *daimyō* — feudal lord
内	内 内	132; 2/3. NAI, DAI, *uchi* inside, within, among, home [NEI⁴ • I: entering 3–4 a house 1–2; P*] 国内 — *kokunai* — within a country, internal 近い内に — *chikai uchi ni* — in the near future
虫	虫 蟲	133; 142/0. CHŪ, *mushi* insect [CH'UNG² • D: big-headed snake (tripled = any ⌞tiny animal); P*⌟ 毛虫 — *kemushi* — caterpillar 水虫 — *mizu-mushi* — water-insect; athlete's foot
風	風	134; 182/0. FŪ, FU, *kaze* wind [FENG¹ • insects shut themselves up (cf. 1338) when the wind comes; P*] 風土 — *fūdo* — regional features/climate 風上の — *kazakami no* (ir.) — windward
足	足	135; 157/0. SOKU, *ashi* foot, leg; *ta(riru)* be sufficient ⌜= the lower leg; P*⌝ [TSU², CHÜ⁴ • the shin 1–3 & foot (cf. 552) 4–7] 不足 — *fusoku* — insufficiency 人足 — *hitoashi* — pedestrian traffic, passersby; *ninsoku* — coolie
平	平	136; 1/4. HEI, BYŌ, *tai(ra na)*, *hira(tai)* even, level, flat ⌜surface of water 4; P*⌝ [P'ING² • D: water plant 1–3 with root 5, on level 平野 — *heiya* — plain; *Hirano* — psn. 不平 — *fuhei* — discontent, complaint

所	所	137; 63/4. SHO, *tokoro* place [SO³ • R axe & P→B] 名所 — *meisho* — famous place 所所 — *tokorodokoro* — in places, here & there
首	首	138; 185/0. SHU head, unit for counting poems; *kubi* neck ⌈1–3 = head → neck; P*⌉ [SHOU³ • D: the nose (cf. 60) 4–9 with hair above 首相 — *shushō* — Prime Minister 首になる — *kubi ni naru* — get the sack
前	前	139; 12/7. ZEN, *mae* before, in front of, previous [CH'IEN² • I] 事前の — *jizen no* — before the event, prior 名前 — *namae* — name
午	午	140; 4/3. GO, noon [WU³ • D→B; P*] 午前 — *gozen* — morning, a.m. 正午 — *shōgo* — noon
道	道	141; 162/9. DŌ, TŌ, *michi* road, way, path [TAO⁴ • I: the head 1–9 of an advance 10–12 finds the way; P*] 国道 — *kokudō* — national highway 近道 — *chikamichi* — short cut
馬	馬	142; 187/0. BA, MA, *uma* horse [MA³ • D: a horse's head 1–3, mane 4–5, back & tail 6, & legs 7–10; P*] 馬力 — *bariki* — horsepower, cart 竹馬 — *takeuma/chikuba* — stilts, bamboo horse
地	地	143; 32/3. CHI*, JI* earth, ground [TI⁴ • R earth & P*] 土地 — *tochi* — land 地元 — *jimoto* — locality, home area
気	気 氣	144; 84/2. KI, KE spirit ⌈rice 5–6; P*⌉ [CH'I⁴ • I: the vapour 1–4 rising from cooking 気持ち — *kimochi* — feeling, mood 天気 — *tenki* — weather

病	病	145; 104/5. BYŌ, HEI, *ya(mu)* be ill with, suffer [PING⁴ • R illness & P*] ⌊from; *yamai* illness 病人 — *byōnin* — sick person 病気 — *byōki* — illness
品	品 品	146; 30/6. HIN* refinement, elegance; *shina* goods [P'IN³ • I: three similar goods → quality; P*] 学用品 — *gakuyōhin* — school goods, student sup- 品物 — *shinamono* — goods ⌊plies
作	作	147; 9/5. SAKU, SA, *tsuku(ru)* make [TSO⁴ • R man & P*] 作品 — *sakuhin* — a (literary, etc.) work 作り病 — *tsukuri-yamai* — fake illness
昨	昨	148; 72/5. SAKU yester-, the past [TSO² • R sun & P*] 昨日 — *kinō/sakujitsu* — yesterday 一昨年 — *issakunen/ototoshi* — year before last
信	信	149; 9/7. SHIN* trust, faith; *shin(zuru)* believe/ trust in [HSIN⁴ • I: a man standing by his word; P*] 信用 — *shin'yō* — trust, reliance 自信 — *jishin* — self-confidence
半	半	150; 3/4. HAN, *naka(ba)* half, middle of (period of time) ⌈half; P*] [PAN⁴ • I: an ox 3–6 (for 534) split in two 1–2→ 半分 — *hanbun* — half 前半 — *zenhan* — first half
家	家	151; 40/7. KA, KE, *ie, ya* house, home [CHIA¹ • I: a pig 4–10 under a roof; P*] 家政 — *kasei* — household management 海の家 — *umi no ie* — seaside [summer] house
森	森	152; 75/8. SHIN, *mori* a wood, grove [SHEN¹ • I: P*] 森林 — *shinrin* — forest, wood 森の中 — *mori no naka* — in the woods

休	休	153; 9/4. KYŪ, *yasu(mu/mi)* rest, take a holiday [HSIU¹ · I: a man beside a tree, resting; P*] 休日 — *kyūjitsu* — holiday, shop closing day 土地を休める — *tochi o yasumeru* — rest land, leave land fallow
村	村	154; 75/3. SON, *mura* village [TS'UN¹ · R tree & P*] 山村 — *sanson* — mountain village; *Yamamura* — 村人 — *murabito* — villager ⌐psn.
長	長	155; 168/0. CHŌ* head, leader; *naga(i)* long [CHANG³ · D: long hair tied & clipped back; P*] 長男 — *chōnan* — eldest son 校長 — *kōchō* — headmaster
北	北	156; 21/3. HOKU, *kita* north [PEI³ · I: two men back to back → face away from (the sunless north); P*] 東北 — *tōhoku* — northeast [region of Japan] 北西の風 — *hokusei no kaze* — a northwest wind
南	南	157; 24/7. NAN, NA, *minami* south [NAN² · R ten & P*] 西南 — *seinan* — southwest 南シナ海 — *Minami Shina-kai* — South China Sea
友	友	158; 29/2. YŪ, *tomo* friend [YU³ · I: hand 1–2 in hand 3–4; P*] 学友会 — *gakuyūkai* — alumni/students' society 友人 — *yūjin* — friend
円	円 圓	159; 13/2. EN* yen; *maru(i)* round, circular [YÜAN² · I] 千四百円 — *sen'yonhyakuen* — 1,400 yen 半円 — *han'en* — semicircle
高	高 高	160; 189/0. KŌ, *taka(i)* high, expensive [KAO¹ · D: tall building, with roof, upper floor, main building 6–7, & lower floor; P*] 高校生 — *kōkōsei* — high-school student 作り高 — *tsukuri-daka* — yield, output, production

重	重	161; 4/8. JŪ, CHŌ, *omo(i)* heavy; *kasa(neru/naru)* pile up; *omo(njiru)* think important, value; *-e, -jū*-fold [CHUNG⁴, CH'UNG² • I; P*]　　　　　　　　ingly 重病 — *jūbyō* — serious illness 重ね重ね — *kasanegasane* — frequently, exceed-
春	春	162; 72/5. SHUN, *haru* spring [CH'UN¹ • I: sun & first shoots 1–5 = spring] 春分の日 — *shunbun no hi* — the Vernal Equinox 　　　　　　　　　　　　　　　　　　[holiday] 春雨 — *harusame* (ir.) / *shun'u* — spring rain
夏	夏	163; 1/9. KA, GE, *natsu* summer [HSIA⁴ • D→E; P*] 夏休み — *natsu yasumi* — summer holiday 夏草 — *natsugusa/natsukusa* — summer grass
秋	秋	164; 115/4. SHŪ, *aki* autumn [CH'IU¹ • R grain & P*] 春秋 — *shunjū* — spring & autumn 秋風 — *akikaze* — autumn wind
冬	冬	165; 34/2. TŌ, *fuyu* winter [TUNG¹ • R ice & P*] 春夏秋冬 — *shunkashūtō* — spring, summer, 　　　　　　　　　　　autumn & winter　　sale 冬物売出し — *fuyumono uridashi* — winter-clothing
丁	丁	166; 1/1. TEI* 4th (in a series); CHŌ* unit of length [109 meters], town/ward sector, leaf (of paper) [TING¹ • D→B; P*] 丁重な — *teichō na* — polite, respectful 一丁目 — *itchōme* — 1st sector, 1-chōme
町	町	167; 102/2. CHŌ* street, ward sector; *machi* town [T'ING³ • R field & P*] 町村会 — *chōsonkai* — town & village assemblies 下町 — *shitamachi* — plebeian section of town
区	区 區	168; 22/2. KU* town ward, sector [CH'Ü¹ • I; P*] 地区 — *chiku* — area, region 千代田区 — *Chiyoda-ku* — Chiyoda Ward

動	動	169; 19/9. DŌ, *ugo(kasu/ku)* move [TUNG⁴ · R strength & P*] 自動車 — *jidōsha* — car, motor vehicle 人の心を動かす — *hito no kokoro o ugokasu* — move a person
働	働 仂	170; 9/11. DŌ, *hatara(ku/ki)* work [- · R man & P*] 働き口 — *hatarakiguchi* — opening, position 働き者 — *hatarakimono* — hard worker
役	役	171; 60/4. YAKU* use, service, role; EKI* battle, service ┌→ service; P*] [I⁴ · I: footstep 1–3 & spear 4–7 = armed patrol 重役 — *jūyaku* — company director 役に立つ — *yaku ni tatsu* — be of use
京	京	172; 8/6. KYŌ*, KEI capital (city) [CHING¹ · D: roofed building 1–5 on high ground 6–8; P*] 上京する — *jōkyō suru* — go up to the capital 東京の人口 — *Tōkyō no jinkō* — the population of Tōkyō
都	都 都	173; 163/8. TO, TSU, *miyako* capital, metropolis [TU¹ · I: a city 9–11 with (many) men 1–8; P*] 首都 — *shuto* — capital 東京都と京都市 — *Tōkyō-to to Kyōto-shi* — Tōkyō metropolis & Kyōto city
間	間 間	174; 169/4. KAN, KEN, *aida* interval, space; *ma* interval, room ┌gate; P*] [CHIEN¹,⁴, HSIEN² · I: the sun shining through a 二重夏時間 — *nijū natsu jikan* — double summer [daylight saving] time ┌months 四カ月の間 — *yonkagetsu no aida* — a period of 4
問	問	175; 169/3. MON, *to(u)* ask about, question [WEN⁴ · I: a mouth at the gate; P*] 学問 — *gakumon* — learning, study 時と所を問わず — *toki to tokoro o towazu* — not querying/regardless of time or place
体	体 體	176; 9/5. TAI, TEI, *karada* body [T'I³ · I: a person's 1–2 main, basic part 3–7; P*] 体力 — *tairyoku* — physical strength 体重 — *taijū* — body weight

世	世	177; 2/4. SE, SEI, *yo* world, age, reign [SHIH[1] • I: orig., three tens = thirty (years) = one generation] 世間の耳目 — *seken no jimoku* — public attention/interest 「the world 世の中へ出る — *yo no naka e deru* — go out into
新	新	178; 69/9. SHIN, *atara(shii)*, *ara(ta na)*, *nii-* new [HSIN[1] • R ax & P*] 新品 — *shinpin* — new article 新聞 — *shinbun* — newspaper
葉	葉	179; 140/9. YŌ, *ha* leaves, foliage [YEH[4] • I: the growth 1–3 on [thirty (see 177) 4–8] trees = leaves; P*] 「(mid 8th-century) 万葉時代 — *Man'yō jidai* — the Man'yōshū period 新しい言葉 — *atarashii kotoba* — new word
話	話	180; 149/6. WA, *hana(su)* speak; *hanashi* talk, story [HUA[4] • I: words 1–7 & tongue (see 878) 8–13; 「P*] 世話 — *sewa* — aid, care, charge 作り話 — *tsukuri-banashi* — made-up story, fabrication
多	多	181; 36/3. TA, *ō(i)* many, plentiful [TO[1] • I: evening 1–3 (see no. 734) after evening = day after day → many; P*] 多少 — *tashō* — to some extent, somewhat 寺の多い京都 — *tera no ōi Kyōto* — Kyōto, where there are many temples
鳥	鳥	182; 196/0. CHŌ, *tori* bird [NIAO[3] • D: big/longtailed bird (cf. R 172: small/short-tailed bird); P*] 野鳥 — *yachō* — wildfowl 小鳥 — *kotori* — small bird
島	島 嶋	183; 4/9. TŌ, *shima* island [TAO[3] • I: a bird 1–7 rests on a mountain (in the 「sea); P*] 半島 — *hantō* — peninsula 島国 — *shimaguni* — island country
空	空	184; 116/3. KŪ, *sora* sky; *a(keru/ku)* empty; *kara* 「*(no)* empty [K'UNG[1, 4] • R hole & P*] 空気 — *kūki* — air, atmosphere 空耳 — *soramimi* — hearing (non-existent) things, pretending not to hear

49

同	同	185; 13/4.　DŌ, *ona(ji)* same [T'UNG² • I: call 4–6 together into one place (cf. 1338) 1–3 = be united → same; P*] 人間同士 — *ningen dōshi* — human beings all of a kind, fellow men　「time as working 働くと同時に — *hataraku to dōji ni* — at the same
発	発 發	186; 105/4.　HATSU emerge, issue [FA¹ • R both feet & P*] 出発する — *shuppatsu suru* — depart, set off 発明する — *hatsumei suru* — invent
周	周	187; 13/6.　SHŪ, *mawa(ri)* circuit, rotation [CHOU¹ • I: ricefields 1–5 in a fixed area 6–8; P*] 一周 — *isshū* — a circuit/lap 円周 — *enshū* — circumference
週	週	188; 162/8.　SHŪ* week [CHOU¹ • R proceed & P*] 先週 — *senshū* — last week 十週間 — *jisshūkan* (ir.) — 10 weeks
駅	駅 驛	189; 187/4.　EKI* station [I⁴, YI⁴ • R horse & P*] 駅長 — *ekichō* — stationmaster 品川駅前で — *Shinagawa ekimae de* — in front of Shinagawa station
訳	訳 譯	190; 149/4.　YAKU* translation; *yaku(suru)* translate; *wake* reason, meaning, circumstances [I⁴, YI⁴ • R words & P*] 訳者 — *yakusha* — translator 訳が分からない — *wake ga wakaranai* — incomprehensible, unreasonable
変	変 變	191; 8/7.　HEN, *ka(eru/waru)* change; *hen (na)*, *ka(watta)* strange [PIEN⁴ • R rap & P*] 変化 — *henka* — change, variation 変動 — *hendō* — change, fluctuation
送	送 逶	192; 162/6.　SŌ, *oku(ru)* send [SUNG⁴ • R proceed & P*] 送金する — *sōkin suru* — send/remit money 〔見〕送る — *[mi]okuru* — see (someone) off/home

陸	陸	193; 170/8. RIKU* land [LU⁴ · R hill & P*] 陸軍軍人 — *rikugun gunjin* — an army man 大陸 — *tairiku* — continent
進	進	194; 162/8. SHIN, *susu(meru/mu)* advance [CHIN⁴ · I: advance 9–11 like a bird 1–8 (see R 172); P*] 進行する — *shinkō suru* — advance, progress 工事を進める — *kōji o susumeru* — advance/press on with construction work
合	合	195; 9/4. GŌ, KATSU, *a(waseru/u)* fit/put together [HO² · I: lid 1–3 & container 4–6 on which it fits; P*] 都合 — *tsugō* — one's arrangements/convenience 問い合わせ — *toi-awase* — inquiry, application
知	知	196; 111/3. CHI, *shi(ru)* know, learn; *shi(raseru)* inform ⌈6–8 of one who knows; P*] [CHIH¹ · I: the arrowlike 1–5 (see 1335) speech 周知 — *shūchi* — common knowledge 知り合い — *shiriai* — an acquaintance
考	考	197; 125/2. KŌ, *kanga(eru/e)* think, consider [K'AO³ · R old & P* = mature consideration] 考古学 — *kōkogaku* — archaeology 思考作用 — *shikō sayō* — thought process
活	活	198; 85/6. KATSU life, activity [HUO² · I: a watery/moist 1–3 tongue 4–9; P*] 活発な — *kappatsu na* — lively, active 活動 — *katsudō* — activity
常	常	199; 42/8. JŌ, *tsune no* normal, regular, continual; *toko-* unending [CH'ANG² · R cloth 9–11 & P 1–8 (cf. 1843); P*] 正常な — *seijō na* — normal, regular 日常生活 — *nichijō seikatsu* — daily life
利	利	200; 115/2. RI* interest (on money), advantage; *ki(ku)* be effective [LI⁴ · I: cutting 6–7 grain 1–5 = gain, profit; P*] 利口 — *rikō* — cleverness 利用する — *riyō suru* — utilize, make good use of

通	通	201; 162/7. TSŪ, TSU, tō(su/ru) pass through/along; kayo(u) go to & fro [T'UNG¹ · R proceed & P*] 交通 — kōtsū — traffic 通り道 — tōrimichi — passage, route
原	原	202; 27/8. GEN origin; hara moor, field [YÜAN² · I: a spring 3–10 (= 915) below a cliff = source → level ground; P*] 高原 — kōgen — plateau 野原 — nohara — field, moor, plain
社	社 社	203; 113/3. SHA association; yashiro Shinto shrine [SHE⁴ · I: god 1–4 of the earth 5–7 → his shrine; P*] 会社 — kaisha — business company 社会 — shakai — society, the public
申	申	204; 2/4. SHIN, mō(su) (dep.) say [SHEN¹ · D: lightning = expression of the gods → declare, say; P*] 上申する — jōshin suru — submit a report 内申書 — naishinsho — (school, etc.) report/record
神	神 神	205; 113/5. SHIN, JIN, kami god [SHEN² · I: god 1–4 of lightning (see 204) → any god; P*] 神社 — jinja — Shinto shrine 神風 — kamikaze — divine wind
音	音	206; 180/0. ON, IN, oto, ne sound [YIN¹ · S: vrt. of 43, with line inside mouth = actual sound; P*] 発音 — hatsuon — pronunciation 足音 — ashioto — footstep
死	死	207; 78/2. SHI* death; shi(nu) die [SSU³, SZU³ · I: R disintegrate & man 5–6] 半死半生の — hanshi hanshō no — half dead 死に神 — shinigami — the god of death, Death
居	居	208; 44/5. KYO, i(ru) be (present), reside [CHÜ¹ · R bent figure & P*] 同居する — dōkyo suru — live together 居心地がいい — igokochi ga ii — be comfortable, feel at home

住	住	209; 9/5. Jū, *su(mu)* reside/live (in) [CHU⁴ • I: a man 1–2 is master 3–7 where he lives; P*] 住所 — *jūsho* — home, house, address 住居 — *sumai/jūkyo* — home, house, address
使	使	210; 9/6. SHI, *tsuka(u)* use [SHIH⁴ • I: one who serves 3–8 (see 1684), who is used; P*] 大使 — *taishi* — ambassador 使役する — *shieki suru* — employ, put to work
親	親	211; 147/9. SHIN, *oya* parent; *shita(shimu/shii)* feel close (to), take pleasure (in) [CH'IN¹ • R see & P*] 親友 — *shin'yū* — good friend 親切な — *shinsetsu na* — kind
全	全	212; 9/4. ZEN, *matta(ku)* completely, entirely [CH'ÜAN² • I: P*] 全訳 — *zen'yaku* — complete translation 安全 — *anzen* — safety
法	法	213; 85/5. Hō*, HATSU-, HOTSU- law, doctrine, method; the law; P*] [FA³,⁴ • I: to wash 1–3 away 5–8 wrong through 方法 — *hōhō* — method 六法全書 — *roppō zensho* — a Compendium of [the 6 Major] Laws
治	治	214; 85/5. JI, CHI, *osa(meru/maru)* rule over, pacify; *nao(su/ru)* cure [CHIH⁴ • R water & P*] 治安 — *chian* — public peace & order 政治 — *seiji* — politics, government
向	向	215; 2/5. Kō, *mu(keru/kau)* turn, face; *mu(ku)* face, be suited (to/for); *mu(kō)* opposite [HSIANG⁴ • D: a high window 4–6 under the roof 1–3 facing the light; P*] 方向 — *hōkō* — direction 都市向きの品 — *toshi-muki no shina* — goods suitable for the town
説	説	216; 149/7. SETSU* view, theory; ZEI, *to(ku)* explain, propound [SHUO¹ • R words & P*] 説明 — *setsumei* — explanation 小説 — *shōsetsu* — a novel, fiction

光	光	**217**; 42/3. KŌ, *hika(ru)* shine; *hikari* light, ray [KUANG¹ • I: a torch 1–3 (= 15) carried by a man 4–6; P*] 日光 — *nikkō* — sunshine, sunlight; pn. 発光する — *hakkō suru* — radiate, emit light
定	定	**218**; 40/5. TEI, JŌ, *sada(meru/maru)* decide, fix [TING⁴ • I: put things right 4–8 (= 123) in the house 1–3; P*] 定休 — *teikyū* — regular/fixed holiday/closing-day 定説 — *teisetsu* — established/accepted theory
公	公	**219**; 12/2. KŌ, *ōyake* public 「it public; P*] [KUNG¹ • I: open up 1–2 a place 3–4, and make 公言 — *kōgen* — open declaration/profession 日本交通公社—*Nihon Kōtsū Kōsha*—Japan Travel Bureau [lit . . . Public Corporation]
貨	貨	**220**; 154/4. KA goods, money [HUO⁴ • I: money 5–11 changed/changeable 1–4 into other things; also R shell/money & P*] 貨物を発送する — *kamotsu o hassō suru* — dispatch goods 十進法通貨—*jisshinhō tsūka* — decimal currency
以	以	**221**; 9/2. I with, by, (pref.) -ward from [I³ • D: a man 4–5 holding something 1–3 → using, with; P*] 首相以下の政治家 — *shushō ika no seijika* — politicians from the Prime Minister down 「weeks 五週間以内に — *goshūkan inai ni* — within 5
電	電	**222**; 173/5. DEN lightning, electricity [TIEN⁴ • I: lightning 9–13 (= 204) from the sky 1–8; P*] 「electricity 火力電気—*karyoku denki*—thermal/steampower 電話で話す—*denwa de hanasu*—talk on the phone
形	形	**223**; 59/4. KEI, GYŌ, *katachi*, *-gata* form, shape [HSING² • R light rays & P*] 長方形 — *chōhōkei* — rectangle, oblong (shape) 形相 — *gyōsō* — features, look, aspect
成	成	**224**; 62/2. SEI, JŌ, *na(ru)* turn (into), be completed/formed (from); *na(su)* do, achieve [CH'ENG² • R lance & P*] 成立 — *seiritsu* — establishment, formation 成長 — *seichō* — growth

意	意	225; 180/4. I* mind, will, heart, meaning [I⁴ · I: a person's sounds (= words) 1–9 & spirit/ 意見 — *iken* — opinion　　　⌊feelings 10–13; P*] 用意 — *yōi* — preparation, arrangement
声	声 聲	226; 32/4. SEI, SHŌ, *koe* voice [SHENG¹ · I: a man 1–3 waiting at the door 4–7 will use his voice; P*] 音声学 — *onseigaku* — phonetics 少年の声変わり — *shōnen no koegawari* — a boy's 　　　　　　　　　change/breaking of voice
号	号 號	227; 30/3. GŌ* pen-name; issue/number (of periodi- [HAO⁴ · R mouth & P*]　　　　　　⌊cal) 交通信号 — *kōtsū shingō* — traffic signals 年号 — *nengō* — era name, year period (of reign)
級	級	228; 120/4. KYŪ* rank, class [CHI² · R thread & P*] 高級 — *kōkyū* — high rank/class 進級する — *shinkyū suru* — be promoted
点	点 點	229; 25/7. TEN* point, mark [TIEN³ · R fire & P*] 重点 — *jūten* — main point, emphasis 出発点 — *shuppatsu-ten* — departure point
決	決	230; 85/4. KETSU, *ki(meru/maru)* decide [CHÜEH² · R water & P*] 決意 — *ketsui* — determination, resolve 決定する — *kettei suru* — decide, determine
語	語	231; 149/7. GO* word; *kata(ru/ri)* tell, relate [YÜ³ · R words & P*] 口語訳 — *kōgoyaku* — colloquial-language trans- 　　　　　　　　lation/version　⌈words 外来語 — *gairaigo* — words from abroad, imported
種	種	232; 115/9. SHU kind, sort; *tane* seed [CHUNG³,⁴ · I: grain 1–5 piled up 6–14, all one kind of seed; P*]　　　　　　　⌈tation 人工変種 — *jinkō henshu* — artificial variety/mu- 種切れになる — *tanegire ni naru* — run out of 　　　　　　　　　　　seed/material

実	実 實	233; 40/5. JITSU* truth, reality; *mi* nut, fruit; *mino-* [SHIH² · R roof & P*] └*(ru)* bear fruit 当人の実話 — *tōnin no jitsuwa* — actual account from the person concerned ┌out an idea 考えを実行する — *kangae o jikkō suru* — carry
兄	兄	234; 30/2. KEI, KYŌ, *ani* elder brother [HSIUNG¹ · I: a man 4-5 who can speak 1-3 with some authority; P*] 実兄 — *jikkei* — one's (own/true) elder brother 父兄 — *fukei* — father & elder brothers, guardians
店	店	235; 53/5. TEN, *mise* shop [TIEN⁴ · R lean-to & P*] 百貨店 — *hyakkaten* — (department) store 神戸支店 — *Kōbe shiten* — Kōbe branch (shop/office)
完	完	236; 40/4. KAN completion [WAN² · R roof & P*] 完全 — *kanzen* — perfection 完成 — *kansei* — completion
院	院	237; 170/7. IN institution [YÜAN⁴ · R hill & P*] 病院へ通う — *byōin e kayou* — attend a hospital 寺院 — *jiin* — Buddhist temple
失	失	238; 4/4. SHITSU, *ushina(u)* lose [SHIH¹ · D: a hand 1-4 (cf. 37) dropping/losing something 5; P*] 失政 — *shissei* — misrule, misgovernment 失意 — *shitsui* — disappointment; adversity
次	次	239; 15/4. JI, SHI, *tsugi (no)* next; *tsu(gu)* be next/rank second (to) ┌3-6; P*] [TZ'U⁴ · I: the second 1-2 (= 2) open mouth 目次 — *mokuji* — table of contents 次点 — *jiten* — second mark/points, runner-up
共	共	240; 12/4. KYŌ, *tomo* together, both [KUNG⁴ · R eight & P*] 共通の — *kyōtsū no* — common, joint ┌action 共同動作 — *kyōdō dōsa* — combined/cooperative

色	色	241; 139/0. SHOKU, SHIKI, *iro* color, passion [SE⁴ · I ; P*] 変色する — *henshoku suru* — change color 色色な — *iroiro na* — various, all kinds of
鉄	鉄 鐵	242; 167/5. TETSU* iron [T'IEH³ · R metal & P*] 鉄道工学 — *tetsudō kōgaku* — railway engineering 国鉄 — *kokutetsu* — national railway
団	団 團	243; 31/3. DAN group, troupe; TON [T'UAN² · I: a closed circle 1–3 with its own rule 4–6; P*]⌐living 団体生活 — *dantai seikatsu* — group/community 公団法 — *Kōdan-hō* — Public Corporation Law
義	義	244; 123/7. GI* justice, integrity, loyalty; (pref.) -in-law, artificial [I⁴ · R sheep & P*]⌐sister-in-law 義兄と義姉 — *gikei to gishi* — elder brother- & 義理 — *giri* — duty, obligation
議	議	245; 149/13. GI debate, consider [I⁴ · R words & P*] 議会 — *gikai* — national assembly, the Diet 不思議な — *fushigi na* — strange, unaccountable
民	民	246; 1/4. MIN, *tami* people, populace [MIN² · R clan & P*] 民主主義 — *minshu shugi* — democracy 住民の意見 — *jūmin no iken* — residents'/inhabitants' views
教	教 敎	247; 66/7. KYŌ, *oshi(eru)* teach [CHIAO⁴ · I: teach piety 1–7 (see 865) by raps 説教 — *sekkyō* — sermon ⌊8–11; P*] 教義 — *kyōgi* — doctrine, dogma
宗	宗	248; 40/5. SHŪ, SŌ founder, sect, religion [TSUNG¹ · I: a roofed shrine 1–3 with its god 4–8; 宗教 — *shūkyō* — religion ⌊P*] 宗家 — *sōke* — (head of a) main family/house

仏	仏 佛	249; 9/2. BUTSU*, *hotoke* Buddha; FUTSU France [FO² • R man & P*] 仏教 — *Bukkyō* — Buddhism ⌈Institute 日仏学院 — *Nichi-Futsu Gakuin* — Japanese-French
場	場 場	250; 32/9. JŌ, *ba* place [CH'ANG²,³ • R earth & P*] ⌈factory 工場で働く — *kōba/kōjō de hataraku* — work in a 場合 — *baai* — case, circumstances
屋	屋	251; 44/6. OKU, *ya* house; *-ya* shop/store (keeper) [WU¹ • a man bent in sleep 1–3 & room 4–9 (= 278) → home, house; P*] 八百屋 — *yaoya* — greengrocer('s shop) 家屋の売買 — *kaoku no baibai* — dealings in houses /buildings/real estate
度	度	252; 53/6. DO degree, limit; *tabi* time, occasion; TAKU, TO [TU⁴, TO⁴ • I: to measure 1–7 with the hand 毎度 — *maido* — every time ⌊8–9; P*] 度度 — *tabitabi* — often, frequently
可	可	253; 1/4. KA* good, right; possible [K'O³, K'E³ • R mouth & P*] 可決する — *kaketsu suru* — pass/approve (a bill) 不可分な — *fukabun na* — indivisible, inseparable
何	何	254; 9/5. KA, *nani, nan* what, how many [HO² • R man & P*] 何でも屋 — *nandemoya* — Jack-of-all-trades 何度も — *nando mo* — any number of times
荷	荷	255; 140/7. KA, *ni* burden, baggage [HO² • R grass & P*] 入荷通知 — *nyūka tsūchi* — goods-arrival notice 荷物の目方 — *nimotsu no mekata* — weight of luggage
歌	歌	256; 76/10. KA poem; *uta(u)* sing; *uta* song [KO¹, KE¹ • R open mouth & P*] 校歌 — *kōka* — school song ⌈ing voice 歌い声がいい — *utaigoe ga ii* — have a good sing-

番	番	257; 165/5. BAN* one's turn, (guard) duty; number [FAN¹ · I: separate 1–7 fields 8–12 → turn by 番号 — *bangō* — number ⌊turn; P*⌋ 交番 — *kōban* — police box
在	在	258; 32/3. ZAI* outskirts, country; (pref.) resident in; *a(ru)* be, exist [TSAI⁴ · R earth & P* 1–3 (vrt. of 574)] 在荷 — *zaika* — goods on hand/in stock 在世中 — *zaiseichū* — during one's life
付	付	259; 9/3. FU, *tsu(keru/ku)* attach, stick [FU⁴ · R man & P*] 付近 — *fukin* — vicinity 利子が付く — *rishi ga tsuku* — yield/bear interest
府	府	260; 53/5. FU* urban prefecture; center, office [FU³ · R lean-to & P*] 政府 — *seifu* — government 府知事 — *fu-chiji* — (urban) prefectural governor
短	短	261; 111/7. TAN, *mijika(i)* short [TUAN³ · I: an arrow (see 1335) as short as a bean (see 1044); P*] 短歌 — *tanka* — Japanese 31-syllable poem 短刀 — *tantō* — short sword
要	要	262; 146/3. YŌ* main point, necessity; *i(ru)* be [YAO¹,⁴ · I; P*] ⌊needed; *yō(suru)* need 要点 — *yōten* — main point, gist 重要な — *jūyō na* — important, weighty, main
帰	帰 歸	263; 58/7. KI, *kae(ru)* return, go home [KUEI¹ · I; P*] 帰国 — *kikoku* — returning to one's country 帰り支度 — *kaeri-jitaku (← -shitaku)* — prepara- tions for one's return (home)
苦	苦	264; 140/5. KU* suffering; *kuru(shii)* painful; [K'U³ · R grass & P*] ⌊*niga(i)* bitter 苦役 — *kueki* — [imprisonment with] hard labor 苦手 — *nigate* — weak point, tough opponent

便	便	265; 9/7. BEN* facilities, excreta; BIN* post, mail, opportunity; *tayo(ri)* news [PIEN⁴, P'IEN² • R man & P*] 交通不便で — *kōtsū fuben de* — communications being inconvenient 「being near 近くて便利 — *chikakute benri* — convenient in
勝	勝	266; 130/8. SHŌ, *ka(tsu)* win (against); *masa(ru)* be superior (to) 「powerful 11–12 who win; P*] [SHENG¹,⁴ • I: flesh 1–4 is cut 5–10 by the 勝利 — *shōri* — victory 「unbeaten 勝ち通す — *kachi-tōsu* — win right through, be
有	有	267; 130/2. YŪ, U, *a(ru)* exist, be held/owned [YU³,⁴ • R moon & P*] 有意義な — *yūigi na* — significant 有史時代 — *yūshi jidai* — historical period
美	美	268; 123/3. BI* beauty; *utsuku(shii)* beautiful [MEI³ • I: a sheep 1–6 (see 1326) that is big 7–9; P*] 都市美化 — *toshi bika* — urban beautification 有名な美人 — *yūmei na bijin* — a famous beauty
界	界	269; 102/4. KAI world [CHIEH⁴ • I: what is between 6–9 (see 941) fields 1–5 = boundary → sphere; also R field & P*] 世界一の — *sekai-ichi no* — first/foremost in the world 社交界 — *shakōkai* — social/fashionable world
辺	辺 邊	270; 162/2. HEN*, *ata(ri)*, *-be* vicinity [PIEN¹ • R proceed & P*] 近辺 — *kinpen* — vicinity 周辺 — *shūhen* — outskirts, perimeter
引	引	271; 57/1. IN, *hi(ku/ki)* pull [YIN³ • I: a bow 1–3 (see 1419) string 4] 引火と発火 — *inka to hakka* — ignition & combustion 引き出し — *hikidashi* — drawer 」bustion
受	受	272; 87/4. JU, *u(keru)* receive; *u(ke)* reception, popularity, receptacle 「from a hand 7–8; P*] [SHOU⁴ • I: claws 1–4 receiving something 5–6 小切手の受理 — *kogitte no juri* — acceptance of a cheque 「a proposal 申し入れを受ける — *mōshi-ire o ukeru* — accept

角	角	273; 148/0. KAKU* angle, square; *kado* (outside) corner; *tsuno* (animal) horn [CHIAO³, CHÜEH²,³ · D] 角度 — *kakudo* — angle 角店 — *kadomise* — corner shop
労	労 勞	274; 19/5. RŌ* work, labor [LAO² · R strength & P*] 労働立法 — *rōdō rippō* — labor legislation 苦労 — *kurō* — trouble, hardship
赤	赤	275; 155/0. SEKI, SHAKU, *aka, aka(i)* red [CH'IH⁴ · I; P*] 赤十字社 — *Sekijūji-sha* — Red Cross Society 赤字を出す — *akaji o dasu* — run into the red, produce a deficit
後	後	276; 60/6. GO,* *nochi* after(wards); KŌ, *ushi(ro)* back, behind; *ato* behind, after, remainder; *oku-(raseru/reru)* make late ⌈after 7–9] [HOU⁴ · I: footsteps 1–3 trailing 4–6 (= 113) 午後 — *gogo* — afternoon ⌈back, face wrong way 後向きになる — *ushiro-muki ni naru* — turn one's
和	和	277; 115/3. WA peace, harmony, Japan; *yawa-(rageru/ragu)*, *nago(meru/mu)* soften; *nago(yaka na)* amiable, genial ⌈peace; P*] [HO²,⁴ · I: grain 1–5 in the mouth 6–8 brings 和歌二首 — *waka nishu* — two Japanese poems 平和会議 — *heiwa kaigi* — peace conference
室	室	278; 40/6. SHITSU* room; *muro* cellar, outhouse [SHIH⁴ · I: a house's 1–3 inner reaches 4–9 (cf. 725); P*] 和室 — *washitsu* — Japanese-style room 室町時代 — *Muromachi jidai* — the Muromachi period (1336–1568)
集	集	279; 172/4. SHŪ, *atsu(meru/maru)*, *tsudo(u)* (vi.) assemble [CHI² · I; small birds 1–8 on a tree; P*] 集団心理 — *shūdan shinri* — group/mass psychology 古今和歌集 — *Kokinwakashū* — the Kokinshū poetry anthology
性	性	280; 61/5. SEI* sex, nature; SHŌ temperament [HSING⁴ · R heart & P*] 天性 — *tensei* — [by] one's nature 相性のいい — *aishō no ii* — compatible, congenial

必

281; 3/4. HITSU, *kanara(zu)* without fail, inevitably
[PI⁴ · I: 'Cross my heart . . .'; P*]
必要 — *hitsuyō* — necessity
必死の — *hisshi no* — frantic, desperate

部

282; 163/8. BU part, section; copy (of publication)
[PU⁴ · R city & P*]
部分 — *bubun* — part ⌜faculty
社会学部 — *shakai-gakubu* — sociology department/

食

283; 184/0. SHOKU* food; *ta(beru)*, *ku(u)*, *ku(rau)*
eat ⌜(cf. 586) underneath; P*]
[SHIH² · I: lid of food dish 1–2 with good things
十分な食事 — *jūbun na shokuji* — good/substantial
定食 — *teishoku* — set/fixed meal ⌞meal

材

284; 75/3. ZAI* timber, material, talent
[TS'AI² · R tree & P*]
小説を教材とする — *shōsetsu o kyōzai to suru* —
treat a novel as teaching material
新聞の取材 — *shinbun no shuzai* — newspaper sub-
ject matter/material

財

285; 154/3. ZAI*, SAI money, wealth
[TS'AI² · R shell/money & P*]
財界の中心 — *zaikai no chūshin* — center of the
financial world
財政 — *zaisei* — [public] finance, financial affairs

黒

286; 203/0. KOKU, *kuro*, *kuro(i)* black
[HEI¹ · I: village 1–7 (see 101) fires 8–11 make
smoke & soot; P*] ⌜right & wrong
黒白 — *kokubyaku* — black & white, good & bad,
黒光り — *kurobikari* — black luster

放

287; 70/4. HŌ, *hana(tsu)*, *hana(su)* set free, release
[FANG⁴ · R rap & P*] ⌜cast
海外放送 — *kaigai hōsō* — overseas/foreign broad-
放火する — *hōka suru* — set fire to, commit arson

別

288; 18/5. BETSU* distinction, separate; *betsu (ni)*
separately, (+ neg.) (not) particularly; *waka(reru)*
[PIEH² · I] ⌞(vi.) part (from)
区別 — *kubetsu* — distinction ⌜arate post
別便で送る — *betsubin de okuru* — send by sep-

関	関 關	289; 169/6. KAN, *seki* barrier [KUAN[1] • R gate & P*] 関西 — *Kansai* — pn. 関所 — *sekisho* — barrier, checkpoint
台	台 臺	290; 28/3. DAI* a stand, unit for counting vehicles, machines, etc.; TAI [T'AI[2] • I: top & base; P*] 台所 — *daidokoro* — kitchen 台風 — *taifū* — typhoon
最	最	291; 72/8. SAI, *motto(mo)* most [TSUI[4] • R say & P*] 最新の — *saishin no* — the latest 最高の — *saikō no* — highest, maximum
業	業	292; 3/12. GYŌ* occupation, study, industry; GŌ* karma; *waza* deed, act ⌈10-13 — all mean work] [YEH[4] • I: plants growing 1-5, sheep 6-11, trees 重工業 — *jūkōgyō* — heavy industry 失業手当法 — *Shitsugyō Teate-hō* — Unemployment Allowance Law
商	商	293; 8/9. SHŌ, *akina(u)* trade/deal in [SHANG[1] • I: to stand 1-4 (= 72) at a curtained stall 5-8 & talk 9-11; P*] 商業用語 — *shōgyō yōgo* — business terminology 引き合う商売 — *hiki-au shōbai* — a paying business/trade
等	等	294; 118/6. TŌ class, grade; *hito(shii)* like, equal [TENG[3] • R bamboo & P*] ⌊(to) 等級 — *tōkyū* — class, grade, rank 平等 — *byōdō* — equality
報	報	295; 32/9. HŌ* report, recompense; *muku(iru/i)* give reward/recompense (for) [PAO[4] • I; P*] 報知する — *hōchi suru* — report, inform 電報 — *denpō* — telegram
告	告	296; 30/4. KOKU, *tsu(geru)* tell, report [KAO[4] • I: come forth 1-4 from the mouth; P*] 告発する — *kokuhatsu suru* — prosecute, indict, 報告 — *hōkoku* — report, statement ⌊charge

由	由	297; 2/4. YŪ, YU, YUI, *yoshi* report, means, reason [YU² • D; P*] 理由 — *riyū* — reason 自由 — *jiyū* — freedom
油	油	298; 85/5. YU, *abura* oil [YU² • R water & P*] 石油工業 — *sekiyu kōgyō* — oil industry 油虫 — *aburamushi* — cockroach
勢	勢	299; 19/11. SEI, *ikio(i)* power [SHIH⁴ • I: layers of earth 1–8 and balls/spheres 9–11 (see 922) have strength 12–13; P*] 大勢で — *ōzei de* — in great strength/numbers; *taisei de* — being the general trend 時勢 — *jisei* — (the trend/conditions of) the times
熱	熱	300; 86/11. NETSU* heat, fever; *nes(suru)* heat, become hot 「P*] [JO⁴, JE⁴ • I: strongly 1–11 (=299) aflame 12–15; 熱中する — *netchū suru* — be mad (on)/engrossed 熱病 — *netsubyō* — fever └(in)
記	記	301; 149/3. KI, *shiru(su)*, *ki(su)* record, write down [CHI⁴ • R words & P*] 記号 — *kigō* — mark, sign, symbol 後記 — *kōki* — postscript
終	終	302; 120/5. SHŪ, *o(waru)* (vt. & vi.) end; *o(wari)* end; *o(eru)* (vt.) end [CHUNG¹ • R thread & P*] 中野が終点です — *Nakano ga shūten desu* — Nakano is the terminus. 最終電車 — *saishū densha* — the last (electric) train
広	広 廣	303; 53/2. KŌ, *hiro(i)* wide, extensive; *hiro(geru/garu)* spread; *hiro(maru)* be spread [KUANG³ • R lean-to & P*] 広告 — *kōkoku* — advertisement 広島出の親友 — *Hiroshima-de no shin'yū* —a good friend who comes/hails from Hiroshima
直	直	304; 24/6. CHOKU, JIKI, *nao(su/ru)* repair, correct; *ji(ki ni)*, *tada(chi ni)* immediately [CHIH² • D & S: an eye 3–8 (= 22) looking straight ahead 1–2; P*] 「angled triangle 直角三角形 — *chokkaku sankakukei* — right- 正直な — *shōjiki na* — honest

洋	洋	305; 85/6. YŌ ocean, the west [YANG² • R water & P*]　　　　　　⌈Western food 和食と洋食 — washoku to yōshoku — Japanese & 西洋文明 — seiyō bunmei — Western civilization
服	服	306; 130/4. FUKU* [Western] dress/clothes [FU² • I: a body 1–4 kneeling 5–6 (before mirror) is dressed by hands 7–8; P*]　　　⌈Western dress 和服と洋服 — wafuku to yōfuku — Japanese & 服役する — fukueki suru — serve time/a term
返	返	307; 162/4. HEN, kae(su) give back; kae(shi) return gift, change, response　　　　⌈also R proceed & P*] [FAN³ • I: return 1–4 (see 42) & proceed 5–7; 二つ返事 — futatsu henji — immediate/eager reply 返信用葉書 — henshin'yō hagaki — reply postcard
表	表	308; 2/7. HYŌ* table, list; omote outside, front; arawa(su) show, reveal, express [PIAO³ • R clothes & P*] 表音字母 — hyōon jibo — phonetic alphabet 代表 — daihyō — representation
様	様 様	309; 75/10. YŌ* likeness, manner; sama Mr., Mrs., Miss, form, state [YANG⁴ • R tree & P*: tree-sheep-water] 死んだも同様 — shinda mo dōyō — the same/as 　　　　　　　　good as dead　⌈Michiko Ueda 上田道子様 — Ueda Michiko-sama — Mrs./Miss
王	王	310; 96/0. Ō* king [WANG² • D: big ax = authority; P*] 王様 — ō-sama — king 法王 — hōō — the Pope
争	争 爭	311; 4/5. SŌ, araso(u/i) compete for, dispute [CHENG¹ • I: use strength 1–2 (= 53) in contest 3–6; P*] 労働争議 — rōdō sōgi — labor dispute　⌈throne 王位を争う — ōi o arasou — contend for the
乗	乗 乘	312; 4/8. JŌ, no(seru/ru) give ride to, carry [CH'ENG² • I: P*] 乗馬服 — jōba-fuku — horse-riding clothes 乗合 — nori-ai — riding together, joint undertaking

婦	婦	313; 38/8 FU woman [FU⁴ · I: woman & broom; also R woman & *P] 婦人界 — *fujin-kai* — women's/ladies' world/sphere 主婦の会 — *shufu no kai* — housewives' society
船	船 船	314; 137/5. SEN, *fune* ship [CH'UAN² · R boat & P*] 船室 — *senshitsu* — cabin 乗合船 — *noriai-bune* — ferryboat
残	残 残	315; 78/6. ZAN, *noko(su/ru/ri)* leave behind, let remain [TS'AN² · R disintegrate & P*] 残業手当 — *zangyō teate* — overtime allowance 残り多い — *nokori-ōi* — regretful, regrettable
念	念	316; 9/6. NEN* thought, idea, wish [NIEN⁴ · R heart & P*] 残念 — *zannen* — regret 記念号 — *kinen-gō* — commemorative number/issue
産	産 産	317; 117/6. SAN* childbearing, product, wealth; *u(mu)* give birth to [CH'AN³ · R birth & P*] 不動産 — *fudōsan* — real estate 公共財産 — *kōkyō zaisan* — public property/assets
官	官	318; 40/5. KAN* government (service) [KUAN¹ · I: roof = building & community 4–8→ public affairs; P*] mental, semiofficial 半官半民の — *hankan hanmin no* — semigovern- 外交官 — *gaikōkan* — diplomat
館	館 館	319; 184/8. KAN building [KUAN³ · R eat & P*] 大使館 — *taishikan* — embassy 別館 — *bekkan* — annex, detached building
習	習 習	320; 124/5. SHŪ, *nara(u)* learn [HSI² · I: fluttering their wings 1–6 (= 967) by themselves 7–11 (= 60), birds learn to fly; P*] 習字を習う — *shūji o narau* — learn calligraphy 常習 — *jōshū* — usage, custom, habit

面	面	321; 176/0. MEN* face, surface, mask, aspect; *omo-(te)*, *tsura* face, surface [MIEN⁴ • D: space enclosing 3–4 & 9 the eyes 5–8 below the hair 1–2 (cf. 138)] 面目 — *menmoku* — face, dignity, pride 表面 — *hyōmen* — surface
楽	楽 樂	322; 75/9. GAKU* music; RAKU* comfort; *tano-(shii)* pleasant [LE⁴ • D: musical fittings 1–9 on wood base; P*] 教会音楽 — *kyōkai ongaku* — church music 楽天家 — *rakutenka* — optimist
薬	薬 藥	323; 140/13. YAKU, *kusuri* medicine, chemicals [YAO⁴ • R grass & P*] 薬品 — *yakuhin* — medicine 薬食い — *kusuri-gui* — nutritious eating
想	想	324; 61/9. SŌ* thought, ideas; SO [HSIANG³ • R heart & P*] 理想 — *risō* — ideal 空想 — *kūsō* — daydream, fantasy
質	質	325; 154/8. SHITSU* quality, nature; SHICHI* pawn; inquire into, check [CHIH²,⁴ • R shell/money & P*] 性質 — *seishitsu* — character, nature 質屋 — *shichiya* — pawnshop/pawnbroker
遠	遠	326; 162/10. EN, ON, *tō(i)* distant [YÜAN³ • R proceed & P*] 遠足 — *ensoku* — excursion, outing 耳が遠い — *mimi ga tōi* — be hard of hearing
園	園	327; 31/10. EN, *sono* garden [YÜAN² • R enclosure & P*] 動物園 — *dōbutsu-en* — animal park, zoo 学園生活 — *gakuen seikatsu* — campus life
花	花	328; 140/4. KA, *hana* flower [HUA¹ • R grass & P*] 花台 — *kadai* — flower-vase stand 花園 — *hanazono* — flower garden

流	流	329; 85/7. RYŪ* (artistic) school; RU, naga(su/reru) set adrift, wash away; naga(re) current [LIU² · R water & P*] 支流 — shiryū — tributary 最新流行 — saishin ryūkō — latest fashion
急	急	330; 61/5. KYŪ* sudden, steep; iso(gaseru/gu) hurry ⌜anxiously 6-9] [CHI² · I: struggle 1-5 (cf. 311) against time, 急流 — kyūryū — swift current, rapids 急変 — kyūhen — sudden change, emergency
青	青 青	331; 174/0. SEI, SHŌ, ao, ao(i) green, blue, immature ⌜by moonlight 5-8; P*] [CHI'ING¹ · I: color of plants 1-4 (vrt. of 67) 青年 — seinen — youth, young man/generation 青空市場 — aozora ichiba — blue-sky/open-air ⌞market
強	強 強	332; 57/8. KYŌ, GŌ, tsuyo(i) strong; shi(iru) [CH'IANG² · I] ⌞compel, force 強熱 — kyōnetsu — intense heat 強度の — kyōdo no — strong, intense
感	感 感	333; 61/9. KAN*, kan(ji) feeling; kan(jiru) feel [KAN³ · R heart & P*] ⌜sensitive 感受性の強い — kanjusei no tsuyoi — highly 感想 — kansō — thoughts, impressions
情	情	334; 61/8. JŌ*, SEI, nasa(ke) (fellow-) feeling [CH'ING² · I: feeling 1-3 blue 4-11 (see 331); also R heart & P*] 強情な — gōjō na — obstinate 感情 — kanjō — feelings, emotions
旅	旅	335; 70/6. RYO, tabi journey [LÜ³ · I: a flag 1-6 (cf. 601) followed by many people 7-10] ⌜world trip 世界一周旅行 — sekai isshū ryokō — round-the- 旅館 — ryokan — Japanese-style inn
夜	夜	336; 8/6. YA, yoru, yo night [YEH⁴ · I: a man 3-4 under a shelter 1-2 at night ← moon 5-8 (= 13); P*] 夜半 — yahan — midnight, dead of night 夜通し — yodōshi — all through the night

港	港	337; 85/9. KŌ, *minato* harbor [CHIANG³ · R water & P*] 入港する — *nyūkō suru* — enter harbor 空港 — *kūkō* — airport
興	興	338; 12/14. KŌ, *oko(su/ru)* raise, revive; KYŌ* interest [HSING¹,⁴ · hands & legs on each side 1–4 & 11–16 lifting something in unison 5–10 (= 185)] 興行 — *kōgyō* — performance, entertainment 興信所 — *kōshinjo* — detective agency
味	味	339; 30/5. MI, *aji* taste [WEI⁴ · R mouth & P*] 興味 — *kyōmi* — interest 薬味 — *yakumi* — spices, flavoring
得	得	340; 60/8. TOKU* profit, gain; *e(ru), u(ru)* gain, ⌐obtain [TE², TEI³ · I] 得意 — *tokui* — one's forte, client, elation 会得する — *etoku suru* — understand, comprehend
経	経經	341; 120/5. KEI longitude; KYŌ* sutra; *he(ru)* spend (time), pass through [CHING¹ · R thread & P*] ⌐via Shanghai 上海経由電報 — *Shanhai keiyu denpō* — telegrams 神経質 — *shinkeishitsu* — nervous temperament
反	反	342; 27/2. HAN anti-; TAN* unit of land/cloth measure; HON, *so(rasu/ru)* bend, warp [FAN³ · R right hand & P*] 反感 — *hankan* — antipathy, animosity 反物屋 — *tanmonoya* — drapery/dry-goods store
坂	坂	343; 32/4. HAN, *saka* slope, hill [FAN³ · R earth & P*] 急坂 — *kyūhan* — steep slope 上り坂 — *noborizaka* — uphill road, upgrade
血	血	344; 143/0. KETSU, *chi* blood [HSIEH³, HSÜEH⁴ · I: a dish 2–6 overflowing 1 with sacrificial blood] 内出血 — *nai-shukketsu* — internal bleeding 血の気の多い — *chi-no-ke no ōi* — full-blooded, hot-headed

置	置	345; 122/8. CHI, *o(ku)* put, place [CHIH⁴ · R net 1–5 & P*] 放置する — *hōchi suru* — leave alone, let be 位置 — *ichi* — position, place
助	助	346; 19/5. JO, *tasu(keru/karu)* help, rescue [CHU⁴ · R strength & P*] 助産婦 — *josanpu* — midwife 助け船 — *tasukebune* — lifeboat, help, rescue
酒	酒	347; 85/7. SHU, *sake* rice-wine, alcoholic drink [CHIU³ · I: water 1–3 & a wine jug; P*] 日本酒と洋酒 — *Nihonshu to yōshu* — rice-wine & Western drink 酒は百薬の長 — *Sake wa hyakuyaku no chō* — Rice-wine is the best of all medicines.
給	給	348; 120/6. KYŪ provide, supply [KEI³, CHI³ · I: join 7–12 (see 195) thread → supply (new thread); P*] 酒場の給仕 — *sakaba no kyūji* — bar waiter/waitress 少ない月給 — *sukunai gekkyū* — small (monthly) salary
式	式	349; 56/3. SHIKI* ceremony, -style, -type [SHIH⁴ · R work & P]* ⌐hall 式場 — *shikijō* — place of the ceremony, reception 形式 — *keishiki* — form, formality
礼	礼 禮	350; 113/1. REI*, RAI salutation, thanks [LI³ · R god & P*] 失礼 — *shitsurei* — rudeness 礼式 — *reishiki* — etiquette, manners
保	保	351; 9/7. HO, *tamo(tsu)* keep, preserve [PAO³ · I: a person 1–2 carrying a child 3–9 → care for, preserve] ⌐security 保安 — *hoan* — preservation of (public) peace/ 保母 — *hobo* — governess, mother's help
守	守	352; 40/3. SHU, SU, *mamo(ru/ri)* defend, protect, uphold; *mori* guard, protector [SHOU³ · I: roof & rule; P*] 保守勢力 — *hoshu seiryoku* — conservative forces 守勢を取る — *shusei o toru* — go/stand on the defensive

非	非	353; 175/0. HI wrong; (neg. pref.) un-, non-, etc. [FEI[1] · D & S: the wings of a flying bird → opposite → neg.; P*] 非合法な — hi-gōhō na — illegal 非常の場合 — hijō no baai — extraordinary/unusual circumstances
試	試	354; 149/6. SHI, kokoro(miru/mi), tame(su) try, ⌊test [SHIH[4] · R words & P*] 非公式試合 — hikōshiki shiai — unofficial match/ contest 試金石 — shikinseki — touchstone, test (case)
験	験 驗	355; 187/8. KEN, GEN effect; test, examine [YEN[4] · R horse & P*] 試験 — shiken — examination ⌈rience 経験が広い — keiken ga hiroi — have wide expe-
険	険 險	356; 170/8. KEN, kewa(shii) steep, fierce [HSIEN[3] · R hill & P*] 保険 — hoken — insurance ⌈expression 険しい表情 — kewashii hyōjō — fierce/severe
計	計	357; 149/2. KEI (suf.) -meter; haka(ru) measure [CHI[4] · I: words & ten (= number) → count; P*] 早計な — sōkei na — hasty, ill-considered 夜光時計 — yakō-dokei — luminous watch
堂	堂	358; 42/8. DŌ* hall [T'ANG[2] · I: lofty 1–8 (vrt. of 1843) & earth = a lofty/exalted place; P*] 公会堂 — kōkaidō — public [meeting] hall 食堂 — shokudō — dining room/hall
結	結	359; 120/6. KETSU, musu(bu) tie, conclude; musu(bi) knot, conclusion; yu(u) dress (the hair) [CHIEH[2] · R thread & P*] ⌈together 団結する — danketsu suru — unite, stand/band 終結する — shūketsu suru — terminate, conclude
第	第 才	360; 118/5. DAI grade; pref. for ordinal numbers [TI[4] · I: bamboo & sequence 7–11 (ab. of 446) = a counter; P*] ⌈mediately 次第 — shidai — order, reason, circumstance, im- 安全第一 — anzen daiichi — safety first

氏	氏	361; 83/0. SHI (lit. suf.) Mr.; *uji* family (name), [SHIH⁴ • R clan; P*] ⌐lineage 氏名 — *shimei* — full name 氏神 — *ujigami* — patron god
紙	紙	362; 120/4. SHI, *kami* paper [CHIH³ • R thread & P*] ⌐covered book 紙表紙の本 — *kami-byōshi no hon* — paper- 紙筆 — *shihitsu* — paper & writing brush
建	建	363; 54/6. KEN, KON, *ta(teru/tsu)* build, set up; -*date* -stories ⌐up laws; P*] [CHIEN⁴ • I: writing 1–6 & Court (=1417)→ set 建議する — *kengi suru* — propose, move, submit 堂堂たる建物 — *dōdō-taru tatemono* — imposing/majestic building
健	健	364; 9/9. KEN, *suko(yaka na)* healthy [CHIEN⁴ • R man & P*] 保健 — *hoken* — (maintenance of) health, hygiene 強健 — *kyōken* — robust health
雑	雑 雑	365; 172/6. ZATSU*, ZŌ miscellany, roughness [TSA² • I: nine (=many) trees full of birds 7–14] 雑音 — *zatsuon* — (unwanted) noise, interference 雑木林 — *zōki-bayashi* — wood of mixed trees
隊	隊 隊	366; 170/9. TAI* unit, squad, group [TUI⁴ • R hill & P*] 軍隊 — *guntai* — the forces/military, an army 部隊長 — *butaichō* — unit/squad leader
私	私	367; 115/2. SHI, *watakushi* I, personal matters [SZU¹, SSU¹ • I: grain 1–5 & private [enclosure] 6–7; P*] ⌐municipal establishment 私立と市立 — *shiritsu to shiritsu* — private & 私財 — *shizai* — private funds/money
過	過	368; 162/9. KA, *su(gosu/giru)* overdo, pass (time); *ayama(tsu/chi)* mistake [KUO⁴ • R proceed & P*] 過労 — *karō* — overwork 過失 — *kashitsu* — error, negligence

包	包	369; 4/4. HŌ, *tsutsu(mu)* wrap; *tsutsu(mi)* parcel [PAO[1] • I: womb 1–2 with fetus 3–5; P*] 包丁 — *hōchō* — kitchen knife, cooking 紙包み — *kamizutsumi* — paper parcel
対	対 對	370; 67/3. TAI* opposing, against; TSUI a pair [TUI[4] • I: literature 1–4 (see 71) & rule (see 1045) 反対 — *hantai* — opposite ⌐= opposites; P*] 一対 — *ittsui* — one pair
程	程	371; 115/7. TEI, *hodo* extent, degree; *-hodo* about [CH'ENG[2] • R grain & P*] 程度 — *teido* — extent, limit 生産の過程 — *seisan no katei* — production process
的	的	372; 106/3. TEKI (adj. suf.); *mato* target, mark [TI[2,4] • R white & P*] 実用的 — *jitsuyō-teki* — practical 目的 — *mokuteki* — aim, object
運	運	373; 162/9. UN* luck, fortune; *hako(bu)* transport [YÜN[4] • I: an advancing 10–12 army 1–9 (see 100) needs luck & transport; P*] 反政府運動 — *han-seifu undō* — antigovernment activity/action 運送保険 — *unsō hoken* — freight/shipping insurance
員	員	374; 30/7. IN personnel, member [YUAN[2] • I: a mouth to feed 1–3 & money = employee; P*] 店員 — *ten'in* — shop assistant, clerk 議員 — *giin* — assemblyman, Diet member
果	果	375; 2/7. KA, *hata(su)* fulfill; *hate* result, end [KUO[3] • D & S: the fruit 1–4 on the tree, P*] 果実 — *kajitsu* — fruit 結果 — *kekka* — result, effect
調	調	376; 149/8. CHŌ, *shira(beru)* investigate; *shira(be)* tone, investigation; *totono(eru/u)* prepare, supply, [TIAO[4] • R words & P*] ⌐arrange 調子 — *chōshi* — tone, condition, way 変調 — *henchō* — change of tone, irregularity

英 英

377; 140/55. EI splendid, England
[YING¹ · R grass & P*]
英才 — *eisai* — [person of] brilliant talent 「reader
英語読本 — *Eigo tokuhon* — English-language

談 談

378; 149/8. DAN talk
[T'AN² · I: fiery 8–15 words; P*]
相談する — *sōdan suru* — consult (with)
非公式対談 — *hi-kōshiki taidan* — unofficial/informal dialogue/talk

銀 銀

379; 167/6. GIN* silver
[YIN² · R metal & P*]
大和銀行 — *Daiwa Ginkō* — The Daiwa Bank
水銀の実験 — *suigin no jikken* — mercury experiment/test

絵 絵 繪

380; 120/6. E*, KAI picture
[HUI⁴ · R thread & P*]
大和絵 — *Yamato-e* — painting in old Japanese
油絵 — *abura-e* — oil painting 「style

県 県 縣

381; 42/6. KEN* prefecture
[HSIEN⁴ · S: vrt. of 138 'head' inverted → downward from the top (national) level; P*]
千葉県 — *Chiba-ken* — Chiba Prefecture
都道府県 — *to-dō-fuken* — the administrative regions (Tōkyō, Hokkaidō & the prefectures)

温 温 温

382; 85/9. ON, *atata(kai)*, *atata(ka na)*, *atata(meru/maru)* warm
[WEN² · R water & P]
温度計 — *ondokei* — thermometer 「at body heat
丁度体温の水 — *chōdo taion no mizu* — water just

連 連

383; 162/7. REN group; *tsu(reru)* take along; *tsu(re)* companion; *tsura(naru)* (vi.) range
[LIAN² · R proceed & P*]
連合 — *rengō* — union, association, alliance
連勝 — *renshō* — a run of victories

真 真 眞

384; 24/8. SHIN, *ma* truth; *ma-, matsu-, man-* (emp. pref.) 「human truth; P*]
[CHEN¹ · I: correctness 1–8 (cf. 304) & legs →
真空 — *shinkū* — vacuum
真っ青な — *massao na* — ashen, deathly pale

科	科	385; 115/4. KA* section, branch, course [K'O¹, K'E¹ · I; P*] ⌐scalpel 外科用小刀 — gekayō kogatana — surgical knife, 教科書 — kyōkasho — textbook
無	無	386; 86/8. MU, BU, na(i), na(shi) (lit.) be not [WU² · R fire & P*] 無理な — muri na — unreasonable, impossible 無礼 — burei — rudeness
命	命	387; 9/6. MEI* order, command; MYŌ, inochi life [MING⁴ · I: mouth 4–6 & order 1–3 & 7–8 (=496)] 生命保険 — seimei hoken — life insurance 運命 — unmei — fate
図	図 圖	388; 31/4. ZU* plan, sketch, table; TO, haka(ru) [T'U² · I] ⌐plan/scheme for/against 図表 — zuhyō — chart, diagram 図書館 — toshokan — library
線	線	389; 120/9. SEN* line [HSIEN⁴ · R thread & P*] 等高線地図 — tōkōsen chizu — contour map 直線を引く — chokusen o hiku — draw a straight line
単	単 單	390; 3/8. TAN single [TAN¹ · D: a single weapon, with forked end 1–3; 単位 — tan'i — unit ⌐P*] 単線鉄道 — tansen tetsudō — single-track railway
達	達	391; 162/9. TATSU, tas(suru) reach, attain [TA² · I: the ground 1–3 is reached by the sheep's 4–9 fleece as it advances 10–12] 科学の発達 — kagaku no hattatsu — development/ advancement of science 友達 — tomodachi — friend
茶	茶	392; 140/6. CHA*, SA tea [CH'A² · I: type of tree 6–9 plant 1–3 used by 番茶 — bancha — coarse tea ⌐man 4–5] 茶道 — sadō, chadō — tea ceremony

題	題	393; 72/14. DAI* topic, subject, title [T'I² · R head/page & P] 題材 — *daizai* — theme, subject matter 問題 — *mondai* — problem, question
農	農	394; 161/6. NŌ agriculture [NUNG² · I: bend 1–6 (see 715) to cut grass with a shell 7–13; P*] 農業 — *nōgyō* — agriculture 農産物 — *nōsanbutsu* — agricultural products
朝	朝	395; 130/8. CHŌ, *asa* morning [CH'AO² · I: rising sun 3–6 amid grass 1–2 & 7–8, seen with the moon; P*] 平安朝 — *Heian-chō* — Heian court/period 明朝 — *myōchō* — tomorrow morning
兵	兵	396; 4/6. HEI*, HYŌ soldier [PING¹ · I: a war-ax 1–4 held in both hands 5–7;⌐P*] 兵役 — *heieki* — military service 兵隊 — *heitai* — soldier, troops
覚	覚 覺	397; 147/5. KAKU, *obo(eru)* remember, under- stand; *sa(masu/meru)* awake [CHÜEH² · R see & P*] 感覚 — *kankaku* — sense, sensation, feeling 自覚する — *jikaku suru* — be aware of, realize
器	器 器	398; 30/12. KI, *utsuwa* vessel ⌐7–9 vessel] [CH'I⁴ · I: for many mouths 1–6 & 10–15, a big 兵器 — *heiki* — arms, military weapons 電熱器 — *dennetsuki* — electric heater/hot plate
戦	戦 戰	399; 62/9. SEN, *tataka(u/i)* fight, struggle; *ikusa* war, battle ⌐P*] [CHAN⁴ · I: forked weapon 1–9 (see 390 & lance; 戦争 — *sensō* — war ⌐membrane] Day 休戦記念日 — *Kyūsen Kinenbi* — Armistice [Re-
具	具 具	400; 109/3. GU* tool, equipment [CHÜ⁴ · I: tools need a good eye 1–5 & two 家具 — *kagu* — furniture ⌐hands 6–8; P*] 具体的 — *gutaiteki* — concrete, tangible

漢	漢	401; 85/10. KAN* [Han] China, (suf.) man [HAN⁴ • R water & P] 漢字 — *kanji* — Chinese character 漢語 — *kango* — Chinese word
庭	庭	402; 53/7. TEI, *niwa* garden [T'ING¹'² • R lean-to & P*] 屋上庭園 — *okujō teien* — roof garden 庭先で — *niwasaki de* — in the garden
着	着	403; 123/6. CHAKU, JAKU, *ki(ru)* wear; *tsu(ku)* arrive. [CHAO¹'², CHE², CHO² • I: the wool of the sheep 1–7 (cf. 1326) is worn, the eye 8–12 sees arrivals] ⌐one] [in a kimono] 着物を着せる — *kimono o kiseru* — dress (some- 着実な — *chakujitsu na* — steady, sound, solid
飛	飛	404; 183/0. HI, *to(bu)* fly [FEI¹ • D: a flying bird] 夜間飛行 — *yakan hikō* — night flight 無着陸飛行 — *muchakuriku hikō* — [without landing →] non-stop flight
存	存	405; 39/3. ZON, SON exist; *zon(jiru)* (dep.) think, [TS'UN² • R child & P*] ⌐know 残存する — *zanson suru* — survive, still exist 存分に — *zonbun ni* — to one's heart's content, freely
論	論	406; 149/8. RON* argument, thesis [LUN²'⁴ • R words & P*] 結論に達する — *ketsuron ni tassuru* — arrive at a conclusion ⌐logic 記号的論理学 — *kigōteki ronrigaku* — symbolic
列	列	407; 78/2. RETSU* row, line [LIEH⁴ • I: cut into pieces 1–4 with a knife 5–6 → put in a row; P*] 列島 — *rettō* — archipelago 直通列車 — *chokutsū ressha* — a through train
省	省	408; 4/8. SHŌ* government ministry; SEI, *kaeri-* *(miru)* reflect (on oneself); *habu(ku)* omit [SHENG³, HSING³ • R eye & P*] 文部省 — *Monbushō* — Ministry of Education 反省する — *hansei suru* — reflect, consider

輸	輸 輸	409; 159/9. YU transport [SHU[1] • I: cart 1–7 & transfer 8–16; also R cart & P*]　「imports & exports 輸入品 と 輸出品 — *yunyūhin to yushutsuhin* — 運輸省 — *Un'yushō* — Ministry of Transport
料	料	410; 119/4. RYŌ materials, fee [LIAO[4] • I: a measure 7–10 of rice 1–6; P*] 料理 — *ryōri* — cooking, preparation of food 原料 — *genryō* — raw materials
特	特	411; 93/6. TOKU special [T'E[4] • R ox & P*] 特別列車 — *tokubetsu ressha* — special train 新年特集号 — *shinnen tokushūgō* — New Year special issue
留	留	412; 102/5. RYŪ, RU, *to(meru)* bring to a stop, [LIU[2] • R field & P*]　　　　　　　　　└fasten 留学する — *ryūgaku suru* — study abroad 留守 — *rusu* — absence (from home), being out
専	専 専	413; 41/6. SEN, *moppa(ra)* solely, mainly [CHUAN[1] • I; P*] 専門家 — *senmonka* — specialist 専用電話線 — *sen'yō denwasen* — exclusive-use/ private telephone line
任	任	414; 9/4. NIN* duty, task; *maka(seru)* entrust/ [JEN[2,4] • R man & P*]　　　　　　　└leave (to) 任命する — *ninmei suru* — appoint, nominate 専任の理事 — *sennin no riji* — [sole appointment →] full-time director
機	機	415; 75/12. KI occasion, machine; *hata* loom [CHI[1] • R tree & P*] 機会 — *kikai* — opportunity 飛行機 — *hikōki* — airplane
能	能	416; 28/8. NŌ* ability, Nō drama [NENG[2] • D → P*] 器官の機能 — *kikan no kinō* — organic function 不可能な — *fukanō na* — impossible

接	接	417; 64/8. SETSU, *ses(suru)* touch, adjoin; *tsu(gu)* join 「woman」 [CHIEH¹ · I: join hands 1–3 with a standing 4–8 直接の — *chokusetsu no* — direct 間接の — *kansetsu no* — indirect
毒	毒 毒	418; 80/4. DOKU* poison [TU² · plants 1–4 (vrt. of 67) which should not 5–8 be touched; P*] 中毒 — *chūdoku* — poisoning 毒薬 — *dokuyaku* — poison
殺	殺	419; 79/6. SATSU, SAI, SETSU, *koro(su)* kill [SHA¹,⁴, SHAI⁴ · I: animal 1–2 in a tree 3–6 is clubbed to death 7–10] 毒殺する — *dokusatsu suru* — (kill by) poison 殺人光線 — *satsujin kōsen* — murder/death ray
権	権 權	420; 75/11. KEN authority; GON deputy [CH'ÜAN² · R tree & P*] 「tonomy 自治権 — *jichiken* — right of self-government, au- 親権 — *shinken* — parental authority
芸	芸 藝	421; 140/4. GEI* arts, artistic skill [I⁴, YI⁴ · I; P*] 文芸 — *bungei* — literary arts 民芸館 — *mingeikan* — folkcraft museum
局	局	422; 44/4. KYOKU* bureau, office [CHÜ² · R bent figure & P] 局員 — *kyokuin* — bureau/post-office staff 薬局 — *yakkyoku* — chemist's, drugstore, dispensary
祭	祭	423; 113/6. SAI, *matsu(ru)* worship, deify; *matsu-(ri)* festival 「offered to the gods 7–11; P*] [CHI⁴ · I: flesh 1–4 (= 533) in the hand 5–6 祭日 — *saijitsu* — festival day 祭礼 — *sairei* — festival [rites]
際	際	424; 170/11. SAI* occasion; *kiwa* edge [CHI⁴ · R hill & P*] 交際 — *kōsai* — friendship, association 国際共産主義 — *kokusai kyōsan-shugi* — inter- national communism

根	根	425; 75/6. KON* perseverance; *ne* root [KEN¹ • R tree & P*] 根 性 — *konjō* — spirit, nature 屋 根 — *yane* — roof
係	係	426; 9/7. KEI, *kaka(ru)* hang, depend (on), cost, affect; *kakari* person in charge [HSI⁴ • R man & P*] 係 争 — *keisō* — contention, dispute 関 係 — *kankei* — connection
妹	妹	427; 38/5. MAI, *imōto* younger sister [MEI⁴ • I: not yet 4–8 (see 626) a woman; also R woman & P*] 姉 妹 — *shimai* — sisters 義 妹 — *gimai* — (younger) sister-in-law
願	願	428; 4/18. GAN, *nega(u/i)* request [YÜAN⁴ • R head/page & P*] 志 願 兵 — *shiganhei* — volunteer soldier 念 願 — *nengan* — cherished wish/desire
数	数 數	429; 66/9. SŪ, SU, *kazu* number; *kazo(eru)* count [SHU³,⁴, SHUO⁴, SU⁴ • I: the rice woman 1–9 taps 10–13 the abacus beads as she counts; P*] 数 学 — *sūgaku* — mathematics ⌐decision/vote 過 半 数 の 議 決 — *kahansū no giketsu* — majority
配	配	430; 164/3. HAI, *kuba(ru)* distribute [P'EI⁴ • R wine jug & P*] 配 達 する — *haitatsu suru* — distribute, deliver 心 配 する — *shinpai suru* — worry
織	織	431; 120/12. SHOKU, SHIKI, *o(ru)* weave; *o(ri)*, -*ori* weave, fabric [CHIH¹ • R thread & P*] 自 動 織 機 — *jidō shokki* — automatic loom 織 物 — *orimono* — cloth, textiles
職	職	432; 128/12. SHOKU* employment, post [CHIH² • R ear & P*] 職 業 — *shokugyō* — profession ⌐sion 休 職 — *kyūshoku* — temporary retirement, suspen-

歩	歩 歩	433; 77/4. HO, BU, FU, *aru(ku)*, *ayu(mu)* walk [PU⁴ · I: a walk in which stops 1–4 (see 552) are few 5–8 (see 129); P*] 歩道 — *hodō* — pavement, sidewalk 歩合 — *buai* — percentage, commission
客	客	434; 40/6. KYAKU*, KAKU guest [K'O⁴, K'E⁴ · R roof & P*] 客間 — *kyakuma* — drawing/hotel room 客員 — *kyakuin* — associate/guest member
臣	臣	435; 131/0. SHIN retainer, subject [CH'EN² · D: an eye watching out (cf. 22) → lookout → retainer] 大臣 — *daijin* — government minister 英国臣民 — *Eikoku shinmin* — British subject
階	階	436; 170/9. KAI* story, floor, level [CHIEH¹ · R hill & P*] 階級 — *kaikyū* — social class, rank 音階 — *onkai* — musical scale
然	然	437; 86/8. ZEN, NEN correct, however; -*zen* (suf.) [JAN² · R fire & P*] ⌐like, resembling 自然の美 — *shizen no bi* — the beauty of Nature 必然の — *hitsuzen no* — inevitable, necessary
植	植	438; 75/8. SHOKU, *u(eru)* plant ⌐R tree & P*] [CHIH² · I: a tree set upright 5–12 (see 304); also 植物園 — *shokubutsuen* — botanical garden 植木屋 — *uekiya* — gardener
歯	歯 齒	439; 211/0. SHI, *ha* tooth ⌐5–12 & P*] [CH'IH³ · D: the two rows of teeth in the mouth 歯科用具 — *shika yōgu* — dental instruments 虫歯 — *mushiba* — decayed tooth
医	医 醫	440; 22/5. I healing [I¹, YI¹ · I: an arrow 2–6 wound 1 & 7; P*] 歯医者 — *ha-isha* — [tooth-doctor→] dentist 内科医 — *naika-i* — physician

例	例	**441;** 9/6. REI* example; *tato(eru)* compare (to); [LI⁴ • R man & P*] ⌐*tato(eba)* for example 例題集 — *reidaishū* — collection of examples/exer- 特例 — *tokurei* — special case, exception ⌐cises
慣	慣 慣	**442;** 61/11. KAN, *na(reru)* become used (to) [KUAN⁴ • R heart & P*] ⌐tional 慣例の — *kanrei no* — customary, usual, conven- 習慣 — *shūkan* — custom
橋	橋	**443;** 75/12. KYŌ, *hashi* bridge [CH'IAO² • R tree & P*] 鉄橋 — *tekkyō* — iron/railway bridge 石橋 — *ishibashi* — stone bridge
注	注	**444;** 85/5. CHŪ, *soso(gu)* pour, shed, concentrate [CHU⁴ • R water & P*] 注意する — *chūi suru* — concentrate/pay attention 定食を注文する — *teishoku o chūmon suru* — order the set meal
州	州	**445;** 2/5. SHŪ* province, state [CHOU¹ • D & S: tracts of land 1, 3 & 5 between 九州 — *Kyūshū* — pn. ⌐rivers; P*] 本州 — *Honshū* — pn. [main island of Japan]
弟	弟	**446;** 12/5. DAI, TEI, DE, *otōto* younger brother [TI⁴ • I: P*] 兄弟 — *kyōdai* — brothers 弟妹 — *teimai* — younger brothers & sisters
術	術 術	**447;** 60/8. JUTSU* art, skill, means, magic [SHU⁴ • R go/do & P*] 美術館 — *bijutsukan* — art museum/gallery 芸術 — *geijutsu* — art, the arts
族	族	**448;** 70/7. ZOKU* clan, tribe [TSU², TS'U² • I: a flag 1–6 (cf. 601) & arrow 7–11, symbols of the clan] 少数民族 — *shōsū minzoku* — minority race 家族連れの旅行 — *kazoku-zure no ryokō* — family trip

損	損	449; 64/10. SON* loss; *son(suru)* suffer a loss; *sokona(u/eru)* (both vt.) harm, spoil [SUN³ • R hand & P*] 損失 — *sonshitsu* — loss 損得 — *sontoku* — loss & gain, profit & loss
害	害	450; 40/7. GAI* harm [HAI⁴ • I: words 8–10 which produce 4–7 (vrt. of 67) harm in the home 1–3; P*] 損害 — *songai* — damage 利害 — *rigai* — advantage & disadvantage
約	約	451; 120/3. YAKU (pref.) about, roughly; promise; [YÜEH¹·⁴ • R thread & P*] ⌐reduce 公約を果す — *kōyaku o hatasu* — fulfill a public promise/pledge ⌐lion yen 約二百万円 — *yaku-nihyakuman'en* — about 2 mil-
条	条 條	452; 34/4. JŌ branch, avenue; clause, edict [T'IAO² • D: branches 1–3 at the top of a tree] 平和条約 — *heiwa jōyaku* — peace treaty 別条がない — *betsujō ga nai* — be unharmed/well
適	適	453; 162/11. TEKI, *teki(suru)* be suitable (for) [SHIH⁴, TI⁴ • R proceed & P*] 適当な — *tekitō na* — suitable, fitting 適切な — *tekisetsu na* — apt, fitting
敵	敵	454; 66/11. TEKI*, *kataki* enemy, rival [TI² • R strike & P*] 敵意 — *tekii* — hostile feeling, enmity 強敵 — *kyōteki* — powerful enemy/rival
構	構	455; 75/10. KŌ, *kama(eru)* take up a stance, build; *kama(e)* stance, structure [KOU⁴ • R tree & P*] 結構な — *kekkō na* — splendid, fine 機構 — *kikō* — mechanism, structure
愛	愛	456; 87/9. AI*, *ai(suru)* love [AI⁴ • I: a person receives 1–6 & 11–13 (vrt. of 272) one's heart 7–10] 愛情 — *aijō* — love, affection 友愛 — *yūai* — friendship, fellowship

精	精 精 精	457; 119/8. SEI*, SHŌ a spirit, vitality [CHING¹ · R rice & P*] 精力 — *seiryoku* — vitality, energy 精神 — *seishin* — spirit, mind
組	組	458; 120/5. SO, *kumi* group, class; *ku(mu)* put/come [TSU³ · R thread & P*] ⌊together 組織 — *soshiki* — structure, organization 労働組合 — *rōdō kumiai* — labor union
退	退	459; 162/6. TAI, *shirizo(keru/ku)* drive back/away [T'UI⁴ · I; P*] 退院する — *taiin suru* — leave hospital ⌈post 退職する — *taishoku suru* — retire from one's work/
皇	皇	460; 106/4. KŌ, Ō emperor [HUANG² · R white & P*] 皇居 — *kōkyo* — Imperial Palace 天皇 — *tennō* — emperor
席	席	461; 53/7. SEKI* seat, place [HSI² · R cloth & P* 1–7] 席次 — *sekiji* — seating order, precedence 着席する — *chakuseki suru* — take one's seat/place
因	因	462; 31/3. IN* cause; *yo(ru)* be due (to), depend (on) [YIN¹ · D & S: a man 3–5 stretched out on a quilt 1–2 & 6 → rest/rely/depend on; P*] 因果 — *inga* — cause & effect, fate, karma 原因 — *gen'in* — origin, cause
技	技	463; 64/4. GI technique, skill; *waza* work, trick [CHI⁴ · R hand & P*] 技能 — *ginō* — technical skill 技術 — *gijutsu* — technique
競	競	464; 117/15. KYŌ, KEI, *kiso(u)* compete (for); *se-(ru/ri)* [bid at] auction [CHING⁴ · I: two men 9–10 & 19–20 in verbal dispute 1–8 & 11–18 (vrts. of 43); P*] 競争 — *kyōsō* — competition 競馬 — *keiba* — horse racing

散	散	**465**; 66/8. SAN, *chi(rasu/ru)* scatter; -*san* powder [SAN³,⁴ · I: to strike 9–12 the flesh 5–8 of plants 1–4 & split them] 散歩する — *sanpo suru* — take a walk 退散する — *taisan suru* — (vi.) disperse, break up (of crowd)
党	党 黨	**466**; 42/7. TŌ* party, faction [TANG³ · R legs & P* 1–8 (vrt. of 1843)] 野党 — *yatō* — party out of office 政党 — *seitō* — political party
功	功	**467**; 48/2. KŌ*, KU merit, achievement [KUNG¹ · R strength & P*] 成功する — *seikō suru* — succeed 功業 — *kōgyō* — achievement, exploit
板	板	**468**; 75/4. HAN, *ita* wooden board [PAN³ · R tree & P*] 合板 — *gōban/gōhan* — plywood, veneer 板紙 — *itagami* — cardboard
黄	黄 黄	**469**; 201/0. KŌ, Ō, *ki* yellow [HUANG² · I; P*] 黄金時代 — *ōgon jidai* — golden age, zenith 黄色の — *kiiro no* — yellow
横	横 横	**470**; 75/11. Ō, *yoko* side [HENG²,⁴ · R tree & P*] 専横な行動 — *sen'ō na kōdō* — arbitrary action 横流しする — *yokonagashi suru* — divert into illegal channels
借	借	**471**; 9/8. SHAKU, *ka(riru/ri)* borrow, rent [CHIEH⁴ · R man & P*] 借財 — *shakuzai* — financial debt, loan 「debt 一時借入金 — *ichiji kariire-kin* — temporary loan/
貸	貸	**472**; 154/5. TAI, *ka(su/shi)* lend, rent [TAI⁴ · R shell/money & P*] 貸借 — *taishaku* — loan, lending & borrowing 貸出し係り — *kashidashi kakari* — person in charge of lending

編	編	473; 120/8. HEN, *a(mu)* knit, compile, edit [PIEN¹ • R thread & P*] 編集する — *henshū suru* — compile, edit 編成 — *hensei* — formation, organization
械	械	474; 75/7. KAI fetters; machine [HSIEH⁴ • R tree & P*] 器械 — *kikai* — apparatus, appliance 編み物機械 — *amimono kikai* — knitting machine
去	去	475; 32/2. KYO, KO, *sa(ru)* (vt.) leave, depart [CH'Ü⁴ • I; P*] ⌊from, (vi.) pass (of time) 去年の今夜 — *kyonen no kon'ya* — this night last 過去 — *kako* — the past ⌊year
暑	暑 暑	476; 72/8. SHO, *atsu(i)* hot [SHU³ • R sun & P*] ⌈by the heat 暑気に当る — *atsuke/shoki ni ataru* — be affected 暑い夏 — *atsui natsu* — hot summer
画	画 畫	477; 1/7. GA picture; KAKU stroke (of Chinese [HUA⁴ • D: a picture in a frame] ⌊character) 絵画 — *kaiga* — pictures, paintings 計画 — *keikaku* — plan
雲	雲	478; 173/4. UN, *kumo* cloud [YÜN² • R rain & P*] 風雲 — *fūun* — wind & cloud, the situation 黒雲 — *kurokumo/kokuun* — black cloud
君	君	479; 30/4. KUN (fam. suf.) Mr.; *kimi* (fam.) you [CHÜN¹ • R mouth & P*] 君主 — *kunshu* — monarch, sovereign ⌈anthem] 君が代 — *Kimi-ga-yo* — [Japanese national
郡	郡	480; 163/7. GUN* country district [CHÜN⁴ • R district & P*] 郡部 — *gunbu* — country district 板坂郡 — *Itasaka-gun* — pn.

顔	顔 顔	481; 181/9. GAN, *kao* face [YEN[2] · R head & P*] 顔面 の 表情 — *ganmen no hyōjō* — facial expres- 横顔 — *yokogao* — profile ⌞sion
練	練 練	482; 120/8. REN, *ne(ru)* train, polish, refine [LIEN[4] · R thread & P*] 練習 — *renshū* — train, practice 試練 — *shiren* — test, ordeal, trial
余	余 餘	483; 9/5. YO* (suf.), *-amari* and more; *ama(ru/ri)* be over/in excess; *ama(su)* leave over [YÜ[2] · D→B; P*] 余計 な — *yokei na* — extra, superfluous, unwanted 余談 — *yodan* — sequel, digression
波	波	484; 85/5. HA, *nami* wave [PO[1] · R water & P*] 余波 — *yoha* — aftereffect, sequel 白波 — *shiranami* — white-topped waves; thief
件	件	485; 9/4. KEN* matter [CHIEN[4] · R man & P*] 事件 — *jiken* — event, matter, incident 要件 — *yōken* — requisite, essential factor
識	識	486; 149/12. SHIKI know, discriminate [SHIH[2,4] · R words & P*] 知識 — *chishiki* — knowledge 常識 — *jōshiki* — common sense
育	育	487; 8/6. IKU, *soda(teru)* bring up, rear [YÜ[4] · I: child 1-4 (inverted vrt. of 61) and flesh; 体育 — *taiiku* — physical training ⌞P*] 教育 — *kyōiku* — education
税	税 税	488; 115/7. ZEI* tax [SHUI[4] · R grain & P*] 税金 — *zeikin* — tax 直接税 — *chokusetsu-zei* — direct tax

飲	飲	489; 184/4. IN, *no(mu)* drink [YIN[3,4] • R eat & P*] 飲 食 税 — *inshoku-zei* — food & drink tax 飲 料 — *inryō* — a drink
汽	汽	490; 85/4. KI steam [CH'I[4] • R water & P*] 汽 船 — *kisen* — steamship 汽 車 — *kisha* — [steam] train
務	務	491; 110/6. MU, *tsuto(meru)* work; *tsuto(me)* work, duty [WU[4] • R strength & P*] 任 務 — *ninmu* — task, function 義 務 — *gimu* — duty, obligation
責	責	492; 154/4. SEKI, *se(meru)* blame, torture, press for; *se(me)* responsibility, blame, torture [TSE[2,4], CHAI[2] • R money & P*] 責 任 — *sekinin* — responsibility 責 務 — *sekimu* — duty, obligation
類	類 類	493; 181/9. RUI* kind, type [LEI[4] • B] 種 類 — *shurui* — kind, type 親 類 — *shinrui* — a relative
写	写 寫	494; 14/3. SHA, *utsu(su)* copy, take (photograph) [HSIEH[3] • R cover & P*] 写 実 的 な — *shajitsu-teki na* — realistic 写 真 — *shashin* — photograph
現	現	495; 96/7 GEN present, existing; *arawa(su/reru)* show, reveal, express [HSIEN[4], HSÜAN[4] • I: jewel 1–4 & see → manifest; P*] 現 在 — *genzai* — the present 現 存 する — *genson suru* — exist, be extant
令	令 令	496; 9/3. REI order, command [LING[4] • I: to gather 1–3 men & affix seal 4–5 = issue orders; P*] 命 令 — *meirei* — order, command 号 令 — *gōrei* — (word of) command, edict

判	判	497; 18/5. HAN* seal, stamp; judgment; BAN [P'AN⁴ · R knife & P*] └(paper) size 判事席 — *hanji-seki* — judge's seat/bench 判決 — *hanketsu* — judgment, decision
準	準 準	498; 24/11. JUN (pref.) semi-, associate; level [CHUN³ · R water & P*] 準急行 — *jun-kyūkō* — semiexpress (train) 水準 — *suijun* — water level
則	則	499; 154/2. SOKU rule, law [TSE² · I: shell 1–7 engraved with a knife → fixed rule/law; P*] 原則 — *gensoku* — basic/general principle 準則 — *junsoku* — standing rule/regulation
案	案	500; 40/7. AN* plan, proposal; *an(jiru)* be anxious [AN⁴ · R tree & P*] └about, worry over 思案する — *shian suru* — think, ponder 議案 — *gian* — bill, measure, proposal
展	展	501; 44/7. TEN stretch/set out [CHAN³ · R bent figure & P] 発展する — *hatten suru* — expand, develop 進展する — *shinten suru* — develop, progress
個	個	502; 9/8. KO, KA individual, unit for counting miscellaneous objects [KO⁴, KE⁴ · R man & P*] 個性 — *kosei* — individuality ┌exhibition 美術個展 — *bijutsu koten* — personal/one-man art
負	負	503; 154/2. FU, *ma(keru)* be defeated, reduce price; *ma(ke)* defeat; *o(u)* bear, be indebted (to) [FU⁴ · R shell & P*] 全負荷電流 — *zen-fuka denryū* — full-load current 勝負 — *shōbu* — victory & defeat, a contest
満	満 満	504; 85/9. MAN, *mi(tasu/chiru)* fill; *man-* full, whole [MAN³ · I: water & level 4–12 = vesselful] 満足する — *manzoku suru* — find satisfaction (in) 満員 — *man'in* — full to capacity, a full house

章	章	505; 180/2. SHŌ* chapter, paragraph [CHANG[1] • D; P*] 文章 — *bunshō* — written text, sentence 第二楽章 — *daini gakushō* — second (musical) movement
順	順	506; 47/9. JUN* sequence, turn [SHUN[4] • R head & P*] 順番 — *junban* — sequence, one's turn 順調 — *junchō* — favorable, satisfactory
序	序	507; 53/4. JO* preface [HSÜ[4] • R lean-to & P*] 序説 — *josetsu* — introduction, preface 順序 — *junjo* — sequence, order
太	太	508; 37/1. TAI, TA, *futo(i)* big, thick; *futo(ru)* grow fat [T'AI[4] • S: something more 4 than big 1–3; P*] 太平洋 — *Taiheiyō* — Pacific Ocean 皇太子 — *kōtaishi* — Crown Prince
景	景	509; 72/8. KEI, KE view, scene [CHING[3] • R sun & P*] 殺風景な — *sappūkei na* — tasteless, vulgar, dreary 景色 — *keshiki* — scenery
査	査	510; 75/5. SA investigate, inspect [CH'A[2] • R tree & P] 査問する — *samon suru* — investigate, inquire into 調査 — *chōsa* — investigation, survey
察	察	511; 40/11. SATSU, *sas(suru)* presume, understand, sympathize with [CH'A[2] • R roof & P*] 査察する — *sasatsu suru* — inspect 考察する — *kōsatsu suru* — consider, study
状	状 狀	512; 90/4. JŌ condition; form; letter [CHUANG[4] • R dog & P* (orig., shape of dog)] 現状 — *genjō* — present/actual state, status quo 案内状 — *annai-jō* — invitation (letter/card), advice notice

弁	弁辨 辨辯 辯	513; 28/3. BEN (a) discriminate; (b) speech; (c) petal; (d) braid [PIEN⁴ • I: two hands 3–5 holding up a cover] 関西弁 — *Kansai-ben* — Kansai speech/dialect 花弁 — *kaben* — petal
参	参 參	514; 28/6. SAN* three (used in documents); *mai(ru)* (dep.) go/come [to worship] [TS'AN¹, SHEN¹, TS'EN¹ • R private & P*] 参加する — *sanka suru* — participate 参考書 — *sankō-sho* — reference book
転	転 轉	515; 159/4. TEN, *koro(bu)*, *koro(garu/geru)* (vi.), *koro(basu/gasu)* (vt.) roll over/about, knock, over, tumble [CHUAN³ • R cart & P*] 転向する — *tenkō suru* — turn/be converted (to) 運転手 — *untenshu* — driver
派	派	516; 85/6. HA* faction, school, group [P'AI⁴ • I: water & streams dividing 4–9] 右派に転向する — *uha ni tenkō suru* — join the rightists 党派 — *tōha* — party, faction, clique
昭	昭	517; 72/5. SHŌ brightness [CHAO¹ • R sun & P*] 昭代 — *shōdai* — brilliant period, glorious reign 昭和 — *Shōwa* — name of reign period (1926–)
雪	雪 雪	518; 173/3. SETSU, *yuki* snow [HSÜEH³,⁴ • R rain & P] 雪害 — *setsugai* — snow damage 雪合戦 — *yuki-gassen* — snow fight/battle
頭	頭	519; 151/9. TŌ, TO, ZU, *atama, kashira* head, top, leader [T'OU² • R head & P*] 頭注 — *tōchū* — headnote (to Japanese text) 店頭 — *tentō* — shop-front/-window
他	他	520; 9/3. TA* other [T'A¹, T'O¹ • R man & P*] 他人の前で — *tanin no mae de* — in front of strangers 他国 — *takoku* — foreign/strange country

統	統	521; 120/6. TŌ, *su(beru)* control [T'UNG³ · R thread & P*] 統治する — *tōchi suru* — rule over, govern 統計報告 — *tōkei hōkoku* — statistical report
選	選	522; 162/12. SEN, *era(bu)* choose [HSÜAN³ · R proceed & P*] 改選 — *kaisen* — fresh/further/re- election ⌈pick 精選する — *seisen suru* — carefully select, hand-
挙	挙 擧	523; 64/6. KYO, *a(geru)* raise, perform, plan; [CHÜ³ · R hand & P*] ⌊*a(garu)* rise 列挙する — *rekkyo suru* — enumerate, list 選挙する — *senkyo suru* — elect
像	像 像	524; 9/12. ZŌ* statue, image, picture [HSIANG⁴ · R man & P*] 仏像 — *butsuzō* — Buddhist image ⌈nation 想像力 — *sōzōryoku* — imaginative power, imagi-
博	博 博	525; 24/10. HAKU, BAKU extensive, universal [PO²,⁴ · R ten & P*] 博愛 — *hakuai* — charity, philanthropy 博物館 — *hakubutsukan* — museum
律	律	526; 60/6. RITSU, RICHI law, rule [LÜ⁴ · R footstep & P*] 法律 — *hōritsu* — law 生の律動 — *sei no ritsudō* — rhythm of life
規	規	527; 147/4. KI standard, measure [KUEI¹ · I: a man 1–4 looking 5–11 to see that things are correct; P*] 規律 — *kiritsu* — discipline, regulations 規則 — *kisoku* — rule, regulation
谷	谷	528; 150/0. KOKU, *tani* valley [KU³ · I: a split 1–4 & mouth = a mouthlike split in the earth; P*] 空谷の足音 — *kūkoku no ashioto* — footsteps in a lonely valley, unexpected help 谷間 — *tanima* — ravine, gorge, slum

拝	拝 拜	529; 64/5. HAI, *oga(mu)* worship ⌈worship⌉ [PAI⁴ • I: a hand holding up a leafy spray 4–8 in 拝見する — *haiken suru* — (dep.) [humbly] look 拝借する — *haishaku suru* — (dep.) borrow
除	除	530; 170/7. JO, JI, *nozo(ku)* exclude, remove [CH'U² • R hill & P*] 除名する — *jomei suru* — strike off a name, expel 除雪する — *josetsu suru* — clear away snow
予	予 豫	531; 6/3. YO beforehand, previously [YÜ² • R & P*] 予想する — *yosō suru* — foresee, anticipate 天気予報 — *tenki yohō* — weather forecast
鉱	鉱 鑛	532; 167/5. KŌ ore [K'UANG⁴, KUNG³ • R metal & P*] 鉱山 — *kōzan* — mine 鉱石 — *kōseki* — ore, mineral
肉	肉	533; 130/0. NIKU* meat [JOU⁴, JU⁴ • D: a piece of flesh 1–2 with sinews 肉体 — *nikutai* — the flesh, the body ⌊3–6⌋ 肉親 — *nikushin* — blood relation
牛	牛	534; 93/0. GYŪ, *ushi* cow, bull, ox ⌈of 4; P*⌉ [NIU² • D: animal with projecting horns 1 & top 牛肉 — *gyūniku* — beef ⌈snail's pace⌉ 牛歩で進む — *gyūho de susumu* — progress at a
欲	欲 慾	535; 150/4. YOKU* greed, desire; *hos(suru)* desire; *ho(shii)* wanted, desired [YÜ⁴ • R open mouth & P*] 欲目 — *yokume* — partial view, partiality 無欲な — *muyoku na* — free from greed, unselfish
済	済 濟	536; 85/8. SAI, *su(masu/mu)* finish, settle [CHI³,⁴ • R water & P*] 返済する — *hensai suru* — repay, refund 経済 — *keizai* — the economy

灯	灯 燈	537; 86/2. TŌ, *hi* light, lamp [TENG[1] • R fire & P*] 灯台守 — *tōdai-mori* — lighthouse keeper 電灯 — *dentō* — electric light
側	側	538; 9/9. SOKU, *kawa* side [TS'E[4], CHAI[1] • R man & P*] 側面 — *sokumen* — side, flank 向こう側 — *mūkōgawa* — opposite/other side
綿	綿	539; 120/8. MEN* *wata* cotton [MIEN[2] • R thread & P*] 綿織り物 — *men-orimono* — cotton goods/textiles 木綿 — *momen* — cotton (cloth)
祖	祖 祖	540; 113/5. SO ancestor [TSU[3] • R god & P*] 先祖 — *senzo* — ancestor　　　　　　　⌈man お祖父さん — *ojiisan* — (hon.) grandfather, old
燃	燃	541; 86/12. NEN, *mo(yasu/eru)* burn [JAN[2] • R fire & P*] 燃料 — *nenryō* — fuel 燃え切る — *moekiru* — burn away
后	后	542; 4/5. KŌ empress, queen [HOU[4] • S: reversed vrt. of 761 = ruler within the 皇后 — *kōgō* — empress　　　　　　⌊Court; P*] 皇太后 — *kōtaikō* — empress dowager
再	再	543; 1/5. SAI, SA, *futata(bi)* twice, again [TSAI[4] • D & S: two weighings 5–6, on a balance 2–4 hanging from a beam 1] 再考する — *saikō suru* — reconsider 再来年 — *sarainen* — year after next
俗	俗	544; 9/7. ZOKU* vulgar, lay; custom [SU[2], HSÜ[2] • R man & P*] 俗語 — *zokugo* — colloquial language, slang 風俗 — *fūzoku* — customs, public behavior

始	始	545; 38/5. SHI, *haji(meru/maru)* begin [SHIH³ • R woman & P*] 始終 — *shijū* — all the time 原始的 — *genshiteki* — primitive, original
宮	宮	546; 40/7. KYŪ, GŪ, KU, *miya* shrine, palace, prince [KUNG¹ • R roof & P*] 神宮 — *jingū* — Shinto shrine 宮参り — *miyamairi* — shrine visit
師	師	547; 2/9. SHI teacher, army [SHI¹ • I; P*] 医師 — *ishi* — doctor 教師 — *kyōshi* — teacher
続	続 續	548; 120/7. ZOKU, *tsuzu(keru/ku/ki)* continue [HSÜ⁴ • R thread & P*] 手続 — *tetsuzuki* — procedure, formalities 相続 — *sōzoku* — succession, inheritance
宿	宿	549; 40/8. SHUKU, *yado* inn; *yado(su/ru)* lodge [SU⁴, HSIU³,⁴, HSÜ¹ • R roof & P*] 下宿 — *geshuku* — lodgings 新宿 — *Shinjuku* — pn.
開	開	550; 169/4. KAI, *hira(keru/ku)*, *a(keru/ku)* open [K'AI¹ • R gate & P*] 開始 — *kaishi* — beginning 開放する — *kaihō suru* — [throw] open
造	造	551; 162/7. ZŌ, *tsuku(ru/ri)* build [TSAO⁴ • I: also R proceed & P*] 造作 — *zōsa* — trouble; *zōsaku* — furnishings 石造 — *ishizukuri* — stone-built
止	止	552; 77/0. SHI, *to(meru/maru)* stop [CHIH³ • D: the foot; P*] 止宿 — *shishuku* — lodgings 中止する — *chūshi suru* — discontinue

処	処 處	553; 34/2. SHO place; *sho(suru)* deal with, act, punish ⌐4-5; P*⌐ [CH'U³,⁴ • I: where one steps along 1–3 & stands 処置 — *shochi* — measures, action 処理する — *shori suru* — manage, settle
伝	伝 傳	554; 9/4. DEN, *tsuta(eru/waru)* transmit, pass on [CH'UAN²,⁴ • R man & P*] 伝統 — *dentō* — tradition 伝聞 — *denbun* — hearsay, report
賃	賃	555; 154/6. CHIN wages, charge [LIN⁴ • R shell/money & P*] 賃金 — *chingin* — wages 汽車賃 — *kishachin* — rail fare
答	答	556; 118/6. TŌ, *kota(eru/e)* answer [TA¹,²,⁴ • R bamboo & P*] 返答 — *hentō* — reply 答案 — *tōan* — (examination) answer paper
落	落	557; 140/9. RAKU, *o(tosu/chiru)* drop [LO⁴, LA⁴, LAO⁴, LE⁴ • R grass & P*] 落物 — *otoshimono* — lost article 落着く — *ochitsuku* — settle down
資	資	558; 154/6. SHI resources; nature, temperament [TZU¹ • R shell/money & P*] 資本 — *shihon* — capital [assets] 物資 — *busshi* — goods
登	登	559; 105/7. TŌ, TO, *nobo(ru/ri)* climb [TENG¹ • I: two feet 1–5 on a step 6–12 = climb in; also R both feet & P*] 登場 — *tōjō* — entry on stage 登山 — *tozan* — mountain climbing
永	永	560; 3/4. EI, *naga(i)* lengthy [YUNG³ • S: river 2 with many tributaries 1 & 3–5 formed over a long period; P*] 永遠 — *eien* — eternity 永続 — *eizoku* — permanence

航	航	561; 137/4. Kō navigation, voyage [HANG² • R boat & P*] 航空 — *kōkū* — aviation 航海 — *kōkai* — sea voyage
泳	泳	562; 85/5. EI, *oyo(gu/gi)* swim [YUNG³ • R water & P*] 水泳 — *suiei* — swimming 泳ぎ手 — *oyogite* — swimmer
修	修	563; 9/8. SHŪ, SHU, *osa(meru)* study, complete [HSIU¹ • R man & P] 修理する — *shūri suru* — repair 修行 — *shugyō* — asceticism
喜	喜	564; 32/9. KI, *yoroko(basu/bu/bi)* delight [HSI³ • I: drum 1–9 (= music) & voices 10–12 = joy; P*] 喜色 — *kishoku* — joyful countenance 大喜び — *ōyorokobi* — great joy
末	末	565; 4/4. MATSU, BATSU power; *sue* end [MO⁴ • S: line at top of tree to mark its end; P*] 年末 — *nenmatsu* — year end 行く末 — *yukusue* — one's fate, future
努	努	566; 19/5. DO, *tsuto(meru)* try hard [NU³ • R strength & P*] 努力 — *doryoku* — effort 努めて — *tsutomete* — with effort & care
観	観 觀	567; 147/11. KAN view [KUAN¹,⁴ • R see & P*] 観念 — *kannen* — concept 観光 — *kankō* — sightseeing
課	課	568; 149/8. KA lesson; section [K'O⁴, K'E⁴ • R words & P*] 課目 — *kamoku* — subject, course 課長 — *kachō* — section head

宣	宣	569; 40/6. SEN announce [HSÜAN¹ · R roof (of palace where announcements made) & P*] 宣伝 — *senden* — publicity, propaganda 宣教師 — *senkyōshi* — missionary
製	製	570; 145/8. SEI manufacture [CHIH⁴ · R clothes & P*] 製造 — *seizō* — manufacture 製品 — *seihin* — manufactured goods
回	回 囙	571; 31/3. KAI turn, time; *mawa(su/ru)* turn [HUI² · D: cf. a wheel; P*] 回答 — *kaitō* — reply 数回 — *sūkai* — several times
協	協	572; 24/6. KYŌ cooperation [HSIEH² · I: many people 1–2 combining their strength 3–8; P*] 協会 — *kyōkai* — society, association 協力 — *kyōryoku* — cooperation
湖	湖	573; 85/9. KO, *mizuumi* lake [HU² · R water & P*] 湖水 — *kosui* — lake 湖辺 — *kohen* — vicinity of a lake
才	才	574; 6/2. SAI* talent [TS'AI² · D→B; P*] 天才 — *tensai* — genius 才能 — *sainō* — ability, talent
示	示	575; 113/0. SHI, JI, *shime(su)* show [SHIH⁴ · D: 3-legged altar stand, the site of revelations; P*] 示教 — *shikyō* — instruction 展示 — *tenji* — display
暗	暗	576; 72/9. AN, *kura(i)* dark [AN⁴ · R sun & P*] 暗記 — *anki* — memorization 暗殺 — *ansatsu* — assassination

解	解	577; 148/6. KAI, *to(ku/keru)* unravel, solve [CHIEH³ · I: remove horns 1–7 of an ox 10–12 with a knife 8–9 = solve dilemma] 解説 — *kaisetsu* — explanation 解散 — *kaisan* — dispersal
犬	犬	578; 94/0. KEN, *inu* dog [CH'ÜAN³ · D; P*] 番犬 — *banken* — watchdog 野犬 — *yaken* — stray dog
起	起	579; 156/3. KI, *o(kiru)* get up, awake; *o(kosu/koru)* raise, begin [CH'I³ · R run & P*] 起原 — *kigen* — source 早起き — *hayaoki* — early rising
著	著 著	580; 140/8. CHO, *ichijiru(shii)* notable; *arawa(su)* write, publish [CHU⁴, CHAO², CHE², CHO² · R grass & P*] 著名 — *chomei* — fame 著者 — *chosha* — author
異	異	581; 102/6. I, *koto(naru)* differ [I,⁴ YI⁴ · I; P*] 異常 — *ijō* — abnormality 異同 — *idō* — difference
庫	庫	582; 53/7. KO, KU, *kura* storehouse [K'U⁴ · I: lean-to 1–3 with a cart 4–10; P*] 兵庫県 — *Hyōgo-ken* — Hyōgo Prefecture 金庫 — *kinko* — a safe
研	研 研	583; 112/4. KEN, *to(gu)* polish, sharpen [YEN² · R stone & P*] 研学 — *kengaku* — study 研修所 — *kenshūjo* — training institute
求	求	584; 3/6. KYŪ, *moto(meru/me)* request, seek [CH'IU² · D→B; P*] 求職 — *kyūshoku* — seeking employment 要求 — *yōkyū* — requirement

折	折	585; 64/4. SETSU, *o(ru/reru)* break, bend; *ori* occasion, opportunity [CHE², CHA³, SHE² · I: hand with an ax 4–7; P*] 折角 — *sekkaku* — at great effort/trouble 折紙 — *origami* — paperfolding
良	良	586; 138/1. RYŌ, *i(i)*, *yo(i)* good [LIANG² · D & S; P*] 良心 — *ryōshin* — conscience 最良 — *sairyō* — best
遊	遊	587; 162/9. YŪ, YU, *aso(bu)* play, enjoy oneself [YU² · R proceed & P] 遊興 — *yūkyō* — enjoyment 遊び相手 — *asobi-aite* — playmate
復	復	588; 60/9. FUKU revert, restore, repeat [FU⁴ · R footstep & P*] 復活 — *fukkatsu* — revival 回復 — *kaifuku* — recovery
比	比	589; 81/0. HI, *kura(beru)* compare [PI³,⁴ · I: two people side by side; P*] 比例 — *hirei* — proportion, ratio 比論 — *hiron* — analogy
底	底	590; 53/5. TEI, *soko* bottom [TI³ · R lean-to & P*] 海底 — *kaitei* — sea bottom 底力 — *sokojikara* — underlying strength
停	停	591; 9/9. TEI stop [T'ING² · R man & P*] 停止する — *teishi suru* — stop, suspend 停留所 — *teiryūjo* — (bus, etc.) stop
徳	徳 德	592; 60/11. TOKU* virtue [TE²,⁴ · R footstep & P*] 徳義 — *tokugi* — integrity　　　「public/civic virtue 公徳を重んじる — *kōtoku o omonjiru* — value

深	深	593; 85/8. SHIN, *fuka(i)* deep [SHEN[1] · R water & P*] 深夜 — *shin'ya* — dead of night ⌐operations 深海作業 — *shinkai sagyō* — deep-sea [salvage]
辞	辞 辭	594; 135/7. JI word; *ji(suru)*, *ya(meru)* resign, give [TZ'U[2] · R bitter & P*] ⌊up 辞書 — *jisho* — dictionary 辞職 — *jishoku* — resignation
弱	弱	595; 15/8. JAKU, *yowa(i)* weak; *yowa(ru)* grow weak, be troubled/overcome (by) ⌐4–5 & 9–10] [JO[4], JE[4] · I: bows 1–3 & 6–8 with decorations 弱点 — *jakuten* — weak point, weakness 弱味 — *yowami* — weakness
武	武	596; 1/7. BU, MU military [WU[3] · I: stop 3–6 revolt by force of arms 1–2 武士 — *bushi* — warrior ⌊& 7–8 (= R lance); P*] 武器 — *buki* — weapon
極	極	597; 75/8. KYOKU, *kiwa(meru/maru)* take to the extreme/end; *kiwa(mi)* extremity, end; GOKU* ex- [CHI[2] · R tree & P*] ⌊tremely 極東 — *Kyokutō* — Far East 北極 — *Hokkyoku* — North Pole
軽	軽	598; 159/5. KEI, *karu(i)*, *karo(yaka na)* light [CH'ING[1] · R cart & P*] 軽油 — *keiyu* — light oil 気軽な — *kigaru na* — light-hearted
究	究	599; 116/2. KYŪ penetrate deeply; *kiwa(meru/ maru)* take to the extreme/end [CHIU[1,4] · R hole & P*] 究明 — *kyūmei* — investigation 研究 — *kenkyū* — research
限	限	600; 170/6. GEN, *kagi(ru/ri)* limit [HSIEN[4] · R hill & P*] 限度 — *gendo* — limit 無限 — *mugen* — infinity

旗	旗	601; 70/10. KI, *hata* flag [CH'I² • R square & P*] 国旗 — *kokki* — national flag 旗行列 — *hata-gyōretsu* — flag procession
誤	誤 誤	602; 149/7. GO, *ayama(ru/ri)* mistake, be mistaken [WU⁴ • R words & P*] 誤解 — *gokai* — misunderstanding 誤訳 — *goyaku* — mistranslation
魚	魚	603; 195/0. GYO, *sakana, uo* fish [YÜ² • D: head 1–2, body 3–7 & tail; P*] 金魚 — *kingyo* — goldfish 魚市場 — *uo-ichiba* — fish market
刊	刊	604; 51/2. KAN publish [K'AN¹ • R knife (for carving printing blocks) & 刊行 — *kankō* — publication ⌐P*] 週刊 — *shūkan* — weekly publication
衣	衣	605; 145/0. I, *koromo* clothing, garment [I¹⸴⁴, YI¹⸴⁴ • D: robe folded over the chest 3–6 below the head & shoulders; P*] 衣食住 — *ishokujū* — clothing, food and shelter 衣類 — *irui* — clothing
断	断 斷	606; 69/7. DAN decision; *kotowa(ru)* refuse, warn; *ta(tsu)* cut off [TUAN⁴ • I: cut 1–7 with an ax 8–11; P*] 判断 — *handan* — judgment 油断 — *yudan* — negligence
移	移	607; 115/6. I, *utsu(su/ru)* move, transfer [I², YI² • R grain & P*] 移住民 — *ijūmin* — immigrant, emigrant 移動 — *idō* — movement, mobility
費	費	608; 154/5. HI expense; *tsuiya(su)* spend [FEI⁴ • R money & P*] 費用 — *hiyō* — expense 旅費 — *ryohi* — traveling expenses

浴	浴	609; 85/7. YOKU, a(biru) bathe oneself [YÜ⁴ · R water & P*] 浴室 — yokushitsu — bathroom 入浴 — nyūyoku — taking a bath
減	減	610; 85/9. GEN, he(rasu/ru) decrease [CHIEN³ · R water & P*] 減少する — genshō suru — decrease, diminish 減退する — gentai suru — decline, subside
待	待	611; 60/6. TAI, ma(tsu) wait for, await [TAI⁴ · R footstep & P*] 接待 — settai — reception 待合室 — machiaishitsu — waiting room
消	消	612; 85/7. SHŌ, ke(su) switch off, extinguish; ki- [HSIAO¹ · R water & P*] ⌊(eru) go/die out 消化 — shōka — digestion 消費 — shōhi — consumption, expenditure
訓	訓	613; 149/3. KUN* Japanese kun reading; instruction [HSÜN⁴ · R words & P*] 訓練 — kunren — training 教訓 — kyōkun — teachings
帯	帯 帯	614; 50/7. TAI belt; obi(ru) wear; obi waist sash [TAI⁴ · I: decorated sash 1–7 & cloth 8–10; P*] 地帯 — chitai — land belt, zone 熱帯 — nettai — tropics
賀	賀	615; 154/5. GA congratulations [HO⁴ · R money (= present) & P*] 賀状 — gajō — greetings card/letter 賀正 — gashō — New Year's greetings
貴	貴	616; 154/5. KI, tatto(i), tōto(i) noble, precious; tatto(bu), tōto(bu) prize, revere [KUEI⁴ · R shell/money & P] 貴族 — kizoku — nobility 貴重な — kichō na — precious

諸	諸 諸	617; 149/8. SHO all, various [CHU[1] • R words & P*] 諸説 — *shosetsu* — various views/theories 諸島 — *shotō* — island group
独	独 獨	618; 94/6. DOKU, *hito(ri)* alone; Germany [TU[2] • R dog & P*] 独立 — *dokuritsu* — independence 独特 の — *dokutoku no* — unique/peculiar to
期	期	619; 130/8. KI, GO period of time [CH'I[1,2] • R moon & P*] 期限 — *kigen* — time limit 学期 — *gakki* — academic term
各	各	620; 34/3. KAKU, *ono-ono* each, every [KO[2,3,4], KE[2,3,4] • I: P*] 各国 — *kakkoku* — each/every country 各駅停車 — *kakueki teisha* — all-stations train
賞	賞	621; 42/12. SHŌ prize; praise [SHANG[3] • R shell & P*] 賞金 — *shōkin* — prize money 文学賞 — *bungakushō* — literary prize
憲	憲	622; 40/13. KEN constitution, law [HSIEN[4] • R heart & P] 憲法 — *kenpō* — constitution 憲政 — *kensei* — constitutional government
効	効	623; 19/6. KŌ, *ki(ku)* be effective [HSIAO[4] • R strength & P*] 有効 な — *yūkō na* — valid, effective 効果 — *kōka* — efficacy
豊	豊 豊	624; 151/6. HŌ, *yuta(ka na)* abundant [FENG[1] • D: a tall vessel 7–13 filled to overflow- 豊年 — *hōnen* — bumper year ⌊ing 1–6; P*] 豊作 — *hōsaku* — rich harvest

拾	拾	625; 64/6. SHŪ, *hiro(u)* pick up; JŪ ten [used in [SHIH² · R hand & P*] ⌊documents, etc.] 拾い物 — *hiroimono* — a find 拾参円 — *jūsan'en* — 13 yen
未	未	626; 4/4. MI not yet [WEI⁴ · D & S: a point 2 not yet at the top of 未来 — *mirai* — future ⌊the tree; P*] 未知 — *michi* — unknown
評	評	627; 149/5. HYŌ, *hyō(suru)* criticize, comment on [P'ING² · R words & P*] 評判 — *hyōban* — reputation 書評 — *shohyō* — book review
息	息	628; 132/4. SOKU son; *iki* breath [HSI¹,² · I: what comes to the nose 1–6 from 息子 — *musuko* — son ⌊the heart 7–10; P*] 休息 — *kyūsoku* — rest
福	福 福	629; 113/9. FUKU* good fortune, wealth [FU² · I: riches 5–13 from the gods 1–4; also R god & P*] 福の神 — *Fuku-no-kami* — God of Wealth 福島 — *Fukushima* — pn.
絶	絶 絶	630; 120/6. ZETSU, *ta(eru)* die out, cease [CHÜEH² · I: thread 1–6 cut 9–12 with a knife 絶対 — *zettai* — absolute ⌊7–8; P*] 絶え間 — *taema* — pause, gap
益	益 益	631; 12/8. EKI, YAKU, *eki(suru)* benefit [I²,⁴, YI²,⁴ · I: water 1–5 overflowing a dish 6– 益虫 — *ekichū* — beneficial insect ⌊10; P*] 利益 — *rieki* — profit
忠	忠	632; 61/4. CHŪ loyalty, faithfulness [CHUNG¹ · I: what is within 1–4 the heart 5–8; also R heart & P*] 忠実 — *chūjitsu* — faithfulness 忠臣 — *chūshin* — loyal retainer

105

河	河	633; 85/5. KA, *kawa* river [HO² • R water & P*] 河口 — *kakō* — river mouth; Kawaguchi — psn. 河底 — *kawazoko/katei* — river bed
系	系	634; 4/6. KEI system, lineage [HSI⁴ • D & S: thread 2–7 caught on something 1 and hanging down; P*] 系統 — *keitō* — system, lineage 系図 — *keizu* — family tree
制	制	635; 18/6. SEI law, system; *sei(suru)* control [CHIH⁴ • I: small branches 1–6 being cut 7–8 = prune, control; P*] 制限 — *seigen* — limit 制度 — *seido* — system
初	初	636; 145/2. SHO, *haji(me)* beginning; *haji(mete)* the first time; *hatsu, ui* first; *-so(meru)* begin to [CH'U¹ • I: cut out 6–7 a robe 1–5 = the first step; P*] 初期 — *shoki* — the early period 最初の — *saisho no* — the first
老	老	637; 125/0. RŌ, *o(iru/i)*, *fu(keru)* grow old [LAO³ • D: long-haired old man 1–4 with stick 5–6; P*] 老人 — *rōjin* — old man 老病 — *rōbyō* — senility
勧	勧 勸	638; 19/11. KAN, *susu(meru)* encourage [CH'ÜAN⁴ • R strength & P*] 勧告 — *kankoku* — advice 勧進帳 — *Kanjinchō* — 'The Offertory Register'
禁	禁	639; 113/8. KIN, *kin(jiru)* prohibit [CHIN¹,⁴ • R god & P*] 禁止 — *kinshi* — prohibition 禁物 — *kinmotsu* — prohibited article
典	典	640; 12/6. TEN code, rule, ceremony [TIEN³ • D & S: sacred books 1–5 on a stand 6–8] 辞典 — *jiten* — dictionary 古典 — *koten* — the classics

季	季	**641; 115/3. KI** season [CHI⁴ • R grain & P*] 四 季 — *shiki* — the four seasons 夏 季 — *kaki* — summer
討	討	**642; 149/3. TŌ,** *u(tsu)* attack [T'AO³ • I: orderly 8-10 discussion 1-7→ dispute → attack; P*] 自由討議 — *jiyū tōgi* — free discussion 討 論 — *tōron* — debate
童	童	**643; 117/7. DŌ,** *warabe* child [T'UNG² • R stand & P*] 童 心 — *dōshin* — child's mind, innocence 童 話 — *dōwa* — children's story
孫	孫	**644; 39/7. SON,** *mago* grandchild [SUN¹ • I: child 1-3 & lineage 4-10; P*] 子 孫 — *shison* — descendants 孫弟子 — *mago deshi* — a pupil's pupil
破	破	**645; 112/5. HA,** *yabu(ru/reru/re)* tear, destroy [P'O⁴ • R stone & P*] 破 産 — *hasan* — bankruptcy 破れ目 — *yabureme* — tear, rent
提	提	**646; 64/9. TEI** present, put forward; *sa(geru)* carry [T'I², TI¹ • R hand & P*] ⌐in the hand 提出する — *teishutsu suru* — present 提 案 — *teian* — proposition, proposal
鏡	鏡	**647; 167/11. KYŌ,** *kagami* mirror [CHING⁴ • R metal & P*] 鏡 台 — *kyōdai* — mirror stand, dressing table 三面鏡 — *sanmenkyō* — triple mirror
詩	詩	**648; 149/6. SHI** poetry [SHIH¹ • R words & P*] 詩 歌 — *shiika/shika* — poetry 漢 詩 — *kanshi* — Chinese poem/poetry

認	認 認	649; 149/7. NIN, *mito(meru)* recognize [JEN⁴ · R words & P*] 認可する — *ninka suru* — approve, authorize 認識 — *ninshiki* — cognition, understanding
墓	墓	650; 140/10. BO, *haka* grave [MU¹ · R earth & P*] 墓地 — *bochi* — cemetery 墓参り — *hakamairi* — visiting a grave
衆	衆	651; 143/6. SHŪ multitude ⌈clan → crowd⌉ [CHUNG⁴ · I: blood 1-6 & many men 7-12 → 衆議院 — *Shūgiin* — Lower House 公衆 — *kōshū* — public
歓	歡 歡	652 ;76/11. KAN pleasure [HUAN¹ · R open mouth & P*] 歓喜 — *kanki* — joy 歓待 — *kantai* — warm welcome, hospitality
投	投	653; 64/4. TŌ, *na(geru)* throw [T'OU² · R hand & P*] 投資 — *tōshi* — investment 投書 — *tōsho* — (written) contribution
清	清 清	654; 85/8. SEI, SHŌ, *kiyo(i)* pure, clear [CH'ING¹ · R water & P*] 清水 — *shimizu* — clear water, sn.; *Kiyomizu* — 清書 — *seisho* — fair copy ⌊pn.
属	属 屬	655; 44/9. ZOKU, *zoku(suru)* belong (to), be [SHU³ · R bent figure & P*] ⌊attached (to) 付属する — *fuzoku suru* — be attached 金属 — *kinzoku* — metal
遺	遺	656; 162/12. I, YUI bequeath [I², YI², WEI⁴ · R proceed & P*] 遺族 — *izoku* — bereaved family 遺言 — *yuigon/igen/igon* — will [& testament]

許 許

657; 149/4. KYO, *yuru(su/shi)* permit, pardon
[HSÜ³ • R words & P*]
許可 — *kyoka* — permission
特許 — *tokkyo* — patent

絹 絹

658; 120/7. KEN, *kinu* silk
[CHÜAN⁴ • R thread & P]
人絹 — *jinken* — artificial silk, rayon
絹糸 — *kinuito/kenshi* — silk thread

液 液

659; 85/8. EKI* liquid
[YEH⁴ • R water & P*]
液体 — *ekitai* — liquid
消毒液 — *shōdokueki* — disinfectant

釈 釈 釋

660; 165/4. SHAKU explain, distinguish
[SHIH⁴ • R separate & P*]
注釈 — *chūshaku* — notes, commentary
解釈 — *kaishaku* — explanation

確 確 確

661; 112/10. KAKU, *tashi(ka na)* certain; *tashi-(kameru)* ascertain
[CH'ÜEH⁴ • R stone & P*]
正確 — *seikaku* — accuracy
確認する — *kakunin suru* — confirm, certify

差 差

662; 123/4. SA* difference; *sa(su)* point to, insert
[CH'A¹,⁴, CH'AI¹, TZ'U¹ • R work & P* 6-10
差別 — *sabetsu* — discrimination   ⌊(= 87)]
差し支え — *sashitsukae* — hindrance, difficulty

聖 聖 聖

663; 96/9. SEI holy
[SHENG⁴ • R ear & P*]
聖書 — *Seisho* — the Bible
神聖 — *shinsei* — holiness, sanctity

管 管

664; 118/8. KAN control; *kuda* pipe, tube
[KUAN³ • R bamboo & P*]
管理 — *kanri* — control, managing
血管 — *kekkan* — blood vessel

録	録	665; 167/8. ROKU record, transcribe [LU⁴ · R metal & P*] 録音 — *rokuon* — sound recording 記録 — *kiroku* — record
紀	紀	666; 120/3. KI narrative, history [CHI⁴ · R thread & P*] 世紀 — *seiki* — century 紀元 — *kigen* — era, epoch
純	純	667; 120/4. JUN purity [CH'UN² · R thread & P*] 純益 — *jun'eki* — net profit 単純 — *tanjun* — simplicity
恩	恩	668; 61/6. ON* kindness, obligation [EN¹ · R heart & P*] 恩返し — *ongaeshi* — returning a favor 恩給 — *onkyū* — pension
兼	兼	669; 12/8. KEN, *ka(neru)* combine, (as suf.) be unable to　　　　　⌈3, 7, 9, & 2, 3, 8, 10; P*⌉ [CHIEN¹ · I: one hand 4–6 holding two plants 1, 兼任 — *kennin* — double appointment/post ⌈for 待ち兼ねる — *machikaneru* — be unable to wait
敗	敗	670; 154/4. HAI, *yabu(ru/reru)* defeat [PAI⁴ · R strike & P*] 失敗 — *shippai* — failure 敗北 — *haiboku* — defeat
焼	焼	671; 86/8. SHŌ, *ya(ku/keru)* burn, grill, be jealous; *-yaki* (pottery) ware [SHAO¹,² · R fire & P*] 焼死 — *shōshi* — death by fire 焼鳥 — *yakitori* — barbecued chicken pieces
潔	潔	672; 85/12. KETSU pure; *isagiyo(i)* gallant [CHIEH² · R water & P*] 潔白 — *keppaku* — integrity, innocence 清潔な — *seiketsu na* — clean

673; 60/7.   JŪ, SHŌ, JU, *shitaga(u)* follow, obey
[TS'UNG[1,2] · I: line of people 4–6 advancing
1–3 & 7–10 (vrt. of R proceed) = follow; P*]
従業員 — *jūgyōin* — employee
従兄弟 — *itoko* — male cousin

674; 109/6.   GAN, GEN, *manako, me* eye
[YEN[3] · R eye & P*]
眼科医 — *ganka-i* — oculist
眼鏡 — *megane* — spectacles

675; 86/9.   SHŌ, *te(rasu/ru)* shine on
[CHAO[4] · R fire & P*]
照明 — *shōmei* — illumination
対照 — *taishō* — contrast, comparison

676; 49/0.   KO, KI, *onore* self
[CHI[3] · D → B; P*]
自己 — *jiko* — one's self
利己 — *riko* — self-interest

677; 157/6.   RO, *ji* road, route
[LU[4] · R foot & P*]
道路 — *dōro* — road
航路 — *kōro* — sea route

678; 102/6.   RYAKU* abbreviation, omission; *ryaku-
[LÜEH[4] · R field & P*]   ⌊*(suru)* omit
略式 — *ryakushiki* — informality
省略 — *shōryaku* — omission

679; 64/5.   SHŌ, *mane(ku)* invite, beckon
[CHAO[1] · R hand & P*]
招待 — *shōtai* — invitation
招待状 — *shōtaijō* — written invitation

680; 170/4.   BŌ, *fuse(gu)* defend, prevent
[FANG[2] · R hill & P*]
予防 — *yobō* — prevention
消防 — *shōbō* — fire fighting

張	張	681; 57/8. CHŌ, *ha(ru)* stretch, spread, affix [CHANG[1] · R bow & P*] 主張 — *shuchō* — emphasis, insistence 引張る — *hipparu* — pull
打	打	682; 64/2. DA, *u(tsu)* strike [TA[3] · R hand & P*] 打ち殺す — *uchikorosu* — beat/shoot to death 打ち敗る — *uchiyaburu* — defeat
節	節 節	683; 118/7. SETSU*, SECHI season, section; *fushi* joint, melody; *ses(suru)* be moderate [CHIEH[2, 3] · R bamboo & P*] 節約 — *setsuyaku* — frugality 季節 — *kisetsu* — season
混	混	684; 85/8. KON, *ma(zeru/jiru)* mix [HUN[4] · R water & P] 混合 — *kongō* — mixture 混雑 — *konzatsu* — disorder
型	型	685; 32/6. KEI, *kata* type, model [HSING[2] · R earth & P*] 小型 — *kogata* — small size 大型 — *ōgata* — large size
衛	衛	686; 60/1. EI defend, protect [WEI[4] · I: go 1–3 & 13–14 around 4–12; P*] 自衛隊 — *Jieitai* — Self-Defence Force 防衛 — *bōei* — defence
岸	岸	687; 46/5. GAN, *kishi* bank, shore [AN[4] · R mountain & cliff 4–5 & P*] 海岸 — *kaigan* — coast 川岸 — *kawagishi* — riverbank
基	基	688; 32/8. KI, *moto(zuku)* be based (on); *motoi* motor, *moto* basis, base [CHI[1] · R earth & P*] 基地 — *kichi* — base 基準 — *kijun* — standard, norm

版	版	689; 91/4. HAN* printing [block] [PAN³ • R split wood (right) & P*] 版画 — *hanga* — woodblock print 出版 — *shuppan* — publishing
低	低	690; 9/5. TEI, *hiku(i)* low, short [TI¹ • R man & P*] 低級 — *teikyū* — low grade 最低 — *saitei* — minimum
改	改	691; 49/4. KAI, *arata(meru/maru)* change, reform [KAI³ • R strike & P*] 改良 — *kairyō* — improvement, reform 改新 — *kaishin* — renovation, reformation
寄	寄	692; 40/8. KI, *yo(seru)* bring close; *yo(ru)* draw [CHI⁴ • R roof & P*] ⌊near (to), call in (at) 寄付 — *kifu* — donation 寄り合う — *yoriau* — (vi.) assemble
増	増 増	693; 32/11. ZŌ, *fu(yasu/eru), ma(su)* (vt. & vi.) [TSENG¹ • R earth & P*] ⌊increase 増減 — *zōgen* — increase & decrease 増進する — *zōshin suru* — promote
供	供	694; 9/6. KYŌ, KU, GU, *tomo* companion; *sona(eru)* [KUNG¹,⁴ • R man & P*] ⌊offer up 提供する — *teikyō suru* — offer 供給する — *kyōkyū suru* — supply
策	策	695; 118/6. SAKU* plan, policy [TS'E⁴ • R bamboo & P*] 政策 — *seisaku* — policy 対策 — *taisaku* — countermeasure
仮	仮 假	696; 9/4. KA, KE, *kari (no)* temporary, assumed [CHIA³,⁴ • R man & P*] 仮面 — *kamen* — mask 仮住居 — *karizumai* — temporary residence

証	証 證	697; 149/5. SHŌ proof, evidence [CHENG⁴ · R words & P*] 証明 — *shōmei* — proof, evidence 保証する — *hoshō suru* — guarantee
救	救	698; 66/7. KYŪ, *suku(u/i)* help, rescue [CHIU⁴ · R strike & P*] 救済 — *kyūsai* — relief, rescue 救急 — *kyūkyū* — first aid
畑	畑	699; 86/5. *hata, hatake* cultivated dry field [- · I: field fertilized by burning 1–4 stubble] 田畑 — *tahata* — fields 茶畑 — *chabatake* — tea plantation/field
容	容	700; 40/7. YŌ looks, contents [JUNG² · R roof & P*] 美容院 — *biyōin* — beauty shop 内容 — *naiyō* — contents
細	細	701; 120/5. SAI, *hoso(i)* slender, narrow; *koma-(kai)* minute, detailed [HSI⁴ · R thread & P*] 細工 — *saiku* — craftsmanship 細長い — *hosonagai* — slender
講	講	702; 149/10. KŌ lecture, study [CHIANG³ · R words & P*] 講師 — *kōshi* — lecturer 講義 — *kōgi* — lecture
静	静 靜	703; 174/6. SEI, JŌ, *shizu(meru/maru)* quieten, calm; *shizu(ka na)* peaceful [CHING⁴ · R blue & P*] 静止 — *seishi* — stillness 絶対安静 — *zettai ansei* — absolute rest
久	久	704; 4/2. KYŪ, KU, *hisa(shii)* long, enduring [CHIU³ · S: long-lasting old man with bent back] 永久 — *eikyū* — permanence 長久 — *chōkyū* — permanence

富 | 富 | 705; 40/9. FU, to(mu/mi) be rich
[FU⁴ · I: abundance 4–12 in the home 1–3; also
富士山 — Fuji-san — Mt. Fuji ⌊R roof & P*]
豊富 — hōfu — abundance

延 | 延 | 706; 54/5. EN, no(basu/biru) extend, postpone
[YEN² · I: feet 1–5 going far 6–8; also R extend
延期 — enki — postponement ⌊& P*]
引延ばす — hikinobasu — prolong, enlarge

故 | 故 | 707; 66/5. KO old, deceased; yue reason
[KU⁴ · R strike & P*]
故人 — kojin — deceased person
事故 — jiko — accident

壱 | 壱 壹 | 708; 32/4. ICHI, ITSU one [used in documents, etc.]
[I¹,²,⁴, YI¹,²,⁴ · I]
拾壱万円 — jūichiman'en — 110,000 yen

芽 | 芽 | 709; 140/5. GA, me bud, shoot
[YA² · I: a plant 1–3 like a tusk 4–8; also R
芽生え — mebae — bud, shoot ⌊grass & P*]
新芽 — shinme — bud, shoot

採 | 採 | 710; 64/8. SAI, to(ru) gather, adopt, engage
[TS'AI³ · I: use hand 1–3 & claw 4–7 to take
from tree 8–11; also R hand & P*]
採用 — saiyō — use, adoption
採集 — saishū — collecting

築 | 築 | 711; 118/10. CHIKU, kizu(ku) build
[CHU²,⁴ · R tree & P*]
築造 — chikuzō — building
建築 — kenchiku — building

幸 | 幸 | 712; 32/5. KŌ, saiwa(i), sachi, shiawa(se) good
[HSING⁴ · I: P*] ⌊fortune
幸福 — kōfuku — happiness
不幸 — fukō — misfortune

欠	欠	713; 76/0. KETSU, *ka(ku/keru)* lack [CH'IEN⁴ • S: vapour 1–2 (= 144) from person 3–4 → yawn → open mouth; P*] 欠点 — *ketten* — fault 欠席 — *kesseki* — absence
鼻	鼻	714; 209/0. BI, *hana* nose [PI² • R nose & P*] 鼻血 — *hanaji* — nosebleed 鼻先 — *hanasaki* — end of the nose
曲	曲	715; 1/5. KYOKU* melody; *ma(geru/garu/gari)* bend, turn [CH'Ü¹˒³ • D: bent receptacle; P*] 曲線 — *kyokusen* — curved line 作曲家 — *sakkyokuka* — composer
格	格	716; 75/6. KAKU* status, standard [KO², KE² • R tree & P*] 格式張る — *kakushiki-baru* — be on one's dignity 性格 — *seikaku* — character
善	善	717; 12/10. ZEN*, *i(i)*, *yo(i)* good [SHAN⁴ • I: fine 1–9 (= 268) words 10–12 (=43)] 善良 — *zenryō* — goodness 改善 — *kaizen* — improvement
応	応 應	718; 53/4. Ō, *ō(zuru)* respond/accede/agree (to) [YING¹˒⁴ • R heart & P*] 応接間 — *ōsetsuma* — reception room 相応 — *sōō* — suitability
我	我	719; 4/6. GA, *ware* I, oneself; *wa(ga)* my, our [WO³ • I: hand 1–4 & lance 2, 5–7 → self-defence; P*] 我等 — *warera* — we 我勝ち — *waregachi* — everyone for himself
算	算	720; 118/9. SAN calculation [SUAN⁴ • I: two hands 12–14 counting money 7–11 (= 44) on bamboo 1–6 abacus] 予算 — *yosan* — estimate, budget 計算 — *keisan* — calculation

収	収 收	721; 29/3. SHŪ, osa(meru/maru) obtain, supply, [SHOU¹ · R rap & P*] ⌐put away 収入 — shūnyū — income 収得する — shūtoku suru — receive
浅	浅	722; 85/6. SEN, asa(i) shallow [CH'IEN³ · R water & P*] 浅見 — senken — superficial view 浅黒い — asaguroi — dusky
弐	弐 貳	723; 1/5. NI two (used in documents, etc.) [ERH⁴ · R shell/money & P*] 拾弐万円 — jūniman'en — 120,000 yen
肥	肥	724; 130/1. HI, ko(yasu/eru) enrich, fatten; koe manure ⌐eating → fleshy; P*] [FEI² · I: (flesh 1-4 =) person kneeling 5-8 → 肥料 — hiryō — fertilizer 肥満 — himan — corpulence
至	至	725; 133/0. SHI extreme; ita(ru) arrive (at), lead (to) ⌐ground 4-6; P*] [CHIH⁴ · D & S: an arrow 1-3 stuck in the 至急 — shikyū — urgency 至極 — shigoku — extremely
勤	勤	726; 19/10. KIN, GON, tsuto(meru/me) serve, work, [CH'IN² · R strength & P*] 勤務 — kinmu — service, duty 通勤 — tsūkin — commuting to work
届	届 屆	727; 44/5. KAI, todo(keru/ke) notify, deliver; todo-(ku) reach [CHIEH⁴ · R bent figure & P*] 届け先 — todokesaki — destination 行き届く — yukitodoku — be thorough
預	預	728; 181/4. YO, azu(keru/karu) deposit, entrust [YÜ⁴ · I; P*] 預金 — yokin — deposited money 預り証 — azukarishō — deposit receipt

指	指	729; 64/6. SHI, *yubi* finger; *sa(su)* point/refer to, [CHIH[1, 2, 3] • R hand & P* └pour 指定席 — *shitei-seki* — designated [=reserved] 親指 — *oyayubi* — thumb └seats
塩	塩 鹽	730; 32/10. EN, *shio* salt [YEN[2] • R earth & P] 食塩 — *shokuen* — table salt 塩水 — *shiomizu* — salt water
株	株	731; 75/6. *kabu* stocks, shares [CHU[1] • R tree & P*] 株式会社 — *kabushiki kaisha* — stock/limited com- 株主 — *kabunushi* — shareholder └pany
倉	倉	732; 9/8. SŌ, *kura* storehouse [TS'ANG[1] • I: food 1-7 (ab. of 283) & enclosure 8-10 → store; P*] 倉庫 — *sōko* — storehouse 正倉院 — *Shōsōin* — The Imperial Storehouse
納	納	733; 120/4. NŌ, TŌ, NA, NAN, *osa(meru/maru)* obtain, supply, put away [NA[4] • R thread & P*] 納得 — *nattoku* — consent, acceptance 出納 — *suitō* — income & expenditure, accounts
夕	夕	734; 36/0. SEKI, *yū* evening [HSI[4] • S: partially risen moon (cf. 13); P*] 夕方 — *yūgata* — evening 夕刊 — *yūkan* — evening paper
厚	厚	735; 27/7. KŌ, *atsu(i)* thick, cordial [HOU[4] • I: thick/dense 3-9 hills & cliffs 1-2; also R cliff & P*] 厚生省 — *Kōseishō* — Welfare Ministry 厚紙 — *atsugami* — cardboard
称	称 稱	736; 115/5. SHŌ, *shō(suru)* name [CH'ENG[1] • R grain & P*] 名称 — *meishō* — name 略称 — *ryakushō* — abbreviated name

布	布	737; 50/2. FU spread; *nuno* cloth [PU⁴ · cloth 3–5 & P* 1–2 (= 90)] 分布 — *bunpu* — distribution 毛布 — *mōfu* — blanket
固	固	738; 31/5. KO, *kata(meru/maru)* harden; *kata(i)* [KU⁴ · R enclosure & P*] ⌐hard 固定する — *kotei suru* — fix 固有の — *koyū no* — peculiar (to), inherent (in)
盟	盟	739; 108/8. MEI oath, alliance [MENG² · I: sacrificial dish 9–13 offered to the heavens 1–8; also R dish & P*] 同盟 — *dōmei* — alliance 連盟 — *renmei* — league
貯	貯	740; 154/5. CHO storage [CHU³ · R shell/money & P] 貯水地 — *chosuichi* — reservoir 貯金 — *chokin* — savings
総	総 總	741; 120/8. SŌ general, entire [TSUNG³ · R thread & P*] 総選挙 — *sōsenkyo* — general election 総長 — *sōchō* — university president
設	設	742; 149/4. SETSU, *mō(keru)* establish [SHE⁴ · I: words & weapon 8–9 in hand 10–11 = organize military camp; P*] 設計 — *sekkei* — plan, design 建設 — *kensetsu* — construction
量	量	743; 72/8. RYŌ* quantity; *haka(ru)* measure [LIANG²,⁴ · measuring box 1–4 & weight 6–12 ⌐(= 161); P*] 分量 — *bunryō* — quantity 重量 — *jūryō* — weight
補	補	744; 145/7. HO, *ogina(u)* supply, supplement [PU³ · R clothes & P*] 補助 — *hojo* — assistance ⌐fill a gap 補欠する — *hoketsu suru* — supply a deficiency,

誠 | 誠 | 745; 149/6. SEI, *makoto* truth 「words & P*」
[CH'ENG² · I: fulfill 9-13 one's words; also R
誠実 — *seijitsu* — truthfulness, honesty
忠誠 — *chūsei* — loyalty

追 | 追 | 746; 162/6. TSUI, *o(u)* chase
[CHUI¹ · R proceed & P*]
追放する — *tsuihō suru* — exile, purge
追い風 — *oikaze* — following wind

券 | 券 | 747; 18/6. KEN ticket, certificate 「P*」
[CH'ÜAN⁴ · R knife 7-8 (to cut tally in two) &
入場券 — *nyūjōken* — admission/platform ticket
旅券 — *ryoken* — passport

罪 | 罪 | 748; 122/8. ZAI, *tsumi* crime, offence
[TSUI⁴ · R net & P*]
罪人 — *zainin* — criminal;
    tsumibito — sinner
有罪 — *yūzai* — guilt

額 | 額 | 749; 181/9. GAKU sum, quantity; framed picture;
[O²,⁴ · R head & P*] ⌊*hitai* forehead
多額 — *tagaku* — large sum
総額 — *sōgaku* — total sum

備 | 備 | 750; 9/10. BI, *sona(eru/waru)* furnish, equip
[PEI⁴ · R man & P]
設備 — *setsubi* — equipment
準備 — *junbi* — preparations

境 | 境 | 751; 32/11. KYŌ, KEI, *sakai* boundary
[CHING⁴ · I: the end 4-14 of a stretch of land
1-3; also R earth & P*]
境界 — *kyōkai* — boundary
国境 — *kokkyō* — frontier

疑 | 疑 | 752; 21/12. GI, *utaga(u/i)* doubt, suspect
[I², YI² · I; P*]
疑問 — *gimon* — doubt
容疑者 — *yōgisha* — a suspect

陽	陽	753; 170/9. YŌ sunshine, positive [YANG² · R hill & P*] 陽気 — *yōki* — liveliness, weather 太陽 — *taiyō* — sun
需	需	754; 173/6. JU require [HSÜ¹ · R rain & P*] 需要供給 — *juyō kyōkyū* — demand and supply 必需品 — *hitsujuhin* — a neccessity
導	導	755; 41/11. DŌ, *michibi(ku)* guide [TAO³, ⁴ · R rule & P*] 導入する — *dōnyū suru* — bring in 指導 — *shidō* — guidance
祝	祝 祝	756; 113/5. SHUKU, SHŪ, *iwa(u/i)* celebrate [CHU⁴ · I: person 8–9 offering words 5–7 to the 祝賀 — *shukuga* — celebration ⌊gods 1–4; P*] 祝福 — *shukufuku* — blessing
志	志	757; 32/4. SHI, *kokoroza(su)* aspire (to), aim (at); *kokorozashi* intention, aim [CHIH⁴ · R heart & P*] 志願 — *shigan* — volunteering, application 意志 — *ishi* — will
測	測	758; 85/9. SOKU, *haka(ru)* measure [TS'E⁴ · R water & P*] 測定 — *sokutei* — measurement 測量 — *sokuryō* — surveying
就	就	759; 8/10. SHŪ, JU take up, fulfill; *tsu(ku)* engage [CHIU⁴ · I; P*] ⌊(in), work (at) 就職 — *shūshoku* — taking up employment 成就 — *jōju* — realization, achievement
旧	旧 舊	760; 2/4. KYŪ old [CHIU⁴ · I: days 2–5 that have gone before 1; P*] 旧式 — *kyūshiki* — old style 復旧 — *fukkyū* — restoration

121

司	司	761; 30/2. SHI administer [SZU[1], SSU[1] · S: 'external administrator,' hence reverse form of 542 (orig., 'ruler within the Court'); P*] 司会者 — shikaisha — chairman, M.C. 司令部 — shireibu — command section, H.Q.
価	価 價	762; 9/6. KA, atai price, value [CHIA[4] · I: a person 1-2 trading 3-8] 価額 — kagaku — valuation, amount 評価 — hyōka — appraisal, assessment
幹	幹	763; 24/11. KAN main part; miki (tree) trunk [KAN[4] · R shield 11-13 (for R tree) & P*] 新幹線 — shinkansen — new trunk/main (railway) 根幹 — konkan — basis, fundamentals ⌊line
複	複	764; 145/9. FUKU repeat, double [FU[4] · R clothes & P*] 複雑な — fukuzatsu na — complicated 複数 — fukusū — plural
謝	謝	765; 149/10. SHA, sha(suru) thank, apologize; ayama(ru) apologize (for/about) [HSIEH[4] · R words & P*] 謝礼 — sharei — remuneration, thanks 感謝 — kansha — thanks
積	積	766; 115/11. SEKI, tsu(mu) load, pile up; tsumo(ru) be piled up; tsumo(ri) intention [CHI[1,4] · R grain & P*] 積極的 — sekkyokuteki — positive 面積 — menseki — area
望	望	767; 96/7. BŌ, MŌ, nozo(mu) hope for, desire, look out (over); nozo(mi) hope, desire [WANG[4] · R moon & P*] 絶望 — zetsubō — hopelessness 望遠鏡 — bōenkyō — telescope
飯	飯 飯	768; 184/4. HAN, meshi boiled rice, a meal [FAN[4] · R eat & P*] 赤飯 — sekihan — rice with red beans 朝飯 — asameshi — breakfast

群	群	769; 123/7. GUN*, *mu(re)* group, crowd; *mu(reru)*, *mura(garu)* crowd, throng [CH'ÜN² · R sheep & P*] 群島 — *guntō* — archipelago 群集 — *gunshū* — crowd
述	述	770; 162/5. JUTSU, *no(beru)* state, speak [SHU⁴ · R proceed & P*] 口述 — *kōjutsu* — oral statement 著述 — *chojutsu* — authorship, literary works
犯	犯	771; 94/2. HAN, *oka(su)* violate, perpetrate [FAN⁴ · R dog & P*] 犯罪 — *hanzai* — crime 防犯 — *bōhan* — crime prevention
副	副	772; 18/9. FUKU deputy, secondary [FU⁴ · R knife & P*] 副題 — *fukudai* — subheading 副産物 — *fukusanbutsu* — byproduct
養	養	773; 123/9. YŌ, *yashina(u)* rear, take care of [YANG³,⁴ · R eat & P*] 養子 — *yōshi* — adopted child 養老院 — *yōrōin* — old people's home
票	票	774; 146/5. HYŌ slip, vote [P'IAO⁴ · R god & P*] 伝票 — *denpyō* — chit 投票 — *tōhyō* — voting
似	似	775; 9/4. JI, *ni(ru)* resemble [SZU⁴, SSU⁴ · R man & P*] 類似 — *ruiji* — similarity 似合う — *niau* — be suited/becoming (to)
拡	拡 擴	776; 64/5. KAKU spread, extend [K'UO⁴ · R hand & P*] 拡声機 — *kakuseiki* — loudspeaker 拡張 — *kakuchō* — extension, expansion

栄	栄 榮	777; 75/5. EI, *saka(eru/e)* prosper; *hae* glory [JUNG[2] • R tree & P*] 栄養 — *eiyō* — nutrition 光栄 — *kōei* — honor
授	授	778; 64/8. JU, *sazu(keru/karu)* grant, award; teach [SHOU[4] • R hand & P*] 授賞 — *jushō* — awarding a prize 授業 — *jugyō* — teaching, classes
蔵	蔵 藏	779; 140/11. ZŌ, *zō(suru)* own, possess; *kura* storehouse [TSANG[4], TS'ANG[2] • R grass & P*] 大蔵省 — *Ōkurashō* — Finance Ministry ⌈ers' 忠臣蔵 — *Chūshingura* — 'League of Loyal Retain-
営	営 營	780; 30/9. EI, *itona(mu)* run (a business, etc.); *itona(mi)* occupation [YING[2] • R mouth & P*] 営業報告 — *eigyō hōkoku* — business report 経営 — *keiei* — management, running (a business)
迷	迷	781; 162/6. MEI, *mayo(wasu/u)* confuse, lead astray [MI[2] • R proceed & P*] 迷信 — *meishin* — superstition 迷路 — *meiro* — maze
児	児 兒	782; 10/5. JI, NI infant [ERH[2] • D: young child with a fontanel-type 児童 — *jidō* — juvenile, child ⌊head] 小児 — *shōni* — infant
臨	臨	783; 131/11. RIN, *nozo(mu)* face (onto), be faced (by), be present (at) [LIN[2,4] • D: a retainer 1–7, seen as a man 8–9 who faces/deals with things 10–18] 臨時 — *rinji* — special, ad hoc 臨席 — *rinseki* — attendance
晴	晴	784; 72/8. SEI, *ha(rasu/reru)* clear away, dispel; *ha(re)* clear skies [CH'ING[2] • R sun & P*] 晴天 — *seiten* — clear sky 秋晴れ — *akibare* — clear autumn weather

検	検 檢	785; 75/8. KEN inspection, investigation [CHIEN³ • R tree & P*] 検査 — *kensa* — inspection, examination 検定 — *kentei* — certification
是	是	786; 72/5. ZE right, just [SHIH⁴ • R sun & P*] 是非 — *zehi* — right or wrong, without fail 是認 — *zenin* — approval
加	加	787; 19/3. KA, *kuwa(eru/waru)* add, increase, join [CHIA¹ • I: strength 1–2 added to the spoken word 3–5; P*] 加減 — *kagen* — condition, health 増加 — *zōka* — increase
災	災	788; 47/4. SAI, *wazawa(i)* disaster, misfortune [TSAI¹ • I: disasters from rivers 1–3 (= 41) & 災害 — *saigai* — disaster ⌊fire 4–7; P*] 天災 — *tensai* — natural disaster
創	創	789; 18/10. SŌ creation [CH'UANG¹,³,⁴ • R knife & P*] 創造 — *sōzō* — creation 独創 — *dokusō* — originality
逆	逆	790; 162/6. GYAKU reverse, opposite; *saka(rau)* be opposed/run counter (to) [NI⁴ • R proceed & P*] 逆転 — *gyakuten* — reversal 反逆 — *hangyaku* — treason
身	身	791; 158/0. SHIN, *mi* body [SHEN¹ • D: a pregnant person; P*] 身体 — *shintai/karada* — the body 身分 — *mibun* — social position
冷	冷	792; 15/5. REI, *hi(yasu/eru)*, *sa(masu/meru)* cool; *tsume(tai)* cold (to the touch) [LENG³ • R ice & P*] 冷蔵庫 — *reizōko* — refrigerator 冷静 — *reisei* — coolness, calmness

粉	粉	793; 119/4. FUN, *kona, ko* powder [FEN[3] · R rice & P*] 粉末 — *funmatsu* — powder 製粉 — *seifun* — flour milling
視	視 視	794; 113/7. SHI sight, vision [SHIH[4] · R see & P*] 視察 — *shisatsu* — observation, inspection 軽視する — *keishi suru* — view lightly, despise
句	句	795; 20/3. KU clause, phrase, line, verse [CHÜ[4] · R mouth & P*] 文句 — *monku* — words, expression; grumble 挙句 — *ageku* — last line of *haiku*, the final thing
護	護	796; 149/13. GO defend [HU[4] · R words & P*] 保護 — *hogo* — protection 弁護士 — *bengoshi* — lawyer
素	素	797; 120/4. SO, SU simple, plain; origin [SU[4], SO[4] · R thread & P] 素質 — *soshitsu* — temperament, character 要素 — *yōso* — main factor, element
卒	卒	798; 8/6. SOTSU* private soldier; completion [TSU[2], TS'U[4] · I: clothes 1-6 (vrt. of 605) with military marks 7-8] 兵卒 — *heisotsu* — private (soldier) 卒業する — *sotsugyō suru* — graduate
牧	牧	799; 93/4. BOKU, *maki* pasture [MU[4] · I: ox 1-4 & strike = rounding up → 牧師 — *bokushi* — pastor, priest　⌊raising cattle] 牧場 — *bokujō* — pasture, stock farm
難	難	800; 172/10. NAN calamity; *muzuka(shii)* difficult; *kata(i)* (lit.), *-gata(i)* (lit.) difficult, impossible [NAN[2, 4] · R small bird & P*] 災難 — *sainan* — calamity, disaster　⌈send 送り難い — *okurigatai* — difficult/impossible to

126

印	印	801; 2/5. IN* seal, stamp; *shirushi* sign, mark [YIN⁴ · I: a hand 1–4 pressing down a kneeling person 5–6; P*] 印判 — *inban* — a seal, stamp 印税 — *inzei* — imprint/book royalties
刷	刷	802; 4/7. SATSU, *su(ru)* print [SHUA¹˒⁴ · I: brush 1–6 & knife 7–8 = carve printing block] 刷新する — *sasshin suru* — reform, renovate 印刷する — *insatsu suru* — print
囲	囲 圍	803; 31/4. I, *kako(mu)* surround [WEI² · R enclosure & P*] 周囲 — *shūi* — circumference, surroundings 取り囲む — *torikakomu* — surround, crowd round
悪	悪 惡	804; 1/10. AKU, O, *waru(i)* bad, evil, wrong [O³˒⁴, WU⁴ · R heart & P*] 善悪 — *zen'aku* — good & evil, right & wrong 悪口 — *warukuchi* — slander, abuse
績	績	805; 120/11. SEKI achievement; spinning [CHI¹˒⁴ · R thread & P*] 成績 — *seiseki* — result, achievement 功績 — *kōseki* — worthy deed, achievement
演	演	806; 85/11. EN, *en(zuru)* perform, act [YEN³ · R water & P*] 演芸 — *engei* — entertainment, performance 演説 — *enzetsu* — speech
詞	詞	807; 149/5. SHI words [TZ'U² · R words & P*] 名詞 — *meishi* — noun 歌詞 — *kashi* — song lyrics
率	率	808; 8/9. RITSU* rate; SOTSU, *hiki(iru)* lead [LÜ⁴, SHUAI⁴ · D & S] 能率 — *nōritsu* — efficiency 率直な — *sotchoku na* — frank, candid

象	象	809; 152/6. SHŌ image; ZŌ* elephant [HSIANG⁴ · D: long-nosed 1–2, big-bodied ele-⌐phant; P*] 印象 — *inshō* — impression 現象 — *genshō* — phenomenon
腸	腸	810; 130/9. CHŌ* the intestines [CH'ANG² · R flesh & P*] 大腸 — *daichō* — the large intestine, the colon 断腸 — *danchō* — heartbreak
革	革	811; 177/0. KAKU reform; *kawa* leather [KO², KE² · D: animal skin stretched out to dry] 革命 — *kakumei* — revolution 改革 — *kaikaku* — reform
耕	耕	812; 127/4. KŌ, *tagaya(su)* till [KENG¹, CHING¹ · R plow & P*] 耕作 — *kōsaku* — cultivation 耕地 — *kōchi* — arable land
脈	脈	813; 130/6. MYAKU* pulse, hope; (geological) vein [MAI⁴, MO⁴ · I: flesh 1–4 & stream 5–10 (cf. 516) → vein → pulse; P*] 動脈 — *dōmyaku* — artery 山脈 — *sanmyaku* — mountain range
唱	唱	814; 30/8. SHŌ, *tona(eru)* recite, advocate [CH'ANG⁴ · R mouth & P*] 合唱団 — *gasshōdan* — choir 独唱 — *dokushō* — vocal solo
穀	穀	815; 79/10. KOKU grain, cereals [KU³ · I: grain 6–10 in the husk 1–3 & 11–14; P*] 穀物 — *kokumotsu* — grain, cereals 穀類 — *kokurui* — cereals
麦	麦 麥	816; 199/0. BAKU, *mugi* barley, wheat [MAI⁴ · I] 麦畑 — *mugibatake/mugibata* — barley/wheat field 小麦 — *komugi* — wheat

嚴	厳 嚴	817; 1/16. GEN, GON, *kibi(shii)* stern, severe; *ogoso(ka na)* solemn, majestic [YEN² · R mouth & P*] 厳禁 — *genkin* — strict prohibition 厳格 — *genkaku* — sternness, severity
奮	奮	818; 37/13. FUN, *furu(u)* be vigorous, be spirited [FEN⁴ · I: many 1–3 birds 4–11 over a field] 奮発 — *funpatsu* — strenuous efforts 興奮 — *kōfun* — excitement
酸	酸	819; 164/6. SAN*, *su(i)* acid [SUAN¹ · R wine jug 1–7 & P*] 酸性 — *sansei* — acidity 酸素 — *sanso* — oxygen
氷	氷	820; 3/4. HYŌ, *kōri, hi* (lit.) ice [PING¹ · I: ice 2 (for R ice) & water 1 & 3–5; P*] 氷山 — *hyōzan* — iceberg 氷点 — *hyōten* — freezing point
岩	岩	821; 46/5. GAN, *iwa* rock, crag [YEN² · I: a mountain 1–3 rock; P*] 岩石 — *ganseki* — rock, crag 岩屋 — *iwaya* — rocky cave
悲	悲	822; 175/4. HI, *kana(shii)* sad [PEI¹ · R heart & P*] 悲喜 — *hiki* — joy & sorrow 悲観 — *hikan* — pessimism
希	希	823; 50/4. KI, desire; scarce ⌈P*⌋ [HSI¹ · I: the fine mesh 1–2 of cloth 3–7 (see 737); 希求する — *kikyū suru* — seek, require 希望 — *kibō* — desire, hope
易	易	824; 72/4. EKI* divination; I, *yasa(shii)* easy [I⁴, YI⁴ · D: the sun 1–4, with rays 5 & 7–8 shining from behind a cloud 6;→B; P*] 易者 — *ekisha* — fortuneteller 容易な — *yōi na* — easy

勇	勇	825; 19/7. YŪ, *isa(mashii)* brave [YUNG³ • R strength & P*] 勇士 — *yūshi* — brave man 勇気 — *yūki* — bravery, boldness
柱	柱	826; 75/5. CHŪ, *hashira* pillar [CHU⁴ • R tree & P*] 電柱 — *denchū* — telegraph pole 大黒柱 — *daikokubashira* — kingpost, mainstay
快	快	827; 61/4. KAI, *kokoroyo(i)* pleasant, agreeable [K'UAI⁴ • R heart & P*] 快活な — *kaikatsu na* — cheerful, lively 全快 — *zenkai* — complete recovery
昼	昼 晝	828; 1/8. CHŪ, *hiru* noon, daytime [CHOU⁴ • I] 昼夜 — *chūya* — day & night 昼間 — *hiruma* — daytime
仁	仁	829; 9/2. JIN, NIN humanity, benevolence [JEN² • R man & P*] 仁愛 — *jin'ai* — benevolence, charity 仁徳 — *jintoku* — benevolence, virtue
否	否	830; 1/6. HI, *ina* no [FOU³, P'I³ • D→B; P*] 否決する — *hiketsu suru* — reject, vote down 安否 — *anpi* — safety, well-being
寒	寒	831; 40/9. KAN* midwinter; *samu(i)* cold [HAN² • I: a house 1–3 sheltering reclining figures 4–10 in icy 11–12 (= R ice) weather] 寒暑の差 — *kansho no sa* — difference between cold & heat/winter & summer 「plant 寒帯植物 — *kantai shokubutsu* — arctic [-region]
走	走	832; 156/0. SŌ, *hashi(ru)* run [TSOU³ • I: earth/ground 1–3 & foot 4–7; P*] 走破する — *sōha suru* — cover a distance by running 走り書き — *hashiri-gaki* — hasty writing, scribble

暴	暴	833; 72/11. BŌ, *aba(reru)* be violent; BAKU, *aba-* [PAO⁴, P'U⁴ · I; P*] ⌊*(ku)* disclose, reveal 暴走列車 — *bōsō ressha* — runaway train 暴挙 — *bōkyo* — violence, recklessness
徒	徒	834; 60/7. TO on foot; companion; empty, useless [T'U² · I: to tread 1–3 & 7–10 the ground 4–6; 徒歩する — *toho suru* — walk, go on foot ⌊P*] 暴徒 — *bōto* — rioters, a mob
態	態	835; 61/10. TAI condition, appearance [T'AI⁴ · R heart & P*] 態度 — *taido* — attitude 状態 — *jōtai* — condition, state, situation
貧	貧	836; 12/9. HIN*, BIN, *mazu(shii)* poor [P'IN² · I money 5–11 divided/dispersed 1–4 (see 35); also R money & P*] 貧弱な — *hinjaku na* — poor, scanty, meager 貧富 — *hinpu* — poverty & wealth, rich & poor
委	委	837; 115/3. I entrust with [WEI³ · R woman & P*] 文化財保存委員会 — *Bunka-zai Hozon Iinkai* — Cultural Properties Protection Committee 副委員会 — *fuku-iinkai* — subcommittee
星	星	838; 72/5. SEI, SHŌ, *hoshi* star [HSING¹ · R sun & P*] 一等遊星 — *ittō yūsei* — primary planet 衛星 — *eisei* — satellite
歴	歴	839; 27/12. REKI travel along [LI⁴ · R stop & P*] 歴史 — *rekishi* — history 経歴 — *keireki* — career [record], personal history
整	整	840; 77/12. SEI, *totono(eru/u)* make ready, arrange [CHENG³ · I: order 1–11 (vrt. of 1478) & put right 12–16; P*] ⌊surgery operation 整形外科手術 — *seikei geka shujutsu* — plastic 調整する — *chōsei suru* — regulate, adjust

賛	賛 賛	841; 154/8. SAN praise [TSAN⁴ · R money & P*] 賛成する — sansei suru — agree/give approval (to) 賞賛する — shōsan suru — praise, admire
炭	炭	842; 46/6. TAN, sumi charcoal [T'AN⁴ · R fire & P*] ⌈bon, decarbonize 炭素を除く — tanso o nozoku — remove the car- 石炭液化 — sekitan ekika — coal liquefaction
銭	銭 銭	843; 167/6. SEN* old unit of money [1/100 of a yen]; [CH'IEN² · R metal & P*] ⌊zeni money 悪銭 — akusen — ill-gotten money ⌈register 金銭登録器 — kinsen tōroku-ki — money/cash
湯	湯	844; 85/9. TŌ, yu hot water [T'ANG¹ · R water & P*] 銭湯 — sentō — public bathhouse ⌈zation 熱湯消毒 — nettō shōdoku — boiling-water sterili-
球	球	845; 96/7. KYŪ, tama ball, sphere, globe [CH'IU² · R jewel & P*] ⌈sphere 南半球 — minami hankyū — the southern hemi- 庭球試合 — teikyū shiai — lawn-tennis match
輪	輪	846; 159/8. RIN, wa wheel, ring [LUN² · R cart & P*] 輪番制 — rinban-sei — job-rotation/shift system 指輪 — yubiwa — ring
池	池	847; 85/3. CHI, ike pond [CH'IH² · R water & P*] 電池 — denchi — battery 貯水池 — chosuichi — reservoir
速	速	848; 162/7. SOKU, haya(i), sumi(yaka na) fast, [SU²,⁴ · R proceed & P*] ⌊speedy 速達 — sokutatsu — express [postal] delivery 快速電車 — kaisoku densha — fast (electric) train

領	領 領	849; 181/5. RYŌ govern, control [LING³ • R head & P*] 領収書/証 — ryōshū-sho/-shō — (certificate of) receipt 副大統領 — fuku-daitōryō — [U.S., etc.] Vice President
漁	漁	850; 85/11. GYO, RYŌ fishing [YÜ² • I: water and fish; also R water & P*] 遠洋漁業 — en'yō gyogyō — deep-sea/ocean fish- 漁師 — ryōshi — fisherman ⌐ing
帳	帳	851; 50/8. CHŌ register, curtain [CHANG⁴ • R cloth & P*] 帳面 — chōmen — account-book, register 帳消しにする — chōkeshi ni suru — cancel/write off accounts/debts
勉	勉 勉	852; 4/9. BEN effort, hard work [MIEN³ • R strength & P*] 勉強する — benkyō suru — study 勤勉な — kinben na — industrious, diligent
胃	胃	853; 102/4. I* stomach [WEI⁴ • I: a full container 1–5 & flesh; P* 6–9] 胃弱 — ijaku — stomach weakness, indigestion 胃腸 — ichō — stomach & intestines/bowels
承	承	854; 4/6. SHŌ, uketamawa(ru) (dep.) hear, agree to [CH'ENG² • R hand & P] 承服する — shōfuku suru — submit/yield to 承認する — shōnin suru — approve, recognize, acknowledge
銅	銅	855; 167/6. DŌ* copper [T'UNG² • R metal & P*] 銅像 — dōzō — bronze/copper statue 銅貨 — dōka — copper coin/coinage
尊	尊 尊	856; 12/10. SON, tatto(bu), tōto(bu) respect, re- vere; tatto(i), tōto(i) respected, revered, valued [TSUN¹ • I: a hand 10–12 offering up a jug of wine 1–9 to the gods; P*] 尊重する — sonchō suru — respect, value 尊称 — sonshō — honorary/honorific title

敬	敬	857; 66/8.　KEI, *uyama(u)* respect [CHING⁴ • R rap & P*] 敬遠する — *keien suru* — keep (someone) at a respectful distance/at arm's length 尊敬する — *sonkei suru* — respect, esteem
標	標	858; 75/11.　HYŌ sign, mark [PIAO¹ • R tree & P*] 標準語 — *hyōjun-go* — standard language 墓標 — *bohyō* — grave post/marker
両	両 兩	859; 1/5.　RYŌ both, two; old unit of money [LIANG³ • D: a hanging balance, showing the two arms for weighing money] 両側 — *ryōgawa, ryōsoku* — both sides 両親 — *ryōshin* — [both] parents
康	康	860; 52/8.　KŌ ease, peace [K'ANG¹ • I; P*] 小康 — *shōkō* — lull, respite 健康そうな — *kenkō-sō na* — healthy-looking
妻	妻	861; 38/5.　SAI* my wife; *tsuma* wife [CH'I¹ • I: a woman 6–8 with a hairpin 1 & 5 in her hand 2–4] 妻子 — *saishi/tsumako* — wife & children, nearest 妻帯 — *saitai* — matrimony　　　└& dearest
候	候	862; 9/8.　KŌ season, weather; *sōrō* classical vb. & [HOU⁴ • R man & P*]　　　　　　　└vb. suf. 候補者 — *kōhosha* — candidate 測候所 — *sokkōjo* — meteorological station
皮	皮	863; 107/0.　HI, *kawa* skin, leather [P'I² • I: a hand 4–5 with an animal skin 1–3; P*] 皮肉 — *hiniku* — sarcasm, irony 皮細工 — *kawa-zaiku* — leatherwork/craft
鳴	鳴	864; 30/11.　MEI, *na(ku)* (of animals, birds, etc.) sing, cry, chirp, etc. [MING² • L: mouth 1–3 and bird; P*] 共鳴する — *kyōmei suru* — resound/be sympathetic (to) 悲鳴をあげる — *himei o ageru* — scream, shriek

孝	孝	865; 24/5. KŌ* filial piety [HSIAO⁴ ・ I: a child 5–7 supporting an old person 1–4 (= 635); P*] 至孝 — shikō — the greatest/utmost filial piety 〔親〕孝行 — [oya]kōkō — filial piety/devotion
倍	倍	866; 9/8. BAI* double, twice the amount; (suf.) [PEI⁴ ・ R man & P*] ⌞times (the amount) 倍率 — bairitsu — magnification 倍増し — baimashi — double, doubling
秒	秒	867; 115/4. BYŌ* a second (of time) [MIAO³ ・ I; P*] 秒速十メートルで — byōsoku jū-mētoru de — at 10 meters speed per second 一分五秒 — ippun gobyō — 1 minute 5 seconds
億	億	868; 9/13. OKU* 100 million [I⁴, YI⁴ ・ R man & P*] ⌜million yen 壱億参百万円 — ichioku-sanbyaku-man'en — 103 億万長者 — okuman chōja — a multi-millionaire
均	均	869; 32/4. KIN equal, level [CHÜN¹ ・ I: to level 4–7 ground 1–3] 平均 — heikin — average, balance, equilibrium 均等 — kintō — uniformity, equality, parity
菜	菜	870; 140/8. SAI, na greens, rape plant [TS'AI⁴ ・ R grass & P*] 野菜 — yasai — vegetables 菜種 — natane — rapeseed
貿	貿	871; 154/5. BŌ trade, exchange [MAO⁴ ・ R money & P*] 貿易 — bōeki — trade 貿易会社 — bōekigaisha — trading company
舎	舎	872; 9/6. SHA house, shelter [SHE⁴ ・ R mouth & P*] 寄宿舎 — kishukusha — boarding house, hostel 田舎 — inaka — country(side)

陛	陛	873; 170/7. HEI steps of the throne [PI⁴ · R mound & P*] 天皇陛下 — *Tennō-heika* — His Majesty the Emperor 「press 皇后陛下 — *Kōgō-heika* — Her Majesty the Em-
圧	圧 壓	874; 27/3. ATSU pressure [YA¹,⁴ · R earth & P*] 気圧 — *kiatsu* — atmospheric pressure 電圧 — *den'atsu* — voltage
往	往	875; 60/5. Ō go [WANG³,⁴ · I; P*] 往復 — *ōfuku* — going & returning, round trip 立往生する — *tachi-ōjō suru* — die on one's feet, be at a standstill/loss
緑	緑 綠	876; 120/8. RYOKU, ROKU, *midori* green [LÜ⁴, LU⁴ · R thread & P*] 新緑 — *shinryoku* — fresh greenery 緑色 — *midori-iro* — green
推	推	877; 64/8. SUI, *o(su)* infer, recommend, support [TʼUI¹ · R hand & P*] 推定 — *suitei* — inference 推理 — *suiri* — reasoning, inference
舌	舌	878; 135/0. ZETSU, *shita* tongue 「mouth; P*] [SHE² · D: the tongue 1–3 sticking out from the 弁舌の才 — *benzetsu no sai* — eloquence 舌打ち — *shitauchi* — clicking the tongue, smacking the lips
俵	俵	879; 9/8. HYŌ, *tawara* straw bag [PIAO³ · R man & P*] 土俵 — *dohyō* — sandbag, sumō ring 炭俵 — *sumidawara* — charcoal sack
蚕	蚕 蠶	880; 1/9. SAN, *kaiko* silkworm [TSʼAN² · R insect & P*] 蚕糸 — *sanshi* — silk thread 養蚕 — *yōsan* — sericulture

央	央	881; 2/4. Ō center, middle [YANG¹ · I; P*] 中央 — chūō — center 中央線 — Chūō-sen — the Central (railway) Line
好	好	882; 38/3. KŌ, kono(mu), su(ku) like [HAO³·⁴ · I: woman & child P*] 好意 — kōi — goodwill 好調 — kōchō — good tone/trend/condition
違	違	883; 162/9. I, chiga(u) be different/wrong [WEI² · R proceed & P*] 違反 — ihan — violation, infringement 相違 — sōi — difference, disparity
松	松	884; 75/4. SHŌ, matsu pine tree [SUNG¹ · R tree & P*] 松林 — matsubayashi — pine forest 門松 — kadomatsu — New Year gate decorations
巻	巻 巻	885; 49/5. KAN, maki volume, book; ma(ku) roll, [CHÜAN³·⁴ · R kneeling figure & P*] ⌐wind 第一巻 — daiikkan — volume 1 絵巻〔物〕— emaki[mono] — picture scroll
城	城	886; 32/6. JŌ, shiro castle [CH'ENG² · R earth & P*] 城下町 — jōkamachi — castle town 宮城県 — Miyagi-ken — Miyagi Prefecture
降	降	887; 170/7. KŌ, fu(ru) fall (of rain, etc.); o(riru) alight/descend from [CHIANG,⁴ HSIANG² · R mound & P] 降参する — kōsan suru — surrender 以降 — ikō — on & after, during & since
及	及	888; 4/2. KYŪ, oyo(bu) attain/come/match up (to); oyo(bi) and ⌐gain, reach; P*] [CHI²·⁴ · I: a man 1–2 seized by a hand 3 → 及第点 — kyūdaiten — examination pass mark 及び難い — oyobigatai — hard/impossible to attain

枝	枝	889; 75/4. SHI, *eda* branch, bough [CHIH¹ • R tree & P*] 枝葉 — *shiyō* — branches & leaves, side issues 小枝 — *koeda* — twig, spray
忙	忙	890; 61/3. BŌ, *isoga(shii)* busy [MANG² • R heart & P*] 忙殺 — *bōsatsu* — being worked to death 多忙な — *tabō na* — busy
暇	暇	891; 72/9. KA, *hima* leisure [HSIA² • R sun & P*] 休暇 — *kyūka* — holiday 余暇 — *yoka* — leisure
殿	殿	892; 4/12. DEN, TEN hall, palace; *-dono* Mr., Esq.; [TIEN⁴ • R kill & P*] ⌊*tono* (feudal) lord 宮殿 — *kyūden* — palace 殿様 — *tonosama* — (feudal) lord
源	源	893; 85/10. GEN, *minamoto* origin, source [YÜAN² • R water & P*] 源平 — *Genpei* — the Minamoto & Taira clans 起源 — *kigen* — origin, source
継	継 繼	894; 120/7. KEI, *tsu(gu)* inherit, succeed to; *tsu(gi)* patch ⌈be joined⌉ [CHI⁴ • I: thread 1–6 in two pieces 7–13, ready to 皇位を継承する — *kōi o keishō suru* — succeed to the throne 受継ぐ — *uketsugu* — inherit, succeed to
遣	遣	895; 162/10. KEN, *tsuka(wasu)* send, present; [CH'IEN³ • R proceed & P*] ⌊*tsuka(u)* use 派遣する — *haken suru* — dispatch 小遣〔銭〕 — *kozukai[sen]* — pocket money
詳	詳	896; 149/6. SHŌ, *kuwa(shii)* detailed, well informed [HSIANG² • R words & P*] 詳細 — *shōsai* — details 未詳 — *mishō* — not [yet] known

渡

897; 85/9. TO, *wata(su/ru)* cross/pass over, transfer
[TU⁴ · R water & P*]
渡来 — *torai* — arrival from abroad
渡し船 — *watashibune* — ferryboat

盛 盛

898; 108/6. SEI, JŌ, *saka(n na)* prosperous; *saka-(ru/ri)* be at the height/prime; *mo(ru)* serve, heap up
[SHENG⁴. CH'ENG² · R dish & P*]
全盛 — *zensei* — full splendor/power, prime
最盛期 — *saiseiki* — richest age, best season

危

899; 4/5. KI, *abu(nai)*, *ayau(i)* dangerous
[WEI² · I: man 1–2 on a cliff 3–4, kneeling 5–6 in ⌊fright]
危険 — *kiken* — danger
危機 — *kiki* — time of danger, crisis

閉

900; 169/3. HEI, *to(jiru)*, *shi(meru/maru)* shut
[PI⁴ · I: to bar the gates 1–8 with timber 9–11; P*]
閉口する — *heikō suru* — be dumbfounded
開閉 — *kaihei* — opening & closing

晩 晩

901; 72/8. BAN* evening
[WAN³ · R sun & P*]
晩秋 — *banshū* — late autumn ⌈late.
大器晩成 — *taiki bansei* — Great talent matures

警

902; 149/12. KEI warn, caution
[CHING³ · R words & P*]
警備する — *keibi suru* — guard, defend
暴風警報 — *bōfū keihō* — storm warning

署 署

903; 122/8. SHO government office, [police, etc.]
[SHU³ · R net & P*] ⌊station; signature
警察署 — *keisatsusho* — police station
消防署 — *shōbōsho* — fire station

払 拂

904; 64/2. FUTSU, *hara(u)* sweep away, pay
[FU² · R hand & P*]
払底 — *futtei* — shortage, scarcity ⌈note
支払い伝票 — *shiharai denpyō* — payment slip/

巡	巡	905; 162/3. JUN, *megu(ru)* go/travel around [HSÜN² · I: a river 1–3 proceeds 4–6 meanderingly; P*] 巡歴する — *junreki suru* — tour/travel around 交通巡査 — *kōtsū junsa* — traffic policeman
帝	帝	906; 8/7. TEI emperor [TI⁴ · D→E; P*] 帝国 — *teikoku* — empire 皇帝 — *kōtei* — emperor, sovereign
浜	浜 濱	907; 85/7. HIN, *hama* beach [PIN¹ · R water & P*] 京浜地区 — *Keihin chiku* — Tōkyō (= *kei*)-Yoko- 横浜 — *Yokohama* — pn. ⌊hama (= *hin*) area
沢	沢 澤	908; 85/4. TAKU, *sawa* swamp, marsh [TSE²′⁴, CHAI² · R water & P*] 光沢 — *kōtaku* — luster, gloss, polish 沢辺 — *sawabe* — edge of a swamp
離	離	909; 172/11. RI, *hana(su/reru)* separate, keep apart [LI² · R small bird & P] ⌈lose one's job 離職する — *rishoku suru* — be separated from 分離する — *bunri suru* — secede, detach oneself
映	映	910; 72/5. EI, *utsu(su/ru)* reflect, project; *ha(eru)* [YING⁴ · R sun & P*] ⌊shine, glow 映画 — *eiga* — film, movie 映写機 — *eishaki* — (cine) projector
段	段	911; 79/5. DAN* grade, step, level [TUAN⁴ · R kill & P*] 段違い — *danchigai* — different level, widely apart 階段 — *kaidan* — stairs, steps
乱	乱 亂	912; 135/1. RAN* civil war, rising; *mida(su/reru)* [LUAN⁴, LAN⁴ · I; P*] ⌊throw into disorder 乱暴な — *ranbō na* — violent, rough 混乱する — *konran suru* — be confused/chaotic

突	突 突	913; 116/3. TOTSU sudden; *tsu(ku)* strike, thrust [T'U⁴ · I: a big dog 6–8 rushing out from a hole/cave 1–5; P*] 突破する — *toppa suru* — break through, surmount 突然 — *totsuzen* — suddenly
煙	煙 烟	914; 86/9. EN, *kemuri* smoke; *kemu(ru)* smoke; *kemu(i)* smoky [YEN¹ · I: flame & incense burner 5–13] 煙突 — *entotsu* — chimney 禁煙 — *kin'en* — smoking prohibited, no smoking
泉	泉	915; 106/4. SEN, *izumi* spring [CH'ÜAN² · I: clear/pure 1–5 water; P*] 冷泉 — *reisen* — cold-water spring 温泉 — *onsen* — hot spring
井	井	916; 4/3. SEI, SHŌ, *i* a well [CHING³ · D: well frame seen from above; P*] 油井 — *yusei* — oil well 井戸 — *ido* — a well 天井 — *tenjō* — ceiling
暖	暖	917; 72/9. DAN, *atata(kai)* warm [NUAN³, NAN³, NANG³ · R sun & P*] 温暖前線 — *ondan zensen* — warm front 寒暖計 — *kandankei* — thermometer
寝	寝 寢	918; 40/10. SHIN, *ne(ru)* lie down, go to bed, sleep [CH'IN³ · I; P*] 寝室 — *shinshitsu* — bedroom 就寝中 — *shūshin-chū* — while sleeping/in bed
誌	誌	919; 149/7. SHI write down, record [CHIH⁴ · R words & P*] 雑誌 — *zasshi* — magazine　⌐a magazine 次号誌上で — *jigō shijō de* — in the next issue of
将	将 將	920; 90/7. SHŌ commander; be about to [CHIANG¹,⁴ · I; P*] 将軍 — *shōgun* — general; military ruler of Japan 将来 — *shōrai* — the future

臟	臓 臓	921; 130/14. ZŌ organs of the body [TSANG⁴ • R flesh & P*] 内臓 — *naizō* — internal organs, intestines 心臓 — *shinzō* — the heart
丸	丸	922; 4/2. GAN, *maru(i)* round; -*maru* suf. for ship [WAN² • I; P*] └names 丸薬 — *gan'yaku* — (medicinal) pill, capsule 丸太 — *maruta* — log
爆	爆	923; 86/15. BAKU burst, explode [PAO⁴ • R fire & P*] 爆発する — *bakuhatsu suru* — explode 原爆 — *genbaku* — atomic bomb
御	御	924; 60/9. GO, GYO, o, on hon. pref.; *gyo(suru)* [YÜ⁴ • I; P* 4–7 (= 140)] └control 御飯 — *gohan* — cooked rice ┌check 制御する — *seigyo suru* — control, suppress,
洗	洗	925; 85/6. SEN, *ara(u)* wash, inquire into [HSI³ • R water & P*] 洗練する — *senren suru* — polish, refine 〔お〕手洗い — *[o]tearai* — toilet
袋	袋	926; 145/5. TAI, *fukuro* bag, sack [TAI⁴ • R clothes & P*] 袋小路 — *fukuro-kōji* — blind alley, cul-de-sac 手袋をはめる — *tebukuro o hameru* — put on gloves
脳	脳 脳	927; 130/7. NŌ* brain ┌P*] [NAO³ • R flesh & (D: brains in the head →) 脳出血 — *nō-shukketsu* — cerebral hemorrhage 頭脳 — *zunō* — brains, intelligence
途	途	928; 162/7. TO road, way [T'U² • R proceed & P*] ┌cut off 途絶する — *tozetsu suru* — be stopped/blocked/ 帰途に — *kito ni* — on one's way home

影	影	929; 59/12. EI, *kage* shadow, image [YING³ · R light rays & P*] 投影する — *tōei suru* — throw/project an image 影法師が映る — *kage-bōshi ga utsuru* — A person's shadow is cast.
奥	奥 奧	930; 4/11. OKU*, ō interior, innermost part [AO⁴ · I; inner room 1–3 (= 278) where the rice 4–9 is brought in 10–12 (←D of two hands)] 奥様 — *okusama* — (hon.) wife 深奥 — *shin'ō* — the depths, secrets, mysteries
免	免	931; 10/6. MEN, *manu(kareru)* escape from, avoid; *men(zuru)* dismiss/exempt from [MIEN³ · I; P*] 御免 — *gomen* — (another's) pardon, permission 運転免許証 — *unten menkyo-shō* — driving licence/certificate
乏	乏	932; 4/2. BŌ, *tobo(shii)* insufficient, scanty [FA² · S: reversed vrt. of 123 = not right, deficient] 欠乏する — *ketsubō suru* — be insufficient/lacking 貧乏な — *binbō na* — poor, poverty-stricken
背	背	933; 130/5. HAI, *se* back, stature; *sei* stature; *somu(ku)* go/act/offend (against); *somu(keru)* avert [PEI¹·⁴ · I: two men back to back 1–5 & flesh 6–9; P*] 背景 — *haikei* — background 背中を流す — *senaka o nagasu* — wash one's back
覧	覧 覽	934; 147/9. RAN see, look at [LAN³ · R see & P*] 遊覧 — *yūran* — excursion, sightseeing 展覧会 — *tenrankai* — exhibition
箱	箱	935; 118/9. *hako* box [HSIANG¹ · R bamboo & P] 箱根 — *Hakone* — pn. 重箱 — *jūbako* — tier of fitted boxes
罰	罰 罰	936; 122/9. BATSU* punishment, penalty; BACHI* punishment (for sin); *bas(suru)* punish [FA² · I: to scold 1–11 and threaten with a sword 12–13] 所罰する — *shobatsu suru* — punish 厳罰 — *genbatsu* — severe punishment

片	片	937; 91/0.　HEN part; *kata-* one (of two) [P'IEN⁴ ・ D&S: right half of a tree split down the middle] 断片的 — *danpenteki* — fragmentary 片寄る — *katayoru* — lean/be partial (toward)
傾	傾	938; 9/11.　KEI, *katamu(keru/ku/ki)* incline (to) [CH'ING¹,² ・ I: a man 1–2 bending 3–4 his head 5–13 → lean; P*] 傾向 — *keikō* — inclination, tendency 傾注する — *keichū suru* — devote, concentrate
慮	慮	939; 141/9.　RYO think, consider [LÜ⁴ ・ I: the presence of a tiger 1–6 (= 1932) gives food for thought 7–15; P*] 遠慮する — *enryo suru* — be reserved/constrained 考慮 — *kōryo* — consideration
秘	秘 祕	940; 115/5.　HI, *hi(meru)* keep secret [MI⁴, PI⁴ ・ R grain & P*] 秘蔵する — *hizō suru* — prize, treasure 極秘 — *gokuhi* — strict secrecy, top secret
介	介	941; 9/2.　KAI* shellfish; stand between; *kai(shite)* through the good offices of 「tween 3–4; P*] [CHIEH⁴ ・ I: a man 1–2 who divides/stands be- 介在する — *kaizai suru* — interpose, intervene 魚介 — *gyokai* — seafood
艦	艦 艦	942; 137/14.　KAN warship [CHIEN⁴ ・ R boat & P*] 艦隊 — *kantai* — naval fleet 旗艦 — *kikan* — flagship
肺	肺	943; 130/5.　HAI* lung [FEI⁴ ・ R flesh & P*] 肺病 — *haibyō* — tuberculosis 肺臓 — *haizō* — the lungs
絡	絡	944; 120/6.　RAKU, *kara(mu)*, *kara(maru)* coil/twist (around), cling (to) [LE⁴, LAO⁴ ・ R thread & P*] 連絡 — *renraku* — communication, contact 脈絡 — *myakuraku* — coherence, logical connection

触	触 觸	945; 148/6. SHOKU, *fu(reru)* (vi.) *sawa(ru)* (vi.) [CH'O⁴, CH'U⁴ · R horn & P*] ⌞touch 接触する — *sesshoku suru* — come in contact/ touch (with) 感触 — *kanshoku* — sense of touch, feel
菓	菓	946; 140/8. KA fruit, cake [KUO³ · R grass & P*] 茶菓子 — *cha-gashi* — tea-cakes, refreshments 製菓 — *seika* — confectionery
掃	掃	947; 64/8. SŌ, *ha(ku)* sweep [SAO³,⁴ · I: hand & broom 4–11; P*] 掃除する — *sōji suru* — clean, sweep 清掃夫 — *seisōfu* — road sweeper, dustman
帆	帆	948; 50/3. HAN, *ho* sail [FAN¹,² · R cloth & P*] 帆船 — *hansen/hobune* — sailboat 出帆する — *shuppan suru* — set sail
緒	緒 緒	949; 120/8. SHO, CHO beginning; *o* cord, string [HSÜ⁴ · R thread & P*] ⌜remarks 緒論 — *shoron/choron* — introductory statement/ 情緒 — *jōcho* — emotion, sentiment
蒸	蒸	950; 140/9. JŌ, *mu(su)* (vt.) steam, (vi.) be close/ [CHENG¹ · R grass & P*] ⌞sultry 蒸発する — *jōhatsu suru* — evaporate 蒸留する — *jōryū suru* — distill
符	符	951; 118/5. FU tally, sign [FU² · R bamboo & P*] ⌜(with) 符合する — *fugō suru* — conform/fit/correspond 切符 — *kippu* — ticket
枚	枚	952; 75/4. MAI unit for counting sheetlike things [MEI² · I: wood & rap 5–8 → cane → count- ing stick; P*] 枚挙する — *maikyo suru* — count, enumerate 枚数 — *maisū* — number of sheets/leaves

145

軒	軒	953; 159/3. KEN unit for counting buildings; *noki* eaves ⌜projecting eaves; also R cart & P*⌝ [HSÜAN¹ • I: cart with projecting 8–10 shafts→ 軒数 — *kensū* — number of houses 軒下に/で — *nokishita ni/de* — under the eaves
芝	芝	954; 140/2. *shiba* lawn, turf [CHIH¹ • R grass & P] 芝生 — *shibafu* — lawn, grass 芝居 — *shibai* — play, drama
郎	郎	955; 163/6. RŌ man, husband; suf. in mn. [LANG² • R city & P*] 太郎 — *Tarō* — mn. 新郎新婦 — *shinrō shinpu* — bridegroom & bride
冊	冊 冊	956; 2/4. SATSU unit for counting books; SAKU [T'SE⁴, CH'AI³ • D: inscribed strips 1–4 tied with string 5; P*] 〔小〕冊子 — *[shō-]sasshi* — booklet, pamphlet 分冊 — *bunsatsu* — separate volume
換	換	957; 64/9. KAN, *ka(eru/waru)* change [HUAN⁴ • R hand & P*] 換算率 — *kansan-ritsu* — exchange/conversion rate 〔電話〕交換局 — *[denwa] kōkankyoku* — telephone exchange
畳	畳 畳	958; 102/7. JŌ unit for counting room mats; *tatami* ⌞room mat; *tata(mu)* fold up [TIEH² • I] 八畳の部屋 — *hachijō no heya* — an 8-mat room 畳み寝台 — *tatami-shindai* — folding bed
床	床	959; 53/4. SHŌ, *toko* bed, alcove; *yuka* floor ⌜P*⌝ [CH'UANG² • I: the wood 4–7 inside a house 1–3] 臨床的研究 — *rinshōteki kenkyū* — clinical study 床板を張る — *yuka-ita o haru* — lay floorboards
誕	誕	960; 149/8. TAN birth [TAN⁴ • I: stretched 8–14 (see 706) words 1–7→ 誕生日 — *tanjōbi* — birthday ⌞B; P*⌝ 降誕 — *kōtan* — royal/holy birth

杯	杯	961; 75/4. HAI unit for counting containerfuls; [PEI¹ • R tree & P*] ⌊sakazuki wine cup 杯洗 — haisen — sink, washing-up bowl 一杯飲む — ippai nomu — have a drink
丈	丈	962; 4/2. JŌ 10 feet; take stature, length [CHANG⁴ • I] 方丈 — hōjō — 10 feet square, [room of] an abbot 気丈な — kijō na — stout-hearted, strong-nerved
勘	勘	963; 19/9. KAN* intuition, sixth sense; consider, [K'AN⁴ • R strength & P*] ⌊investigate 勘弁する — kanben suru — pardon, tolerate 勘定 — kanjō — account, bill
郵	郵	964; 163/8. YŪ post, mail [YU² • I: remote 1–8 (see 1214) district 9–11→ settlement → post town; P*] 航空郵便 — kōkū yūbin — air mail ⌈post-free 郵送無料 — yūsō muryō — post without charge,
婚	婚	965; 38/8. KON marriage [HUN¹ • I: a woman enters the family line 4–7 from that day 8–11] 結婚する — kekkon suru — marry (with) 離婚する — rikon suru — divorce (from)
企	企	966; 9/4. KI, kuwada(teru/te) plan, scheme [CH'I³,⁴ • D & S; P*] 企図 — kito — plan, scheme 企画 — kikaku — plan, planning
羽	羽	967; 124/0. U, ha, hane feather, wing [YÜ³ • D: a bird's wings; P*] 羽毛 — umō — feathers, plumage 羽織 — haori — a haori jacket
舟	舟	968; 137/0. SHŪ, fune boat [CHOU¹ • D: boat with mooring rope 1, hull 2–3, planking 4 & 5, & stern oar 6] 川舟 — kawabune — river-boat; barge 舟遊び — funa-asobi — boating

困	困	969; 31/4. KON, *koma(ru)* be in difficulties, be at a loss ⌈P*⌉ [K'UN⁴ • I: tree restricted by cramped enclosure; 困難 — *konnan* — difficulty 貧困 — *hinkon* — poverty
攻	攻	970; 48/4. KŌ, *se(meru/me)* attack [KUNG¹ • R strike & P*] 攻勢 — *kōsei* — an offensive, aggression 専攻 — *senkō* — special [subject of] study
骨	骨	971; 188/0. KOTSU, *hone* bone [KU²·³ • I: flesh 7–10 & bone 1–6; P*] 骨格 — *kokkaku* — frame, physique 骨折り — *honeori* — efforts, trouble
狂	狂	972; 94/4. KYŌ, *kuru(u/i)* be mad; *-kyō* enthusiast [K'UANG² • R dog & P*] 狂犬病 — *kyōkenbyō* — rabies 狂喜 — *kyōki* — wild joy, exultation
秀	秀	973; 115/2. SHŪ, *hii(deru)* surpass, excel [HSIU⁴ • I: grain 1–5 growing 6–7 well; P*] 秀才 — *shūsai* — gifted person, genius 秀美 — *shūbi* — outstanding beauty
染	染	974; 75/5. SEN, *so(meru/maru)* dye; *shi(miru)* soak (into), be infected (by), smart; *shi(mi)* stain [JAN³ • I: nine liquids 1–5 obtained from trees & plants 6–9 = vegetable dyes] 伝染病 — *densenbyō* — communicable disease 染物屋 — *somemonoya* — dyer's, dyer
津	津	975; 85/6. SHIN, *tsu* harbor, ferry [CHIN¹, CHING¹ • R water & P*] 津波 — *tsunami* — tidal wave 津軽平野 — *Tsugaru heiya* — the Tsugaru plain
浄	浄 淨	976; 85/6. JŌ pure [CHING⁴ • R water & P*] 浄土宗 — *Jōdoshū* — Pure Land sect 清浄 — *seijō* — purity

148

為	為 爲	977; 3/8. I do, make; cause; purpose [WEI^{2,4} • I; P*] 行為 — kōi — act, conduct 無為 — mui — inactivity
皆	皆	978; 81/5. KAI, mina all ⌐the same; P*] [CHIEH¹ • I: person after person 1–4 says 5–9 皆納 — kainō — full payment 皆様 — minasama — all/everyone (present)
亡	亡	979; 8/1. BŌ, MŌ die, perish; na(i) be not [WANG², WU² • I; P*] 死亡者 — shibōsha — the dead, fatalities 興亡 — kōbō — rise & fall, vicissitudes
潮	潮	980; 85/12. CHŌ, shio tide, salt water [CH'AO² • R water & P*] 満潮 — manchō — high tide 黒潮 — Kuroshio — the Black/Japan Current
宝	宝 寶	981; 40/5. HŌ, takara treasure [PAO³ • R roof & P*] 宝石 — hōseki — precious stone 宝船 — takarabune — treasureship [picture]
若	若	982; 140/5. JAKU, NYAKU, waka(i) young; mo- [JO⁴, JE⁴ • I; P*] ⌐(shiku wa) or 若年者 — jakunenmono — youngster; novice 若盛り — wakazakari — bloom of youth
与	与 與	983; 1/2. YO, ata(eru) give, provide [YÜ^{1,2,3} • I; P*] 与党 — yotō — government party, party in power 給与 — kyūyo — allowance, pay
穴	穴	984; 116/0. KETSU, ana hole [HSÜEH⁴ • D: entrance to cave dwelling; P*] 穴居 — kekkyo — cave dwelling 穴蔵 — anagura — cellar

占	占	985; 25/3. SEN, *shi(meru)* occupy; *urana(u/i)* divine ⌜P*⌝ [CHAN[1,4] • I: to inquire into 3–5 the omens 1–2; 占領 — *senryō* — occupation 独占 — *dokusen* — exclusive possession, monopoly
頂	頂	986; 181/2. CHŌ, *itada(ku)* (dep.) receive; *itadaki* [TING[3] • R head & P*] ⌊head, peak 頂点 — *chōten* — apex, peak 絶頂 — *zetchō* — summit, pinnacle
込	込	987; 162/2. *ko(meru)* put into, include; *ko(mu)* be crowded, be contained [- • I: advance 3–5 & enter 1–2] 申込む — *mōshikomu* — apply for 見込み — *mikomi* — prospect, hope, likelihood
昔	昔	988; 72/4. SEKI, SHAKU, *mukashi* former times [HSI[2] • I: layer after layer 1–4 of days 5–8 = past days; P*] 今昔 — *konjaku* — present & past 昔話 — *mukashibanashi* — old tale; reminiscences
射	射	989; 158/3. SHA, *i(ru)* shoot [SHE[4], SHIH[2] • I: body 1–7 (see 791) & hand 8–10 (see 1045), used to fire arrow; P*] 注射 — *chūsha* — injection 発射 — *hassha* — firing, discharge
吉	吉	990; 32/3. KICHI*, KITSU good fortune ⌜P*⌝ [CHI[2] • I: a male 1–3 birth announcement 4–6] 吉日 — *kichinichi* — lucky/auspicious day 吉報 — *kippō* — good tidings
浮	浮	991; 85/7. FU, *uka(beru/bu)*, *u(kasu/ku)* float [FOU[2], FU[2] • R water & P*] 浮動 — *fudō* — floating, drifting 浮世絵 — *ukiyoe* — 'Floating-world'/genre pictures
宅	宅	992; 40/3. TAKU* home, husband [CHAI[2] • R roof & P*] 住宅 — *jūtaku* — house, housing 帰宅 — *kitaku* — returning home

砲	砲	993; 112/5.　HŌ gun, cannon [P'AO⁴ · R stone & P*] 大砲 — taihō — gun, cannon, artillery 鉄砲 — teppō — gun
江	江	994; 85/3.　KŌ, e inlet, bay [CHIANG¹ · R water & P*] 江戸 — Edo — pn. [old name for Tōkyō] 入江 — irie — inlet, creek
堅	堅	995; 32/8.　KEN, kata(i) hard, firm [CHIEN¹ · R earth & P*] 堅固な — kengo na — strong, solid 堅実な — kenjitsu na — steadfast, sound
幾	幾	996; 52/9.　KI, iku(tsu) how many?; iku(ra) how much?; iku- some, several, how many/much? [CHI¹,³ · R fine thread & P*]　⌈many? 幾何 — kika — geometry; iku-baku — how much/ 幾分〔か〕— ikubun [ka] — partly, somewhat
撃	撃 撃	997; 64/11.　GEKI, u(tsu) strike, attack, fire (gun, etc.)　⌈physical attack⌉ [CHI¹ · I: carts 1–7 colliding 8–11 & hand = 爆撃 — bakugeki — bombing 攻撃 — kōgeki — attack
並	並 竝	998; 12/6.　HEI, nara(beru/bu) line up; nara(bi ni) and; nami ordinary, average [PING⁴ · I: 72 repeated & combined = stand 並行 — heikō — parallel　　　⌊side by side] 並列 — heiretsu — row, parallel
娘	娘	999; 38/7.　musume daughter, girl [NIANG² · I: a woman who is still good 4–10; P*] 娘盛り — musumezakari — bloom of young wo- 　　　　　　　　　　　　　　　　manhood 孫娘 — magomusume — granddaughter
呼	呼	1000; 30/5.　KO, yo(bu) call, summon, invite [HU¹ · R mouth & P] 点呼 — tenko — roll-call 呼び声 — yobigoe — call, cry

刑	刑	1001; 18/4. KEI punishment [HSING² • I; P*] 刑事 — *keiji* — criminal case; detective 刑罰 — *keibatsu* — punishment
呉	呉 呉	1002; 12/5. GO, *Kure* pn.; *Wu* ancient Chinese pn. [WU² • I; P*] 呉服屋 — *gofukuya* — drapery/dry goods store 呉呉も — *kuregure mo* — repeatedly, earnestly
舞	舞	1003; 136/8. BU, *ma(u)*, *mai* dance [WU³ • R oppose & P*] 舞台効果 — *butai kōka* — stage effect 舞い狂う — *mai-kuruu* — dance wildly
忘	忘	1004; 8/5. BŌ, *wasu(reru)* forget [WANG⁴ • R heart & P*] 忘年会 — *bōnenkai* — year-end party 忘れ形見 — *wasuregatami* — keepsake
尾	尾	1005; 44/4. BI, *o* tail [WEI³, I³ • I: bent figure 1–3 & fur 4–7; P*] 尾行する — *bikō suru* — (vi.) follow, trail, shadow 首尾よく — *shubi yoku* — successfully, smoothly
戒	戒	1006; 62/3. KAI, *imashi(meru/me)* warn, admonish [CHIEH⁴ • I: two hands 2–4 brandishing a spear 1 & 5–7; P*] 訓戒する — *kunkai suru* — warn, admonish 警戒する — *keikai suru* — warn, caution
僧	僧 僧	1007; 9/11. SŌ Buddhist priest, monk [SENG¹ • R man & P*] 僧正 — *sōjō* — Buddhist bishop, high priest 小僧 — *kozō* — young priest; (errand) boy
傷	傷	1008; 9/11. SHŌ, *kizu* wound, injury; *ita(meru/ mu/mi)* hurt, injure [SHANG¹ • R man & P*] 傷害 — *shōgai* — wound, injury 負傷 — *fushō* — wound, injury

腰	腰	1009; 130/9. YŌ, *koshi* waist, hips, lumbar region [YAO[1] · R flesh & P*] 腰部 — *yōbu* — waist, hips, lumbar region 腰布 — *koshinuno* — loincloth
腹	腹	1010; 130/9. FUKU, *hara* stomach [FU[3,4] · R flesh & P*] 立腹 — *rippuku* — anger 腹巻 — *haramaki* — bellyband
威	威	1011; 62/5. I authority, majesty [WEI[1] · I: woman & battle-axe 1–3 & 7–9; P*] 威厳 — *igen* — majesty, dignity 権威 — *ken'i* — authority
恋	恋 戀	1012; 8/8. REN, *koi(shii)* beloved; *koi* love [LIEN[4], LUAN[4], LÜAN[4] · R heart & P*] 恋愛結婚 — *ren'ai kekkon* — love marriage 恋路 — *koiji* — the path of love, romance
沿	沿	1013; 85/5. EN, *so(u)* run/lie (along) [YEN[2,4] · R water & P*] 沿岸 — *engan* — coast, shore 沿革 — *enkaku* — history, development
飾	飾 飾	1014; 184/5. SHOKU, *kaza(ru/ri)* decorate, ornament [a cloth 11–13; P*] [SHIH[4] · I: when eating 1–8, a person 9–10 uses 服飾 — *fukushoku* — dress & accessories 飾り気 — *kazarike* — affectation, showing off
浦	浦	1015; 85/7. HO, *ura* bay, beach [P'U[3] · R water & P*] 浦波 — *uranami* — waves on a beach, breakers 浦和 — *Urawa* — pn.
泊	泊	1016; 85/5. HAKU, *to(meru/maru)* lodge, accommodate; *toma(ri)* lodging, anchorage [PO[2], P'O[4] · R water & P*] 一泊 — *ippaku* — overnight stay 泊り賃 — *tomarichin* — accommodation charge

域	域	1017; 32/8.　IKI area, region [YÜ⁴ ・ I: earth & break/division 4–11; P*] 配達区域 — haitatsu kuiki — delivery area 領域 — ryōiki — domain, sphere
了	了	1018; 6/1.　RYŌ understanding; finish [LIAO³, LE³ ・ D & S: reeled thread] 了解 — ryōkai — understanding, comprehension 終了 — shūryō — end, completion
殊	殊	1019; 78/6.　SHU, koto (ni) especially, particularly [SHU¹ ・ R disintegrate & P*] 殊勝な — shushō na — admirable, commendable 特殊事情 — tokushu jijō — special situation
痛	痛	1020; 104/7.　TSŪ, ita(meru/mu/mi) hurt, pain [T'UNG⁴ ・ R illness & P*] 頭痛 — zutsū — headache 痛手 — itade — severe wound, heavy blow
越	越	1021; 156/5.　ETSU, ko(su/eru) pass, cross, exceed [YÜEH⁴ ・ R run & P] 越境 — ekkyō — border violation 追い越す — oikosu — overtake
施	施	1022; 70/5.　SHI, SE, hodoko(su) grant, bestow, per- [SHIH¹ ・ I; P*]　　　　　　　⌐form, carry out 施行する — shikō suru — carry out 施設 — shisetsu — institution; facilities
狩	狩	1023; 94/6.　SHU, ka(ru/ri) hunt [SHOU⁴ ・ R dog & P*] 狩り小屋 — karigoya — hunting lodge 狩り込み — karikomi — roundup
惜	惜	1024; 61/8.　SEKI, o(shimu) regret; o(shii) regret- [HSI² ・ R heart & P*]　　　　　⌐table, precious 惜敗 — sekihai — regrettable/narrow defeat ⌐ness 骨惜しみ — honeoshimi — withholding effort, lazi-

渋	渋 渋	1025; 85/8. JŪ, *shibu(i)* astringent, in sober taste; *shibu* astringency, sober taste ⌈water & P*⌉ [SE⁴ • I: water 1–3 stops 4–11 → dry; also R] 渋面 — *jūmen/shibuzura* — wry face, grimace 渋味 — *shibumi* — astringency, sober taste
盗	盗 盗	1026; 108/6. TŌ, *nusu(mu)* steal [TAO⁴ • I: to want the next 1–6 dish 7–11 & steal Lit; P*] 盗難 — *tōnan* — robbery, burglary 強盗 — *gōtō* — burglar, burglary
珍	珍	1027; 96/5. CHIN, *mezura(shii)* rare, unusual [CHEN¹ • R jewel & P*] 珍品 — *chinpin* — rarity, curio 珍重する — *chinchō suru* — prize, value highly
荒	荒	1028; 140/6. KŌ, *a(rasu/reru)* devastate; *ara(i)* violent, rough ⌈tation; also R grass & P*⌉ [HUANG¹ • I: grasses 1–3 spread 4–9 over devas- 荒野 — *areno/kōya* — wilderness 荒仕事 — *arashigoto* — rough work
窓	窓 窓 窗	1029; 116/6. SŌ, *mado* window [CH'UANG¹ • R roof & P*] 同窓 — *dōsō* — same school, alumni 窓飾り — *madokazari* — window dressing
郊	郊	1030; 163/6. KŌ suburbs [CHIAO¹ • R city & P*] 郊外 — *kōgai* — suburbs 近郊 — *kinkō* — suburbs
陰	陰	1031; 170/8. IN negative; *kage* shadow [YIN¹ • I: the dark 4–11 side of the hill 1–3; also R mound & P*] 陰性 — *insei* — negative; dormant 日陰 — *hikage* — shade
互	互	1032; 1/3. GO, *taga(i ni)* mutually [HU⁴ • D: frame for winding rope into a figure-of-eight skein] 互選 — *gosen* — co-option, mutual election 相互条約 — *sōgo jōyaku* — mutual/reciprocal treaty

慶	慶	1033; 53/12. KEI rejoice, congratulate [CH'ING⁴ · I] 慶祝 — *keishuku* — congratulation, celebration 慶賀 — *keiga* — congratulation
庁	庁 廳	1034; 53/2. CHŌ government office/agency [T'ING¹ · R lean-to & P*] 府県庁 — *fukenchō* — prefectural office 警視庁 — *Keishichō* — Metropolitan Police Office
踊	踊	1035; 157/7. YŌ, *odo(ru/ri)* dance, jump [YUNG³ · R foot & P*] 日本舞踊 — *Nihon buyō* — Japanese dance/danc- 踊り子 — *odoriko* — girl dancer ⌊ing
誓	誓	1036; 149/7. SEI, *chika(u/i)* vow, swear [SHIH⁴ · R words & P*] 誓文 — *seimon* — written oath, covenant 誓約 — *seiyaku* — vow, oath
瀬	瀬 瀨	1037; 85/16. *se* shallows, rapids [LAI⁴ · R water & P*] 瀬戸内海 — *Seto-naikai* — the Inland Sea 早瀬 — *hayase* — swift current, rapids
霧	霧	1038; 173/11. MU, *kiri* fog, spray [WU⁴ · R rain & P*] 夕霧 — *yūgiri* — evening mist 朝霧 — *asagiri* — morning mist
敷	敷 敷	1039; 66/11. FU, *shi(ku)* spread, lay [FU¹ · I: spread 1–11 & strike/push down 12–15 = spread out; also R strike & P*] 敷設 — *fusetsu* — construction, laying [railway,etc.] 敷地 — *shikichi* — site
隣	隣	1040; 170/12. RIN, *tonari* next door; *tona(ru)* adjoin [LIN² · R mound (orig.,R city) & P*] ⌐work 隣保事業 — *rinpo jigyō* — neighborhood/social 隣接する — *rinsetsu suru* — be adjacent (to)

到 | 到 | 1041; 133/2. TŌ reach, arrive at
[TAO⁴ · R reach & P* 7-8 (= 34)]
到底 — *tōtei* — finally; absolutely, (not) at all
到着 — *tōchaku* — arrival

宜 | 宜 | 1042; 40/5. GI good, right
[I²,⁴, YI²,⁴ · I; P*]
便宜 — *bengi* — convenience, expedience
適宜 — *tekigi* — suitable, appropriate

吟 | 吟 | 1043; 30/4. GIN, *gin(zuru)* sing, recite
[YIN² · R mouth & P*]
吟味する — *ginmi suru* — inquire into, scrutinize
独吟 — *dokugin* — solo song

豆 | 豆 | 1044; 151/0. TŌ, ZU, *mame* peas, beans; *mame-*
baby-, midget- ⌈P*⌉
[TOU⁴ · D: lid 1 & dish 2-4 on tall stand 5-7→B;
大豆 — *daizu* — soy bean
豆電球 — *mame-denkyū* — miniature electric bulb

寸 | 寸 | 1045; 41/0. SUN* 1.193 inches, 3.03 cms.
[TS'UN⁴ · D & S: the pulse 3 (an inch) below
the hand 1-2; P*]
寸法通りに — *sunpō-dōri ni* — as arranged/
寸暇 — *sunka* — brief leisure ⌊planned

侵 | 侵 | 1046; 9/7. SHIN, *oka(su)* invade, violate
[CH'IN¹ · R man & P*]
侵略 — *shinryaku* — aggression
侵害 — *shingai* — violation, infringement

趣 | 趣 | 1047; 156/8. SHU, *omomuki* meaning, taste, ap-
[CH'Ü⁴ · R run & P*] ⌊pearance
趣向 — *shukō* — plan, scheme
趣味 — *shumi* — [good] taste; interest, hobby

奇 | 奇 | 1048; 37/5. KI strange, wonderful, curious
[CH'I² · R big & P*]
好奇心 — *kōkishin* — curiosity
珍奇な — *chinki na* — curious, strange

泣	泣	1049; 85/5. KYŪ, *na(ku)* cry, weep [CH'I⁴ · R water & P*] 感泣する — *kankyū suru* — be moved to tears 泣き顔 — *nakigao* — tearful face
桜	桜 櫻	1050; 75/6. Ō, *sakura* cherry tree [YING¹ · I: tree with blossom falling 5–7 on a 桜色 — *sakura-iro* — pink ⌊woman below] 八重桜 — *yaezakura* — double cherry blossom
超	超	1051; 156/5. CHŌ super-; *ko(su/eru)* exceed [CH'AO¹ · R run & P*] 超音波 — *chōonpa* — supersonic waves 超過 — *chōka* — excess
綱	綱	1052; 120/8. KŌ, *tsuna* rope, cable [KANG¹ · R thread & P* (N.B. a rope is needed to climb a mountain 12–14: cf. 1282)] 要綱 — *yōkō* — main principles, outline 綱引 — *tsunahiki* — rope pulling, tug of war
樹	樹	1053; 75/12. JU tree [SHU⁴ · R tree & P] 樹木 — *jumoku* — trees & shrubs 果樹 — *kaju* — fruit tree
謀	謀	1054; 149/9. BŌ, MU, *haka(ru)* plan, plot [MOU² · R words & P*] 参謀 — *sanbō* — military staff officer; adviser 陰謀 — *inbō* — plot, conspiracy
聴	聴 聽	1055; 128/11. CHŌ, *ki(ku)* listen [T'ING¹,⁴ · R ear & P*] 聴講 — *chōkō* — attendance at lectures 聴衆 — *chōshū* — audience
闘	闘 鬭	1056; 169/10. TŌ, *tataka(u)* fight (with) [TOU⁴ · R fight & P*] 戦闘 — *sentō* — fight, battle 奮闘 — *funtō* — hard fighting; strenuous efforts

看	看	1057; 4/8. KAN watch, see [K'AN[1,4] · D & I: a hand 1-4 shading the eyes 5-9 to see out; P*] 看板 — *kanban* — signboard 看護婦 — *kangofu* — nurse
莊	莊 莊	1058; 140/6. SŌ solemn, majestic; villa [CHUANG[1] · R grass & P*] 荘重 — *sōchō* — solemnity 別荘 — *bessō* — (country) villa
香	香	1059; 186/0. KŌ* incense; *kaori, ka* fragrance, smell ⌐grain 1-5; P*] [HSIANG[1] · I: the sweet smell 6-9 (= 1333) of 香料 — *kōryō* — spices; perfumery 香港 — *Honkon* — Hongkong
忍	忍	1060; 61/3. NIN, *shino(bu)* bear, endure; hide one- [JEN[3] · R heart & P*] ⌊self 忍苦 — *ninku* — endurance, stoicism ⌐ing 忍び泣き — *shinobi-naki* — silent/suppressed weep-
驚	驚	1061; 187/12. KYŌ, *odoro(kasu/ku/ki)* surprise [CHING[1] · R horse & P*] 驚天動地 — *kyōten dōchi* — world-shaking 驚異 — *kyōi* — wonder[ment], miracle
迎	迎	1062; 162/4. GEI, *muka(eru/e)* welcome, greet [YING[2] · R proceed & P*] 歓迎 — *kangei* — welcome ⌐back 迎え撃つ — *mukae-utsu* — await an attack & fight
禅	禅 禪	1063; 113/9. ZEN* Zen Buddhism [CH'AN[2], SHAN[4] · R god & P*] 禅宗 — *zenshū* — Zen sect 禅僧 — *zensō* — Zen priest
鼓	鼓	1064; 207/0. KO, *tsuzumi* hand drum [KU[3] · I: drum on stand 1-9 & strike 10-13 (= R strike); P*] 鼓動 — *kodō* — pulsation, beat 鼓舞 — *kobu* — encouragement, stimulation

淡	淡	1065; 85/8. TAN, *awa(i)* light, faint, pale [TAN⁴ · R water & P*] 淡水湖 — *tansuiko* — fresh-water lake 冷淡 — *reitan* — indifference, apathy, coldness
慰	慰	1066; 61/11. I, *nagusa(meru/me)* comfort, console; *nagusa(mi)* amusement, pastime [WEI⁴ · R heart & P*] 慰問 — *imon* — condolence, consolation 慰み半分に — *nagusami-hanbun ni* — partly for pleasure
範	範	1067; 118/9. HAN pattern; limit [FAN⁴ · R cart & P*] 規範 — *kihan* — pattern, model 範囲 — *han'i* — sphere, scope
怒	怒	1068; 61/5. DO, *oko(ru)*, *ika(ru)* (lit.) become [NU⁴ · R heart & P*] ⌐angry 喜怒 — *kido* — joy & anger, emotions 怒り争う — *ikari-arasou* — quarrel
旨	旨	1069; 21/4. SHI, *mune* purport, [main] principle, in- [CHIH³ · I; P*] ⌐structions 要旨 — *yōshi* — the gist, essentials 趣旨 — *shushi* — aim, purpose
遂	遂	1070; 162/9. SUI, *to(geru)* accomplish, achieve [SUI²·⁴ · R proceed & P*] 遂行する — *suikō suru* — accomplish, carry out 未遂罪 — *misuizai* — attempted/unsuccessful crime
謡	謡 謡	1071; 149/9. YŌ song; *utai* Nō singing [YAO² · R words & P*] 民謡 — *min'yō* — folk song 童謡 — *dōyō* — children's song
賢	賢	1072; 154/8. KEN, *kashiko(i)* wise [HSIEN² · R shell & P*] 賢明 — *kenmei* — wisdom 賢聖 — *kensei* — wise men & saints

簿	簿 簿	1073; 118/13.　BO notebook, register [PU⁴　·　R bamboo & P*] 名簿 — *meibo* — name register, roll 帳簿 — *chōbo* — account book
露	露	1074; 173/13.　RO open, exposed; *tsuyu* dew [LU⁴, LOU⁴　·　R rain & P*] 露骨な — *rokotsu na* — frank, plain 朝露 — *asatsuyu* — morning dew
没	没 没	1075; 85/4.　BOTSU, *bos(suru)* sink, die [MEI², MO⁴, MU²,⁴　·　R water & P*] 没収 — *bosshū* — confiscation 没落 — *botsuraku* — ruin, downfall
裏	裏 裡	1076; 8/11.　RI, *ura* reverse side, back [LI³　·　R clothes 1–2 & 10–13, & P* 3–9 (cf. 1809)] 表裏 — *hyōri* — back & front, two sides, double-dealing 裏付け — *urazuke* — backing, proof, lining
旋	旋	1077; 70/7.　SEN revolve [HSÜAN²,⁴　·　R roll of cloth & P*] 旋律 — *senritsu* — melody 旋回 — *senkai* — rotation
劇	劇	1078; 4/14.　GEKI* play, drama; intense, severe [CHÜ⁴, CHI²,⁴　·　R knife & P*] 演劇 — *engeki* — the theater, drama 悲劇 — *higeki* — tragedy
併	併	1079; 9/6.　HEI, *awa(seru)* (vt.) combine, join [PING⁴　·　R man & P*] 併用 — *heiyō* — combined/joint use 合併 — *gappei* — combination, amalgamation
喫	喫	1080; 30/9.　KITSU eat, drink, smoke [CH'IH¹　·　R mouth & P*] 喫茶店 — *kissaten* — tea/coffee shop 喫煙 — *kitsuen* — tobacco smoking

診	診	1081; 149/5. SHIN, *mi(ru)* examine, look over/up [CHEN[1,3] • R words & P*] 診断 — *shindan* — diagnosis 診察料 — *shinsatsuryō* — medical examination fee
甲	甲	1082; 2/4. KŌ* lst (in a series), 'A'; armor; KAN high (voice) ⌐P*⌐ [CHIA[3,2] • D: seed in shell 1–4, taking root 5; 甲鉄 — *kōtetsu* — armor plate 甲板 — *kanpan* — deck
吸	吸	1083; 30/3. KYŪ, *su(u)* suck, smoke (tobacco) [HSI[1] • R mouth & P*] 呼吸 — *kokyū* — breathing; a knack 吸取紙 — *suitorigami* — blotting paper
怠	怠	1084; 28/7. TAI, *okota(ru)*, neglect; *nama(keru)* be [TAI[4] • R heart & P*] ⌊idle [about] 怠業戦術 — *taigyō senjutsu* — go-slow tactics 怠り勝ちの — *okotarigachi no* — neglectful
架	架	1085; 75/5. KA, *ka(suru)*, *ka(keru/karu)* erect, [CHIA[4] • R tree & P*] ⌊construct 架空 — *kakū* — aerial, overhead; fictitious, fanciful 十字架像 — *jūjikazō* — crucifix
柔	柔	1086; 110/4. JŪ, NYŪ, *yawa(raka i)*, *yawa(raka na)* soft, gentle ⌐6–9 → pliable; P*⌐ [JOU[2] • I: a spearlike 1–5 (see 1813) sapling 柔道 — *jūdō* — judo, jujitsu 柔和 — *nyūwa* — gentleness, mildness
盆	盆	1087; 12/7. BON* Bon summer festival, tray [P'EN[2] • R dish & P*] 盆景 — *bonkei* — tray landscape 煙草盆 — *tabako-bon* — tobacco tray; busybody
緊	緊	1088; 120/8. KIN hard, tight, strict [CHIN[3] • R thread & P*] 緊急 — *kinkyū* — emergency; urgency 緊張 — *kinchō* — tension, strain

座	座	1089; 53/7. ZA* seat; theater; *suwa(ru)* sit down [TSO⁴ • I: seating 4–10 inside a building 1–3; P*] 銀座 — *Ginza* — pn.: the Ginza (Street) 座敷 — *zashiki* — drawing room
遅	遅 遲	1090; 162/9. CHI, *oso(i)* late, slow; *oku(reru)* be late, be behind (schedule), be slow (of watches) [CH'IH² • I: proceed 10–12 slowly 1–9] 遅延 — *chien* — delay, postponement 遅着 — *chichaku* — late arrival
薄	薄 薄	1091; 140/13. HAKU, *usu(i)* thin, pale, weak [PAO², PO²,⁴ • R grass & P*] 薄弱 — *hakujaku* — flimsiness; weakness 薄情 — *hakujō* — heartlessness
繁	繁 繁	1092; 120/10. HAN profusion, frequency [FAN² • R thread & P] 繁忙な — *hanbō na* — extremely busy 繁栄 — *han'ei* — prosperity 繁盛 — *hanjō* — prosperity
騒	騒 騒	1093; 187/8. SŌ, *sawa(gu/gi)* make a noise/dis- turbance ⌐pound an insect 13–18] [SAO¹ • I: a horse 1–10 uses its hoof 11–12 to 騒動 — *sōdō* — disturbance, riot ⌐fuss 騒ぎ立てる — *sawagi-tateru* — make an outcry/
襲	襲	1094; 212/6. SHŪ, *oso(u)* attack, inherit, succeed [HSI² • R clothes & P*] ⌊(to) 空襲警報 — *kūshū keihō* — air-raid alarm 世襲財産 — *seshū zaisan* — hereditary property
吹	吹	1095; 30/4. SUI, *fu(ku)* blow [CH'UI¹ • R mouth & P*] 吹雪 — *fubuki* — snowstorm 吹き寄せ — *fukiyose* — drift (of snow/sand)
択	択 擇	1096; 64/4. TAKU selection [TSE²,⁴, CHAI² • R hand & P*] 採択 — *saitaku* — selection, adoption ⌐course 選択科目 — *sentaku kamoku* — optional/elective

沈	沈	1097; 85/4. CHIN, *shizu(meru/mu)* sink [SHEN[2], CH'EN[2] · R water & P*] 沈没 — *chinbotsu* — sinking 沈着 — *chinchaku* — calmness, composure
偉	偉	1098; 9/9. I, *era(i)* great, remarkable [WEI[3] · R man & P*] 偉丈夫 — *ijōfu* — hero, great man 偉物 — *eramono/erabutsu* — great man
弾	弾	1099; 57/9. DAN, *tama* projectile; *hi(ku)* play (string instrument); *hazu(mu)* rebound, bounce [T'AN[2], TAN[4] · R bow & P*] 弾丸列車 — *dangan ressha* — bullet/superexpress train 爆弾投下 — *bakudan tōka* — bomb-dropping, bombing
廃	廃 廢	1100; 53/9. HAI abandon, abolish; *suta(reru)*, *suta(ru)* die out, decline [FEI[4] · R lean-to & P*] 廃置 — *haichi* — abolition & establishment 森林荒廃 — *shinrin kōhai* — forest devastation
蓄	蓄	1101; 140/10. CHIKU, *takuwa(eru)* store up, save [HSÜ[4] · I: grass & store up 4–13 (cf. 1740); also R grass & P*] 蓄積する — *chikuseki suru* — accumulate 相互貯蓄銀行 — *sōgo chochiku ginkō* — mutual savings bank
普	普	1102; 12/10. FU universal [P'U[3] · R sun & P*] 普及する — *fukyū suru* — (vt. & vi.) spread, diffuse 普通の — *futsū no* — usual, ordinary
簡	簡	1103; 118/12. KAN simple, concise [CHIEN[3] · R bamboo & P*] 簡単な — *kantan na* — simple 簡潔な — *kanketsu na* — concise, brief
悟	悟	1104; 61/7. GO, *sato(ru/ri)* comprehend, become enlightened [WU[4] · R heart & P*] 悟了 — *goryō* — enlightenment, perception 覚悟 — *kakugo* — resolve, readiness; perception

帽	帽 帽	1105; 50/9. BŌ hat [MAO⁴ • R cloth & P*] 帽子〔入れ〕箱 — *bōshi* [-*ire*]-*bako* — hat-box 帽章 — *bōshō* — cap badge
零	零 零	1106; 173/5. REI* zero, nought; spill over [LING² • R rain & P*] ⌐posits/savings 零細な貯金 — *reisai na chokin* — small/trifling de- 零落する — *reiraku suru* — be ruined, come down in the world
刃	刃 刃 刄	1107; 4/2. JIN, *ha* blade, cutting edge [JEN⁴ • D: sword, with line 3 indicating the blade 刀刃 — *tōjin* — sword blade ⌐2; P*] 刃物 — *hamono* — edged tool, cutlery
哲	哲	1108; 30/7. TETSU wisdom [CHE² • R mouth & P*] 哲学 — *tetsugaku* — philosophy 賢哲 — *kentetsu* — sage, wise man
鉛	鉛 鉛	1109; 167/5. EN, *namari* lead [CH'IEN¹ • R metal & P*] 鉛毒 — *endoku* — lead poisoning 鉛筆 — *enpitsu* — pencil
距	距	1110; 157/4. KYO distance [CHÜ⁴ • R foot & P*] 短距離 — *tan-kyori* — short distance 長距離 — *chō-kyori* — long distance
響	響	1111; 180/10. KYŌ, *hibi(ku/ki)* echo, vibrate [HSIANG³ • R sound & P*] 交響曲ハ短調 — *kōkyōkyoku ha-tanchō* — sym- 影響 — *eikyō* — influence ⌐phony in C minor
偶	偶	1112; 9/9. GŪ doll; spouse; by chance [OU³ • R man & P*] 偶像 — *gūzō* — image, idol 偶然 — *gūzen* — by chance

玄	玄	1113; 95/0.　GEN dark, obscure [HSÜAN² ・ D: black thread; P*] 玄米 — *genmai* — unhulled/unpolished rice 玄関 — *genkan* — porch, entrance hall
致	致	1114; 133/4.　CHI, *ita(su)* (dep.) do, make, cause [CHIH⁴ ・ R strike (orig., R step) & P*] 致命傷を受ける — *chimeishō o ukeru* — suffer a fatal wound 合致する — *gatchi suru* —accord/correspond(with)
召	召	1115; 18/3.　SHŌ, *me(su)* general hon. vb.: wear, summon, ride, etc. [CHAO⁴ ・ R mouth & P*] 召致する — *shōchi suru* — call together, summon 臨時国会を召集する — *rinji kokkai o shōshū suru* — convene a special Diet session
房	房	1116; 63/4.　BŌ room; *fusa* tuft, bunch, cluster [FANG² ・ R door & P*] 蒸気暖房 — *jōki danbō* — steam heating 官房長 — *kanbō-chō* — secretariat head, secretary general
衝	衝	1117; 60/12.　SHŌ strike against, attack [CH'UNG¹ ・ R go/do & P*] 電柱に衝突する — *denchū ni shōtotsu suru* — collide with a telegraph pole 折衝する — *sesshō suru* — negotiate/parley (with)
密	密	1118; 40/8.　MITSU secret, dense, minute [MI⁴ ・ R mountain & P*] 秘密 — *himitsu* — secret 禁制品を密輸する — *kinseihin o mitsuyu suru* — smuggle contraband goods
蚊	蚊	1119; 142/4.　*ka* mosquito [WEN² ・ R insect & P] 蚊屋 — *kaya* — mosquito net　　　　　「coil 蚊取り線香 — *katori senkō* — mosquito [smoke]
匹	匹	1120; 22/2.　HIKI unit for counting animals/rolls of cloth; HITSU equal, lowly [P'I³ ・ D: hindquarters of a horse; P*] 蚊一匹 — *ka ippiki* — one mosquito 匹敵する — *hitteki suru* — be equal/compare (to)

棒	棒	1121; 75/8. Bō stick, pole [PANG⁴ • R tree & P*] 棒暗記 — bō-anki — rote learning, sheer memori- 鉄棒 — tetsubō — iron bar ⌊zation
冗	冗	1122; 14/2. Jō superfluous ⌈working, P*] [JUNG³ • I: a person 3–4 in the house 1–2, not 冗長な — jōchō na — prolix, verbose 冗談 — jōdan — joke, witticism
震	震	1123; 173/7. SHIN, furu(waseru) (vt.) shake; furu- (u/i), furu(eru/e) (vi.) shake [CHEN⁴ • R rain & P*] 地震 — jishin — earthquake 震央 — shin'ō — earthquake center, epicenter
封	封	1124; 41/6. FŪ* seal; fū(jiru) seal up; HŌ fief [FENG¹ • I; P*] 開封する — kaifū suru — unseal/open (a letter) 封建制度 — hōken seido — feudal system
筒	筒	1125; 118/6. TŌ, tsutsu tube, pipe [T'UNG²,³ • R bamboo & P*] 封筒 — fūtō — envelope 竹筒 — takezutsu — bamboo tube/pipe
束	束	1126; 4/6. SOKU*, taba bundle, bunch, sheaf [SHU⁴ • D: wood 1 & 5–7 bound together with rope 2–4; P*] 約束する — yakusoku suru — promise 花束 — hanataba — bunch of flowers
砂	砂	1127; 112/4. SA, SHA, suna sand [SHA¹ • R stone & P*] 砂金採集権 — sakin saishū-ken — gold-dust/allu- vial-gold collection right 砂浜 — sunahama — sandy beach
糖	糖	1128; 119/10. TŌ sugar [T'ANG² • R rice & P*] 砂糖 — satō — sugar 丸薬に糖衣を施こす — gan'yaku ni tōi o hodo- kosu — put a sugar-coating on a pill

裁	裁	1129; 24/10. SAI, *saba(ku)* judge, decide (a case); *ta(tsu)* cut out (cloth) [TS'AI² · R clothes & P*] 裁判官 — *saiban-kan* — court judge
紹	紹	1130; 120/5. SHŌ introduction [SHAO⁴ · R thread & P*] 紹介する — *shōkai suru* — introduce, present 紹介状 — *shōkaijō* — letter of introduction
惑	惑	1131; 61/8. WAKU, *mado(wasu/u)* confuse, lead astray (cf. 781 *mayowasu*) [HUO⁴ · R heart & P*] 迷惑 — *meiwaku* — trouble, annoyance 疑惑 — *giwaku* — suspicion, doubt
契	契	1132; 37/6. KEI, *chigi(ru/ri)* pledge, promise [CH'I⁴ · R big & P*] 契約 — *keiyaku* — contract, agreement 契機 — *keiki* — opportunity, chance
姿	姿	1133; 38/6. SHI, *sugata* form, shape, appearance [TZU¹ · R woman & P*] 姿勢 — *shisei* — posture, carriage 容姿 — *yōshi* — face & figure, person's appearance
訂	訂	1134; 149/2. TEI correction [TING⁴ · R words & P*] 改訂増補 — *kaitei zōho* — revision & enlargement 訂正 — *teisei* — correction, revision
依	依	1135; 9/6. I, E depend on, be according to [I¹, YI¹ · R man & P*] 依然〔として〕— *izen [to shite]* — as ever, as before 帰依 — *kie* — religious conversion
湾	湾 湾	1136; 85/9. WAN bay 「bow 10-12」 [WAN¹ · I: water 1–3 bent 4–9 in the shape of a 台湾 — *Taiwan* — pn.: Taiwan, Formosa 港湾 — *kōwan* — harbors

筋	筋	1137; 118/6.　KIN, *suji* sinew, vein, story [-line] [CHIN[1] · I: bamboo 1-6 & what gives the flesh 7-10 strength 11-12 = grain, vein; P*] 筋肉 — *kinniku* — muscles, sinew 筋違い — *sujichigai* — sprain, illogicality; *sujikai* — obliqueness
項	項	1138; 48/9.　KŌ item, section [HSIANG[4] · R head & P*] 項目 — *kōmoku* — item, clause 条項 — *jōkō* — articles & clauses, provisions
刺	刺	1139; 18/6.　SHI, *sa(su)* poke forward, stab, sting [TZ'U[4] · I: pointed weapon 1-6 & knife → stab; P*] 名刺 — *meishi* — visiting card 刺身 — *sashimi* — sliced raw fish
暮	暮	1140; 140/11.　BO, *ku(rasu)* live, make a living; *ku(reru)* grow dark, end; *ku(re)* year's end [MU[4] · R sun & P* 1-10] 薄暮 — *hakubo* — dusk, twilight 夕暮 — *yūgure* — evening
祈	祈	1141; 113/4.　KI, *ino(ru/ri)* pray for [CH'I[2] · R god & P*] 祈願 — *kigan* — prayer, supplication 祈誓 — *kisei* — vow, pledge
縮	縮	1142; 120/11.　SHUKU, *chiji(meru/mu)* shrink [SO[1] · R thread & P*] 縮刷版 — *shukusatsuban* — reduced-size edition 緊縮 — *kinshuku* — shrinkage; economy; curtailment
掛	掛	1143; 64/8.　*ka(keru)* hang, apply, sit (on); *ka(karu)* be hanging, cost; *kakari* person in charge, [KUA[4] · R hand & P] expense 掛け布団 — *kakebuton* — bedspread, eiderdown 腰掛 — *koshikake* — seat, chair; stopgap job
眠	眠	1144; 109/5.　MIN, *nemu(ru/ri)* sleep [MIEN[2] · R eye & P*] 安眠 — *anmin* — peaceful sleep 眠り薬 — *nemurigusuri* — sleeping medicine

障	障	1145; 170/11. SHŌ, *sawa(ru/ri)* be a hindrance (to), have a bad effect (on) [CHANG⁴ · R mound & P*] 故 障 — *koshō* — defect, breakdown 障 害 — *shōgai* — obstacle, difficulty
憶	憶	1146; 61/13. OKU remember, think [I⁴, YI⁴ · R heart & P*] 憶 病 — *okubyō* — cowardice, timidity 記 憶 — *kioku* — memory
笑	笑	1147; 118/4. SHŌ, *wara(u/i)* laugh; smile; *e(mu)*, ⌐*emi* smile [HSIAO⁴ · R bamboo & P*] 冷 笑 — *reishō* — cold smile, sneer 笑 い 草 — *waraigusa* — laughingstock
優	優	1148; 9/15. YŪ, *sugu(reru)* be superior (to); *yasa-(shii)* gentle, elegant [YU¹ · R heart & P*] 優 秀 — *yūshū* — superiority, excellence 優 等 — *yūtō* — superiority, excellence
胸	胸	1149; 130/6. KYŌ, *mune* chest [HSIUNG¹ · R flesh & P*] 度 胸 — *dokyō* — courage 胸 飾 り — *munekazari* — brooch
姓	姓	1150; 38/5. SEI* family name; SHŌ [HSING⁴ · R woman & P*] 姓 氏 — *seishi* — family name, surname 百 姓 — *hyakushō* — farmer
謹	謹 謹	1151; 149/10. KIN, *tsutsushi(mu)* be respectful/cautious/restrained about [CHIN³ · R words & P*] 謹 賀 新 年 — *Kinga Shinnen* — Happy New Year 謹 聴 す る — *kinchō suru* — listen respectfully/attentively
透	透	1152; 162/7. TŌ, *su(ku)* be transparent [T'OU⁴ · R proceed & P*] 透 明 — *tōmei* — transparency 透 き 通 る — *suki-tōru* — be transparent

隻	隻	1153; 172/2. SEKI unit for counting ships, etc.; single, solitary [CHIH¹ · I: one bird 1–8 in the hand 9–10; P*] 数隻の船 — sūseki no fune — several ships 一隻眼 — issekigan — a discerning eye
抵	抵	1154; 64/5. TEI resist [TI³ · R hand & P*] 抵当 — teitō — mortgage ⌈tradictory (to) 抵触する — teishoku suru — run counter/be con-
較	較	1155; 159/6. KAKU, KŌ compare [CHIAO³·⁴ · R cart & P*] 比較 — hikaku — comparison 較量 — kōryō — comparison
飼	飼	1156; 184/5. SHI, ka(u) keep (animals) [SZU⁴ · R eat & P*] 飼育 — shiiku — breeding, rearing 飼い主 — kainushi — (animal) owner, keeper
偽	偽 偽	1157; 9/9. GI, itsuwa(ru) deceive, lie; nise sham, [WEI³·⁴ · R man & P*] ⌊imitation 偽造 — gizō — forgery, counterfeiting 真偽 — shingi — truth or falsehood, authenticity
菊	菊	1158; 140/8. KIKU* chrysanthemum [CHÜ² · R grass & P*] 菊人形 — kiku ningyō — chrysanthemum-flower doll 菊作り — kikuzukuri — chrysanthemum growing/ grower
姻	姻	1159; 38/6. IN marriage [YIN¹ · R woman & P*] 姻族 — inzoku — relative by marriage 婚姻統計 — kon'in tōkei — marriage statistics
圏	圏	1160; 31/9. KEN sphere, range, orbit [CH'ÜAN¹, CHÜAN⁴ · R enclosure & P*] 圏内 — kennai — within the orbit 北極圏 — Hokkyokuken — Arctic circle

	詠	1161; 149/5. EI, *yo(mu)* recite/chant/compose a [YUNG³ • R words & P*] ⌐poem 詠草 — *eisō* — draft of a poem ⌐hymn 詠歌 — *eika* — composing a poem/song; pilgrim's
	梅 梅	1162; 75/6. BAI, *ume* plum tree [MEI² • R tree & P*] 梅雨 — *baiu/tsuyu* — rainy season 梅酒 — *umeshu* — plum wine
	恐	1163; 61/6. KYŌ, *oso(reru/re)* fear; *oso(roshii)* [K'UNG³ • R heart & P*] ⌐fearsome 恐英病 — *kyōeibyō* — Anglophobia 恐れ入る — *osore-iru* — be overwhelmed/afraid; hesitant [to impose]
	削	1164; 18/7. SAKU, *kezu(ru)* plane, pare, delete [HSIAO¹, HSÜEH¹,⁴ • R knife & P*] 削減 — *sakugen* — reduction, curtailment 鉛筆削り — *enpitsu-kezuri* — pencil sharpener
	郷 郷	1165; 163/8. KYŌ village, native place; GŌ country- [HSIANG¹ • I; P*] ⌐side 故郷 — *kokyō* — native place ⌐crafts 郷土芸術 — *kyōdo geijutsu* — folk/rural arts &
	悔 悔	1166; 61/6. KAI, *ku(iru), kui* regret; *ku(yamu/yami)* regret, condole with [HUI³ • R heart & P*] 悔悟 — *kaigo* — repentance, remorse 後悔 — *kōkai* — regret, repentance
	彫	1167; 4/10. CHŌ, *ho(ru)* carve, engrave [TIAO¹ • I: to envelop 1–8 with decoration 9–11; also R light rays & P*] 彫像 — *chōzō* — sculpture, statue 一刀彫り — *ittō-bori* — single-knife carving
	柄	1168; 75/5. HEI, *gara* design, pattern, character; *e* [PING³,⁴ • R tree & P*] ⌐handle 人柄 — *hitogara* — personality, character 事柄 — *kotogara* — circumstances, situation

逃	逃	1169; 162/6. TŌ, *ni(gasu)/no(gasu)* (vt.), *ni(geru)* (vi.) let go/escape, set free; *no(gareru)* (vt.) escape (from), evade [T'AO² · R proceed & P*] 逃亡 — *tōbō* — escape, desertion 逃走 — *tōsō* — escape, desertion
冠	冠	1170; 14/7. KAN, *kanmuri* crown [KUAN¹,⁴ · I: what the hand 7–9 covers 1–2 the head 3–6 with; also R cover & P*] 王冠 — *ōkan* — crown ⌈victory 勝利の栄冠 — *shōri no eikan* — crown/laurels of
懇	懇	1171; 61/13. KON, *nengo(ro)* courtesy, cordiality [K'EN³ · R heart & P*] 懇意 — *kon'i* — kindness, friendship 懇願 — *kongan* — entreaty, appeal
頼	頼 賴	1172; 181/7. RAI, *tano(mu/mi)* make request (to), rely (on); *tayo(ru/ri)* rely/depend (on) [LAI⁴ · R money & P*] 依頼する — *irai suru* — make request/entrust (to) 頼みの綱 — *tanomi no tsuna* — lifeline, one's last hope
脱	脱 脱	1173; 130/7. DATSU omit; *nu(gu)* take off (clothes) [T'O¹,³ · R flesh & P*] 脱誤 — *datsugo* — omissions & mistakes 脱線 — *dassen* — derailment; deviation
騎	騎	1174; 187/8. KI unit for counting horsemen; horse-riding [CH'I² · R horse & P*] 一騎打ち — *ikki-uchi* — man-to-man fight on horseback 単騎旅行 — *tanki ryokō* — lone journey by horse
沼	沼	1175; 85/5. SHŌ, *numa* swamp [CHAO³ · R water & P*] 沼沢 — *shōtaku* — marsh, swamp 沼地 — *numachi/shōchi* — marsh land
怪	怪	1176; 61/5. KAI weird, mysterious; *aya(shimu)* suspect, doubt; *aya(shii)* suspicious, strange; KE [KUAI⁴ · R heart & P*] 奇怪な — *kikai na* — strange, weird 怪我 — *kega* — wound, injury

盲	盲	1177; 8/6. MŌ, *mekura* blindness, blind person [MANG² • I: without/lost 1–3 sight 4–8; also R eye & P*] 盲目 — *mōmoku* — blindness 盲腸 — *mōchō* — the appendix
棄	棄 棄	1178; 8/11. KI discard [CH'I⁴ • R tree & P*] 放棄する — *hōki suru* — abandon, relinquish 自暴自棄 — *jibō jiki* — self-neglect, despair
煮	煮 煮	1179; 86/8. SHA, *ni(ru)* boil, cook [CHU³ • R fire & P*] 煮直す — *ni-naosu* — reboil, recook 生煮えの — *namanie no* — undercooked
腕	腕	1180; 130/8. WAN, *ude* arm, ability [WAN⁴ • R flesh & P*] 腕輪 — *udewa* — bracelet 腕前 — *udemae* — ability, skill
街	街	1181; 60/9. GAI, KAI, *machi* street [CHIEH¹ • R go/do & P*] 街路掃除夫 — *gairo sōjifu* — street cleaner 甲州街道 — *Kōshū kaidō* — the Kōshū highway
訴	訴	1182; 149/5. SO, *utta(eru/e)* sue, complain of, appeal/resort (to) [SU⁴, SUN⁴ • R words & P*] 告訴 — *kokuso* — accusation 訴願 — *sogan* — petition, appeal
層	層 層	1183; 44/11. SŌ stratum [TS'ENG² • R bent figure & P*] 下層 — *kasō* — substratum; lower classes 地層 — *chisō* — land stratum
漸	漸	1184; 85/11. ZEN gradually, finally [CHIEN¹,⁴ • R water & P*] 漸増 — *zenzō* — gradual increase 漸減 — *zengen* — gradual decrease

銃	銃	1185; 167/6. JŪ gun [CH'UNG⁴ • R metal & P*] 小銃弾 — *shōjū-dan* — rifle bullet 銃殺 — *jūsatsu* — shooting to death
踏	踏	1186; 157/8. TŌ, *fu(mu)* step/tread on [T'A⁴ • R foot & P] 舞踏会 — *butōkai* — dance party, ball 踏切り — *fumikiri* — level crossing
維	維	1187; 120/8. I fasten; support [WEI² • R thread & P*] 維持 — *iji* — support, maintenance 明治維新 — *Meiji Ishin* — Meiji Restoration
懐	懐 懷	1188; 61/13. KAI, *natsu(kashii)* nostalgic, yearned for; *natsu(kashimu)* yearn for; *natsu(keru/ku)* win over, tame; *futokoro* breast pocket, purse [HUAI² • R heart & P*] 述懐 — *jukkai* — reminiscences 懐中電灯 — *kaichū dentō* — pocket torch
倒	倒	1189; 9/8. TŌ, *tao(su/reru)* fell, bring down [TAO³,⁴ • R man & P*] 圧倒的 — *attōteki* — overwhelming 卒倒する — *sottō suru* — faint, fall unconscious
請	請 請	1190; 149/8. SEI, SHIN, *u(keru)* receive, undertake; ⌊*ko(u)* request [CH'ING³ • R words & P*] 請求書 — *seikyūsho* — bill, written claim 普請 — *fushin* — building, construction
奉	奉	1191; 4/7. HŌ, BU, *hō(zuru)* present, serve, obey; *tatematsu(ru)* present, revere [FENG⁴ • I: offer up 1–5 with the hand 6–8; P*] 奉仕 — *hōshi* — service 奉納 — *hōnō* — presentation; offering
寛	寛	1192; 40/10. KAN generous, liberal [K'UAN¹ • R roof & P*] 寛容 — *kan'yō* — generosity, tolerance 寛厚 — *kankō* — magnanimity, cordiality

隆	隆	1193; 170/8. RYŪ prosperous, high [LUNG² · R mound & P] 隆盛 — *ryūsei* — prosperity 隆運 — *ryūun* — good fortune
慈	慈	1194; 12/11. JI, *itsuku(shimu)* have love/compas- [TZ'U² · R fire & P*] ⌐sion for 慈悲 — *jihi* — compassion, charity 慈愛 — *jiai* — kindness, love
乾	乾	1195; 24/9. KAN, *kawa(kasu)* dry; *kawa(ku)* be- [CH'IEN², KAN¹ · I; P*] ⌐come dry/thirsty 乾杯 — *kanpai* — a toast 乾物 — *kanbutsu* — groceries, dry goods
概	概 概	1196; 75/10. GAI general, approximate [KAI⁴ · R tree & P*] 概略 — *gairyaku* — outline, gist; roughly 概算 — *gaisan* — rough estimate
浪	浪	1197; 85/7. RŌ wave, drifting [LANG⁴ · R water & P*] 浪費 — *rōhi* — waste, extravagance 流浪生活 — *rurō seikatsu* — a wandering life
貫	貫 貫	1198; 80/7. KAN, *tsuranu(ku)* pierce, go through, achieve ⌐5–11 on a string; P*] [KUAN⁴ · I: pierced 1–4 (vrt. of 1206 1–7) money 貫通する — *kantsū suru* — pierce, perforate 貫流する — *kanryū suru* — flow through
烈	烈	1199; 86/6. RETSU violent, brave [LIEH⁴ · R fire & P*] 熱烈な — *netsuretsu na* — passionate, ardent 烈震 — *resshin* — violent earthquake
涙	涙 涙	1200; 85/7. RUI, *namida* tear [LEI⁴ · I: water 1–3 returns 4–10 (vrt. of 1850) 感涙 — *kanrui* — tears of emotion ⌐as tears] 涙声 — *namidagoe* — tearful voice

般	般	1201; 137/4. HAN general; carry [PAN[1] • I; P*] 先般 — *senpan* — the other day 全般 — *zenpan* — the whole
誇	誇	1202; 149/6. KO, *hoko(ru/ri)* be proud, boast [K'UA[1] • I: words & bigness 8–13] 誇示 — *koshi/koji* — display, ostentation 誇張 — *kochō* — exaggeration
誉	誉 譽	1203; 149/6. YO, *homa(re)* honor, glory, fame [YÜ[2,4] • I: give 1–6 (vrt. of 983) words 7–13 of praise; also R words & P*] 名誉 — *meiyo* — honor, honorary 栄誉 — *eiyo* — honor
雷	雷	1204; 173/5. RAI, *kaminari* thunder [LEI[2] • R rain & P*] 雷鳴 — *raimei* — thunder 落雷 —*rakurai* — being struck by lightning
啓	啓	1205; 30/8. KEI enlighten, address [CH'I[3] • I: push open 5–8 the door 1–4 of under- standing by words 9–11; also R mouth & P*] 啓発する — *keihatsu suru* — enlighten, develop 拝啓 — *Haikei* — Respectfully, Dear Sir (in letters)
患	患	1206; 61/7. KAN, *wazura(u/i)* be troubled over, suffer from; *wazura(wasu)* trouble [HUAN[4] • R heart & P (cf. 1198)] 患者 — *kanja* — patient 急患手当 — *kyūkan teate* — first-aid treatment
陣	陣	1207; 170/7. JIN* military camp/position [CHEN[4] • R mound & P* (orig., vrt. of 1647)] 円陣 — *enjin* — (people in) a circle 陣営 — *jin'ei* — camp, barracks
傑	傑	1208; 9/10. KETSU excel [CHIEH[2] • R man & P] 傑作 — *kessaku* — masterpiece; blunder 傑出する — *kesshutsu suru* — excel

促	促	1209; 9/7. SOKU, *unaga(su)* urge [TS'U⁴ · R man & P*] 促成 — *sokusei* — promotion of growth 促進する — *sokushin suru* — promote, stimulate
掌	掌	1210; 42/9. SHŌ control; palm of the hand [CHANG³ · R hand & P* 1–8 (vrt. of 1843)] 車掌 — *shashō* — (bus, etc.) conductor 掌中の玉 — *shōchū no tama* — apple of one's eye
雅	雅	1211; 92/8. GA elegance, grace [YA³ · R small bird & P*] 雅楽 — *Gagaku* — Imperial Court music 優雅 — *yūga* — elegance, grace
侮	侮 侮	1212; 9/6. BU, *anado(ru)* despise [WU³ · R man & P*] 侮言 — *bugen* — insult 軽侮 — *keibu* — contempt
詔	詔	1213; 149/5. SHŌ, *mikotonori* imperial edict [CHAO⁴ · R words & P*] 聖詔 — *seishō* — imperial command/decree 詔書 — *shōsho* — imperial rescript/edict
垂	垂	1214; 4/7. SUI, *ta(rasu/reru)* suspend, [let] hang [CH'UI² · R earth & P*] ⌊down 垂直降下 — *suichoku kōka* — vertical descent 垂線 — *suisen* — vertical/perpendicular line
肩	肩	1215; 63/4. KEN, *kata* shoulder [CHIEN¹ · I: D of shoulder 1–4 & flesh; P*] 肩書 — *katagaki* — title 肩身が広い — *katami ga hiroi* — feel proud/big
乳	乳	1216; 5/7. NYŪ, *chichi/chi* milk, breasts [JU³ · I; P*] 牛乳 — *gyūnyū* — (cow's) milk 乳離れ — *chibanare/chichibanare* — weaning

憎	憎 憎	1217; 61/11. ZŌ, *niku(mu)* hate [TSENG⁴ • R heart & P*] 憎悪〔心〕— *zōo[shin]* — hatred 生憎 — *ainiku* — unfortunately
模	模	1218; 75/10. MO, BO model, imitation [MO¹, MA¹, MAO¹ • R tree & P*] 模範 — *mohan* — model, example 規模 — *kibo* — scale
獄	獄	1219; 94/11. GOKU* prison [YÜ⁴ • I: dogs 1–3 & 11–14 exchanging words/ snarls 4–10 → complaint → prison; P*] 出獄する — *shutsugoku suru* — leave prison 地獄 — *jigoku* — hell
姫	姫 姫	1220; 38/6. *hime* princess [CHI¹ • I: type of woman 1–3 Court official 4–10] 姫君 — *himegimi* — princess 舞姫 — *maihime* — dancing-girl, dancer
浸	浸	1221; 85/7. SHIN, *hita(su/ru)* soak, wet [CHIN¹,⁴, CH'IN⁴ • R water & P*] 浸水家屋 — *shinsui kaoku* — flooded houses 浸透 — *shintō* — permeation, saturation, osmosis
誘	誘	1222; 149/7. YŪ, *saso(u/i)* invite, tempt [YU⁴ • R words & P*] 誘惑 — *yūwaku* — temptation, seduction 勧誘する — *kan'yū suru* — canvass, solicit
嫁	嫁	1223; 38/10. KA, *yome* bride, young wife; *totsu-* *(gu)* marry [of woman] [CHIA⁴ • R woman & P*] 花嫁 — *hanayome* — bride　　　　⌐tions/trousseau 嫁入り支度 — *yomeiri-jitaku* — wedding prepara-
髪	髪 髪	1224; 190/4. HATSU, *kami* the hair [FA³ • R long 1–7 (=155) hair 8–10 & P*] 理髪用具 — *rihatsu yōgu* — hairdressing equip- 髪結い — *kamiyui* — hairdresser/dressing ⌊ment

恒	恒 恒	1225; 61/6. KŌ constant, permanent [HENG² · I: heart 1–3 unchanging one 4 day 5–8 after another 9; P*] 恒久 — kōkyū — permanency 恒例 — kōrei — usual practice, common usage
鬼	鬼	1226; 194/0. KI, oni devil ⌐(vrt. of 4); P*] [KUEI³ · D & S: a weirdfaced 1–6 figure 7–10] 鬼才 — kisai — genius, prodigy 鬼百合 — oni-yuri — tiger lily
恨	恨	1227; 61/6. KON, ura(mu/mi) hate, resent [HEN⁴ · R heart & P*] 悔恨 — kaikon — remorse, regret 痛恨 — tsūkon — deep sorrow, bitter regret
滅	滅	1228; 85/10. METSU, horo(bosu/biru) ruin, destroy [MIEH⁴ · I: water 1–3, battle-ax 4–6 & 11–13, & fire 7–10] 破滅 — hametsu — ruin, destruction 滅亡 — metsubō — downfall, destruction
裸	裸	1229; 145/8. RA, hadaka naked, penniless [LO³ · R clothes & P*] 裸体画 — rataiga — nude picture ⌐all 裸一貫で — hadaka ikkan de — with no money at
飽	飽 飽	1230; 184/5. HŌ, a(kiru/ki) become tiresome/boring, become tired (of) [PAO³ · R eat & P*] ⌐well clothed 飽食暖衣の — hōshoku dan'i no — overfed & 飽き飽きする — aki-aki suru — become tired (of)
執	執	1231; 32/8. SHITSU, SHŪ, to(ru) seize, grasp, take (on), carry out [CHIH² · D & S: kneeling figure 9–11 holding out manacled hands 1–8; P*] 執権 — shikken — regent 執着 — shūjaku/shūchaku — attachment, tenacity
尉	尉	1232; 4/10. I junior/company officer [WEI⁴, YÜ⁴ · R rule & P*] 陸軍中尉 — rikugun chūi — army lieutenant 空軍大尉 — kūgun taii — air-force captain

紅	紅	1233; 120/3. Kō, KU, *kurenai* crimson; *beni* rouge, [HUNG[2] • R thread & P*] ⌐lipstick 紅茶 — *kōcha* — black/Indian-type tea 口紅 — *kuchibeni* — lipstick
幅	幅	1234; 50/9. FUKU* unit for counting scrolls; *haba* width, influence [FU[2,4] • R cloth & P*] 幅利き — *habakiki* — person of influence 半幅 — *hanhaba* — half width
縫	縫	1235; 120/9. Hō, *nu(u/i)* sew [FENG[2,4] • R thread & P*] 裁縫 — *saihō* — sewing, needlework 縫い模様 — *nui-moyō* — embroidered design
探	探	1236; 64/8. TAN, *sagu(ru), saga(su)* search for/through [T'AN[1,4] • I: use a hand 1–3 to search a hole 4–7 (vrt. of 984) for wood 8–11; P*] 探究 — *tankyū* — search, inquiry ⌐pedition 南極探険 — *Nankyoku tanken* — Antarctic ex-
胞	胞	1237; 130/5. Hō placenta [PAO[1], P'AO[1] • R flesh & P*] 胞衣 — *ena/hōi* — placenta 細胞 — *saihō* — (physiological/political) cell
貞	貞	1238; 25/7. TEI chaste, constant [CHEN[1] • R divination & P*] 貞節 — *teisetsu* — chastity, fidelity 貞潔 — *teiketsu* — chastity, purity
噴	噴	1239; 30/12. FUN, *fu(ku)* emit [P'EN[1,4], FEN[4] • R mouth & P*] 噴出する — *funshutsu suru* — gush/spout forth, 噴煙 — *fun'en* — belching smoke ⌐emit
墜	墜	1240; 32/11. TSUI fall [CHUI[4] • R earth & P*] 墜落する — *tsuiraku suru* — fall, crash 撃墜する — *gekitsui suru* — shoot down (a plane)

撮	撮	1241; 64/12. SATSU pinch, pick; *to(ru)* take (photo) [TS'O¹,⁴, TSO¹ • R hand & P*] 撮要 — *satsuyō* — outline, summary 撮影 — *satsuei* — photography
暫	暫	1242; 72/11. ZAN for a while [CHAN⁴ • R sun → day & P*] 暫定 — *zantei* — provisional, tentative 暫時 — *zanji* — (for) a short time
締	締	1243; 120/9. TEI *shi(meru/maru)* tie, shut, tighten [TI⁴ • R thread & P*] 締め切り — *shimekiri* — shut, closing, time limit 条約の締結 — *jōyaku no teiketsu* — treaty conclusion
縁	縁 縁	1244; 120/9. EN relationship, marriage; veranda; [YÜAN² • R thread & P*] *fuchi* edge, rim 縁談 — *endan* — marriage discussion/proposal 額縁 — *gakubuchi* — (picture) frame
顕	顕 顯	1245; 181/9. KEN manifest, important [HSIEN³ • R head & P*] 顕著な — *kencho na* — outstanding, conspicuous 露顕 — *roken* — discovery, exposure
枯	枯	1246; 75/5. KO, *ka(rasu/reru)* wither, dry up [K'U¹ • R tree & P*] 枯芝 — *kareshiba* — withered grass 枯葉 — *kareha/koyō* — dead leaf
耐	耐	1247; 126/3. TAI, *ta(eru)* endure, withstand [NAI⁴ • R rule & P*] 忍耐 — *nintai* — perseverance 耐熱の — *tainetsu no* — heat proof
虐	虐	1248; 141/3.. GYAKU cruelty; *shiita(geru)* oppress [NÜEH⁴ • I: tiger 1–6 (ab. of 1932) claws 7–9 虐待 — *gyakutai* — ill-treatment (vrt.of 1887)] 暴虐 — *bōgyaku* — tyranny, atrocity

哀	哀	1249; 8/7. AI, *awa(remu/re)* pity [AI[1] · I: a robe 1–2 & 6–5 covering the mouth 3–5 in distress; also R mouth & P*] 喜怒哀楽 — *kido airaku* — emotion, feelings 悲哀 — *hiai* — sorrow, pathos
幕	幕	1250; 140/10. MAKU* curtain, act; BAKU military, Shōgunate ⌈cloth & P*⌉ [MU[4] · I: cover up 1–10 & cloth 11–13; also R 開幕 — *kaimaku* — curtain-raising 幕府 — *Bakufu* — Shōgunate government
滞	滞 滞	1251; 85/10. TAI residence (in); *todokō(ru/ri)* stagnate, be in arrears [CHIH[4] · R water & P*] 滞在 — *taizai* — stay, residence 滞納 — *tainō* — nonpayment, default
儀	儀	1252; 9/13. GI* ceremony; rule; matter [I[2], YI[2] · R man & P*] 儀式 — *gishiki* — ceremony, ritual 礼儀〔作法〕— *reigi [sahō]* — etiquette, courtesy
審	審	1253; 40/12. SHIN investigate, judge [SHEN[3] · R roof & P*] 審判官 — *shinpankan* — umpire, referee 審議 — *shingi* — inquiry, review, deliberation
憤	憤	1254; 61/12. FUN, *ikidō(ru)* be angry/indignant/ [FEN[4] · R heart & P*] ⌊resentful 憤然と — *funzen to* — angrily, indignantly 義憤 — *gifun* — righteous indignation
艇	艇	1255; 137/7. TEI small boat [T'ING[3] · R boat & P*] 舟艇 — *shūtei* — boat 艦艇 — *kantei* — naval vessel
潤	潤	1256; 85/12. JUN, *uruo(su/u/i)* moisten, profit, enrich; *uru(mu)* be moist/clouded ⌈& P*⌉ [JUN[4] · I: water 1–3 in excess 4–15; also R water 浸潤 — *shinjun* — permeation, saturation 利潤 — *rijun* — profit (margin)

載	載	1257; 24/11. SAI, *no(seru/ru)* load, carry, publish, [TSAI³,⁴ · R cart & P*] ⌐record 積載 — *sekisai* — loading, carrying 連載読物 — *rensai yomimono* — serial(ized story)
軸	軸	1258; 159/5. JIKU* axis, axle, scroll [CHOU², CHU² · R cart & P*] 車軸 — *shajiku* — wheel axle 掛け軸 — *kakejiku* — hanging scroll
窮	窮	1259; 116/10. KYŪ, *kiwa(meru/maru)* take to an extreme, follow through [CH'IUNG² · I: extremely small hole 1–5 entered by bending the body 6–12 like a bow 13–15; *P] 窮極の — *kyūkyoku no* — final, ultimate 窮境 — *kyūkyō* — extremity, dilemma, plight
偏	偏	1260; 9/9. HEN, *katayo(ru)* incline (to), be one-sided/partial (toward) [P'IEN¹ · R man & P*] 偏見 — *henken* — prejudice ⌐derance 偏重 — *henchō/henjū* — over-emphasis, prepon-
閲	閲 閲	1261; 169/7. ETSU inspect, examine, peruse [YÜEH⁴ · R gate & P*] 検閲 — *ken'etsu* — inspection, censorship ⌐ticket 図書閲覧券 — *tosho etsuran-ken* — library reading
婆	婆	1262; 38/8. BA old woman [P'O² · R woman & P*] 産婆 — *sanba* — midwife ⌐cern 老婆心 — *rōbashin* — old-womanish/excessive con-
崇	崇	1263; 46/8. SŪ worship; lofty, noble [CH'UNG² · R mountain & P*] 祖先崇拝 — *sosen sūhai* — ancestor worship 崇敬 — *sūkei* — reverence, veneration
輝	輝	1264; 42/12. KI, *kagaya(ku)* shine, be radiant [HUI¹ · R cart & P*] 光輝 — *kōki* — brilliance, splendor ⌐wide 輝き渡る — *kagayaki-wataru* — shine out far &

掘	掘	1265; 64/8. KUTSU, ho(ru) dig [CHÜEH[2] • R and & P*] 石炭採掘 — sekitan saikutsu — coal mining 掘り出し物 — horidashimono — lucky find, bargain
渇	渇 渴	1266; 85/8. KATSU, kawa(kasu) dry; kawa(ku) become dry/thirsty [K'O[3], K'E[3] • R water & P*] 枯渇する — kokatsu suru — run dry, be exhausted 知的渇望 — chiteki katsubō — intellectual thirst/ longing
況	況 況	1267; 85/5. KYŌ situation; still more [K'UANG[4] • R water & P*] 状/情況 — jōkyō — situation, circumstances 概況 — gaikyō — general situation/conditions
涼	涼 涼	1268; 85/8. RYŌ, suzu(shii) cool; suzu(mu/mi) cool oneself [LIANG[2] • R water & P*] 清涼飲料 — seiryō inryō — cooling drink 夕涼み — yūsuzumi — (enjoying) the evening cool
斎	斎 齋	1269; 210/3. SAI purification; room [CHAI[1] • R god & P*] 斎戒 — saikai — purification 書斎 — shosai — study
峡	峡 峽	1270; 46/6. KYŌ gorge, ravine [HSIA[4] • R mountain & P*] 津軽海峡 — Tsugaru Kaikyō — the Tsugaru Straits 峡湾 — kyōwan — fiord
駆	駆 驅	1271; 187/4. KU, ka(keru) run, gallop [CH'Ü[1] • R horse & P*] 駆除 — kujo — extermination, destruction 駆け足で — kakeashi de — at the double, at a run
峰	峰 峰	1272; 46/7. HŌ, mine peak [FENG[1] • R mountain & P*] 連峰 — renpō — series/row of mountain peaks 富士山の峰 — Fuji-san no mine — the peak of Mt. Fuji

献	献 戲	1273; 94/9. KEN, KON present, dedicate [HSIEN⁴ · R dog & P*] 奉献する — *hōken suru* — consecrate, dedicate 献立 — *kondate* — menu; arrangements, plan
割	割	1274; 18/10. KATSU, *wa(ru)*, *sa(ku)* divide, split; *wari* proportion; percentage, 10%; profit [KO¹, KE¹ · R knife & P*] ⌐ments 分割払い — *bunkatsu-barai* — installment/easy pay- 割引券 — *waribiki-ken* — discount coupon
募	募	1275; 140/9. BO, *tsuno(ru)* raise, collect, levy [MU⁴ · R strength & *P] 募金運動 — *bokin undō* — fund-raising campaign 募集 — *boshū* — recruitment, enrollment
愉	愉 愉	1276; 61/9. YU enjoyment, pleasure [YÜ² · R heart & P*] 愉快 — *yukai* — enjoyment, pleasure 愉楽 — *yuraku* — pleasure, joy
裂	裂	1277; 145/6. RETSU, *sa(ku/keru)* tear, rend [LIEH⁴ · R clothes & P*] 破裂する — *haretsu suru* — explode, burst 裂目 — *sakeme* — tear, split, crack
詐	詐	1278; 149/5. SA lie, deceive [CHA³ · R words & P*] 詐称 — *sashō* — false name/title, misrepresentation 詐取 — *sashu* — fraud, swindle
遍	遍	1279; 162/9. HEN wide, general [PIEN⁴, P'IEN⁴ · R proceed & P*] 遍歴 — *henreki* — travels, pilgrimage 普遍的真理 — *fuhenteki shinri* — universal truth
閑	閑	1280; 169/4. KAN quietness, peace, leisure [HSIEN² · I: gate 1–8 secured with wooden bar 閑散 — *kansan* — leisure, inactivity ⌊9–12; P*] 閑静 — *kansei* — tranquillity

漂	漂	1281; 85/11.　HYŌ, *tadayo(u)* drift, float [P'IAO¹,³,⁴ · R water & P*] 漂流 — *hyōryū* — drifting 漂白液 — *hyōhakueki* — bleaching liquid
網	網	1282; 120/8.　MŌ, *ami* net [WANG³ · R thread & P* (cf. 1052)] 通信網 — *tsūshin-mō* — communication/news net- 網袋 — *amibukuro* — net bag　　　⌐work
懸	懸	1283; 61/16.　KEN, KE, *ka(keru/karu)* hang, apply, [HSÜAN² · R heart & P*]　　　　　⌐spread 一生懸命に — *isshō kenmei ni* — for dear life 懸念 — *kenen* — fear, anxiety
累	累	1284; 102/6.　RUI successive; involvement, trouble [LEI²,³,⁴ · I; P*] 累積 — *ruiseki* — accumulation, pile 係累 — *keirui* — dependents, ties; complicity
遇	遇	1285; 162/9.　GŪ meeting; treatment [YÜ⁴ · R proceed & P*] 奇遇 — *kigū* — chance/surprise meeting 待遇 — *taigū* — treatment, service
宇	宇	1286; 40/3.　U the heavens, sky [YÜ³ · R roof & P*] 宇内 — *udai* — the whole world 宇治 — *Uji* — pn.
苗	苗	1287; 140/5.　BYŌ, *nae* seedling [MIAO¹ · I: plants 1–3 in a rice field 4–8; P*] 苗床 — *naedoko* — seedbed 苗代〔田〕 — *nawashiro[da]* — rice-seedling bed
磁	磁	1288; 112/9.　JI magnet; porcelain [TZ'U² · R stone & P*] 磁石 — *jishaku/jiseki* — magnet, compass 磁気 — *jiki* — magnetism

慢	慢	1289; 61/11. MAN* idle; haughty [MAN⁴ · R heart & P*] 怠慢 — *taiman* — negligence, neglect 我慢 — *gaman* — patience, tolerance, self-control
盤	盤	1290; 108/10. BAN* dish, board [P'AN² · R dish & P*] 円盤 — *enban* — disc, discus 基盤 — *kiban* — basis, foundation
茎	茎 莖	1291; 140/5. KEI, *kuki* stem, stalk [CHING¹ · R grass & P*] 花茎 — *kakei* — flowering stem 球茎植物 — *kyūkei shokubutsu* — bulb plant
嘆	嘆 嘆	1292; 30/10. TAN, *nage(ku)* sigh/be sad over, deplore [T'AN⁴ · R mouth & P*] 詠嘆 — *eitan* — admiration, exclamation 驚嘆する — *kyōtan suru* — feel admiration (for)
稲	稲 稻	1293; 115/9. TŌ, *ine* rice plant [TAO⁴ · R grain & P] 陸稲 — *rikutō/okabe* — upland/hill rice 稲荷 — *Inari* — fox/harvest god
韻	韻	1294; 180/10. IN* rhyme; meter, echo, tone [YÜN⁴ · R sound & P*] 音韻組織 — *on'in soshiki* — sound system 韻律的 — *inritsuteki* — rhythmic
貢	貢	1295; 48/7. KŌ, KU, *mitsu(gu)* donate, contribute; *mitsugi* tribute [KUNG⁴ · R money & P*] 貢献 — *kōken* — contribution, service 年貢 — *nengu* — annual tribute, land tax
勲	勲 勳	1296; 86/11. KUN merit [HSÜN¹ · R strength & P*] 勲章 — *kunshō* — decoration, order, medal 殊勲 — *shukun* — distinguished service

嘱	囑 囑	1297; 30/12. SHOKU entrust, request [CHU³ · R mouth & P*] 委嘱する — *ishoku suru* — entrust/give a commission (to) 「expect much (of) 嘱望する — *shokubō suru* — pin one's hopes (on),
戯	戯 戲	1298; 4/14. GI, *tawamu(reru/re)* be playful/joking/flirtatious (toward) [HSI⁴ · R lance & P*] 戯曲 — *gikyoku* — drama, play 遊戯 — *yūgi* — game, pastime
霊	靈 靈	1299; 173/7. REI, RYŌ, *tama* spirit, ghost, soul [LING² · I: in the heavens 1–8, lines 9–15 (cf. 998) of spirits] 亡霊 — *bōrei* — dead spirit, ghost 慰霊祭 — *ireisai* — memorial service
寂	寂	1300; 40/8. JAKU, SEKI, *sabi(shii)* lonely [CHI⁴ · R roof & P*] 閑寂 — *kanjaku* — tranquillity 静寂 — *seijaku* — silence, tranquillity
宴	宴	1301; 40/7. EN banquet [YEN⁴ · I: to relax 1–3 & 8–10 (see 98) after the day 4–7 & enjoy oneself] 宴会場 — *enkaijō* — banquet hall 酒宴 — *shuen* — drinking party
庸	庸	1302; 53/8. YŌ mediocre, ordinary [YUNG¹ · R lean-to & P*] 庸才 — *yōsai* — mediocre talent 中庸 — *chūyō* — middle path, the (golden) mean
宙	宙	1303; 40/5. CHŪ the heavens, space [CHOU⁴ · R roof & P*] 宙返り — *chūgaeri* — somersault 宇宙旅行 — *uchū ryokō* — space travel
惨	惨 慘	1304; 61/8. SAN, ZAN, *miji(me na)* piteous, wretched [TS'AN³ · R heart & P*] 惨事 — *sanji* — tragedy, disaster 悲惨な — *hisan na* — wretched, sad, tragic

涉	涉 涉	1305; 85/8. SHŌ cross over, link [SHE⁴ · I: walk/step 4–11 (see 433) across a stream 1–3; P*] 涉外 — *shōgai* — public relations, liaison 交涉 — *kōshō* — negotiations, relations (with)
笛	笛	1306; 118/5. TEKI, *fue* flute [TI² · R bamboo & P*] 警笛 — *keiteki* — alarm-whistle, (car, etc.) horn 口笛 — *kuchibue* — whistling, a whistle
讓	讓 讓	1307; 149/13. JŌ, *yuzu(ru)* hand over, give up, [JANG⁴ · R words & P*] ⌊yield 讓步 — *jōho* — concession 讓り渡す — *yuzuri-watasu* — hand over
臭	臭 臭	1308; 132/3. SHŪ, *kusa(i)* ill-smelling; *-kusa(i)* smacking of ⌈dog 7–9 (ab. of 578), sniffing; P*] [CH'OU⁴ · HSIU⁴ I: the nose 1–6 (see 60) of a 惡臭 — *akushū* — bad smell ⌈sanctimonious 宗教臭い — *shūkyō-kusai* — smacking of religion,
既	既 既 既	1309; 138/5. KI, *sude (ni)* already [CHI⁴ · R limit & P] 既製衣類 — *kisei irui* — ready-made clothes 既定事実 — *kitei jijitsu* — established fact
鑑	鑑	1310; 167/14. KAN discernment; take warning from, have regard to [CHIEN⁴ · R metal & P*] 鑑賞 — *kanshō* — appreciation 年鑑 — *nenkan* — year book
更	更	1311; 1/6. KŌ repeat; *sara (ni)* anew, again; *fu- (kasu)* (vt.) be up deep into (the night); *fu(keru)* [KENG¹,⁴, CHING¹ · R sun & P*] ⌊grow late 更生 — *kōsei* — rebirth 變更 — *henkō* — change, alteration
辛	辛	1312; 160/0. SHIN painful, hard; *kara(i)* spicy, salty; *karō(jite)* barely, with difficulty [HSIN¹ · D; P*] 辛酸 — *shinsan* — hardship, privation 辛辛 — *karagara* — barely, with difficulty

妥	妥	1313; 87/3. DA peace, contentment [T'O³ · I: a hand 1–4 placed on a woman to pacify her; P*] 妥当な — *datō na* — proper, appropriate, sound 妥協 — *dakyō* — compromise
妊	妊 姙	1314; 38/4. NIN conception, pregnancy [JEN² · R woman & P*] 妊婦 — *ninpu* — pregnant woman 懐妊 — *kainin* — conception, pregnancy
伺	伺	1315; 9/5. SHI, *ukaga(u)* (vi.) visit, (vt.) ask/hear [TZ'U⁴, SZU⁴ · R man & P*] ⌐about 伺候する — *shikō suru* — wait (upon), pay one's respects (to) ⌐after a person's health] 暑中伺い — *shochū-ukagai* — hot-season inquiry
芳	芳	1316; 140/4. HŌ hon. pref.; *kanba(shii)* fragrant [FANG¹ · R grass & P*] 芳志 — *hōshi* — your kindness 芳香 — *hōkō* — perfume, fragrance
沖	沖	1317; 85/4. CHŪ, *oki* open sea, offshore sea [CH'UNG¹ · R water & P*] 沖合 — *okiai* — offshore, offing ⌐waves 沖津白波 — *okitsu shiranami* — offshore white
抑	抑	1318; 64/4. YOKU, *osa(eru)* restrain, hold down [I⁴, YI⁴ · R hand & P*] 抑圧 — *yokuatsu* — suppression 抑制する — *yokusei suru* — restrain, repress
充	充	1319; 8/4. JŪ fill; *a(teru)* apply, strike home [CH'UNG¹ · I: the full growth of a child 1–4 (inverted vrt. of 61) into a man 5–6; P*] 充分に — *jūbun ni* — in full measure, satisfactorily 充足 — *jūsoku* — sufficiency
抗	抗	1320; 64/4. KŌ resist [K'ANG⁴ · R hand & P*] 反抗 — *hankō* — resistance, opposition ⌐(against) 抵抗する — *teikō suru* — offer resistance (to), fight

妙	妙	1321; 38/4. MYŌ* wondrous, strange [MIAO⁴ · I: the beauty of a woman 1–3 of few 4–7 years; P*] 妙技 — *myōgi* — outstanding skill 功妙 — *kōmyō* — skill
佐	佐	1322; 9/5. SA assist [TSO³ · R man & P*] 補佐 — *hosa* — assistance 佐賀 — *Saga* — pn.
邦	邦	1323; 163/4. HŌ homeland, Japan [PANG¹ · R district & P*]　　　　⌜wealth 英国連邦 — *Eikoku Renpō* — British Common- 在留邦人 — *zairyū hōjin* — overseas Japanese
劣	劣	1324; 4/5. RETSU, *oto(ru)* be inferior (to) [LIEH⁴ · I: less 1–4 strength 5–6 than others; P*] 劣等感 — *rettō-kan* — inferiority complex 優勝劣敗 — *yūshō reppai* — the strong win & the weak fail, survival of the fittest
灰	灰 灰	1325; 27/4. KAI, *hai* ashes [HUI¹ · R fire & P*] 石灰 — *sekkai* — lime 灰色の — *hai-iro no* — ashen, gray
羊	羊	1326; 123/0. YŌ, *hitsuji* sheep [YANG² · D: sheep with horns 1–2; P*] 羊毛 — *yōmō* — wool 羊飼 — *hitsujikai* — shepherd
旬	旬	1327; 20/4. JUN ten-day period　　　⌜P*⌝ [HSÜN² · I: sun/day 3–6 & revolve/repeat 1–2] 下旬 — *gejun* — last ten days of a month 旬刊 — *junkan* — published every ten days
汗	汗	1328; 85/3 KAN, *ase* sweat [HAN⁴ · R water & P*] 発汗 — *hakkan* — sweating 冷汗 — *hiya-ase* — cold sweat

壮	壮 壮	1329; 90/3. SŌ powerful, brave [CHUANG⁴ · R scholar & P*] 壮健な — sōken na — healthy, robust 強壮な — kyōsō na — sturdy, robust
扱	扱	1330; 64/3. atsuka(u) deal with [HSI² · R hand & P*] 扱い人 — atsukainin — person in charge 取り扱う — toriatsukau — deal with, treat
伏	伏	1331; 9/4. FUKU, fu(seru/su) lay face down ⌐P*⌐ [FU² · I: a man 1–2 lying down like a dog 3–6; 起伏 — kifuku — ups & downs, undulations 伏し拝む — fushi-ogamu — bow down in worship
仲	仲	1332; 9/4. CHŪ, naka personal relations [CHUNG⁴ · R man & P*] 仲裁 — chūsai — arbitration, mediation 仲良く — nakayoku — on cordial terms
甘	甘	1333; 99/0. KAN, ama(i) sweet, indulgent, mild [KAN¹ · I: something 4 held in the mouth 1–3 & 5 (vrt. of 38) ; P*] 甘味料 — kanmiryō — sweetening material 甘口 — amakuchi — sweet flavor/tooth/words
幼	幼	1334; 52/2. YŌ, osana(i) infant, juvenile [YU⁴ · I: slender/little 1–3 strength 4–5; P*] 幼児 — yōji — infant, child 幼恋 — osanagoi — calf love
矢	矢	1335; 111/0. SHI, ya arrow [SHIH³,⁴ · D; P*] 矢張 — yahari/yappari — likewise, after all 矢印 — yajirushi — arrow mark, direction arrow
孔	孔	1336; 39/1. KŌ hole; Confucius ⌐4; P*⌐ [K'UNG³ · I: a child 1–3 sucking at the breast 鼻孔 — bikō — nostril ⌐of Confucius 孔子の論語 — Kōshi no Rongo — the Analects

凶	凶	1337; 17/2. KYŌ evil, bad luck, calamity [HSIUNG¹ • R receptacle & P*] 凶報 — *kyōhō* — bad news 吉凶 — *kikkyō* — good & bad luck, one's fortune
凡	凡	1338; 16/1. BON, HAN general, ordinary [FAN² • D; P*] 凡庸 — *bon'yō* — mediocrity 平凡 — *heibon* — mediocrity, commonness
乙	乙	1339; 5/0. OTSU 2nd (in a series), 'B' [I⁴, YI⁴ • D→B] 甲乙 — *kō-otsu* — A & B 乙女 — *otome* — maiden
騰	騰	1340; 130/16. TŌ [price] rise [T'ENG² • R horse & P*] 暴騰 — *bōtō* — violent/sharp rise 「crease 物価騰貴 — *bukka tōki* — commodity-price in-
顧	顧	1341; 181/12. KO, *kaeri(miru)* look back, review [KU⁴ • R head & P*] 顧問 — *komon* — adviser 顧慮 — *koryo* — concern, care
躍	躍	1342; 157/14. YAKU, *odo(ru)* leap, jump [YÜEH⁴ • R foot & P*] 躍進 — *yakushin* — rush/leap forward 飛躍 — *hiyaku* — leap, jump, activity
籍	籍	1343; 118/14. SEKI (household) register [CHI²,⁴ • R bamboo & P*] 戸籍 — *koseki* — household/census register 書籍目録 — *shoseki mokuroku* — book catalogue
麗	麗	1344; 198/8. REI, *uruwa(shii)* beautiful, lovely [LI⁴ • D & S: a deer 9–19 with beautifully dec- orated antlers 1–8; P*] 秀麗な — *shūrei na* — graceful, beautiful 美辞麗句 — *biji reiku* — flowery words, rhetoric

鯨	鯨	1345; 195/8. GEI, *kujira* whale [CHING¹, CH'ING² • R fish & P*] 鯨油 — *geiyu* — whale oil 鯨狩り — *kujira-gari* — whale hunting, whaling
譜	譜	1346; 149/12. FU* musical notation, genealogy [P'U³ • R words & P*] 楽譜 — *gakufu* — musical score 系譜 — *keifu* — genealogy
繰	繰	1347; 120/13. *ku(ru)* reel, spin, turn over (pages) [SAO² • R thread & P*] 繰り返す — *kuri-kaesu* — repeat, do again 繰り越す — *kuri-kosu* — transfer, carry forward
鎮	鎮 鎮	1348; 167/10. CHIN, *shizu(meru/maru)* quieten, [CHEN⁴ • R metal & P*] ⌊suppress 鎮守 — *chinju* — local Shinto god/shrine 鎮圧 — *chin'atsu* — suppression, subjugation
贈	贈 贈	1349; 154/11. ZŌ, SŌ, *oku(ru)* present, award [TSENG⁴ • R money & P*] 寄贈する — *kizō suru* — present, donate 贈り物 — *okurimono* — gift, present
鮮	鮮	1350; 195/6. SEN freshness, Korea; *azaya(ka na)* [HSIEN¹,³ • R fish & P*] ⌊bright, fine 鮮魚 — *sengyo* — fresh fish 北朝鮮 — *Kita Chōsen* — North Korea
鍛	鍛	1351; 167/9. TAN, *kita(eru)* forge, temper, train [TUAN⁴ • R metal & P*] 鍛工 — *tankō* — metalworker 鍛え上げる — *kitae-ageru* — temper/train well
霜	霜	1352; 173/9. SŌ, *shimo* frost [SHUANG¹ • R rain & P*] 霜焼け — *shimoyake* — chilblains, frostbite 霜解け — *shimodoke* — thawing

購	購	1353; 154/10. KŌ purchase [KOU⁴ · R money & P*] 購買 — *kōbai* — purchasing 購読料 — *kōdoku-ryō* — (newspaper, etc.) sub- scription charge
齢	齢 齡	1354; 211/5. REI age, years [LING² · R tooth & P*] 老齢 — *rōrei* — old age 高齢 — *kōrei* — advanced age
償	償	1355; 9/15. SHŌ, *tsuguna(u/i)* indemnify, atone for [CH'ANG² · R man & P*] 代償 — *daishō* — compensation 弁償 — *benshō* — compensation
擬	擬	1356; 64/14. GI, *gi(suru)* (vt.) model (on), regard [NI³ · R hand & P*] ⌐(as) 模擬試験 — *mogi shiken* — sham/mock examina- 擬音効果 — *gion kōka* — sound effects ⌐tion
諭	諭 諭	1357; 149/9. YU, *sato(su)* warn/caution about, [YÜ⁴ · R words & P*] ⌐reprove for 諭告 — *yukoku* — counsel, warning 説諭 — *setsuyu* — reproof, admonition
衡	衡	1358; 60/13. KŌ measure, weigh [HENG² · I: a balance 1–3 & 14–16 containing fish 4–13 (cf. 603); P*] 度量衡 — *doryōkō* — weights & measures 平衡 — *heikō* — equilibrium, balance
融	融	1359; 193/6. YŪ melt, dissolve [JUNG² · R 3-legged urn 1–10 & P*] 金融 — *kin'yū* — money circulation, finance 融通 — *yūzū* — circulation, transfer, adaptability
薫	薫 薫	1360; 140/13. KUN, *kao(ru/ri)* be fragrant [HSÜN¹ · R grass & P*] 薫風 — *kunpū* — balmy breeze 薫香 — *kunkō* — incense, fragrance

縛	縛 縛	1361; 120/10. BAKU, *shiba(ru)* bind, tie [FU² • R thread & P*] 束縛 — *sokubaku* — restraint, restriction 縛り首 — *shibarikubi* — hanging
膨	膨	1362; 130/12. BŌ, *fuku(ramasu/ramu)*, *fuku(reru)* (vi.) swell, expand [PENG² • R flesh & P] 膨大 — *bōdai* — swelling, expansion 腹部膨満 — *fukubu bōman* — abdominal swelling
巧	巧	1363; 48/2. KŌ, *taku(mi)* skill [CH'IAO³ • I: work 1–3 & bent 4–5 = twisted/ complicated work; also R work & P*] 巧妙 — *kōmyō* — skill, cleverness 精巧な — *seikō na* — elaborate, delicate
獲	獲	1364; 94/13. KAKU, *e(ru)* gain, obtain [HOU⁴ • R dog & P*] 獲得 — *kakutoku* — acquisition 獲物 — *emono* — catch, prize, spoils
激	激	1365; 85/13. GEKI, *geki(suru)* be excited/angry; *hage(shii)* violent [CHI¹ • I: water 1–3 sends white 4–8 spray in all directions 9–12 as it strikes 13–16] 急激な — *kyūgeki na* — sudden, hasty ⌐impressed 感激する — *kangeki suru* — be deeply moved/
獣	獣 獸	1366; 94/12. JŪ, *kemono* beast, brute [SHOU⁴ • I: a forked weapon 1–12 (cf. 390) & dog → hunting; P*] 獣医学校 — *jūi gakkō* — veterinary college 野獣 — *yajū* — wild animal
操	操	1367; 64/13. SŌ, *ayatsu(ru)* manipulate; *misao* [TS'AO¹ • R hand & P*] ⌐chastity, virtue 貞操 — *teisō* — chastity, virtue 体操 — *taisō* — gymnastics, physical training
嬢	嬢 嬢	1368; 38/13. JŌ daughter, young lady; (as suf.) [NIANG² • R woman & P*] ⌐Miss 令嬢 — *reijō* — daughter, young lady 御嬢様 — *ojōsama* — daughter, young lady

壁	壁	1369; 32/13. HEKI, *kabe* wall [PI⁴ • R earth & P*] ⌐paintings 法隆寺壁画 — *Hōryūji hekiga* — the Hōryūji wall 壁紙 — *kabegami* — wallpaper
凝	凝	1370; 15/14. GYŌ, *ko(ru)* be stiff, be absorbed (in); [NING²,⁴ • R ice & P*] ⌊*ko(ri)* stiffness 凝視 — *gyōshi* — stare, gaze 凝り性の — *kori-shō no* — enthusiastic, fastidious
魅	魅	1371; 194/5. MI, *mi(suru)* enchant, fascinate [MEI⁴ • R devil & P*] 魅力 — *miryoku* — fascination, charm 魅惑 — *miwaku* — fascination, lure
駐	駐	1372; 187/5. CHŪ stop, stay [CHU⁴ • R horse & P*] 駐車場 — *chūshajō* — parking area 駐仏 — *chū-Futsu* — posted to/resident in France
閣	閣	1373; 169/6. KAKU tower, palace, (government) [KO², KE² • R gate & P*] ⌊cabinet 閣下 — *Kakka* — Your/His Excellency 内閣 — *naikaku* — cabinet
隠	隠 隠	1374; 170/11. IN, *kaku(su/reru)* hide [YIN³ • R mound & P*] 隠居 — *inkyo* — retirement, old retired person 隠し芸 — *kakushi-gei* — a hidden skill/stunt/trick
閥	閥	1375; 169/5. BATSU* clique, faction [FA² • R gate & P*] 財閥 — *zaibatsu* — zaibatsu, financial combine 郷土閥 — *kyōdobatsu* — local/provincial clan/clique
遭	遭	1376; 162/11. SŌ, *a(u)* (vi.) meet, encounter [TSAO¹ • R proceed & P*] 遭遇 — *sōgū* — an encounter ⌐nal, SOS 遭難信号 — *sōnan shingō* — disaster/distress sig-

1377; 8/12. GŌ strength, power, splendor
[HAO² • R pig & P* 1–7 (cf. 160)]
豪壮な — gōsō na — splendid, magnificent
豪傑 — gōketsu — great man, hero

1378; 53/11. FU, kusa(rasu/ru) rot, decay, depress, discourage
[FU³ • R flesh & P*]
豆腐 — tōfu — bean curd
気を腐らす — ki o kusarasu — be depressed/discouraged

1379; 130/10. MAKU* membrane
[MO⁴ • R flesh & P*]
角膜 — kakumaku — cornea
網膜 — mōmaku — retina

1380; 117/9. TAN right, correct; hashi, ha, hata edge, side
[TUAN¹ • R stand & P*]
端午の節句 — Tango no sekku — Boys' Festival
端折る — hashoru/hashioru — tuck up, abridge

1381; 85/11. TEKI, shizuku a drop, drip; shitata(ru) (vi.) drip, trickle
[TI¹ • R water & P*]
滴下する — tekika suru — drip/trickle down
滴薬 — tekiyaku — drops (of medicine)

1382; 140/11. BO, shita(u) yearn/long for, adore
[MU⁴ • R grass & P*]
恋慕する — renbo suru — love
敬慕 — keibo — respect & love, admiration

1383; 27/12. REKI, koyomi calendar, almanac
[LI⁴ • R sun/day & P*]
旧暦 — kyūreki — old [lunar] calendar
暦改正 — koyomi kaisei — calendar reform

1384; 60/11. CHŌ summon; sign, omen
[CHENG¹ • R footstep & P* (see & cf. 1668)]
徴兵制〔度〕 — chōhei-sei[do] — conscription system
象徴 — shōchō — symbol

嫡	嫡	1385; 38/11. CHAKU heir, legal child [TI² · R woman & P*] 嫡男 — *chakunan* — eldest/legal son, heir 廃嫡する — *haichaku suru* — disinherit
彰	彰	1386; 59/11. SHŌ clear, manifest [CHANG¹ · R light rays & P*] 表彰式 — *hyōshō-shiki* — commendation ceremony 顕彰する — *kenshō suru* — manifest, display
雄	雄	1387; 172/4. YŪ strong, brave; *osu, o-, on-* male [HSIUNG² · R small bird & P*] ⌊(animal) 英雄崇拝 — *eiyū sūhai* — hero worship 雄鳥 — *ondori* — cock, rooster
鈍	鈍	1388; 167/4. DON, *nibu(i)* dull, blunt, slow [TUN⁴ · R metal & P*] 鈍感な — *donkan na* — insensible, dull, stolid 鈍色 — *nibu-iro/nibi-iro* — dark gray
漫	漫	1389; 85/11. MAN wide-ranging, random; invol- [MAN⁴ · R water & P*] ⌊untary 連載漫画 — *rensai manga* — serialized cartoon, comic strip 漫談 — *mandan* — random/comic talk
蛮	蛮 蠻	1390; 8/10. BAN barbarian [MAN² · R insect & P*] 南蛮 — *nanban* — southern barbarians 野蛮な — *yaban na* — savage, barbarous
装	装 裝	1391; 145/6. SŌ, SHŌ, *yosō(u/i)* wear, put on, [CHUANG¹ · R clothes & P*] ⌊assume 服装 — *fukusō* — clothing, dress ⌈appearance 装束 — *shōzoku* — costume, furnishings, personal
紫	紫	1392; 120/6. SHI, *murasaki* purple, violet [TZU³ · R thread & P*] 紫外線 — *shigaisen* — ultraviolet rays 紫式部 — *Murasaki Shikibu* — Lady Murasaki

琴	琴	1393; 96/8. KIN, *koto* Japanese harp [CH'IN[2] • D: upright harp 9–10 with keys 1–8, & P* 11–12] 手風琴 — *te-fūkin* — hand organ, concertina 〔胸底の〕琴線 — *[kyōtei no] kinsen* — heartstrings
絞	絞	1394; 120/6. KŌ, *shibo(ru/ri)* wring, squeeze, scold; *shi(meru)* strangle [CHIAO[3] • R thread & P*] 絞殺 — *kōsatsu* — strangulation, hanging 絞り染め — *shiborizome* — tie-dyeing
滋	滋 滋	1395; 85/9. JI luxuriant, rich [TZU[1] • R water & P*] 滋養 — *jiyō* — nourishment 滋賀県 — *Shiga-ken* — Shiga Prefecture
殖	殖	1396; 78/8. SHOKU, *fu(yasu/eru)* increase [CHIH[2] • R disintegrate & P*] 増殖する — *zōshoku suru* — increase, multiply 繁殖 — *hanshoku* — breeding, propagation
欺	欺	1397; 76/8. GI, *azamu(ku)* cheat, deceive [CH'I[1] • R open mouth & P*] 保険詐欺 — *hoken sagi* — insurance fraud 欺き惑わす — *azamuki-madowasu* — deceive & lead astray
替	替	1398; 72/8. TAI, *ka(eru)* exchange [T'I[4] • R sun & P*] 両替する — *ryōgae suru* — change money 着替える — *ki-kaeru* — change one's clothes
慨	慨 慨	1399; 61/10. GAI deplore, lament [K'AI[3,4] • R heart & P*] 憤慨 — *fungai* — indignation, resentment 慨嘆する — *gaitan suru* — deplore
幣	幣	1400; 50/12. HEI Shinto offerings; money [PI[4] • R cloth & P*] 貨幣 — *kahei* — money, coin 紙幣 — *shihei* — paper money

揚 揚
1401; 64/9. YŌ, a(geru) raise, fry
[YANG² · R hand & P*]   「equipment
揚水装置 — yōsui sōchi — [water-] pumping
揚げ油 — age-abura — frying oil

湿 湿 濕
1402; 85/9. SHITSU, shime(ru) become damp/moist
[SHIH¹ · R water & P*]
湿気 — shikke — humidity   「mate
湿潤〔な〕気候 — shitsujun [na] kikō — humid cli-

媒 媒
1403; 38/9. BAI intermediary
[MEI² · R woman & P*]
媒介 — baikai — mediation, intervention
触媒反応 — shokubai hannō — catalytic reaction

堤 堤
1404; 32/9. TEI, tsutsumi bank, dike
[T'I¹ · R earth & P*]
堤防 — teibō — bank, dike
防波堤 — bōhatei — breakwater

喚 喚
1405; 30/9. KAN call, summon
[HUAN⁴ · R mouth & P*]
喚問 — kanmon — (legal) summons
喚起する — kanki suru — arouse, stir up

傍 傍
1406; 9/10. BŌ, katawa(ra) side
[P'ANG² · R man & P*]   「etc.) free
傍聴無料 — bōchō muryō — admission (to lecture,
傍系 — bōkei — collateral line

針 針
1407; 167/2. SHIN, hari needle
[CHEN¹ · I: metal 1–8 & thread 9 going through
the eye of a needle 10; P*]
方針 — hōshin — magnetic needle; course, policy
針金製造 — harigane seizō — wire manufacture

託 託
1408; 149/3. TAKU entrust
[T'O¹ · R words & P*]   「someone)
託送する — takusō suru — consign, send (by
嘱託 — shokutaku — (temporary) post/person for
special work

202

華	華	1409; 140/7. KA, KE, *hana* flower; brilliant, gay [HUA[1,2] · I: grass 1–3 & luxuriant tree 4–10] 華氏寒暖計 — *kashi kandankei* — Fahrenheit thermometer 豪華な — *gōka na* — splendid, luxurious
被	被	1410; 145/5. HI passive pref.; *kōmu(ru)* suffer, receive [PEI[4] · R clothes & P*] 被抑留者 — *hiyokuryūsha* — detainee, internee 被選挙資格 — *hisenkyo shikaku* — electoral qualifications
迫	迫	1411; 162/5. HAKU, *sema(ru)* press for, urge, draw near [P'O[4] · R proceed & P*] 窮迫 — *kyūhaku* — poverty, financial straits 切迫する — *seppaku suru* — become imminent/tense
訪	訪	1412; 149/4. HŌ, *otozu(reru)*, *tazu(neru)* visit [FANG[3] · R words & P*] 訪問する — *hōmon suru* — visit 訪客 — *hōkyaku* — visitor
狹	狹 狭	1413; 94/6. KYŌ, *sema(i)* narrow, small; *seba(meru/maru)* narrow, contract [HSIA[2] · R dog & P*] 偏狹な — *henkyō na* — narrow-minded 肩身が狹い — *katami ga semai* — feel small/ashamed
値	値	1414; 9/8. CHI, *ne* price; *atai* value, price [CHIH[2] · R man & P*] 価値 — *kachi* — worth, value 値段 — *nedan* — price
紡	紡	1415; 120/4. BŌ, *tsumu(gu)* spin (thread) [FANG[3] · R thread & P*] 紡績工場 — *bōseki kōjō* — spinning mill 紡織機 — *bōshoku-ki* — spinning & weaving machinery
歐	欧 歐	1416; 76/4. Ō Europe [OU[1] · R open mouth & P*] 欧州 — *Ōshū* — Europe 欧米 — *Ō-Bei* — Europe & America

廷	廷	1417; 54/4. TEI court, government office [T'ING[1,2] · I; P*] 宮廷 — kyūtei — the Court 法廷 — hōtei — law court
歳	歳 歳	1418; 77/9. SAI year, years old, SEI year [SUI[4] · R stop & P*] 万歳 — banzai — Banzai!, Long life! 歳暮 — seibo — year-end (present)
弓	弓	1419; 57/0. KYŪ, yumi bow, archery [KUNG[1] · D; P*] 弓術の試合 — kyūjutsu no shiai — archery contest 弓矢 — yumiya — bow & arrow, arms
猛	猛	1420; 94/8. MŌ strong, fierce [MENG[3] · R dog & P*] 猛烈な — mōretsu na — violent, fierce ⌈hunting 猛獣狩り — mōjū-gari — wild-animal/big-game
翌	翌	1421; 124/5. YOKU the next/following (day, etc.) [I[4], YI[4] · R stand & P*] 翌年 — yokunen — the next/following year 翌翌日 — yokuyokujitsu — the next day but one
脚	脚	1422; 130/7. KYAKU, KYA, ashi leg [CHIAO[3], CHÜEH[2,4] · R flesh & P*] 失脚する — shikkyaku suru — lose one's position, be ruined ⌈version 脚色 — kyakushoku — dramatization, stage/screen
鋳	鋳 鑄	1423; 167/7. CHŪ, i(ru) cast (metal) [CHU[4] · R metal & P*] 鋳造 — chūzō — casting 鋳型 — igata — mold, matrix, die
捨	捨 捨	1424; 64/8. SHA, su(teru) throw away, abandon [SHE[3] · R hand & P*] 捨て値 — sutene — giveaway/sacrifice price 捨台詞 — sutezerifu — exit line, parting remark/threat

夢	夢	1425; 140/10. MU, *yume* dream [MENG⁴ • R evening & P*] 夢中になる — *muchū ni naru* — become ecstatic/ possessed 「reading 夢判断 — *yume handan* — dream interpretation/
賊	賊	1426; 154/6. ZOKU bandit, thief [TSE²,⁴, TSEI² • I: taking money 1-7 by sword 9-10 (vrt. of 34) and lance 8 & 11-13] 賊徒 — *zokuto* — bandit, rebel 盗賊 — *tōzoku* — thief, burglar
俳	俳	1427; 9/8. HAI actor, humor 「others; P*] [P'AI² • I: a man 1-2 who is not 3-10 like 俳優 — *haiyū* — actor, actress 俳句 — *haiku* — haiku (17-syllable verse)
桃	桃	1428; 75/6. TŌ, *momo* peach [T'AO² • I: also P tree & P*] 「gri-La 桃源境/郷 — *tōgenkyō* — a heaven on earth, Shan- 桃園 — *momozono* — peach orchard
敏	敏 敏	1429; 66/6. BIN quick, alert [MIN³ • R strike & P*] 敏速な — *binsoku na* — prompt, brisk 敏腕家 — *binwanka* — able person
扇	扇	1430; 63/6. SEN, *ōgi* folding fan [SHAN⁴ • I: door 1-4 that opens & closes like wings 5-10 → fan: P*] 扇風機 — *senpūki* — electric fan 扇の骨 — *ōgi no hone* — ribs of a fan
恥	恥 耻	1431; 128/4. CHI, *ha(jiru)* be ashamed of; *haji* [CH'IH³ • R heart & P*] 「shame 恥じ入る — *haji-iru* — be ashamed 恥知らず — *haji-shirazu* — shameless person
捜	捜 搜	1432; 64/7. SŌ, *saga(su)* search for [SOU¹ • I: take a torch 4-8 in the hands 1-3 & 9-10 & search] 捜査する — *sōsa suru* — investigate, search 捜し回る — *sagashi-mawaru* — search about for

	伴	1433; 9/5. BAN, HAN, *tomona(u)* (vt.) be accompanied by, take along, (vi.) attend [PAN⁴ · R man & P*] 同伴する — *dōhan suru* — be in company (with) 伴食大臣 — *banshoku daijin* — figurehead/puppet minister
	剛	1434; 2/9. GŌ strong, hard [KANG¹ · R knife & P*] 剛健な — *gōken na* — strong, manly 金剛石 — *kongōseki* — diamond
	凍	1435; 15/8. TŌ, *kō(rasu/ru)* freeze; *kogo(eru)* be chilled/numbed [TUNG⁴ · R ice & P*] 凍結資産 — *tōketsu shisan* — frozen assets 凍え死にする — *kogoe-jini suru* — freeze to death
	劍 劍 劔	1436; 18/8. KEN, *tsurugi* sword [CHIEN⁴ · R knife & P*] 剣劇 — *kengeki* — a sword play/drama 短剣 — *tanken* — short sword, dagger
	揺 搖	1437; 64/9. YŌ, *yu(suru/reru/re)*, *yu(suburu/suburer)*, *yu(saburu/saburer)* shake, rock, swing [YAO² · R hand & P*] 動揺する — *dōyō suru* — tremble, shake, waver 揺すり起す — *yusuri-okosu* — shake (someone) awake
	奔	1438; 37/5. HON run 「4–8」 [PEN¹,⁴ · I: a man 1–3 running with flying feet 奔走する — *honsō suru* — be busy/active 出奔する — *shuppon suru* — abscond
	拒	1439; 64/4. KYO, *koba(mu)* refuse, decline [CHÜ⁴ · R hand & P*] 拒否 — *kyohi* — denial, rejection 拒絶する — *kyozetsu suru* — refuse, reject
	拍	1440; 64/5. HAKU, HYŌ clap, beat time [P'O⁴, P'AI¹ · R hand & P*] 拍手 — *hakushu* — clapping, applause 拍子 — *hyōshi* — rhythm, beat; moment

昇	昇	1441; 72/4. SHŌ, *nobo(ru)* rise [SHENG¹ • R sun & P*] 昇 進 — *shōshin* — promotion, advancement 昇 騰 する — *shōtō suru* — rise, soar
枢	枢 樞	1442; 75/4. SŪ pivot, center [SHU¹ • R tree & P*] 枢 軸 — *sūjiku* — pivot, axle 枢 密 — *sūmitsu* — affairs/helm of state
抽	抽	1443; 64/5. CHŪ extract, pull out [CH'OU¹ • R hand & P*] 抽 出 する — *chūshutsu suru* — extract, abstract 抽 象 名 詞 — *chūshō meishi* — abstract noun
刻	刻	1444; 18/6. KOKU, *kiza(mu)* carve, cut [K'O¹, K'E¹ • R knife & P*] 彫 刻 — *chōkoku* — sculpture, engraving 時 刻 表 — *jikokuhyō* — time table
叔	叔	1445; 29/6. SHUKU uncle [SHU² • R right hand & P*] 叔 父 — *oji/shukufu* — uncle 叔 母 — *oba/shukubo* — aunt
侍	侍	1446; 9/6. JI, *samurai* samurai; *ji(suru)* attend (on), be in the service (of) [SHIH⁴ • R man & P*] 侍 従 — *jijū* — chamberlain 侍 気 質 — *samurai katagi* — samurai spirit
遷	遷	1447; 162/12. SEN, change, transfer [CH'IEN¹ • R proceed & P] 遷 都 — *sento* — moving the capital 変 遷 する — *hensen suru* — change
拘	拘	1448; 64/5. KŌ seize; be concerned in, cling to [CHÜ¹ • R hand & P*] 拘 束 — *kōsoku* — restriction, duress 拘 置 — *kōchi* — detention, confinement

鋭	鋭 鋭 鋭	1449; 167/7. EI, *surudo(i)* pointed, sharp, acute [JUI⁴ • R metal & P*] 鋭敏な — *eibin na* — sharp, sensitive, acute 鋭利な — *eiri na* — sharp, trenchant
佳	佳	1450; 9/6. KA good, beautiful [CHIA¹ • R man & P*] 佳境 — *kakyō* — climax (of story) 風光絶佳 — *fūkō zekka* — scenic excellence
輩	輩	1451; 175/7. HAI colleagues, companions [PEI⁴ • R cart & P*] 先輩 — *senpai* — senior/older person 後輩 — *kōhai* — junior/younger person
諾	諾	1452; 149/8. DAKU consent [NO⁴ • R words & P*] 諾否 — *dakuhi* — consent or refusal, yes or no 承諾する — *shōdaku suru* — consent to, accept
賜	賜	1453; 154/8. SHI, *tama(waru)* bestow, grant [TZ'U⁴ • R money & P*] 下賜する — *kashi suru* — bestow, grant, give 恩賜 — *onshi* — Imperial gift
緩	緩	1454; 120/9. KAN, *yuru(i), yuru(yaka na)* loose, slack, slow; *yuru(meru/mu)* loosen, slacken [HUAN³ • R thread & P*] 緩和する — *kanwa suru* — relieve, mitigate, ease 緩慢な — *kanman na* — slow, slack
澄	澄	1455; 85/12. CHŌ, *su(mu)* become clear/serene [CH'ENG², TENG⁴ • R water & P*] 清澄な — *seichō na* — limpid, clear 澄み渡る — *sumi-wataru* — be perfectly clear
撤	撤	1456; 64/12. TETSU, *tes(suru)* withdraw, remove [CH'E⁴ • R hand & P* pierce (cf. 1638)] 撤退する — *tettai suru* — withdraw from, evacuate 撤廃する — *teppai suru* — abolish

弊	弊	1457; 55/12. HEI humble pref.; evil, abuse [PI⁴ · R folded hands & P*] 弊村 — *heison* — my poor village 弊害 — *heigai* — evil, abuse
潜	潜	1458; 85/12. SEN, *mogu(ru)* dive/creep (into); *hiso-(meru/mu)* conceal [CH'IEN² · R water & P*] 潜水艦 — *sensuikan* — submarine 潜伏する — *senpuku suru* — be concealed, lie hidden
寮	寮	1459; 40/12. RYŌ* hostel, dormitory [LIAO² · R roof & P*] 寮生 — *ryōsei* — boarding student 寮長 — *ryōchō* — head of hostel/dormitory
監	監 監	1460; 108/9. KAN watch over, supervise [CHIEN¹,⁴ · I: a man 8–10 looking 1–7 (vrt. of 22 'eye') at reflection in water dish 11–15; P*] 監禁する — *kankin suru* — imprison 総監 — *sōkan* — inspector general, commissioner
墳	墳	1461; 32/12. FUN tumulus [FEN² · R earth & P*] 古墳 — *kofun* — tumulus, old burial mound 墳墓 — *funbo* — tomb
辱	辱	1462; 161/3. JOKU, *hazuka(shimeru)* shame, dis- [JU³,⁴ · I; P*] ⌐grace 恥辱 — *chijoku* — disgrace, dishonor 侮辱 — *bujoku* — insult, contempt
冒	冒	1463; 72/5. BŌ, *oka(su)* risk, brave, damage, [MAO⁴ · I; P*] ⌐desecrate 冒険小説 — *bōken shōsetsu* — adventure story/ novel ⌐cold 悪性の感冒 — *akusei no kanbō* — a bad/severe
撲	撲	1464; 64/12. BOKU strike, beat [P'U¹ · R hand & P*] 打撲傷 — *dabokushō* — bruise 相撲取り — *sumōtori* — sumō wrestler

軌	軌軌	1465; 159/2. KI vehicle/wheel track [KUEI[3] • R cart & P*] 広軌鉄道 — *kōki tetsudō* — broad-gauge railway 軌範 — *kihan* — model, standard, pattern
胆	胆膽	1466; 130/5. TAN liver, courage [TAN[3] • R flesh & P*] 胆力 — *tanryoku* — courage 落胆する — *rakutan suru* — be discouraged/dis- ⌐appointed
砕	砕砕	1467; 12/4. SAI, *kuda(ku/keru)* smash, crush [SUI[4] • I: smash rock 1–5 into nine 6–7 or ten 8–9 pieces; P*] 粉砕する — *funsai suru* — pulverize 破砕する — *hasai suru* — smash, crush
殴	殴毆	1468; 79/4. Ō beat, strike [OU[1,3] • R kill & P*] 殴打 — *ōda* — blow, assault 殴殺する — *ōsatsu suru* — beat to death
疫	疫	1469; 104/4. EKI, YAKU epidemic [I[4], YI[4] • R illness & P*] 疫病 — *ekibyō/yakubyō* — epidemic, plague 防疫 — *bōeki* — prevention of epidemics
某	某	1470; 99/4. BŌ a certain, some [MOU[3], MU[3] • I; P*] 某氏 — *bōshi* — a certain person, Mr. X 某所 — *bōsho* — a certain place
柳	柳	1471; 75/5. RYŪ, *yanagi* willow tree [LIU[3] • R tree & P*] 川柳 — *senryū* — senryū [humorous 17-syllable ⌐poem] 柳行李 — *yanagi-gōri* — wicker trunk
俊	俊	1472; 9/7. SHUN excel, surpass [CHÜN[4], TSÜN[4] • R man & P*] 俊才 — *shunsai* — genius, talented person 俊傑 — *shunketsu* — great/outstanding person

峠	峠	**1473**; 46/6. *tōge* mountain pass/ridge [- · S: mountain 1–3 & above & below] 乙女峠 — *Otome-tōge* — pn. 「peak 峠を越す — *tōge o kosu* — go over a pass/ridge/
括	括	**1474**; 64/6. KATSU fasten together, bind [K'UO⁴ · R hand & P*] 「gether 一括する — *ikkatsu suru* — bundle up, lump to- 包括保険 — *hōkatsu hoken*—inclusive/comprehen- sive insurance
咲	咲 唉	**1475**; 30/6. *sa(ku)* bloom, blossom [HSIAO⁴ · R mouth & P 4–9 (vrt. of 1147)] 咲き乱れる — *saki-midareru*— bloom in profusion 狂い咲きする — *kurui-zaki suru* — bloom out of season
叙	叙 敍 敘	**1476**; 29/7. JO, *jo(suru)* describe, confer (a rank) [HSÜ⁴ · R right hand & P*] 「poem 叙事詩 — *jojishi* — descriptive/narrative poetry/ 叙情詩 — *jojōshi* — lyric poetry/poem
胎	胎	**1477**; 30/5. TAI womb, fetus [T'AI¹ · R flesh & P*] 胎児 — *taiji* — fetus 母胎 — *botai* — [mother's] womb
勅	勅 敕	**1478**; 19/7. CHOKU Imperial edict [CH'IH⁴ · R strength & P*] 勅命 — *chokumei* — Imperial order/command 詔勅 — *shōchoku* — Imperial rescript/proclamation
侯	侯	**1479**; 9/7. KŌ feudal lord; marquis [HOU² · R man & P*] 諸侯 — *shokō* — feudal lords 「splendor 王侯の栄華 — *ōkō no eiga* — princely/royal
麻	麻	**1480**; 200/0. MA, *asa* hemp, flax [MA² · R lean-to & P*] 「ics Control Law 麻薬取締法 — *Mayaku Tori-shimari-hō* — Narcot- 麻綱 — *asazuna* — hemp rope

陶	陶	1481; 170/8. TŌ pottery, porcelain [T'AO² • R mound & P*] 陶〔磁〕器 — tō[ji]ki — porcelain, pottery 薫陶する — kuntō suru — train, instruct
軟	軟	1482; 159/4. NAN, yawa(rakai), yawa(raka na) [JUAN³ • R cart & P*] ⌊soft 軟骨 — nankotsu — cartilage, gristle 柔軟な — jūnan na — soft, pliable
訟	訟	1483; 149/4. SHŌ accuse, sue [SUNG⁴ • R words & P*] 訴訟費用 — soshō hiyō — lawsuit/litigation costs 離婚訴訟 — rikon soshō — divorce suit/action
虚	虚 虚	1484; 141/5. KYO, KO empty ⌈7-11; P*] [HSÜ¹ • I a tiger 1-6 waiting in an empty grove 虚栄〔心〕 — kyoei[shin] — (a sense of) vanity 虚弱な — kyojaku na — weak, feeble, frail
舶	舶	1485; 137/5. HAKU ship [PO¹'⁴ • R boat & P*] 舶来品 — hakuraihin — imported goods 船舶 — senpaku — vessel, shipping
窒	窒	1486; 116/6. CHITSU block, obstruct; nitrogen [CHIH⁴ • R hole & P*] 窒息する — chissoku suru — be suffocated/stifled 窒素肥料 — chisso hiryō — nitrogen fertilizer
淑	淑	1487; 85/8. SHUKU graceful; pure [SHU²'⁴ • R water & P*] 貞淑 — teishuku — chastity, womanly virtue 私淑する — shishuku suru — look up (to), model oneself (on)
斜	斜	1488; 68/7. SHA, nana(me) slanting [HSIEH², HSIA² • R scoop & P*] 斜陽 — shayō — the setting sun 傾斜 — keisha — slope, slant, inclination

描	描	1489; 64/8.　BYŌ, *ega(ku)* picture, describe [MIAO² • R hand & P*] 描写 — *byōsha* — description, portrayal 素描 — *sobyō* — rough sketch/drawing
崩	崩	1490; 46/8.　HŌ, *kuzu(su/reru)* destroy, demolish [PENG¹ • R mountain & P*] 崩御 — *hōgyo* — death (of emperor, etc.) 崩落 — *hōraku* — cave-in, slump
巣	巣 巢	1491; 3/10.　SŌ, *su* nest, den, cobweb [CH'AO² • D: feather-filled 1–3 nest 4–7 at the top of a tree; P*]　　　　　┌come independent 巣立ちする — *sudachi suru* — leave the nest, be- 巣箱 — *subako* — nest box, hive
培	培	1492; 32/8.　BAI, *tsuchika(u)* cultivate [P'EI² • R earth & P*] 培地 — *baichi* — (bacteria) culture medium 培養 — *baiyō* — cultivation, nurture
唯	唯	1493; 30/8.　YUI solitary, only [WEI² • I: the crying 1–3 of a small bird 4–11; 唯理論 — *yuiriron* — rationalism　　　　└P*] 唯物論 — *yuibutsuron* — materialism
墨	墨 墨	1494; 203/3.　BOKU, *sumi* ink block, India ink [MO⁴ • I: black 1–11 → soot, & earth 12–14; also R earth & P*] 白墨の線 — *hakuboku no sen* — chalk line 墨絵 — *sumie* — India-ink painting
励	励 勵	1495; 4/6.　REI, *hage(mu)* work hard (at); *hage- (masu)* encourage [LI⁴ • R strength & P*] 励行する — *reikō suru* — enforce strictly 鼓舞激励 — *kobu gekirei* — encouragement
愚	愚	1496; 61/9.　GU, *oro(ka na)* foolish [YÜ² • R heart & P*] 愚劣 — *guretsu* — foolishness, stupidity 愚連隊 — *gurentai* — (gang of) hooligans

劑	剤 劑	1497; 210/2. ZAI medicine, drug [CHI⁴ · R knife & P*] 鎮静剤 — *chinseizai* — sedative 殺虫剤 — *satchūzai* — insecticide
惠	恵 惠	1498; 61/6. KEI, E, *megu(mu/mi)* favor, show kindness, aid; *megu(mareru)* be blessed [HUI⁴ · R heart & P*] 慈恵 — *jikei* — charity, benevolence 恵方 — *ehō* — lucky direction
紛	紛	1499; 120/4. FUN, *magi(reru)* be distracted/con- [FEN¹ · R thread & P*] ⌐fused 紛争 — *funsō* — dispute, quarrel 紛議 — *fungi* — dissension, controversy
胴	胴	1500; 130/6. DŌ* trunk (of the body) [TUNG⁴ · R flesh & P*] 胴体 — *dōtai* — torso, body, hull 胴忘れ — *dōwasure* — momentary forgetfulness
衰	衰 衰	1501; 8/8. SUI, *otoro(eru)* become weak, decline [SHUAI¹ · I: a robe 1–2 & 7–10 (see 605) with a hole 3–4 & 6, & a tear 5; P*] 神経衰弱 — *shinkei suijaku* — nervous breakdown/ 衰滅 — *suimetsu* — decline & fall ⌐exhaustion
跡	跡	1502; 157/6. SEKI, *ato* trace, remains, ruins [CHI⁴ · R foot & P*] 遺跡 — *iseki* — remains, ruins, relics 跡継ぎ — *atotsugi* — successor, heir
濃	濃	1503; 85/13. NŌ, *ko(i)* dark, heavy, thick, strong [NUNG² · R water & P*] 濃淡 — *nōtan* — light & shade, shading 濃厚な — *nōkō na* — thick, dense, heavy
該	該	1504; 149/6. GAI (pref.) the relevant —, the — in [KAI¹ · R words & P*] ⌐question 該当者 — *gaitōsha* — the relevant person 該博な知識 — *gaihaku na chishiki* — profound/extensive learning

	稿	1505; 115/10. KŌ draft, manuscript [KAO³ • R grain & P*] 原稿 — genkō — manuscript 投稿する — tōkō suru — contribute (manuscript)
	措	1506; 64/8. SO place, dispose of [TS'O⁴ • R hand & P*] 措置 — sochi — measure, step, move 措辞の妙 — soji no myō — felicity of expression/ phrasing
	詰	1507; 149/6. KITSU interrogate; tsu(meru) close up, [CHIEN⁴ • R words & P*] ⌊stuff, fill 詰問 — kitsumon — cross-examination 詰め替える — tsume-kaeru — refill, repack
	熟	1508; 86/11. JUKU, juku(suru), u(reru) mature [SHOU² • R fire & P*] 熟練 — jukuren — skill, mastery 未熟 — mijuku — unripe, immature
	鋼	1509; 167/8. KŌ, hagane steel [KANG¹ • R metal & P*] 鋼鉄 — kōtetsu — steel 製鋼 — seikō — steel manufacture
	懲 懲	1510; 62/14. CHŌ, ko(rasu) punish, chasten [CH'ENG²,³ • R heart & P*] 懲罰 — chōbatsu — discipline, punishment 勧善懲悪 — kanzen chōaku — encouragement of good & the chastisement of evil
	堕 堕	1511; 32/8. DA fall, drop [TO⁴ • R earth & P*] 堕落 — daraku — degradation, (moral) corruption 堕胎 — datai — abortion, miscarriage
	滑	1512; 85/10. KATSU, sube(rasu/ru) let slip, slide; name(raka na) smooth [HUA²,⁴ • R water & P*] 滑走する — kassō suru — slide, glide 潤滑 — junkatsu — lubrication

215

稚 | 1513; 115/8. CHI infant, childish
[CHIH⁴ · R grain & P*]
稚気 — *chiki* — childishness
稚心 — *chishin* — childish mind

廉 | 1514; 53/10. REN pure, honest; cheap
[LIEN² · R lean-to & P*]
廉売値段 — *renbai nedan* — bargain price
清廉 — *seiren* — integrity

債 | 1515; 9/11. SAI debt
[CHAI⁴ · R man & P*]
債権者 — *saikensha* — creditor
負債 — *fusai* — debt

肝 | 1516; 130/3. KAN vital; *kimo* liver, courage
[KAN¹ · R flesh & P*]
肝臓 — *kanzō* — liver
肝要な — *kan'yō na* — important, vital

溶 | 1517; 85/10. YŌ, *to(kasu/keru)* melt
[JUNG² · R water & P*]
溶解する — *yōkai suru* — melt, dissolve
溶液 — *yōeki* — solvent, solution

憂 | 1518; 1/14. YŪ, *ure(eru/i)* grieve, worry; *u(i)* unhappy
[YU¹ · I: grief 9–12 under a roof 7–8 (=indoors), in the middle of summer 1–6 & 13–15 (see 163); P*]
憂慮する — *yūryo suru* — fear, dread
憂い顔 — *urei-gao* — anxious expression

奨 | 1519; 37/10. SHŌ encourage, promote
[CHIANG³ · R big & P*]
奨学金 — *shōgakukin* — scholarship
奨励する — *shōrei suru* — encourage, promote

邪 | 1520; 92/2. JA evil, wrong
[HSIEH² · R city & P*]
邪宗 — *jashū* — heretical religion, heresy
風邪 — *kaze* — a cold

睡	睡	1521; 109/8.　SUI sleep [SHUI⁴ • I: the eye (lids) 1–5 drop 6–13 (see 1214); also R eye & P*] 睡眠不足 — *suimin fusoku* — sleep deficiency 熟睡 — *jukusui* — sound sleep
忌	忌 忌	1522; 49/4.　KI, *i(mu)* avoid, abhor [CHI⁴ • R heart & P*] 七回忌 — *shichikai-ki* — 7th anniversary of death 忌み言葉 — *imi-kotoba* — taboo word
批	批	1523; 64/4.　HI criticism [P'I¹ • R hand & P*] 批判 — *hihan* — criticism, comment 批評 — *hihyō* — criticism, critique
坑	坑	1524; 32/4.　KŌ cave, pit [K'ENG¹ • R earth & P*] 坑〔内〕夫 — *kō[nai] fu* — miner 炭坑浸水 — *tankō shinsui* — [coal] mine flood
抜	抜	1525; 64/4.　BATSU, *nu(ku)* extract, outstrip [PA² • I: extricated by the hand 1–3 of a friend 4–7; P*] 抜群の — *batsugun no* — preeminent, outstanding 堅忍不抜の — *kennin fubatsu no* — indomitable
呈	呈	1526; 30/4.　TEI, *tei(suru)* present [CH'ENG² • R mouth & P*] 進呈する — *shintei suru* — present 贈呈する — *zōtei suru* — present, donate
卵	卵	1527; 4/6.　RAN, *tamago* egg [LUAN³ • D: frog spawn; P*] 産卵する — *sanran suru* — spawn, lay eggs 女優の卵 — *joyū no tamago* — prospective actress
伸	伸	1528; 9/5.　SHIN, *no(basu/biru)* stretch, extend [SHEN¹ • R man & P*]　　　　　　⌐elastic 伸縮する — *shinshuku suru* — expand, be flexible/ 伸伸する — *nobinobi suru* — feel at ease/relaxed

催	催	**1529**; 9/11. SAI, *moyō(su)* organize, prepare; *moyō(shi)* meeting, entertainment [TS'UI[1] • R man & P]　　　　　　　　「sorship 政府の主催 — *seifu no shusai* — government spon- 催促する — *saisoku suru* — urge, press for
尽	尽 盡	**1530**; 44/3. JIN, *tsu(kusu/kiru)* exhaust [CHIN[4] • I; P*] 無尽蔵の — *mujinzō no* — inexhaustible, unlimited 論じ尽す — *ronji-tsukusu* — discuss exhaustively
汚	汚	**1531**; 85/3. O, *kitana(i)*, *yogo(su/reru)* dirty; *kega-(su/reru)* soil, disgrace　　　　　　　　「water] [WU[1] • I: water & hollow 4–6 = dirty puddle 汚職 — *oshoku* — bribery, corruption 汚染 — *osen* — stain
匠	匠	**1532**; 22/4. SHŌ craftsman [CHIANG[4] • I: basket 1 & 6 for tools, & ax 2–5; 師匠 — *shishō* — teacher, master　　　　　　「P*] 意匠 — *ishō* — design, idea
妃	妃	**1533**; 38/3. HI (married) princess [FEI[1] • R woman & P*]　　　　　　　　　「ness 妃殿下 — *hidenka* — Imperial Highness, Her High- 皇太子妃 — *kōtaishihi* — Crown Princess
仰	仰	**1534**; 9/4. GYŌ, KŌ, *ao(gu)* look up (at/to); *ō(se)* another's instructions [YANG[3] • R man & P*] 仰天する — *gyōten suru* — be amazed 信仰する — *shinkō suru* — believe in, have faith in
伐	伐	**1535**; 9/4. BATSU attack, cut down [FA[1] • R man & P* lance 3–6] 採伐 — *saibatsu* — felling (trees) 討伐する — *tōbatsu suru* — subjugate, suppress
札	札	**1536**; 75/1. SATSU* paper money; *fuda* label, tag [CHA[2] • R tree & P*] 札束 — *satsutaba* — bundle of paper money 改札口 — *kaisatsuguchi* — ticket barrier, wicket

巨	巨	1537; 22/2. KYO giant [CHÜ⁴ • D; P*] 巨匠 — *kyoshō* — master 巨額 — *kyogaku* — enormous sum
囚	囚	1538; 31/2. SHŪ prisoner [CH'IU² • I: man in an enclosure; P*] 囚人 — *shūjin* — prisoner 死刑囚 — *shikeishū* — condemned criminal
如	如	1539; 38/3. JO, NYO be like/equal [JU² • R mouth & P*] 如何 — *ikaga* — how 「abruptly 突如〔として〕— *totsujo* [*to shite*] — suddenly,
刈	刈	1540; 18/2. *ka(ru)* mow, reap, cut (hair) [I⁴, YI⁴ • R knife & P] 稲刈り — *inekari* — rice reaping 刈り込む — *karikomu* — trim, prune, cut
双	双 雙	1541; 29/2. SŌ, *futa* two, both, a pair [SHUANG¹ • S; P*] 双眼鏡 — *sōgankyō* — binoculars 双生児 — *sōseiji* — twins
干	干	1542; 51/0. KAN, *ho(su)*, *hi(ru)* dry, drain away [KAN¹ • D; P*] 干渉する — *kanshō suru* — interfere (in) 干潮 — *kanchō* — ebb tide
妊娠	娠	1543; 38/7. SHIN conception, pregnancy [SHEN¹ • R woman & P*] 妊娠中絶 — *ninshin chūzetsu* — pregnancy termi- nation 「control 妊娠調節 — *ninshin chōsetsu* — pregnancy/birth
脅	脅	1544; 19/8. KYŌ, *obiya(kasu)*, *odo(kasu)*, *odo(su)* menace, threaten 「1–6; also R flesh & P*] [HSIEH² • I: physical 7–10 strength in abundance 脅迫する — *kyōhaku suru* — blackmail, threaten 脅威 — *kyōi* — threat, menace

謙	謙	1545; 149/10. KEN humility, modesty [CH'IEN¹ · R words & P*] 謙虚な — kenkyo na — modest, humble 謙譲 — kenjō — modesty
魔	魔	1546; 201/10. MA* devil, evil spirit [MO² · R devil & P*] 悪魔 — akuma — devil 邪魔する — jama suru — interfere with, hinder
醸	醸 醸	1547; 164/13. JŌ, kamo(su) brew [NIANG²,⁴ · R wine jug & P*] 醸造 — jōzō — brewing 醸成する — jōsei suru — brew, ferment
鶏	鶏 鶏	1548; 196/8. KEI, niwatori chicken [CHI¹ · R bird & P*] 鶏卵 — keiran — hen's egg 鶏肉 — keiniku — chicken meat
藩	藩	1549; 140/15. HAN* [feudal] clan/fief [FAN² · R grass (= boundary hedge) & P*] 幕藩 — bakuhan — Bakufu [Shōgunate] & the clans 藩閥 — hanbatsu — clanship
繕	繕	1550; 120/12. ZEN, tsukuro(u) mend, patch up [SHAN⁴ · I: use thread 1–6 to make good 7–18; also R thread & P*] 修繕する — shūzen suru — repair 繕い物 — tsukuroi-mono — things to be mended
翻	翻 翻	1551; 124/12. HON, hirugae(su/ru) wave, flutter [FAN¹ · R wings & P*] 翻訳する — hon'yaku suru — translate 翻案 — hon'an — adaptation
糧	糧	1552; 119/12. RYŌ, RŌ, kate provisions, food [LIANG² · R rice & P* quantity (see 743)] 食糧 — shokuryō — food 糧道を断つ — ryōdō o tatsu — cut the supply lines

轄	轄	1553; 160/10. KATSU control, manage [HSIA² · R cart ; & P*] 所轄警察署 — *shokatsu keisatsusho* — the super- 　　　　　　vising/controlling police station 管轄 — *kankatsu* — jurisdiction
謄	謄	1554; 130/13. TŌ copy, transfer [T'ENG² · R words & P* relay] 戸籍謄本 — *koseki tōhon* — copy of one's family 謄写版 — *tōshaban* — mimeograph 　└register
翼	翼	1555; 124/11. YOKU, *tsubasa* wing [I⁴, YI⁴ · R wings & P*] 左翼 — *sayoku* — left wing 鳥の翼 — *tori no tsubasa* — wings of a bird
瞬	瞬	1556; 110/12. SHUN, *matata(ku)* wink, flicker; [SHUN⁴ · R eye & P*]　　　　　　└instant 瞬間 — *shunkan* — moment, instant 瞬刻 — *shunkoku* — moment, instant
還	還	1557; 162/13. KAN return [HUAN² · R proceed & P* circuit] 　┌year 還暦 — *kanreki* — one's 60th birthday, one's 61st 領土返還 — *ryōdo henkan* — return of territory
諮	諮	1558; 149/9. SHI, *haka(ru)* consult [TZU¹ · R words & P*] 諮問機関 — *shimon kikan* — consultative organi- 諮議 — *shigi* — discussion 　　　　　└zation
縦	縦 縱	1559; 120/10. JŪ, *tate* vertical [direction/length/ [TSUNG⁴ · R thread & P*]　　　　　└height] 縦横 — *tateyoko/jūō* — lengthwise and crosswise 縦覧 — *jūran* — inspection
薪	薪	1560; 140/13. SHIN, *takigi* firewood [HSIN¹ · R grass & P*] 薪材 — *shinzai* — branches for firewood 薪炭 — *shintan* — wood and charcoal

篤	篤	1561; 118/10. TOKU, sincere, cordial [TU³,⁴ • R horse & P*] 危篤 — *kitoku* — seriously ill 篤志家 — *tokushika* — volunteer
祥	祥 祥	1562; 113/6. SHŌ good fortune, omen [HSIANG² • R god & P*] 発祥地 — *hasshōchi* — cradle, birthplace 吉祥 — *kisshō* — good omen
症	症	1563; 104/5. SHŌ symptoms, illness [CHENG⁴ • R illness & P*] 症状 — *shōjō* — condition of illness 病症 — *byōshō* — nature of a disease
援	援	1564; 64/9. EN help [YÜAN² • R hand & P*] 応援 — *ōen* — aid, help, assistance 援護 — *engo* — support, backing
揮	揮	1565; 64/9. KI shake, scatter, command [HUI¹ • R hand & P*] 指揮する — *shiki suru* — command, direct 揮発 — *kihatsu* — volatilization
握	握	1566; 64/9. AKU, *nigi(ru)* hold, grasp, seize [WO⁴ • R hand & P*] 掌握する — *shōaku suru* — hold, grasp, seize 握り飯 — *nigiri-meshi* — rice ball
廊	廊	1567; 53/8. RŌ corridor, gallery [LANG² • R lean-to & P*] 画廊 — *garō* — picture gallery 回廊 — *kairō* — corridor
環	環	1568; 86/13. KAN ring, surround [HUAN² • R jewel & P* circuit] 環境 — *kankyō* — environment 環状線 — *kanjōsen* — loop/circle line

尋	尋	1569; 58/9. JIN, *tazu(neru)* look for, visit, ask [HSÜN² • I: right hand 1–3 & 7–9 (vrt. of 88) & left hand 4–6 & 10–12 (vrt. of 87)] 尋常の — *jinjō no* — ordinary, common 尋ね求める — *tazune-motomeru* — seek for
塔	塔	1570; 32/9. TŌ* tower [T'A³ • R earth & P*] 五重塔 — *gojū-no-tō* — five-storied pagoda 塔婆 — *tōba* — wooden grave tablet
塁	塁	1571; 102/7. RUI fort, (baseball) base [LEI³ • I: piled-up 1–9 earth; also R earth & P] 塁審 — *ruishin* — umpire on bases (baseball) 敵塁 — *tekirui* — enemy fortress
喪	喪	1572; 2/11. SŌ lose; *mo* mourning [SANG¹ • I: many mouths 3–8 covered by robes 1–2 & 9–12 (vrt. of 605) in grief (cf. 1249)] 喪失 — *sōshitsu* — loss 喪服 — *mofuku* — mourning dress
逐	逐	1573; 162/7. CHIKU chase [CHU²,⁴ • to proceed/follow after 8–10 = hunt a pig/boar 1–7; P*] 駆逐艦 — *kuchikukan* — destroyer 放逐する — *hōchiku suru* — drive out, expel
租	租	1574; 115/5. SO tribute, levy [TSU¹ • R grain & P*] 租税 — *sozei* — taxes, rates ⌈leased territory 租借地返還 — *soshakuchi henkan* — return of
曇	曇	1575; 72/12. DON, *kumo(ru/ri)* become cloudy/dull [T'AN² • I: clouds 5–16 below the sun 1–4; P*] 花曇り — *hanagumori* — cloudy weather in spring 晴曇 — *seidon* — fine & cloudy
墾	墾	1576; 32/13. KON reclaim (land), cultivate [K'EN³ • R earth & P*] 開墾する — *kaikon suru* — bring under cultivation 墾田 — *konden* — new rice fields

脂	脂	1577; 130/6. SHI, *abura* fat, grease [CHIH¹ • R flesh & P*] 合成樹脂 — *gōsei jushi* — synthetic resins, plastics 油脂 — *yushi* — oils and fats
壊	壊 壞	1578; 32/13. KAI, *kowa(su/reru)* destroy, break [HUAI⁴ • R earth & P* collapse] 崩壊 — *hōkai* — collapse, fall 破壊 — *hakai* — destruction, demolition
儒	儒	1579; 9/14. JU Confucianism [JU² • R man & P*] 儒教 — *jukyō* — Confucianism 儒学者 — *jugakusha* — Confucian scholar
餓	餓 餓	1580; 184/7. GA starvation [O⁴ • R eat & P*] 餓死する — *gashi suru* — die of starvation 餓鬼 — *gaki* — hungry ghost, kid [slang]
黙	黙 默	1581; 86/11. MOKU, *dama(ru)* be[come] silent [MO⁴ • R dog & P* black/dark & silent 1–7 & 12–15] 黙秘権 — *mokuhiken* — right to keep silent 黙認 — *mokunin* — tacit approval
晶	晶	1582; 72/8. SHŌ brightness, crystal [CHING¹ • D: group of twinkling stars; P*] 結晶 — *kesshō* — a crystal, crystallization 紫水晶 — *murasaki-suishō* — amethyst
暁	暁 暁 曉	1583; 72/8. GYŌ, *akatsuki* dawn [HSIAO³ • R sun & P*] 暁星 — *gyōsei* — morning star, Venus 暁天 — *gyōten* — dawn
魂	魂	1584; 194/4. KON, *tamashii* spirit, soul [HUN² • R devil & P*] 大和魂 — *Yamato-damashii* — the Japanese spirit 霊魂 — *reikon* — soul, spirit

珠	珠	1585; 96/6.　SHU pearl [CHU¹ • R jewel & P*] 珠算 — *shuzan* — abacus calculation 真珠 — *shinju* — pearl
雌	此隹	1586; 77/10.　SHI, *me-*, *mesu* female (animal, bird) [TZ'U² • R small bird & P*] 雌雄 — *shiyū* — male & female 雌象 — *mezō* — cow elephant
畔	畔	1587; 102/5.　HAN edge, path [P'AN⁴ • R field & P* divide] 湖畔 — *kohan* — lakeside 不忍池畔 — *Shinobazu-chihan* — side of the Shino- 「bazu Pond
銑	銑	1588; 167/6.　SEN pig iron [HSIEN³ • R metal & P*] 銑鉄 — *sentetsu* — pig iron 銑鋼 — *senkō* — pig iron
酵	酵	1589; 164/7.　KŌ yeast, lees, fermentation [CHIAO⁴ • R wine jug & P*] 酵素 — *kōso* — enzyme 発酵 — *hakkō* — fermentation
跳	跳	1590; 157/6.　CHŌ, *ha(neru)*, *to(bu)* leap, jump [T'IAO⁴ • R foot & P*] 跳躍する — *chōyaku suru* — spring, jump 飛び跳ねる — *tobi-haneru* — leap/jump up
酷	酷	1591; 164/7.　KOKU severe, harsh, cruel [K'U⁴ • R wine jug & P*] 酷評 — *kokuhyō* — severe criticism 残酷な — *zankoku na* — cruel
裕	裕	1592; 145/7.　YŪ abundance [YÜ⁴ • R clothes & P*] 裕福な — *yūfuku na* — rich, wealthy 余裕 — *yoyū* — surplus, margin

葬	葬	1593; 140/9. sō, *hōmu(ru)* bury [TSANG⁴ · I: a corpse 4–9 amid grasses 1–3 & 10–12; P*] 葬儀 — *sōgi* — funeral 冠婚葬祭 — *kankonsō-sai* — principal [coming-of-age, marriage & funeral] ceremonies
翁	翁	1594; 12/8. ō [hon. suf. for an] old man [WENG¹ · R wings & P*] 老翁 — *rōō* — old man 村翁 — *son'ō* — village elder
粧	粧	1595; 119/6. SHŌ makeup [CHUANG¹ · R rice & P*] 化粧する — *keshō suru* — put on makeup 化粧品 — *keshō-hin* — cosmetics
硫	硫	1596; 112/7. RYŪ sulfur [LIU² · R stone & P* flow 6–12 (= 329)] 硫酸 — *ryūsan* — sulfuric acid 硫黄島 — *Iō-jima* — pn. [lit., sulfur island]
漆	漆	1597; 85/11. SHITSU, *urushi* lacquer [CH'I¹ · R water & P*] 漆器 — *shikki* — lacquer ware 漆黒の — *shikkoku no* — jet black
硬	硬	1598; 112/7. KŌ, *kata(i)* hard, firm [YING⁴ · R stone & P*] 強硬な — *kyōkō na* — strong, positive 硬質の — *kōshitsu no* — hard, scleroid
漏	漏	1599; 85/11. RŌ, *mo(rasu/reru/ru)* leak [LOU⁴ · I: water 1–3 & rain 7–14 leaking through the roof 4–6 (vrt. of 126)] 漏電 — *rōden* — short circuit 遺漏なく — *irō naku* — without omission, exhaus- ⌐tively
摘	摘	1600; 64/11. TEKI reveal; *tsu(mu)* pick, pluck [CHAI¹ · R hand & P*] 指摘する — *shiteki suru* — point out 茶摘 — *chatsumi* — tea-picking

疎	疎	1601; 103/7. SO, *uto(mu)* neglect, shun; *uto(i)* distant, estranged, uninformed [SHU¹, SU¹ • R roll of cloth & P*] 疎漏 — *sorō* — carelessness 疎開者 — *sokaisha* — evacuee, refugee
寧	寧 寧	1602; 40/11. NEI peace, quiet; rather [NING² • R roof & P*] 丁寧な — *teinei na* — polite, careful 安寧 — *annei* — public peace
奪	奪	1603; 37/11. DATSU, *uba(u)* seize, rob 「12–14] [TO² • I: a man 1–3 with a bird 4–11 in the hand] 略奪する — *ryakudatsu suru* — plunder, pillage 争奪戦 — *sōdatsu-sen* — contest, challenge
雇	雇	1604; 63/8. KO, *yato(u)* employ [KU⁴ • R small bird & P*] 解雇する — *kaiko suru* — dismiss, discharge 雇用と失業 — *koyō to shitsugyō* — employment and unemployment
酢	酢	1605; 164/5. SAKU, *su* vinegar [TSO⁴ • R wine jug & P*] 酢酸 — *sakusan* — acetic acid 酢の物 — *su no mono* — pickles
焦	焦	1606; 172/4. SHŌ, *ko(gasu/geru)* burn; *ase(ru)* be hasty/impatient 「flame 9–12; P*] [CHIAO¹ • I: a small bird 1–8 roasted over a flame 9–12; P*] 焦慮する — *shōryo suru* — be anxious/impatient 焦熱地獄 — *shōnetsu jigoku* — burning hell
款	款 款 欵	1607; 76/8. KAN friendship; clause, section [K'UAN³ • I; P*] 借款 — *shakkan* — loan 定款 — *teikan* — articles of association
核	核	1608; 75/6. KAKU nucleus, core [HO², HU² • R tree & P*] 結核 — *kekkaku* — tubercle, tuberculosis 核分裂 — *kaku-bunretsu* — nuclear fission

桑	桑	1609; 29/8. sō, *kuwa* mulberry [SANG¹ • I: many hands 1–6 plucking the leaves of the mulberry tree; P*] 桑畑 — *kuwa-batake* — mulberry field 桑門 — *sōmon* — priesthood
朗	朗 朗	1610; 130/6. RŌ, *hogara(ka na)* clear, bright [LANG³ • R moon & P* bright] 朗詠する — *rōei suru* — recite 明朗な — *meirō na* — bright, cheerful
捕	捕	1611; 64/7. HO, *tora(eru)*, *to(ru)*, *tsuka(maeru/ [PU³,⁴ • R hand & P*] ⌊*maru)* catch, seize 捕獲する — *hokaku suru* — capture, seize 捕鯨船 — *hogeisen* — whaling vessel
振	振	1612; 64/7. SHIN, *fu(ru/ri)* shake, swing; *-buri* [CHEN⁴ • R hand & P*] ⌊after [a lapse of] 振替貯金 — *furikae chokin* — transfer savings 久し振りに — *hisashiburi ni* — after a long time
徐	徐	1613; 60/7. JO slowly, steadily [HSÜ² • R footstep & P*] 徐歩する — *joho suru* — walk slowly 徐行する — *jokō suru* — go slowly
宰	宰	1614; 40/7. SAI administer, control [TSAI³ • R roof & P*] 宰相 — *saishō* — prime minister 主宰 — *shusai* — supervision, control
埋	埋	1615; 32/7. MAI, *u(meru/maru)* bury [MAI² • R earth & P*] 埋葬する — *maisō suru* — bury 埋没する — *maibotsu suru* — be buried/entombed, remain obscure
倣	倣	1616; 9/8. HŌ, *nara(u)* imitate [FANG³ • R man & P*] 模倣する — *mohō suru* — imitate, copy ⌈dent 先例に倣う — *senrei ni narau* — follow a prece-

悩	悩 悩	1617; 61/7. NŌ, *naya(mu/mi)* suffer (from), be dis-[NAO³ • R heart & P*] └tressed (at) 悩殺する — *nōsatsu suru* — charm, bewitch 悩み苦しむ — *nayami-kurushimu* — be distressed & pained
恭	恭	1618; 61/6. KYŌ, *uyauya(shii)* respectful, reverent [KUNG¹ • R heart & P* offering] 恭賀新年 — *kyōga shinnen* — A Happy New Year 恭順 — *kyōjun* — allegiance
栽	栽	1619; 24/8. SAI plant [TSAI¹ • R tree & P*] 栽培する — *saibai suru* — grow, cultivate 盆栽 — *bonsai* — dwarfed potted plant
倹	倹 倹	1620; 9/8. KEN frugal, humble [CHIEN³ • R man & P*] 倹約する — *ken'yaku suru* — economize, save 節倹 — *sekken* — economy, frugality
邸	邸	1621; 163/5. TEI mansion, residence [TI³ • R city & P*] 邸宅 — *teitaku* — residence 官邸 — *kantei* — official residence
享	享	1622; 8/6. KYŌ enjoy; receive [HSIANG³ • D; P*] 享楽する — *kyōraku suru* — enjoy 享受する — *kyōju suru* — enjoy, be given
迭	迭	1623; 162/5. TETSU alternation, rotation [TIEH² • R proceed & P*] 更迭 — *kōtetsu* — change, shake-up 迭起する — *tekki suru* — happen alternately
弦	弦	1624; 57/5. GEN, *tsuru* string (of musical instru-[HSIEN² • R bow & P*] └ment), bowstring 弓弦 — *yumizuru* — bowstring 管弦楽 — *kangengaku* — orchestra

肯	肯	1625; 77/4. KŌ agree, consent [K'EN³ · I→B; P*] 肯定する — *kōtei suru* — affirm, answer 'yes' to 首肯する — *shukō suru* — agree/assent (to)
炊	炊	1626; 86/4. SUI, *ta(ku)* burn, kindle, cook [CH'UI¹ · R fire & P* 5–8 (ab. of 1095)] 炊飯器 — *suihan-ki* — rice-cooking machine 自炊する — *jisui suru* — cook for oneself
沸	沸	1627; 85/5. FUTSU, *wa(kasu/ku)* boil [FEI⁴ · R water & P*] 沸騰する — *futtō suru* — become boiling/agitated 煮沸する — *shafutsu suru* — boil, heat to boiling
坪	坪	1628; 32/5. *tsubo* unit of area [3.31 sq. meters] [P'ING² · R earth & P*] 建坪 — *tate-tsubo* — floor space 延べ坪 — *nobe-tsubo* — total floor space
屈	屈	1629; 44/5. KUTSU, *kus(suru)* (vt. & vi.) bend, defeat, bow/submit (to); *kaga(meru/mu)* bend, stoop [CH'Ü¹ · R bent figure & P*] 窮屈な — *kyūkutsu na* — narrow, cramped, strict 屈辱 — *kutsujoku* — insult, humiliation
径	径 徑	1630; 60/5. KEI path; diameter [CHING⁴ · R footstep & P*] 径路 — *keiro* — route, course 直径 — *chokkei* — diameter
担	担 擔	1631; 64/5. TAN carry, shoulder [TAN¹ · R hand & P*] 負担 — *futan* — burden, responsibility 担任 — *tannin* — charge, responsibility
押	押	1632; 64/5. Ō, *o(su)* push; *osa(eru)* check, suppress; *o(shi)* weight, authority, boldness [YA¹,³ · R hand & P*] 押収する — *ōshū suru* — seize, confiscate 押し倒す — *oshi-taosu* — push down, overwhelm

抱	抱	1633; 64/5. HŌ, *da(ku)*, *ida(ku)* (lit.) embrace, hug; *kaka(eru)* carry in the arms [PAO⁴ • R hand & P* wrap/envelop] 辛抱する — *shinbō suru* — bear, be patient about 抱負 — *hōfu* — aspiration, ambition
析	析	1634; 75/4. SEKI take apart, divide [HSI¹ • I: tree 1–4 & ax 5–8; P*] 解析 — *kaiseki* — analysis 分析する — *bunseki suru* — analyze
賦	賦	1635; 154/8. FU tribute, payment; ode [FU⁴ • R money & P*] 賦税 — *fuzei* — tax, levy 月賦 — *geppu* — monthly installment/payment
緯	緯	1636; 120/9. I horizontal thread, [lines of] latitude [WEI³·⁴ • R thread & P*] 経緯 — *keii* — longitude & latitude 緯度 — *ido* — latitude
穂	穂 穗	1637; 115/10, SUI, *ho* ear (of rice, etc.) [SUI⁴ • R grain & P*] 稲穂 — *inaho* — ears of rice 穂波 — *honami* — waving grain
徹	徹	1638; 60/12. TETSU pierce, penetrate [CH'E⁴ • R footstep & P* pierce (cf. 1456)] 貫徹する — *kantetsu suru* — accomplish, achieve 徹頭徹尾 — *tettō-tetsubi* — thoroughly
履	履	1639; 44/12. RI, footwear, tread; *ha(ku)* wear on the feet ⌈588), to put both shoes on; P*] [LI³, LÜ³ • I: bent figure 1–3 repeated 4–15 (see 履歴 — *rireki* — one's personal history 麻裏草履 — *asaura-zōri* — hemp-soled straw sandals
糾	糾	1640; 120/3. KYŪ twist, entwine; examine, investi- [CHIU¹·³ • R thread & P*] ⌊gate 紛糾 — *funkyū* — complication, disorder 糾弾する — *kyūdan suru* — impeach, denounce

窃	窃 竊	1641; 116/4.　SETSU rob, steal [CH'IEH⁴ ・ R hole & P*] 窃盗 — settō — theft, thief 窃取する — sesshu suru — purloin, steal
拷	拷	1642; 29/6.　GŌ hit, beat [K'AO³ ・ R hand & P*]　「fession) 拷問する — gōmon suru — torture (to extract con- 拷責する — gōseki suru — torture
奏	奏	1643; 37/6.　SŌ, sō(suru), kana(deru) play (musical instrument) [TSOU⁴ ・ I: two hands 1–5 making offerings to Heaven 6–9; P*]　「(music) 伴奏する — bansō suru — (vi.) accompany with 演奏する — ensō suru — play/perform (music)
粘	粘	1644; 119/5.　NEN, neba(ru) be sticky, stick (to/at [NIEN², CHAN¹ ・ R rice & P*]　└ a task) 粘膜 — nenmaku — mucous membrane 粘り強い — nebari-zuyoi — tenacious
紳	紳	1645; 120/5.　SHIN gentleman; official sash [SHEN¹ ・ R thread & P*] 紳士 — shinshi — gentleman 紳商 — shinshō — merchant prince
陵	陵	1646; 170/8.　RYŌ, misasagi imperial tomb [LING² ・ R mound & P*] 天皇の陵 — tennō no misasagi — tomb of an em- 陵墓 — ryōbo — imperial tomb　└peror
陳	陳	1647; 170/8.　CHIN state, show; old [CH'EN² ・ R mound & P*] 陳列する — chinretsu suru — display, exhibit 新陳代謝 — shinchin taisha — renewal, metabolism
酔	酔 醉	1648; 164/4.　SUI, yo(u) become drunk/sick [TSUI⁴ ・ R wine jug & P*] 酔払い — yopparai — drunkard 麻酔 — masui — anesthesia

232

逮	逮	1649; 162/8. TAI chase [TAI⁴, TI⁴ • R proceed & P*] 逮夜 — *taiya* — eve of the anniversary of a death 逮捕する — *taiho suru* — arrest
販	販	1650; 154/4. HAN sell, trade [FAN⁴ • R money & P*] 販路 — *hanro* — market, outlet 市販する — *shihan suru* — (put on the) market
菌	菌	1651; 140/8. KIN fungus, germ [CHÜN³ • R grass & P*] 細菌 — *saikin* — bacteria, germ 菌毒 — *kindoku* — mushroom-poison
肅	肅 肅	1652; 2/10. SHUKU quiet, solemn [SU⁴ • R writing & P*] 厳粛な — *genshuku na* — grave, solemn 粛然と — *shukuzen to* — quietly, solemnly
紺	紺	1653; 120/5. KON* dark blue [KAN¹ • R thread & P*] 紫紺 — *shikon* — purple-blue 濃紺 — *nōkon* — dark blue
粒	粒	1654; 119/5. RYŪ, *tsubu* grain, drop [LI⁴ • R rice & P*] 飯粒 — *meshitsubu* — boiled rice-grain 粒状の — *ryūjō no* — granular
猟	猟 獵 獵	1655; 94/8. RYŌ hunting [LIEH⁴ • I: a dog 1–3 is repeatedly 4–6 used 7–11 (see 110)] 狩猟 — *shuryō* — hunting 猟銃 — *ryōjū* — hunting gun
添	添	1656; 85/8. TEN, *so(eru)* add, append [T'IEN¹ • R water & P*] 添加する — *tenka suru* — annex, append 添削する — *tensaku suru* — amend, correct

排	排	1657; 64/8. HAI reject, eject [P'AI[2] • R hand & P*] 排液 — *haieki* — drainage 排撃する — *haigeki suru* — denounce
控	控	1658; 64/8. KŌ, *hika(eru)* refrain from, wait, write [K'UNG[4] • R hand & P*] ⌊down 控訴する — *kōso suru* — (vi.) appeal 控え室 — *hikae-shitsu* — waiting room
揭	揭	1659; 64/8. KEI, *kaka(geru)* hoist, fly (flag, etc.), [CHIEH[1] • R hand & P*] ⌊present 揭載する — *keisai suru* — publish, insert, print 国旗揭揚 — *kokki keiyō* — raising of national flag
彩	彩	1660; 59/8. SAI, *irodo(ru/ri)* color [TS'AI[3] • R light rays & P*] 鮮彩な — *sensai na* — brightly colored 色彩 — *shikisai* — color
庶	庶	1661; 53/8. SHO multitude [SHU[4] • R fire & P*] 庶務 — *shomu* — general affairs 庶系 — *shokei* — illegimate line
剩	剩	1662; 18/9. JŌ surplus [SHENG[4] • R knife & P*] 過剩 — *kajō* — surplus, excess 剩余 — *jōyo* — surplus, balance
痴	痴 癡	1663; 104/8. CHI foolish [CH'IH[1,2] • R illness & P*] 愚痴 — *guchi* — grumble, complaint 痴情 — *chijō* — foolish passion, blind love
滝	滝 瀧	1664; 85/10. *taki* waterfall [LUNG[2] • R water & P] 滝登り — *taki-nobori* — climbing a waterfall 白糸の滝 — *Shiraito no Taki* — Shiraito ['White Thread'] Waterfall

摂	摂 攝	1665; 64/10. SETSU proxy; take [SHE⁴ • R hand & P*] 摂政 — *sesshō* — regency, regent 摂取する — *sesshu suru* — take in, ingest, adopt
携	携	1666; 64/10. KEI, *tazusa(eru)* carry in the hand, take/bring with one ⌜bow 12–13 (see 1962)⌝ [HSIEH², HSI¹ • I: a hand 1–3, with a bird 4–11 & 携帯する — *keitai suru* — take/bring with one 提携する — *teikei suru* — act in concert (with)
搬	搬	1667; 64/10. HAN transport, remove [PAN¹ • R hand & P*] 運搬する — *unpan suru* — carry, transport 搬送する — *hansō suru* — convey
微	微	1668; 60/10. BI minute, slight [WEI¹,² • R footstep & P* (cf. 1384, which is read (CH)ō & contains ō 'king' 7–10)] 微妙な — *bimyō na* — subtle, delicate 顕微鏡 — *kenbikyō* — microscope
慎	慎 愼	1669; 61/10. SHIN, *tsutsushi(mu)* be careful/cautious about, abstain from [SHEN⁴ • R heart & P*] 謹慎する — *kinshin suru* — be penitent 慎み深い — *tsutsushimi-bukai* — careful, prudent
塊	塊	1670; 32/10. KAI, *kata(mari)* clod, lump [K'UAI⁴ • R earth & P*] 肉塊 — *nikkai* — lump of flesh/meat 塊根 — *kaikon* — tuberous root
嗣	嗣	1671; 30/10. SHI inherit, succeed to [SZU⁴ • R mouth & P*] 後嗣 — *kōshi* — heir, successor 嗣君 — *shikun* — heir
肖	肖	1672; 42/4. SHŌ resemble ⌜4–7; P*⌝ [HSIAO⁴ • I: a small 1–3 (= 33) flesh/body/figure 肖像画 — *shōzōga* — portrait [painting] 不肖の — *fushō no* — unworthy

克	克	1673; 24/5. KOKU conquer ⌈or 3–5⌉ [K'O⁴, K'E⁴ • D: a man 1–2 & 6–7 wearing arm- 克己 — kokki — self-denial, self-control 克服する — kokufuku suru — conquer, subjugate
妨	妨	1674; 38/4. BŌ, samata(geru) obstruct, prevent [FANG¹⋅² • R woman & P*] 妨害する — bōgai suru — obstruct, interfere with 事故妨止 — jiko bōshi — prevention of accident
抄	抄	1675; 64/4. SHŌ excerpt, extract [CH'AO¹ • I: extract by hand 1–3 a few parts 4–7; 詩抄 — shishō — selected poems ⌊P*⌋ 抄録 — shōroku — quotation, selection
坊	坊	1676; 32/4. BŌ [residence of] priest [FANG¹ • R earth & P*] ⌈priest 生臭坊主 — namagusa-bōzu — worldly / depraved 宿坊 — shukubō — visitor's lodgings (in temple)
含	含	1677; 9/5. GAN, fuku(mu) contain, imply, bear (a feeling) [HAN² • I: what is now 1–4 in the mouth; P*] 包含する — hōgan suru — include, comprise, im- 含蓄 — ganchiku — implication ⌊ply
即	即 卽 卽	1678; 138/2. SOKU immediate; accession; namely [CHI²⋅⁴ • I; P*] 即刻 — sokkoku — instantly, at once 即位する — sokui suru — accede to the throne
伯	伯	1679; 9/5. HAKU eldest brother, count [PO²⋅⁴ • R man & P*] 伯仲する — hakuchū suru — (vi.) match, be equal 画伯 — gahaku — master painter
却	却	1680; 26/5. KYAKU reject; contrary [CH'ÜEH⁴ • I: the going/withdrawal 1–5 (see 475) of a kneeling man 6–7; P*] 償却 — shōkyaku — repayment 忘却する — bōkyaku suru — forget

朱	朱	1681; 4/5. SHU vermilion [CHU¹ • D & S: a redwood tree 2 & 4–6 with trunk cut 1 & 3, exposing color; P*] 朱筆 — shuhitsu — vermilion writing brush 朱印 — shuin — red seal
芋	芋	1682; 140/3. imo potato [YÜ⁴ • R grass & P] 焼芋 — yakiimo — baked sweet potato 里芋 — satoimo — taro
朽	朽	1683; 75/2. KYŪ, ku(chiru) rot, decay [HSIU³ • R tree & P*]　　　　　　┌annuated 老朽の — rōkyū no — senile, worn-out, super- 腐朽する — fukyū suru — rot, decompose
吏	吏	1684; 4/5. RI an official　　┌2–6 (see 81); P*] [LI⁴ • I: one 1 who deals with records & annals 官吏 — kanri — government official 吏党 — ritō — party of officials
叫	叫 叫 叫	1685; 30/3. KYŌ, sake(bu) cry out, shout [CHIAO⁴ • R mouth & P*] 叫喚 — kyōkan — shout, scream, cry 絶叫する — zekkyō suru — scream, exclaim
吐	吐	1686; 30/3. TO, ha(ku) vomit, utter [T'U³ • R mouth & P*] 吐露する — toro suru — express, speak, lay bare 吐息 — toiki — sigh
兆	兆	1687; 15/4. CHŌ*, kizashi sign, omen; billion [Brit.], trillion [U. S.]; kiza(su) (vi.) show signs [CHAO⁴ • D: divination cracks in tortoise shell; 兆候 — chōkō — indication, sign, symptom　　┌P*] 前兆 — zenchō — omen, foreshadow
尼	尼	1688; 44/2. NI, ama nun [NI² • I: bent figure 1–3 & D of nun kneeling with hands held up in prayer 4–5] 尼僧 — nisō — nun 尼寺 — amadera — nunnery, convent

丘	丘	1689; 4/4. KYŪ, *oka* hill [CH'IU¹ · D; P*] 丘陵 — *kyūryō* — hill, hillock 丘辺 — *okabe* — vicinity of a hill
弔	弔	1690; 2/3. CHŌ, *tomura(u)* mourn, condole; *tomura(i)* funeral, condolence ⌈string 4⌉ [TIAO⁴ · S: grief over a life broken like a bow 1-3] 慶弔 — *keichō* — congratulations & condolences 弔辞 — *chōji* — message of condolence
幻	幻	1691; 52/1. GEN, *maboroshi* phantom, vision [HUAN⁴ · D & S; P*] 幻滅 — *genmetsu* — disillusion 幻影 — *gen'ei* — vision, illusion
慌	慌	1692; 61/9. KŌ, *awa(teru)*, *awatada(shii)* be agitated/confused [HUANG¹ · I: one's feelings 1-3 in turmoil 4-12 (see 1028); also R heart & P*] 恐慌 — *kyōkō* — panic, alarm 慌忙 — *kōbō* — being very busy
陪	陪	1693; 170/8. BAI attend upon, serve [P'EI² · R mound & P*] 陪審 — *baishin* — jury ⌈act as an associate 陪席する — *baiseki suru* — sit with (a superior),
憾	憾	1694; 61/13. KAN regret [HAN⁴ · R heart & P* feelings] 遺憾な — *ikan na* — regrettable, unsatisfactory 憾恨 — *kankon* — grudge
鐘	鐘	1695; 167/12. SHŌ, *kane* bell [CHUNG¹ · R metal & P*] 暁鐘 — *gyōshō* — morning/dawn bell 晩鐘 — *banshō* — evening bell
欄	欄 欄	1696; 75/16. RAN* (newspaper, etc.) column; railing [LAN² · R tree & P*] 投書欄 — *tōshoran* — correspondence column 空欄 — *kūran* — blank column

髄	髄 髄	1697; 188/8.　ZUI* marrow, pith [SUI³ • R bone & P*] 脳髄 — *nōzui* — brain 骨髄 — *kotsuzui* — bone marrow
鎖	鎖 鎖	1698; 167/10.　SA shut, close; *kusari* chain [SO³ • R metal & P] 封鎖 — *fūsa* — blockade 閉鎖 — *heisa* — closure, lockout
覆	覆 覆	1699; 146/12.　FUKU, *ō(u)* cover, hide; *kutsuga(esu/* [FU²,⁴ • R cover & P*]　　　　　　　⌐*eru)* overturn 覆面 — *fukumen* — mask, disguise 覆没する — *fukubotsu suru* — be capsized & sunk
繭	繭	1700; 140/15.　KEN, *mayu* silkworm cocoon [CHIEN³ • I: grass/leaves 1–3 are eaten by grubs 13–18 to make silk thread 7–12 for cloth 4–6 (= R cloth)] 繭糸 — *kenshi* — cocoon & silk thread 繭価 — *mayuka* — price of cocoons
礎	礎	1701; 112/13.　SO, *ishizue* foundation, cornerstone [CH'U³ • R stone & P] 基礎 — *kiso* — basis, foundation 礎石 — *soseki* — foundation stone
癖	癖	1702; 104/13.　HEKI, *kuse* habit, idiosyncrasy [P'I³ • R illness & P*] 潔癖な — *keppeki na* — fastidious, habitually clean 性癖 — *seiheki* — mental habit, propensity
醜	醜	1703; 164/10.　SHŪ, *miniku(i)* ugly　　⌐8–17; P*] [CH'OU³ • I: a drunken 1–7 (= R wine jug) devil 醜態 — *shūtai* — disgraceful behavior, ugly sight 醜聞 — *shūbun* — scandal
繊	繊 繊	1704; 120/11.　SEN slender, fine [HSIEN¹ • R thread & P*] 繊維 — *sen'i* — (textile) fiber 繊細な — *sensai na* — delicate

療	療	1705; 104/12. RYŌ heal, cure [LIAO² • R illness & P*] 荒療治 — *ara-ryōji* — rough treatment 医療 — *iryō* — medical treatment
礁	礁 礁	1706; 112/12. SHŌ submerged rock/reef/shoal [CHIAO¹ • R stone & P*] 暗礁 — *anshō* — unknown reef, deadlock 岩礁 — *banshō* — (shore) reef
循	循	1707; 60/9. JUN rotate, follow [HSÜN² • R footstep & P*] 循環する — *junkan suru* — circulate 因循 — *injun* — indecision, vacillation
燥	燥	1708; 86/13. SŌ dry [TSAO⁴ • R fire & P*] 乾燥する — *kansō suru* — become dry 焦燥 — *shōsō* — fretfulness, impatience
擦	擦	1709; 64/14. SATSU, *su(ru/reru)* rub, chafe [TS'A¹, CH'A¹ • R hand & P*] 擦傷 — *sasshō* — abrasion, scratch 擦剤 — *satsuzai* — liniment
憩	憩	1710; 61/12. KEI, *ikoi* rest [CH'I⁴ • I: a time to talk (← tongue 878) 1–6 & catch one's breath 7–16; P*] 休憩 — *kyūkei* — intermission 少憩 — *shōkei* — brief rest
壇	壇	1711; 32/13. DAN platform, dais [T'AN² • R earth & P] 演壇 — *endan* — platform 花壇 — *kadan* — flower bed
随	随 隨	1712; 170/8. ZUI follow [SUI² • R mound & P*] 随筆 — *zuihitsu* — jottings, essays 「at will/free 傍聴随意 — *bōchō zui-i* — [lecture, etc.] admission

敢	敢	1713; 66/8. KAN daringly, boldly [KAN³ · I: P*] 勇敢な — yūkan na — brave, courageous 敢闘する — kantō suru — fight courageously
惰	惰	1714; 61/9. DA idle, lazy [TO⁴ · R heart & P*] 怠惰な — taida na — idle, lazy 惰性 — dasei — inertia
痘	痘	1715; 104/7. TŌ smallpox [TOU⁴ · R illness & P*] 種痘 — shutō — vaccination, inoculation 天然痘 — tennentō — smallpox
痢	痢	1716; 104/7. RI diarrhea [LI¹ · R illness & P*] 疫痢 — ekiri — summer/children's dysentery 下痢 — geri — diarrhea
飢	飢 飢	1717; 184/2. KI, u(eru/e) be starved/hungry [CHI¹ · R eat & P*] 飢餓 — kiga — hunger, starvation 飢死する — uejini suru — starve to death
陥	陥 陥	1718; 170/7. KAN, ochii(ru) fall (into), yield (to) [HSIEN⁴, HSÜAN⁴ · R mound & P] 陥没する — kanbotsu suru — sink, collapse 欠陥 — kekkan — defect, fault
婿	婿	1719; 38/9. SEI, muko son-in-law [HSÜ⁴ · R woman & P*] 婿探し — muko-sagashi — looking for a son-in-law 婿養子 — muko-yōshi — adopted son-in-law
耗	耗	1720; 127/4. MŌ, KŌ decrease, decline [HAO⁴ · R plow & P*] 消耗する — shōmō suru — consume, exhaust 損耗 — sonmō — loss

唆	唆	1721; 30/7. SA, *sosono(kasu)* tempt, entice, incite [SO¹ · R mouth & P*] 示唆する — *shisa suru* — suggest 教唆する — *kyōsa suru* — instigate, incite to
秩	秩	1722; 115/5. CHITSU order, sequence 「plants)] [CHIH⁴ · R grain & P* (= regular rows of rice 秩序 — *chitsujo* — order, discipline 秩父 — *Chichibu* — pn.
逸	逸 逸	1723; 162/8. ITSU excel; be fast; stray [I⁴, YI⁴ · I: a hare 1–8 proceeds/flees 9–11; P*] 放逸 — *hōitsu* — self-indulgence, debauchery 独逸 — *Doitsu* — Germany
粗	粗	1724; 119/5. SO, *ara(i)* coarse, rough [TS'U¹ · R rice & P*] 粗雑な — *sozatsu na* — coarse, rough 粗末な — *somatsu na* — humble, shabby
拠	拠 據 據	1725; 64/5. KYO, KO depend on, be based on [CHÜ⁴ · R hand & P*] 証拠 — *shōko* — evidence, proof 根拠 — *konkyo* — basis, ground
炉	炉 爐	1726; 86/4. RO hearth, furnace [LU² · R fire & P*] 暖炉 — *danro* — fireplace 溶鉱炉 — *yōkōro* — furnace
炎	炎	1727; 86/4. EN, *honoo* flame [YEN² · I: leaping flames; P*] 炎症 — *enshō* — inflammation 腹膜炎 — *fukumakuen* — peritonitis
卸	卸	1728; 26/7. *oro(su)* sell wholesale; *oroshi* whole- [HSIEH⁴ · R kneeling figure & P*] ⌊sale 卸値 — *oroshine* — wholesale price 卸商 — *oroshi-shō* — wholesaler

弧	弧	1729; 57/5. KO* arc [HU² • R bow & P*] 括弧 — *kakko* — parentheses 弧状の — *kojō no* — arc-shaped
棺	棺	1730; 75/8. KAN* coffin [KUAN¹ • R tree & P*] 寝棺 — *negan* — coffin (for a lying body) 棺掛け — *kankake* — coffin cover
銘	銘	1731; 167/6. MEI* inscription, signature, motto [MING² • R metal & P*] 銘柄 — *meigara* — brand [name], description 心に銘記する — *kokoro ni meiki suru* — impress/ engrave on one's mind
賓	賓 賓	1732; 40/12. HIN guest [PIN¹ • I: a guest's 1–8 money/gift 9–15→guest/ visitor himself; P*] 貴賓席 — *kihin-seki* — VIPs' gallery/seat 賓客 — *hinkyaku* — guest of honor
拙	拙	1733; 64/5. SETSU clumsy, inexpert, poor [CHO¹,² • R hand & P*] 稚拙な — *chisetsu na* — unskillful, childish 拙策 — *sessaku* — poor plan
征	征	1734; 60/5. SEI subjugate [CHENG¹ • R footstep & P*] 征伐する — *seibatsu suru* — subjugate, conquer 遠征 — *ensei* — expedition, foray, invasion
幽	幽	1735; 2/8. YŪ quiet, profound [YU¹ • I: a dark, dim 2–7 mountain 1 & 8–9; P*] 幽霊 — *yūrei* — ghost 幽閉する — *yūhei suru* — confine, imprison
殉	殉	1736; 78/6. JUN, *jun(zuru)* follow in death, sacrifice [HSÜN⁴ • R disintegrate & P*]⌐oneself 殉職する — *junshoku suru* — die at one's post 殉死する — *junshi suru* — follow one's lord in death

督	督	1737; 109/8. TOKU supervise, command [TU[1] • R eye & P*] 「direct 監督する — *kantoku suru* — control, supervise, 督促する — *tokusoku suru* — press for, urge
豚	豚	1738; 130/7. TON, *buta* pig [T'UN[2] • I: flesh 1–4 & pig 5–11; P*] 養豚 — *yōton* — swine raising 豚箱 — *butabako* — police (station) cell
赦	赦	1739; 155/4. SHA forgive, pardon [SHE[4] • R strike & P*] 恩赦 — *onsha* — amnesty 「charge 赦免する — *shamen suru* — pardon, remit, dis-
畜	畜	1740; 95/5. CHIKU raise livestock [CH'U[4] • R field & P*] 畜産 — *chikusan* — livestock industry 家畜 — *kachiku* — domestic animals, livestock
帥	帥	1741; 2/8. SUI supreme commander [SHUAI[4] • R cloth & P*] 元帥 — *gensui* — field marshal, admiral of the fleet 統帥 — *tōsui* — supreme command
倫	倫	1742; 9/8. RIN principles, code [LUN[2] • R man & P*] 倫理 — *rinri* — ethics, moral 人倫道徳 — *jinrin dōtoku* — ethics and morality
准	准 準	1743; 15/8. JUN semi-, secondary; imitate [CHUN[3] • R ice & P*] 批准する — *hijun suru* — ratify 准尉 — *jun'i* — warrant officer
楼	楼 樓	1744; 75/9. RŌ tower, tall building [LOU[2] • R tree & P*] 鐘楼 — *shōrō* — bell tower 楼閣 — *rōkaku* — many-storied building

錠	錠	1745; 167/8. JŌ* lock; (unit for) medical tablet [TING⁴ · R metal & P*] 錠前 — *jōmae* — lock 錠剤 — *jōzai* — medical tablet
避	避	1746; 162/13. HI, *sa(keru)* avoid, evade [PI⁴ · R proceed & P*] 逃避する — *tōhi suru* — escape 避雷針 — *hiraishin* — lightning rod/conductor
錯	錯	1747; 167/8. SAKU mixed, disordered [TS'O⁴ · R metal & P*] 錯覚 — *sakkaku* — illusion, hallucination 錯誤 — *sakugo* — mistake, error
薦	薦	1748; 140/13. SEN, *susu(meru)* urge, recommend [CHIEN⁴ · I→B] 推薦する — *suisen suru* — recommend 自薦 — *jisen* — self-recommendation
濁	濁	1749; 85/13. DAKU, *nigo(ru)* become muddy/murky; *nigo(ri)* murkiness, voiced sound [CHO³ · R water & P*] 混濁する — *kondaku suru* — become turbid 濁流 — *dakuryū* — turbid current
擁	擁	1750; 64/13. YŌ, *yō(suru)* embrace, hold [YUNG³ · I: a hand 1–3 covering 4–5 & shading 6–8 a small bird 9–16] 擁護する — *yōgo suru* — protect 抱擁する — *hōyō suru* — embrace
錘	錘	1751; 167/8. SUI weight, sinker; *tsumu* spindle [CH'UI² · R metal & P*] 紡錘 — *bōsui* — spindle 錘状の — *suijō no* — spindle-shaped
僚	僚	1752; 9/12. RYŌ official; companion, associate [LIAO² · R man & P*] 閣僚 — *kakuryō* — Cabinet ministers 同僚 — *dōryō* — colleague

隔	隔	1753; 170/10. KAKU, *heda(teru/taru)* separate by, interpose [KO², KE² • R mound & P*] 隔離する — *kakuri suru* — isolate, insulate 疎隔する — *sokaku suru* — estrange, alienate
酪	酪	1754; 164/6. RAKU dairy produce [LAO³ • R wine jug & P*] 酪農 — *rakunō* — dairy farming 乳酪 — *nyūraku* — butter
虜	虜	1755; 141/7. RYO captive [LO³, LU³ • I: tiger 1–6 (ab. of 1932) & man 7–13; P*] 捕虜 — *horyo* — prisoner of war 虜囚 — *ryoshū* — captive, prisoner
禍	禍	1756; 113/9. KA disaster, misfortune [HUO⁴ • R good & P*] 災禍 — *saika* — accident, disaster 禍福 — *kafuku* — fortune and/or misfortune
碁	碁	1757; 112/8. GO* the game of *go* [CH'I² • R stone & P*] 碁盤 — *goban* — *go* board 囲碁 — *igo* — game of *go*
碑	碑	1758; 112/9. HI* monument, memorial stone [PEI¹ • R stone & P*] 墓碑 — *bohi* — gravestone 記念碑 — *kinenhi* — monument
塗	塗	1759; 32/10. TO, *nu(ru)* paint, coat [T'U² • R earth & P* water 1–3 which is thick/muddy 4–10] 塗装 — *tosō* — coating with paint 漆塗りの — *urushi-nuri no* — lacquered
硝	硝	1760; 112/7. SHŌ niter, gunpowder [HSIAO¹ • R stone & P*] 硝酸 — *shōsan* — nitric acid 硝煙 — *shōen* — gunpowder smoke

卓	卓	1761; 25/6. TAKU excel; table [CHO[1,4] • I: a man 1–2 who is quick 3–8 (see 117) & therefore excels; P*] 卓越する — *takuetsu suru* — be superior (to), 卓球 — *takkyū* — table tennis ⌞excel (over)
索	索	1762; 24/8. SAKU rope; search for ⌐P* [SO[1,2,3] • I: two hands 1–4 plaiting rope 5–10; 捜索令状 — *sōsaku reijō* — search warrant 探索する — *tansaku suru* — search/look for, investigate
紋	紋	1763; 120/4. MON* family crest/sign [WEN[2] • R thread & P*] 指紋 — *shimon* — fingerprint 紋章 — *monshō* — crest, coat of arms
彼	彼	1764; 60/5. HI, *kare* he; *ka(no)* that [PI[3] • R footstep & P*] 彼岸 — *higan* — equinoctial week 彼等は皆 — *karera wa mina* — they all
泰	泰	1765; 85/5. TAI* Thailand, Siam; peace [T'AI[4] • I; P*] 天下泰平 — *tenka taihei* — peace over the land 泰然自若 — *taizen jijaku* — imperturbability
匿	匿	1766; 22/8. TOKU conceal [NI[4] • R box & P*] 隠匿する — *intoku suru* — hide, conceal 匿名の — *tokumei no* — anonymous
阻	阻	1767; 170/5. SO, *haba(mu)* obstruct [TSU[3] • R mound & P*] 阻止する — *soshi suru* — obstruct, hinder 阻害する — *sogai suru* — impede, hinder
孤	孤	1768; 39/5. KO lone, solitary [KU[1] • R child & P*] 孤独な — *kodoku na* — lonely 孤村 — *koson* — lonely village

岐	岐	1769; 46/4. KI road fork [CH'I¹ · R mountain & P*] 岐路 — *kiro* — forked road 分岐点 — *bunkiten* — dividing point
尿	尿	1770; 44/4. NYŌ* urine [NIAO⁴ · I: bent figure 1–3 & water 4–7; P*] 排尿 — *hainyō* — urination 糖尿病患者 — *tōnyōbyō kanja* — diabetic patient
悼	悼	1771; 61/8. TŌ, *ita(mu)* mourn/lament [for/over] [TAO⁴ · R heart & P*] 哀悼する — *aitō suru* — mourn, grieve 追悼の辞 — *tsuitō no ji* — memorial address
岳	岳	1772; 4/7. GAKU, *take* peak, mountain [YÜEH⁴ · I: a hill 1–5 (see 1689) on top of a mountain 6–8; P*] 山岳 — *sangaku* — mountains 八が岳 — *Yatsu-ga-take* — pn.
舗	舗 舗 舗	1773; 9/13. HO shop, store; paving [P'U⁴ · R mouth & P*] 店舗 — *tenpo* — shop, store 「metal a road 道路を舗装する — *dōro o hosō suru* — pave/
酬	酬	1774; 164/6. SHŪ reward, remuneration [CH'OU² · R wine jug & P*] 報酬 — *hōshū* — remuneration, reward 応酬する — *ōshū suru* — respond/reply (to)
鈴	鈴	1775; 167/5. REI, RIN, *suzu* small bell [LING² · R metal & P*] 振鈴 — *shinrei* — ringing a bell 呼鈴 — *yobirin* — call bell
賄	賄	1776; 154/6. WAI bribery; *makana(u)* provide/ supply (meals) [HUI⁴ · I: money 1–7 in one's possession 8–13 (see 267); also R money & P*] 収賄する — *shūwai suru* — accept a bribe 贈賄罪 — *zōwaizai* — crime of bribery

搾	搾	1777; 64/10. SAKU, *shibo(ru)* squeeze, wring, press [CHA³ • R hand & P*] 圧搾する — *assaku suru* — press, compress 搾乳 — *sakunyū* — milking
愁	愁	1778; 61/9. SHŪ, *ure(i)* grief [CH'OU² • R heart & P*] 郷愁 — *kyōshū* — homesickness, nostalgia 哀愁 — *aishū* — sadness, sorrow
斥	斥	1779; 4/4. SEKI expel, rebuff [CH'IH⁴ • I: an ax 1-4 (see 1818) blow 5; P*] 排斥する — *haiseki suru* — expel, reject 斥候 — *sekkō* — scout, patrol
拓	拓	1780; 64/5. TAKU reclaim/develop (land) [T'O¹,² • I: remove by hand 1-3 all the stones 4-8; P*] 拓殖 — *takushoku* — colonization, exploitation 干拓する — *kantaku suru* — reclaim (land) by drainage
尺	尺	1781; 44/1. SHAKU* old unit of length [30.3 cm.] [CH'IH³, CH'E⁴ • D: span made by a hand 1-2 with thumb & fingers stretched 3-4; P*] 尺貫法 — *shakkanhō* — old Japanese weights & measures 尺度 — *shakudo* — standard, measure
丙	丙	1782; 1/4. HEI 3rd (in a series), 'C' [PING⁴ • D; P*] 甲乙丙 — *kō-otsu-hei* — Nos. 1, 2, 3; A, B, C. 丙種 — *heishu* — Class C
摩	摩 摩	1783; 200/4. MA rub, scrape [MO¹,² • R hand & P*] 摩擦する — *masatsu suru* — rub, chafe 摩天楼 — *matenrō* — skyscraper
怖	怖	1784; 61/5. FU, *kowa(i)* fearsome, frightening [PU⁴ • R heart & P*] 孤独恐怖症 — *kodoku kyōfushō* — fear of solitude, monophobia 恐怖観念 — *kyōfu kannen* — fear complex

机	机	1785; 75/2. KI, *tsukue* desk [CHI¹ • R tree & P*] 机上空論 — *kijō kūron* — desk theory 勉強机 — *benkyō-zukue* — study desk
寿	寿 壽	1786; 4/6. JU, *kotobuki* longevity, felicitations [SHOU⁴ • D & S: hand 5-7 with creases 1-3 & long lifeline 4; P*] 平均寿命 — *heikin jumyō* — average span of life 長寿 — *chōju* — long life
泌	泌	1787; 85/5. HITSU, HI flow, secrete [PI⁴ • R water & P*] 泌尿 — *hinyō* — urination 分泌 — *bunpi[tsu]* — secretion
亜	亜 亞	1788; 1/6. A (as pref.) subordinate, sub-; Asia [YA³ • D; P*] 亜鉛 — *aen* — zinc 東亜 — *Tōa* — East Asia
疾	疾	1789; 104/5. SHITSU illness; speed [CHI² • R illness & P*] 疾患 — *shikkan* — disease, ailment 疾風 — *shippū* — gale, hurricane
粋	粋 粋	1790; 119/4. SUI* pure essence, elegance, style [TS'UI⁴ • R rice & P*] 粋美 — *suibi* — exquisite beauty 純粋な — *junsui na* — pure
塑	塑	1791; 32/10. SO clay figure [SU⁴ • R earth & P*] 彫塑 — *chōso* — carving & modeling 塑像 — *sozō* — clay/plaster figure
穏	穏 穩	1792; 115/11. ON, *oda(yaka na)* calm, gentle [WEN³ • R grain & P*] 平穏無事な — *heion buji na* — peaceful 穏健な — *onken na* — moderate, sound

郭	郭	1793; 163/8. KAKU enclosure, redlight district [KUO¹,³ • I: pleasure 1–8 district 9–11; also R district & P*] 郭公〔鳥〕— *kakkō[dori]/hototogisu* — cuckoo 輪郭 — *rinkaku* — outline
棋	棋	1794; 75/8. KI Japanese chess [CH'I² • R tree & P*] 将棋 — *shōgi* — Japanese chess 棋客 — *kikyaku* — chess player
卑	卑	1795; 4/8. HI, *iya(shimeru)* despise; *iya(shii)* low, mean, vulgar ⌈low, humble; P*] [PEI¹ • I: level land with tool 1–7 by hand 8–9→ 卑劣漢 — *hiretsukan* — despicable person 男尊女卑 — *danson johi* — predominance of men over women
扶	扶	1796; 64/4. FU help [FU² • R hand & P*] 扶養家族 — *fuyō kazoku* — dependent family 扶助料 — *fujoryō* — pension
赴	赴	1797; 156/2. FU, *omomu(ku)* go (toward) [FU⁴ • R run & P*] ⌈pointment 赴任する — *funin suru* — proceed to a new ap- 赴援する — *fuen suru* — go to rescue, reinforce
疲	疲	1798; 104/5. HI, *tsuka(reru/re)* become tired/ex- [P'I² • R illness & P*] ⌊hausted 疲労 — *hirō* — fatigue 疲弊 — *hihei* — exhaustion
茂	茂	1799; 140/5. MO, *shige(ru)* grow thickly/luxuriantly [MAO⁴ • R grass & P*] 繁茂 — *hanmo* — luxuriance 茂生する — *mosei suru* — grow luxuriantly
膚	膚	1800; 141/9. FU, *hada* skin [FU¹ • I: tiger 1–6 (ab. of 1932) & stomach 7–15 (see 853), where the skin shows; also R flesh & P*] 皮膚 — *hifu* — skin 膚寒い — *hada-samui* — chilly

娯	娯 娯	1801; 38/7.　GO enjoyment [YÜ² ・ R woman & P*] 娯楽と遊戯 — *goraku to yūgi* — amusements & games「amusements 健全な娯楽 — *kenzen na goraku* — healthy
践	践 践	1802; 157/6.　SEN tread on, perform [CHIEN⁴ ・ R foot & P*]「ing 実践の理性 — *jissenteki risei* — practical reason- 実践道徳 — *jissen dōtoku* — practical morality
祉	祉 祉	1803; 113/4.　SHI good fortune, blessing [CHIH³ ・ R good & P*] 社会福祉 — *shakai fukushi* — social welfare 福祉事業 — *fukushi jigyō* — welfare work
班	班	1804; 96/6.　HAN spot, group, squad [PAN¹ ・ I: a knife 5–6 separating two jewels; P*] 班長 — *hanchō* — group leader 班点 — *hanten* — spot, speck
剖	剖	1805; 18/8.　BŌ dissect [P'OU¹,³ ・ R knife & P*]「postmortem 遺体解剖 — *itai kaibō* — remains/corpse dissection, 解剖学 — *kaibōgaku* — anatomy
肪	肪	1806; 130/4.　BŌ fat, grease [FANG² ・ R flesh & P*] 脂肪過多 — *shibō kata* — fatty excess, obesity 脂肪蓄積 — *shibō chikuseki* — fat accumulation
穫	穫	1807; 115/13.　KAKU harvest [HOU¹ ・ R grain & P*] 収穫予想 — *shūkaku yosō* — harvest estimate 収穫が少ない — *shūkaku ga sukunai* — have a bad/poor harvest
賠	賠	1808; 154/8.　BAI compensate [P'EI² ・ R money & P*]「tion 損害賠償 — *songai baishō* — damage compensa-

衷	衷	1809; 2/8. CHŪ inner/true feelings [CHUNG[1] • I: inside/inner 3–6 (see 1809) robe 1–2 & 7–10 → what is near/in one's heart; also R clothes & P*] ⌐be eclectic 折衷する — setchū suru — make a compromise, 衷心／衷情 — chūshin/chūjō — inner true feelings
猶	猶 獝	1810; 94/9. YŪ hesitate, delay; moreover, still [YU[2] • R dog & P*] ⌐ment, probation 執行猶予 — shikkō yūyo — executive postpone- 猶予出来る — yūyo dekiru — deferrable
犧	犧 犠	1811; 93/13. GI sacrifice [HSI[1] • R ox & P*] 犠打 — gida — sacrifice hit (baseball)
牲	牲	1812; 93/5. SEI sacrifice [SHENG[1] • R ox & P*] 犠牲的精神 — giseiteki seishin — sacrificing spirit 犠牲者 — giseisha — victim
矛	矛 鉾	1813; 110/0. MU, hoko halberd [MAO[2] • D: long-handled pointed weapon; P*] 矛を収める — hoko o osameru — lay down/put aside one's arms 矛先 — hokosaki — the point of a spear/argument
盾	盾	1814; 4/8. JUN, tate shield ⌐P*] [TUN[4] • I: a cover/shield 1–4 over the eyes 5–9; 矛盾 — mujun — contradiction 盾の半面を見る — tate no hanmen o miru — see only one side (of the shield)
斗	斗	1815; 68/0. TO* old unit of capacity [18 liters] [TOU[3] • D: a scoop with handle 4 P*] 北斗〔七〕星 — hokuto[shichi]sei — the Great Bear, 斗酒 — toshu — kegs of sake ⌊the Plow
升	升	1816; 4/3. SHŌ*, masu old unit of capacity [1.8 liters] ⌐of 1815]; P*] [SHENG[1] • D: the contents 1 of a scoop 2–4 (vrt. 一升びん — isshō-bin — a one-shō bottle of (sake) 酒一升 — sake isshō — one shō of sake

勺	勺	1817; 20/1. SHAKU* old unit of capacity [0.018 liters]/area [330 sq. cm.] ⌐tainer; P*] [SHUO², ⁴, SHAO² • D: the contents 3 of a con- 五勺 — go-shaku — five shaku
斤	斤	1818; 69/0. KIN* old unit of weight [600 gr.]; ax [CHIN¹ • D: an ax/adz with blade 1–2 & curved 一斤 — ikkin — one kin ⌐handle 3–4; P*] 斤量 — kinryō — weight
匁	匁	1819; 4/3. monme old unit of weight [3.75 gr.] [Combination of MON 1, top of 2, & 3–4 (vrt. of 71), & katakana sign me (2nd part of 2, & 4)] 百匁 — hyaku-monme — one hundred monme
厘	厘	1820; 27/7. RIN* old unit of money [0.001 yen]/ length [0.303 mm.] [LI² • R cliff & P*] 厘毛 — rinmō — farthing, trifle 一銭五厘 — issen gorin — one sen & five rin
窯	窯	1821; 116/10. YŌ, kama kiln [YAO² • R hole & P*] 窯業 — yōgyō — ceramic manufacture/industry 明朝の名窯 — Min-chō no meiyō — a famous kiln of the Ming period
畝	畝	1822; 8/8. se old unit for land area [99.3 sq. meters]; [MU³ • I] ⌐une ridge (between fields) 一反二畝 — ittan nise — 1 tan 2 se (in area) 畝織り — une-ori — rep, ribbed fabric
渦	渦	1823; 85/9. KA, uzu whirlpool [WO¹ • R water & P*] 戦渦 — senka — evils/horrors of war 渦巻 — uzumaki — swirl, convolution
涯	涯	1824; 85/8. GAI water's edge, extremity [YAI², YA² • R water & P*] 生涯 — shōgai — life, lifetime 際涯 — saigai — limits, end

挑	挑	1825; 64/6. CHŌ inflict/press on (someone) [T'IAO¹,³ · R hand & P*] 挑発する — *chōhatsu suru* — arouse, stir up 挑戦者 — *chōsensha* — challenger
亭	亭	1826; 8/7. TEI* arbor, hostelry [T'ING² · R lid & P*; also D: ab. of 160 = tall 亭主 — *teishu* — husband, host ⌊building] 料亭 — *ryōtei* — Japanese-style restaurant
矯	矯	1827; 111/12. KYŌ straighten, correct [CHIAO³ · R arrow & P* bent] 矯正する — *kyōsei suru* — reform, correct 矯風 — *kyōfū* — reform of morals
朴	朴	1828; 75/2. BOKU plain, simple, straightforward [P'U²,³ · R tree & P*] 素朴な — *soboku na* — simple, naive 質朴な — *shitsuboku na* — unsophisticated
厄	厄	1829; 27/2. YAKU* calamity, misfortune, bad luck [O⁴ · I: a kneeling/injured figure 3–4 below a 厄介 — *yakkai* — trouble, burden ⌊cliff 1–2] 厄払い — *yakubarai* — exorcism
竜	竜 龍 竜	1830; 212/0. RYŪ*, RYŌ, *tatsu* dragon; (see also 1992) [tail 10; P*] [LUNG² · D: head 1–5, body 6–9 and curled 竜宮 — *Ryūgū* — Dragon's (Sea-god's) palace 竜巻 — *tatsumaki* — water/wind spout
据	据	1831; 64/8. *su(eru)* place, position, set up [CHÜ¹ · R hand & P*] 据え置く — *sue-oku* — leave as it is 据え付け — *suetsuke* — installation
殻	殻 殻	1832; 79/7. KAKU, *kara* shell, husk, slough [K'O², K'E², CH'ÜEH⁴ · I; P*] 貝殻 — *kaigara* — shell 殻を破る — *kara o yaburu* — cast off shell/skin

洪	洪	1833; 85/6. KŌ flood, greatness [HUNG[2] · R water & P*] 洪水 — *kōzui* — flood 洪恩 — *kōon* — great benevolence
桟	桟	1834; 75/6. SAN* door bolt, framework [CHAN[4] · R tree & P*] 桟橋 — *sanbashi* — pier, jetty 障子の桟 — *shōji no san* — *shōji* frame
酌	酌	1835; 164/3. SHAKU serve/draw wine [CHO[2], CHAO[1,4] · R wine jug & P* filled container (see 1817)] 晩酌 — *banshaku* — evening drink 独酌 — *dokushaku* — drinking alone
釣	釣 釣	1836; 167/3. *tsuri* change (in money), angling [TIAO[4] · R metal & P] 釣銭 — *tsurisen* — change 沖釣り — *okizuri* — offshore fishing
堀	堀	1837; 32/8. *hori* moat [K'U[1] · R earth & P*] 釣堀 — *tsuribori* — fishing pond 堀端 — *horibata* — side of moat
僕	僕	1838; 9/12. BOKU* (boys' word) I, me; servant [P'U[2,3] · R man & P*] 従僕 — *jūboku* — servant, attendant 僕達 — *bokutachi* — (boys' word) we
偵	偵	1839; 9/9. TEI spy, investigate [CHEN[1], CHENG[1] · R man & P*] 探偵小説 — *tantei shōsetsu* — detective novel 偵察する — *teisatsu suru* — scout, reconnoiter
泥	泥	1840; 85/5. DEI, *doro* mud [NI[2,4] · R water & P*] 泥炭沼 — *deitan-numa* — peat bog 泥棒 — *dorobō* — thief

披	披	1841; 64/5.　HI open up [P'EI¹, P'I¹ ・ R hand & P*] 披露宴 — *hirōen* — reception [wedding, etc.] 披歴する — *hireki suru* — express
俸	俸	1842; 9/8.　HŌ salary [FENG⁴ ・ R man & P*] 俸給 — *hōkyū* — salary, pay 年俸 — *nenpō* — annual salary
尚	尚 尚	1843; 42/5.　SHŌ respect; still (more); long-con- [SHANG⁴ ・ I; P*]　　　　⌐tinued; (see also 1948) 尚早の — *shōsō no* — premature, untimely 尚武の気 — *shōbu no ki* — martial spirit, mili- tarism
壌	壌 壌	1844; 32/13.　JŌ soil, earth [JANG³ ・ R earth & P*] 土壌 — *dojō* — soil　　　　⌐heaven & earth 天壌無窮 — *tenjō mukyū* — limitless/eternal as
斉	斉 齊	1845; 210/0.　SEI, SAI equal, level; arrange; (see [CH'I¹, CHAI¹ ・ D; P*]　　　　⌐also 1958) 均斉 — *kinsei* — symmetry 斉唱 — *seishō* — unison
渓	渓 溪	1846; 85/8.　KEI valley, ravine [CH'I¹, HSI¹ ・ R water & P*] 渓流 — *keiryū* — mountain torrent/stream 渓谷 — *keikoku* — valley
杉	杉	1847; 75/3.　*sugi* cryptomeria, Japanese cedar; (see [SHA¹, SHAN¹ ・ R tree & P]　　　　⌐also 1941) 杉板 — *sugiita* — cedar board 杉並木 — *suginamiki* — avenue of cedar trees
汁	汁	1848; 85/2.　JŪ, *shiru* soup, juice, sap [CHIH¹ ・ R water & P*] 墨汁 — *bokujū* — India ink 汁粉 — *shiruko* — red-bean soup with rice cake

宵	宵 寶	1849; 40/7. SHŌ, *yoi* early evening [HSIAO¹ • R roof & P*] 春宵 — *shunshō* — spring evening 宵越しの — *yoigoshi no* — kept/left overnight
戻	戻 戾	1850; 63/3. *modo(su)* (vt.) return, vomit; *modo(ru)* (vi.) return ⌈the door/gate 1–4 on its return⌉ [LI⁴ • I: a dog 5–7 (ab. of 578) comes in under 払い戻す — *haraimodosu* — pay back, refund 呼び戻す — *yobimodosu* — call back
又	又	1851; 29/0. *mata* again, also, then too [YU⁴ • D: right hand] 又貸し — *matagashi* — sublease 又隣 — *matadonari* — next door but one
丹	丹	1852; 4/3. TAN cinnabar, red [TAN¹ • D & S: red mineral 3 & the pit from which it is obtained 1–2 & 4] 丹念に — *tannen ni* — carefully, elaborately 丹精 — *tansei* — sincerity
但	但	1853; 9/5. *tada(shi)* but, except that [TAN⁴ • I] 但書き — *tadashigaki* — proviso 但馬 — *Tajima* — pn.
堪	堪	1854; 32/9. KAN, *ta(eru)* be resistant/equal (to), [K'AN¹ • R earth & P*] ⌊hold out (against) 堪忍 — *kannin* — pardon, patience 堪能 — *kannō* (lit.)/*tannō* — skill, mastery
寡	寡	1855; 40/11. KA alone, widowed; few, small [KUA³ • R roof & P* 3–14 (vrt. of 163)] 寡婦 — *kafu, yamome* — widow 寡黙な — *kamoku na* — taciturn, reserved
唐	唐	1856; 53/7. TŌ* T'ang [Dynasty/China]; *Kara* [T'ANG² • I; P*] ⌊Cathay, China 遣唐使 — *kentōshi* — envoy to T'ang China 唐詩 — *tōshi* — T'ang-dynasty poem/poetry

悦	悦 悦	1857; 61/7. ETSU* rejoice [YÜEH⁴ • R heart & P*] 満悦 の — man'etsu no — delighted, satisfied 喜悦 — kietsu — joy, rapture
濫	濫	1858; 85/14. RAN inundate, excess, wanton [LAN⁴ • R water & P*] 濫用する — ran'yō suru — abuse, misuse 濫費する — ranpi suru — waste, dissipate
煩	煩	1859; 86/9. HAN*, BON trouble, worry; wazura- (washii) troublesome, annoying [FAN² • I: fire & head 5–13 = feverish headache] 煩雑 — hanzatsu — trouble, complexity 煩忙 な — hanbō na — busy
箇	箇	1860; 118/8. KO, KA item; unit for counting mis- cellaneous objects [KO⁴, KE⁴ • R bamboo & P*] 箇条 — kajō — items, articles 箇数 — kosū — number of articles
脹	脹	1861; 130/8. CHŌ swell up [CHANG⁴ • R flesh & P*] 膨脹する — bōchō suru (vi.) — expand, swell
謁	謁	1862; 149/8. ETSU* an audience (with emperor, etc.) [YEH⁴ • R words & P*] 拝謁 — haietsu — audience (with emperor) 謁見室 — ekkenshitsu — audience chamber
逓	逓 遞 遞	1863; 162/7. TEI proceed by relays/stages [TI⁴ • R proceed & P] 報酬逓減 の 法則 — hōshū teigen no hōsoku — law of diminishing returns 「ward 逓送する — teisō suru — convey (by post), for-
遵	遵	1864; 162/12. JUN obey, follow, observe [TSUN¹ • R proceed & P*] 遵守する — junshu suru — obey, observe 遵法精神 — junpō seishin — law-abiding spirit

且	且	1865; 1/4. *katsu* furthermore, besides [CHʼIEH³ • D→B] 且又 — *katsumata* — moreover
璽	璽	1866; 1/18. JI imperial seal [HSI³ • R jewel & P*] 御璽 — *gyoji* — imperial seal
劾	劾	1867; 19/6. GAI investigate wrongdoing [HO²،⁴ • R strength & P*] 弾劾する — *dangai suru* — impeach, denounce 劾奏する — *gaisō suru* — report an official's offence to the emperor
嚇	嚇	1868; 30/14. KAKU threaten　　　　　⌈rage; & P*] [HO⁴, HSIA⁴ • I; shout 1–3 in a red-hot 4–17 威嚇する — *ikaku suru* — menace, threaten, in- 嚇怒 — *kakudo* — fierce anger　　　　⌊timidate
奴	奴	1869; 34/2. DO servant　　　　　⌈a slave; P*] [NU² • I: woman & hand 4–5 = a seized woman, 奴僕 — *doboku* — slave, manservant 奴鳴る — *donaru* — roar, shout
罷	罷	1870; 122/10. HI stop, withdraw [PA⁴ • R net & P*] 罷免する — *himen suru* — dismiss 罷業 — *higyō* — strike, walkout
迅	迅	1871; 162/3. JIN fast, quick [HSÜN⁴, HSIN⁴ • R proceed & P] 迅速な — *jinsoku na* — swift, prompt 迅雷 — *jinrai* — thunderclap, suddenness
錬	錬	1872; 167/8. REN temper/forge (metal), polish, [LIEN⁴ • R metal & P*]　　　　　⌊train 錬金術 — *renkinjutsu* — alchemy 精錬所 — *seirenjo* — refinery, smeltery

隷	隷 隷	1873; 171/8. REI slave, follower [LI⁴ • R capture & P*] 奴隷 — *dorei* — slave 隷属 — *reizoku* — subordination
頒	頒	1874; 181/4. HAN divide, distribute [PAN¹ • R head & P*] 頒布する — *hanpu suru* — distribute
爵	爵 爵	1875; 87/14. SHAKU* peerage, noble rank [CHÜEH² • I] 爵位 — *shakui* — peerage 伯爵 — *hakushaku* — a count
朕	朕 朕	1876; 130/6. CHIN* We (the Emperor) [CHEN⁴ • I; P*]
虞	虞 虞	1877; 141/7. *osore* anxiety, apprehension [YÜ² • R tiger & P*]
附	附	1878; 170/5. FU attach/fix to (= 259, q.v.) [FU⁴ • R mound & P*]
々	々	1879; 4/2. Repetition sign used with Chinese 密々に — *mitsumitsu ni* — secretly └characters 黙々と — *mokumoku to* — silently
〆	〆	1880; 3/1. *shime* total figure; bundle, ream; *shi-(meru)* total up 〆切 — *shimekiri* — shut, closing, time limit 〆高 — *shimedaka* — total

辻	辻	1881; 162/2. *tsuji* crossroads [· · I: where one can proceed 3–5 in any of four directions 1–2] 辻堂 — *tsujidō* — wayside shrine 辻強盗 — *tsujigōtō* — highway robbery
凸	凸	1882; 2/4. TOTSU, *deko* prominent forehead [TIEH[4] · D] 凸面鏡 — *totsumenkyō* — convex mirror 凸版印刷 — *toppan insatsu* — relief printing
凹	凹	1883; 17/3. Ō, *boko, heko(mi)* hollow, dent, de- [YAO[1,2] · D]　　　　　　　　⌐pression 凹凸 — *ōtotsu* — unevenness 凹眼鏡 — *ōgankyō* — concave glasses
尻	尻	1884; 44/2. KŌ, *shiri* buttocks [K'AO[1] · R bent figure & P*] 尻押し — *shirioshi* — boosting, pushing 尻軽な — *shirigaru na* — wanton, loose
詣	詣	1885; 149/6. KEI, *mō(deru/de)* visit a shrine/temple [I[4], YI[4] · R words & P*] 参詣する — *sankei suru* — make a visit (to a shrine/temple)　⌐the year/after birth 初詣で — *hatsu-mōde* — first shrine/temple visit of
叱	叱	1886; 30/2. SHITSU, *shika(ru)* scold, rebuke [CH'IH[4] · R voice & P*] 叱責する — *shisseki suru* — rebuke, reprove 叱り飛ばす — *shikari-tobasu* — scold severely
爪	爪	1887; 87/0. SŌ, *tsume* nail, claw, hooked catch [CHAO[3], CHUA[3] · D: a hand with fingers stretched to pick something up; P*] 爪弾き — *tsumahajiki suru* — fillip, shun, scorn 爪跡 — *tsumeato* — nailmark, scratch
瓜	瓜	1888; 97/0. KA, *uri* melon [KUA[1] · D: a melon 4–5 hanging from the vine 西瓜 — *suika* — watermelon　　⌐1–3 & 6; P*] 瓜実顔 — *urizanegao* — oval face

岡	岡	1889; 13/6. KŌ, *oka* hill, rise [KANG¹ • R water & P*] 静岡 — *Shizuoka* — pn. 岡焼き — *okayaki* — jealousy
肌	肌	1890; 130/2. KI, *hada* skin, texture [CHI¹ • R flesh & P*] 肌着 — *hadagi* — underwear ⌈skin) 肌触り — *hadazawari* — the touch/feel (on the
皿	皿	1891; 108/0. *sara* dish [MIN³ • D; P*] 皿洗い — *sara-arai* — dishwashing ⌈tables 野菜一皿 — *yasai hito-sara* — one dish of vege-
旦	旦	1892; 72/1. TAN dawn [TAN⁴ • I: the sun 1–4 rising over the horizon 5; 元旦 — *gantan* — New Year's day ⌊P*] 旦夕 — *tanseki* — day & night
阪	阪	1893; 170/4. HAN, *saka* slope (= 343) [FAN³ • R mound & P*] 大阪 — *Ōsaka* — pn. 阪神 — *Hanshin* — Ōsaka-Kōbe
或	或	1894; 62/4. WAKU, *a(ru)* a [certain]; *arui(wa)* or, [HUO⁴ • I; P*] ⌊perhaps 或る者 — *aru mono* — a certain person 或る時 — *aru toki* — once
匂	匂	1895; 20/2. *nio(u)*, *nioi* smell, scent [- • I: what envelops 1–2 a kneeling figure 匂い袋 — *nioibukuro* — sachet ⌊3–4] 新鮮な匂い — *shinsen na nioi* — fresh smell
註	註	1896; 85/3. CHŪ* notes, annotation; *chū(suru)* [CHU⁴ • R words & P*] ⌊annotate 註記する — *chūki suru* — record, write down 註釈 — *chūshaku* — commentary, notes

宛	宛	1897; 40/5. EN, *a(teru)* address letter, *-ate* ad- [WAN³ · R roof & P*] ⌐dressed to 宛転たる — *enten taru* — smoothly rolling 宛名 — *atena* — address
崎	崎	1898; 72/2. KI, *saki* cape, promontory [CH'I² · R mountain & P*] 崎戸 — *Sakito* — pn. 長崎 — *Nagasaki* — pn. 広崎 — *Hirosaki* — sn.
闇	闇	1899; 169/9. AN, *yami* darkness, black market [AN⁴ · R gate & P*] 闇取引 — *yami-torihiki* — shady dealings/trans- 暗闇 — *kurayami* — darkness ⌐actions
枕	枕	1900; 75/4. CHIN, *makura* pillow [CHEN³ · R tree & P*] 枕詞 — *makurakotoba* — a fixed poetic epithet 枕許 — *makuramoto* — bedside
嫌	嫌	1901; 38/10. KEN, *kira(u/i)* dislike; *iya (na)* dis- liked, disagreeable [HSIEN² · R woman & P*] 嫌疑 — *kengi* — suspicion 機嫌 — *kigen* — state of health/mood
嵐	嵐	1902; 46/9. RAN, *arashi* storm [LAN² · I: a mountain 1–3 wind 4–12; P*] 嵐山 — *Arashiyama* — pn. 政界の嵐 — *seikai no arashi* — political storm
貰	貰	1903; 154/5. SEI, *mora(u)* receive [SHIH⁴ · R money & P*] 貰い涙を流す — *morai-namida o nagasu* — shed tears of/in sympathy 友人に探して貰う — *yūjin ni sagashite morau* — have a friend look for it (for you)
泡	泡	1904; 85/5. HŌ, *awa* bubble, foam [P'AO⁴ · R water & P*] 泡立つ — *awadatsu* — foam, froth, lather 泡雪 — *awayuki* — light snow

嘘	嘘	1905; 30/12. KYO, *uso* lie [HSÜ¹ • R mouth & P* empty] 真赤な嘘 — *makka na uso* — barefaced lie 嘘つき — *usotsuki* — liar
頃	頃	1906; 21/9. KEI, *koro* (period of) time; -*goro* about [CH'ING³ • R head & P*] └[of time] 今頃 — *imagoro* — (about) this time 何時頃 — *nanji-/itsu-goro* — about what time?
靴	靴	1907; 177/4. KA, *kutsu* shoes, boots [HSÜEH¹ • R rawhide & P*] 革靴 — *kawagutsu* — leather shoes 靴下 — *kutsushita* — socks, stockings
蔭	蔭	1908; 140/10. IN, *kage* shade, help, kind interest [YIN⁴ • R grass & P*] 御蔭様で — *okagesama de* — thanks to (a person) 日蔭で — *hikage de* — in the shade
伊	伊	1909; 9/4. I (ab. for *Itaria/Itarii*) Italy [I¹, YI¹ • R man & P] 伊太郎 — *Itarō* — mn. 伊勢 — *Ise* — psn. 伊達 — *Date* — sn.
郁	郁	1910; 163/6. IKU cultured; scented [YÜ⁴ • R city & P*] 郁子 — *Ikuko* — fn. 郁夫 — *Ikuo* — mn. 郁次郎 — *Ikujirō* — mn.
寅	寅	1911; 40/8. IN, *tora* 3rd sign of the zodiac, tiger [YIN² • I; P*] 寅吉 — *Torakichi* — mn. 寅雄 — *Torao* — mn. 寅治 — *Toraji* — mn.
胤	胤	1912; 4/8. IN, *tane* descendant, offspring [YIN⁴ • I] 胤信 — *Tanenobu* — mn. 義胤 — *Yoshitane* — mn. 雅胤 — *Masatane* — mn.

亦	亦	1913; 8/4. EKI, *mata* also, again [I[4], YI[4] • D & S; P*] 亦人 — *Matahito* — mn. 亦三郎 — *Matasaburō* — mn. 亦野 — *Matano* — sn.
艶	艷 豓色	1914; 139/13. EN, *tsuya* fn., gloss, shine [YEN[4] • I: an abundance 1–13 (see 624) of color/ お艶 — *O-Tsuya* — fn. ⌊good looks 14–19; P*] 艶子 — *Tsuyako* — fn. 艶太 — *Tsuyata* — mn.
嘉	嘉	1915; 32/11. KA fine, happy, auspicious; *yoshi* [CHIA[1] • I: strength 10–11, & joy 1–9 & 12–14 嘉治郎 — *Kajirō* — mn. ⌊(see 564); P*] 嘉子 — *Yoshiko* — fn. 嘉基 — *Yoshimoto* — mn.
亥	亥	1916; 8/4. GAI, *i* 12th sign of the zodiac, hog [HAI[4] • D; P*] 亥三 — *Izō/Isamu* — mn. 亥三郎 — *Isaburō* — mn. 亥吉 — *Ikichi* — mn.
鶴	鶴 鶴	1917; 196/10. KAKU, *tsuru* crane, stork [HAO[2] • R bird & P*] 鶴吉 — *Tsurukichi* — mn. 千鶴 — *Chizuru* — fn. 舞鶴 — *Maizuru* — pn.
巖	巖 巖	1918; 46/17. GAN, *iwao* mn., *iwa* crag, rock [YEN[2] • R mountain & P*] 巖太郎 — *Gantarō* — mn. 巖谷 — *Iwaya* — sn. 巖崎 — *Iwasaki* — sn.
毅	毅	1919; 79/11. KI strong; *Takeshi/Tsuyoshi* mn.; [I[4], YI[4] • R kill & P] ⌊*take, tsuyo* 正毅 — *Masaki* — mn. 毅雄 — *Takeo/Tsuyoo* — mn.
磯	磯	1920; 112/12. KI, *iso* beach, strand [CHI[1] • R stone & P*] 磯吉 — *Isokichi* — mn. 磯永 — *Isonaga* — sn. 大磯 — *Ōiso* — psn.

亀	亀 龜	1921; 213/0. KI, *kame* tortoise, turtle [KUEI[1] • D] 亀三 — *Kamezō* — mn. 亀五郎 — *Kamegorō* — mn. 亀沢 — *Kamezawa* — sn.
橘	橘	1922; 75/12. KITSU, *tachibana* psn., mandarin [CHÜ[2] • R tree & P] ⌊orange 橘田 — *Kitsuda* — sn. 橘谷 — *Kitsuya* — sn. 橘屋 — *Tachibanaya* — sn.
匡	匡	1923; 22/4. KYŌ true, correct; *Tadasu/Tadashi* mn.; [K'UANG[1] • R basket & P*] ⌊*masa* 匡子 — *Masako* — fn. 匡四郎 — *Kyōshirō* — mn. 匡助 — *Kyōsuke* — mn.
欣	欣	1924; 69/4. KIN rejoice; *yoshi* [HSIN[1] • R open mouth & P*] 欣一 — *Kin'ichi* — mn. 欣造 — *Kinzō* — mn. 欣子 — *Yoshiko* — fn.
欽	欽	1925; 167/4. KIN respect [CH'IN[1] • R open mouth & P*] 欽二 — *Kinji* — mn. 欽太郎 — *Kintarō* — mn. 欽明 — *Kinmei* — mn.
錦	錦	1926; 167/8. KIN, *nishiki* brocade [CHIN[3] • R cloth & P* 1–8 gold/metal] 錦次 — *Kinji* — mn. 錦太郎 — *Kintarō* — mn. 錦部 — *Nishikibe* — sn.
駒	駒	1927; 187/5. KU, *koma* pony [CHÜ[1] • R horse & P*] 駒子 — *Komako* — fn. 駒込 — *Komagome* — pn. 駒吉 — *Komakichi* — mn.
圭	圭	1928; 32/3. KEI, *tama* jewel [KUEI[1] • D: jade scepter; P*] 圭三 — *Keizō* — mn. 圭子 — *Keiko* — fn. 圭雄 — *Tamao* — mn.

桂	桂	1929; 75/6. KEI, *katsura* fn./mn./psn., Judas/cin- [KUEI⁴ • R tree & P*] ⌐namon tree 桂 皮 油 — *keihiyu* — cinnamon oil ⌐Palace 桂 離 宮 — *Katsura Rikyū* — Katsura Detached
馨	馨	1930; 186/11. KEI fragrance; *Kaoru* msn.; *yoshi* [HSIN¹ • I; P*] 馨 一 — *Keiichi* — mn.
彦	彦 彦	1931; 117/4. GEN, *hiko* (old word for) man, boy [YEN⁴ • R light rays & P*] 彦 部 — *Hikobe* — sn. 勝 彦 — *Katsuhiko* — mn. 毅 彦 — *Takehiko* — mn.
虎	虎	1932; 141/2. KO, *tora* fn., tiger; *Takeshi* mn. [HU³ • D; P*] 虎 尾 — *Torao* — mn. 虎 明 — *Toraakira* — mn. 虎 岩 — *Toraiwa* — sn.
吾	吾	1933; 1/6. GO, *waga* my; *ware* I; *a* [WU² • R mouth & P*] 吾 郎 — *Gorō* — mn. 吾 平 — *Ahira* — pn. 吾 妻 — *Azuma* — sn.
亨	亨	1934; —. KYŌ, KŌ, pass through, offer up; *Tōru* [HENG¹,² • D: P*] ⌐mn.; *michi, yuki* 亨 吉 — *Kōkichi* — mn. 亨 子 — *Michiko* — fn. 亨 江 — *Yukie* — fn.
亘	亘	1935; 1/5. KŌ, *wata(ru)* extend/range (over); *Wa- taru/Watari* mn. [KENG⁴ • I: the two extremities 1 & 6 of the crescent moon 2–5 (vrt. of 13); P*] 亘 理 — *Watari* — sn.
宏	宏	1936; 40/4. KŌ wide, expansive; *Hiroshi* mn.; *hiro* [HUNG² • R roof & P*] 宏 平 — *Kōhei* — mn. 宏 枝 — *Hiroe* — fn. 宏 富 — *Hiroto* — mn.

弘	弘	1937; 57/2. KŌ wide, expansive; *Hiroshi* mn.; *hiro* [HUNG² • R bow & P* bend] 弘道館 — *Kōdōkan* — pn. 弘世 — *Hirose* — psn. 弘岡 — *Hirooka* — sn.
晃	晃	1938; 72/6. KŌ brightness; *Akira* mn.; *aki, teru* [HUANG³ • R sun & P* shine] 晃治 — *Kōji* — mn. 晃夫 — *Akio* — mn. 晃年 — *Terutoshi* — mn.
浩	浩	1939; 85/7. KŌ wide, expansive; *Hiroshi* mn.; *hiro* [HAO⁴ • R water & P*] 浩一郎 — *Kōichirō* — mn. 浩二 — *Kōji* — mn. 浩子 — *Hiroko* — fn.
哉	哉	1940; 24/7. SAI, *kana* (lit.) alas!; *Hajime* mn.; *ya, chika* [TSAI¹ • R mouth & P*] 哉女 — *Kaname* — fn.
杉	杉	1941; 75/3. *sugi* sn., cryptomeria, Japanese cedar; [SHA¹, SHAN¹ • R tree & P*] (see also 1847) 杉山 — *Sugiyama* — sn. 杉森 — *Sugimori* — sn. 上杉 — *Uesugi* — sn.
之	之	1942; 8/1. SHI, *kore* this; *no, yuki, yoshi* [CHIH¹ • D] 虎之助 — *Toranosuke* — mn. 貫之 — *Tsurayuki* — mn. 之元 — *Yoshimoto* — mn.
只	只	1943; 30/2. *tada* only, free [CHIH³ • I] 只八 — *Tadahachi* — mn. 只見 — *Tadami* — psn. 只野 — *Tadano* — sn.
巳	巳	1944; 49/0. SHI, *mi* 6th sign of the zodiac, serpent [SZU⁴, ssu⁴ • D: big-headed snake] 巳代治 — *Miyoji* — mn. 巳野 — *Mino* — sn. 巳喜男 — *Mikio* — mn.

爾	爾	1945; I'/13. JI, *Chikashi* mn.; *chika* [ERH[3] · D: spinning wheel; P*] 爾来 — *jirai* — since then 爾後 — *jigo* — thereafter
須	須	1946; 59/9. SU [used for its sound] [HSÜ[1] · D: a head/face 4–12 with whiskers 1–3] 須之内 — *Sunouchi* — sn. 須崎 — *Susaki* — psn. 横須賀 — *Yokosuka* — pn.
淳	淳	1947; 85/8. JUN mn., pure, sincere; *Atsushi* mn.; *Kiyoshi* mn.; *atsu, kiyo* [CH'UN[2] · R water & P*] 淳之助 — *Junnosuke* — mn. 淳国 — *Atsukuni* — mn. 淳浩 — *Kiyohiro* — mn.
尚	尚	1948; 42/5. SHŌ, *Hisashi* mn.; *Naoshi* mn.; *nao, hisa;* (see also 1843) [SHANG[4] · I; P*] 尚一 — *Naoichi* — mn. 尚住 — *Naozumi* — mn. 尚嘉 — *Hisayoshi* — mn.
庄	庄	1949; 53/3. SHŌ countryside [CHUANG[1] · I: lean-to 1–3 & earth = farmhouse; P*] 庄司 — *Shōji* — sn. 庄野 — *Shōno* — sn. 庄蔵 — *Shōzō* — mn.
昌	昌	1950; 72/4. SHŌ brightness; *masa* [CH'ANG[1] · I: two suns; P*] 昌吉 — *Shōkichi* — mn. 昌三 — *Masami* — mn. 昌岡 — *Masaoka* — sn.
丞	丞	1951; 1/4. JŌ help; *suke* [CH'ENG[2] · I; P*] 鉄之丞 — *Tetsunojō* — mn. 兵丞 — *Hyōsuke* — mn. 伊之丞 — *Inosuke* — mn.
穰	穰 穰	1952; 115/13. JŌ abundance; *Minoru* mn.; *shige* [JANG[2] · R grain & P*] 豊穣 — *Toyoshige* — mn.

晋	晋 晉	1953; 1/9. SHIN advance; *Susumu* mn. [CHIN⁴ · I; P*] 晋之助 — *Shinnosuke* — mn. 晋次郎 — *Shinjirō* — mn.
辰	辰	1954; 161/0. SHIN, *tatsu* 5th sign of the zodiac, [CH'EN² · D; P*] ⌊dragon 辰之助 — *Tatsunosuke* — mn. 辰巳 — *Tatsumi* — sn. 辰岡 — *Tatsuoka* — sn.
甚	甚	1955; 2/8. JIN, *hanaha(da)* greatly, extremely [SHEN⁴ · I: a big container 1–6 on a stove 6–9; 甚三郎 — *Jinzaburō* — mn. ⌊P*] 甚太郎 — *Jintarō* — mn. 甚吾 — *Jingo* — mn.
瑞	瑞	1956; 96/9. ZUI auspicious; *tama, mizu* [JUI⁴ · R jewel & P*] 瑞併 — *Tamao/Mizuo* — mn. 瑞西 — *Suisu* — pn.: Switzerland
靖	靖	1957; 117/8. SEI, *yasu(i)* peaceful [CHING⁴ · R stand & P*] 靖国神社 — *Yasukuni Jinja* — Yasukuni Shrine 靖道 — *Yasumichi* — mn.
斉	斉 齊	1958; 210/0. SAI, SEI, *Hitoshi* mn.; *nari;* (see also [CH'I², CHAI¹ · D; P*] ⌊1845) 斉宮 — *Saigū* — sn. 斉藤 — *Saitō* — sn. 斉匡 — *Narimasa* — mn.
仙	仙	1959; 9/3. SEN hermit, mystic [HSIEN¹ · R man & P* mountain] 仙四郎 — *Senshirō* — mn. 仙台 — *Sendai* — pn. 仙波 — *Senba/Sennami* — sn.
惣	惣	1960; 61/8. SŌ all, general [TSUNG³ · R heart & P*] 惣一 — *Sōichi* — mn. 惣三郎 — *Sōsaburō* — mn. 惣助 — *Sōsuke* — mn.

聰	聡 聰	1961; 128/8.　SŌ, *sato(i)* wise, quick; *Satoshi* mn.; ⌞*aki* [TS'UNG¹ · R ear & P*] 聡敏 な — *sōbin na* — clever, quick-minded 聡善 — *Akiyoshi* — mn.
乃	乃	1962; 4/1.　DAI, NAI, *no* [NAI³ · D: the loose string 2–3 of a bow 1] A 乃至 B — A *naishi* B — from A to B 乃木坂 — *Nogizaka*— pn.
琢	琢	1963; 96/8.　TAKU gem cutting/polishing [CHO² · R jewel & P*] 琢之助— *Takunosuke* — mn.
智	智	1964; 72/8.　CHI* wisdom; *Satoru* mn. [CHIH⁴ · R sun & P*] 国民 の 智恵 — *kokumin no chie* — wisdom of the 智津子 — *Chizuko* — fn.　　　　　　⌞people
丑	丑	1965; 1/3.　CHŪ, *ushi* 2nd sign of the zodiac, ox [CH'OU³ · D→B] 丑二 — *Ushiji* — mn. 丑次郎 — *Ushijirō* — mn.
猪	猪 猪	1966; 94/8.　CHO, *i, inoshishi* wild boar [CHU¹ · R dog & P*] 猪首 — *ikubi* — short & thick/bull neck 猪飼 — *Ikai* — sn.
暢	暢	1967; 2/13.　CHŌ stretch, extend; *nobu* [CH'ANG³,⁴ · R sun & P*] 暢気 な — *nonki na* — happy-go-lucky 暢夫 — *Nobuo* — mn.
肇	肇	1968; 129/8.　CHŌ beginning; *Hajime* mn.; *hatsu* [CHAO⁴ · R writing & P*] 肇国 — *chōkoku* — founding a nation/state 肇子 — *Hatsuko* — fn.

蔦	蔦	1969; 140/11. CHŌ, *tsuta* ivy, creeper [NIAO³ • R grass & P*] 蔦沢 — *Tsutazawa* — sn. 蔦松 — *Tsutamatsu* — sn. 蔦屋 — *Tsutaya* — sn.
蝶	蝶	1970; 142/9. CHŌ butterfly [TIEH², T'IEH³ • R insect & P*] 蝶子 — *Chōko* — fn. 蝶蝶 — *chōchō* — butterfly
鯛	鯛	1971; 195/8. CHŌ, *tai* sea bream [T'IAO² • R fish & P*] 鯛二 — *Taiji* — mn. 鯛飯 — *taimeshi* — sea bream pieces with rice
悌	悌	1972; 61/7. TEI obedience to one's seniors [T'I⁴ • R heart & P* younger brother] 孝悌 — *kōtei* — filial piety & brotherly love 悌吉 — *Teikichi* — mn.
禎	禎 禎	1973; 113/9. TEI good fortune; *yoshi* [CHEN¹, CHENG¹ • R god & P*] 禎次 — *Teiji* — mn. 禎次郎 — *Teijirō* — mn. 禎栄 — *Yoshie* — fn.
桐	桐	1974; 75/6. TŌ, *kiri* paulownia tree [T'UNG² • R tree & P*] 桐林 — *Kiribayashi* — sn. 桐原 — *Kirihara* — sn. 桐島 — *Kirishima* — sn.
藤	藤	1975; 140/15. TŌ, *fuji* wisteria [T'ENG² • R grass & P*] 藤井 — *Fujii* — sn. 藤枝 — *Fujieda* — psn., *Fujie* — sn. 藤原 — *Fujiwara* — sn.
敦	敦	1976; 66/8. TON sincerity; *Atsushi* mn.; *atsu* [TUN¹ • R strike & P*] 敦厚 — *tonkō* — simple honesty 敦盛 — *Atsumori* — mn.

奈	奈	1977; 37/5.　NA what? [NAI⁴ ・ R big & P*] 奈良朝 — *Nara-chō* — Nara Court/period (710–794) 奈落 — *naraku* — Hell
楠	楠	1978; 75/9.　NAN, *kusu*[*noki*] psn., camphor tree [NAN² ・ R tree & P*] 楠久 — *Kusuku* — sn. 楠木 — *Kusunoki* — sn. 楠見 — *Kusumi* — sn.
稔	稔	1979; 115/8.　NEN harvest, ripen; *Minoru* mn.; *toshi* [JEN³,⁴ ・ R grain & P*] 稔足 — *Toshitari* — mn. 稔男 — *Toshio* — mn.
弥	弥 彌	1980; 57/5.　MI, BI more; *ya* [MI² ・ R bow & P] 弥三郎 — *Yasaburō* — mn. 弥永 — *Yanaga* — sn. 弥富 — *Yatomi* — psn.
輔	輔	1981; 159/7.　HO help; *suke* [FU³ ・ R cart & P*] 輔佐/輔翼する — *hosa/hoyoku suru* — help, advise 輔子 — *Sukeko* — fn.
朋	朋	1982; 130/4.　HŌ, *tomo* friend, companion [P'ENG² ・ I: a pair; P*] 朋輩 — *hōbai* — companion, colleague 朋来 — *Tomoki* — mn.
卯	卯	1983; 26/3.　BŌ, *u* 4th sign of the zodiac, hare [MAO³ ・ D→B] 卯三郎 — *Usaburō* — mn. 卯月 — *uzuki* — sn., 4th lunar month
睦	睦	1984; 109/8.　BOKU, *mutsu(majii)* friendly, cordial [MU⁴ ・ R eye & P*] 睦子 — *Mutsuko* — fn. 睦月 — *mutsuki* — fn., 1st lunar month

磨	磨	1985; 200/5. MA, *miga(ku)* polish, train; *Migaku* [MO²,⁴ • R stone & P*] ⌊mn. 磨耗する — *mamō suru* — be worn/rubbed away 須磨源氏 — *Suma Genji* — (Prince) Genji at Suma
也	也	1986; 2/2. YA, *nari* (classical vb.) be [YEH³ • D→B] 也寸志 — *Yasushi* — mn. 爾也 — *Chikaya* — mn.
熊	熊	1987; 86/10. YŪ, *kuma* bear [HSIUNG² • R fire & P*] 熊狩り — *kumagari* — bear hunting 熊沢 — *Kumazawa* — sn.
祐	祐 祐	1988; 113/5. YŪ help; *suke* [YU⁴ • R god & P*] 祐六 — *Yūroku* — mn. 祐彦 — *Sukehiko* — mn. 祐靖 — *Sukeyasu* — mn.
酉	酉	1989; 164/0. YŪ, *tori* 10th sign of the zodiac, cock [YU³ • D: wine jug→B; P*] 酉三 — *Yūzō/Torizō* — mn. 酉の市 — *tori no ichi* — year-end fair
蘭	蘭 蘭	1990; 140/16. RAN* orchid; Dutch [LAN² • R grass & P*] 蘭方〔医学〕— *Ranpō [igaku]* — Dutch medicine 蘭領東印度諸島 — *Ranryō Higashi-Indo Shotō* ⌊— Dutch East Indies
鯉	鯉	1991; 195/7. RI, *koi* carp [LI³ • R fish & P*] 鯉三郎 — *Risaburō* — mn. 鯉江 — *Koie* — sn. 鯉沼 — *Koinuma* — sn.
竜	竜 龍	1992; 212/0. RYŪ sn., RYŌ sn., *tatsu* sn., dragon; [LUNG² • D; P*] ⌊(see also 1830) 竜ケ岳 — *Ryūgadake* — pn. 竜安寺 — *Ryōanji* — pn. 竜起 — *Tatsuoki* — pn.

亮	亮	1993; 8/7. RYŌ clear; *suke, aki* [LIANG⁴ • R lid & P] 亮策 — *Ryōsaku* — mn. 亮澄 — *Sukezumi* — mn. 亮道 — *Akimichi* — mn.
綾	綾	1994; 120/8. RYŌ, *aya* psn., design, figured cloth [LING² • R thread & P*] 綾也 — *Aya* — fn. 綾部 — *Ayabe* — psn. 綾瀬 — *Ayase* — psn.
玲	玲 玲	1995; 96/5. REI the sound of jade pendants; *tama* [LING² • R jewel & P*] 玲子 — *Reiko* — fn. 玲枝 — *Tamae* — fn.
鎌	鎌 鎌	1996; 167/10. REN, *kama* sickle, scythe [LIEN² • R metal & P*] 鎌倉 — *Kamakura* — psn. 鎌原 — *Kamahara* — sn. 鎌滝 — *Kamataki* — sn.
呂	呂	1997; 30/4. RO backbone; *tomo* [LÜ³ • D: two vertebrae; P*] 風呂の加減 — *furo no kagen* — the bath tem- 呂久 — *Tomohisa* — mn.　　⌊perature
禄	禄 禄	1998; 113/8. ROKU good fortune; grant, fief; *yoshi* [LU⁴ • I; P*] 禄盗人 — *roku-nusubito* — one who draws an 禄夫 — *Yoshio* — mn.　　⌊unearned salary
鹿	鹿	1999; 198/0. ROKU, *shika* deer; *ka* [LU⁴ • D; P*] 鹿鳴館 — *Rokumeikan* — pn. 鹿又 — *Shikamata* — sn. 鹿児島 — *Kagoshima* — pn.
麿	麿	2000; 200/7. *maro* mn. [Combined form of 1480 & 1997] 人麿 — *Hitomaro* — mn. 桐麿 — *Kirimaro* — mn. 麿枝 — *Maroe* — fn.

Part II

From Readings to Characters

—A—

A	亜	*1788*
	(悪)	AKU
a	吾	1933
aba(ku)	暴	833
aba(reru)		
	暴	833
a(biru)	浴	609
abu(nai)	危	899
abura	油	298
	脂	1577
a(garu)	上	29
	挙	523
a(geru)	上	29
	挙	523
	揚	1401
AI	哀	*1249*
	(衣)	I
	(口)	KŌ
	(衷)	CHŪ
	愛	*456*
ai	相	97
aida	間	174
ai(suru)	愛	456
aji	味	339
aka(i)	赤	275
aka(rui)	明	58
a(kasu)	明	58
akatsuki	暁	1583
a(keru)	明	58
	空	184
	開	550
aki	秋	164
	晃	1938
	聡	1961
	亮	1993
akina(u)	商	293
akira	晃	1938
aki(raka)		
	明	58
a(kiru)	飽	1230
AKU	悪	*804*
	(亜)	A
	握	*1566*
	(屋)	OKU
a(ku)	空	184
	開	550
ama	尼	1688
ama(i)	甘	1333

ama(ri/ru/su)		
	余	483
ame	天	78
	雨	114
ami	網	1282
	(綱)	*tsu-na*
a(mu)	編	473
AN	安	*98*
	案	*500*
	(女)	JO
	(妥)	DA
	暗	*576*
	闇	*1899*
	(音)	ON
	行	24
ana	穴	984
anado(ru)		
	侮	1212
ane	姉	120
ani	兄	234
an(jiru)	案	500
ao(gu)	仰	1534
ao(i)	青	331
ara(i)	荒	1028
	粗	1724
arashi	嵐	1902
araso(i/u)		
	争	311
ara(ta)	新	178
arata(maru/me-ru)	改	691
ara(u)	洗	925
arawa(reru)		
	現	495
arawa(su)		
	表	308
	or 現	495
	著	580
a(reru)	荒	1028
a(ru)	在	258
	有	267
	或	1894
arui(wa)	或	1894
aru(ku)	歩	433
asa	朝	395
	麻	1480
asa(i)	浅	722
ase	汗	1328
ase(ru)	焦	1606

ashi	足	135
or	脚	1422
aso(bu)	遊	587
ata(eru)	与	983
atai	価	762
or	値	1414
atama	頭	519
atara(shii)		
	新	178
ata(ri)	辺	270
a(taru)	当	96
atata(ka)	温	382
atata(kai)		
	温	382
or	暖	917
atata(maru/me-ru)	温	382
ate	宛	1897
a(teru)	当	96
	充	1319
ato	後	276
	跡	1502
ATSU	圧	*874*
	(圧)	SHŌ
atsu	淳	1947
	敦	1976
atsu(i)	熱	300
	暑	476
	厚	735
atsuka(u)		
	扱	1330
atsu(maru/me-ru)	集	279
atsushi	淳	1947
	敦	1976
a(u)	会	116
	合	195
	遭	1376
awa	泡	1904
awa(i)	淡	1065
awa(re/remu)		
	哀	1249
awa(seru)		
	併	1079
awatada(shii)		
	慌	1692
awa(teru)	慌	1692
aya	綾	1994
ayama(chi)		

	過	368
ayama(ri)		
	誤	602
ayama(ru)		
	誤	602
	謝	765
ayama(tsu)		
	過	368
aya(shii/shimu)		
	怪	1176
ayatsu(ru)		
	操	1367
aya(ui)	危	899
ayu(mu)		
	歩	433
aza	字	121
azamu(ku)		
	欺	1397
azaya(ka)		
	鮮	1350
azu(karu/keru)		
	預	728

—B—

BA	馬	*142*
	(篤)	TO-KU
	婆	*1262*
	(波)	HA
ba	場	250
BACHI	罰	936
BAI	倍	*866*
	培	*1492*
	陪	*1693*
	賠	*1808*
	(部)	BU
	(剖)	BŌ
	梅	*1162*
	(毎)	MAI
	(海)	KAI
	(敏)	BIN
	売	*47*
	買	*48*
	(読)	DO-KU
	媒	*1403*
	(某)	BŌ
ba(kasu/keru)		
	化	76
BAKU	暴	833

279

	爆 923	(大) DAI		(奉) HŌ		奉 1191
	(暴) BŌ	備 750		(俸) HŌ	BUN	文 71
	幕 1250	微 1668		暴 833		(交) KŌ
	麦 816	(徴) CHŌ		(爆) BA-		分 35
	縛 1361	鼻 714	BIN	KU		(盆) BON
	(博) HA-	便 265		膨 1362		(貧) HIN
	KU	敏 1429	BOKU	撲 1464		聞 109
	(専) SEN	(毎) MAI		僕 1838		(耳) JI
BAN	判 497	(海) KAI		木 17	buta	豚 1738
	伴 1433	(梅) BAI		目 22	BUTSU	仏 249
	(半) HAN	貧 836		朴 1828		(払) FU-
	盤 1290	BO	墓 650		(赴) FU		TSU
	(般) HAN		暮 1140		牧 799		(私) SHI
	万 84		模 1218		睦 1984		(公) KŌ
	板 468		募 1382		(陸) RI-		物 74
	晩 901		慕 1382		KU	BYAKU	白 79
	(免) MEN		母 89		墨 1494	BYŌ	苗 1287
	(逸) ITSU		(毒) DO-		(黒) KO-		描 1489
	番 257		KU		KU		(田) DEN
	(藩) HAN		(毎) MAI	BON	凡 1338		平 136
	(審) SHIN		簿 1073		帆 HAN		秒 867
	蛮 1390	BŌ	防 680		盆 1087		(少) SHŌ
	(変) HEN		紡 1415		(分) BUN		(砂) SA
	(虫) CHŪ		坊 1676		煩 1859		病 145
bas(suru)			妨 1674	bos(suru)			(丙) HEI
	罰 936		肪 1806		没 1075		
BATSU	伐 1535		房 1116	BOTSU	没 1075	—C—	
	閥 1375		傍 1406		(設) SE-	CHA	茶 392
	抜 1525		(方) HŌ		TSU	CHAKU	着 403
	(友) YŪ		亡 979		(役) YA-		嫡 1385
	(髪) HA-		忙 890		KU		(適) TEKI
	TSU		忘 1004		(投) TŌ	CHI	知 196
	罰 936		望 767	BU	無 386		痴 1663
	末 565		卯 1983		舞 1003		智 1964
-be			賀 871		不 130		地 143
BEI	米 112		(卵) RAN		分 35		池 847
	(迷) MEI		(柳) RYŪ		侮 1212		(也) YA
BEN	弁 513		(留) RYŪ		(毎) MAI		値 1414
	便 265		某 1470		(海) KAI		置 345
	(更) KŌ		謀 1054		(敏) BIN		(直) CHO-
	勉 852		(媒) BAI		武 596		KU
	(免) MEN		冒 1463		(止) SHI		治 214
beni	紅 1233		帽 1105		(賦) FU		恥 1431
BETSU	別 288		乏 932		歩 433		(心) SHI-
BI	尾 1005		剖 1805		部 282		N
	(毛) MŌ		(部) BU		(剖) BŌ		致 1114
	弥 1980		(倍) BAI		(倍) BAI		(至) SHI
	美 268		棒 1121				遅 1090

稚 1513
(進) SHIN
(准) JUN
chi 千 83
血 344
(皿) sara
chichi 父 90
乳 1216
chiga(u) 違 883
chigi(ru) 契 1132
chii(sai) 小 33
chiji(meru/mu)
縮 1142
chika 哉 1940
爾 1945
chika(i) 近 127
誓 1036
chikara 力 53
chikashi 爾 1945
chika(u) 誓 1036
CHIKU 竹 68
築 711
畜 1740
蓄 1101
(玄) GEN
(田) DEN
逐 1573
(家) KA
(遂) SUI
(豚) TON
CHIN 沈 1097
枕 1900
珍 1027
(診) SHIN
陳 1647
(東) TŌ
朕 1876
(送) SŌ
賃 555
(任) NIN
鎮 1348
(真) SHIN
chi(rasu/ru)
散 465
CHITSU 秩 1722
(失) SHI-TSU

(鉄) TETSU
窒 1486
(至) SHI
(屋) OKU
CHO 著 580
緒 949
猪 1966
(者) SHA
貯 740
CHŌ 丁 166
町 167
頂 986
庁 1034
長 155
張 681
帳 851
脹 1861
兆 1687
跳 1590
挑 1825
(逃) TŌ
調 376
彫 1167
鯛 1971
(周) SHŪ
朝 395
潮 980
腸 810
暢 1967
(場) JŌ
徴 1384
懲 1510
(微) BI
鳥 182
蔦 1969
(鳴) MEI
弔 1690
(弓) KYŪ
重 161
超 1051
(召) SHŌ
澄 1455
(登) TŌ
蝶 1970
(葉) YŌ
聴 1055
(徳) TO-KU

肇 1968
(啓) KEI
CHOKU 直 304
(値) CHI
(置) CHI
勅 1478
(速) SO-KU
(疎) SO
CHŪ 中 31
虫 133
忠 632
沖 1317
仲 1332
衷 1809
(哀) AI
注 444
柱 826
註 1896
駐 1372
(主) SHU
(住) Ō
宙 1303
抽 1443
(由) YŪ
(笛) TEKI
丑 1965
昼 828
鋳 1423
(寿) JU
chū(suru)
註 1896

—D—

DA 惰 1714
堕 1511
(随) ZUI
打 682
(丁) TEI
(灯) TŌ
妥 1313
(女) JO
(安) AN
DAI 弟 446
第 360
(悌) TEI
大 32
(美) BI

乃 1962
内 132
代 85
(袋) TAI
(貸) TAI
台 290
(治) JI
(胎) TAI
題 393
DAKU 諾 1452
(若) JA-KU
濁 1749
(独) DO-KU
(触) SHO-KU
da(ku) 抱 1633
dama(ru)
黙 1581
DAN 団 243
(寸) SUN
男 63
(田) DEN
(力) RYO-KU
段 911
(没) BO-TSU
(設) SE-TSU
断 606
(斤) KIN
弾 1099
(単) TAN
暖 917
(援) EN
(緩) KAN
談 378
(炎) EN
(火) KA
壇 1711
da(su) 出 40
-date 建 363
DATSU 脱 1173
(説) SE-TSU
奪 1603

DE	弟 446		(雲) UN		益 *631*		(渇) KA-
DEI	泥 *1840*	dono	殿 892		液 *659*		TSU
	(尼) NI	doro	泥 1840		(夜) YA		
DEN	田 *52*				駅 *189*		**—F—**
	電 222		**—E—**		(尺)SHA-	FU	付 *259*
	(男) DAN	E	会 116		KU		府 *260*
	伝 554		絵 *380*		(訳) YA-		符 *951*
	(芸) GEI		(会) KAI		KU		腐 *1378*
	(雲) UN		回 571		(沢) TA-		附 *1878*
	殿 892		依 *1135*		KU		夫 *51*
de(ru)	出 40		恵 *1498*	eki(suru)	益 631		扶 *1796*
DO	奴 *1869*	e	江 *994*	e(mu)	笑 1147		布 737
	努 566		柄 *1168*	EN	沿 *1013*		怖 *1784*
	怒 *1068*		重 161		鉛 *1109*		(希) KI
	土 19	eda	枝 889		遠 326		普 *1102*
	(吐) TO	ega(ku)	描 *1489*		園 327		譜 *1346*
	(社) SHA	EI	永 560		円 159		(晋)SHIN
	度 252		泳 562		炎 *1727*		父 90
	(渡) TO		詠 *1161*		(火) KA		(交) Kō
	(席) SEKI		(氷) HYō		(談) DAN		不 *130*
Dō	同 185		英 377		延 706		(杯) HAI
	銅 855		映 910		(正) SEI		歩 *433*
	胴 *1500*		(央) ō		(廷) TEI		負 503
	(筒) Tō		栄 777		宛 *1897*		(敗) HAI
	動 169		営 780		腕 WAN		風 134
	働 170		(労) Rō		宴 *1301*		赴 *1797*
	(重) JŪ		(学) GA-		塩 *730*		(朴) BO-
	(力)RYO-		KU		煙 914		KU
	KU		影 *929*		演 806		浮 *991*
	道 *141*		(景) KEI		(寅) IN		(乳)NYŪ
	導 755		衛 686		援 *1564*		婦 *313*
	(首) SHU		(違) I		(暖) DAN		(掃) Sō
	堂 358		鋭 *1449*		(緩) KAN		(帰) KI
	(党) Tō		(悦) E-		縁 *1244*		富 705
	童 643		TSU		(緑)RYO-		(福) FU-
	(鐘) SHō		(説) SE-		KU		KU
DOKU	毒 418		TSU		艶 *1914*		(副) FU-
	(母) BO		亦 *1913*	en(zuru)	演 806		KU
	(毎) MAI		(変) HEN	era(bu)	選 522		敷 *1039*
	独 618		(恋) REN	era(i)	偉 *1098*		賦 *1635*
	(虫) CHŪ		易 *824*	e(ru)	得 340		(武) BU
	(触)SHO-		(賜) SHI	ETSU	閲 *1261*		膚 *1800*
	KU	EKI	役 171		悦 *1857*		(胃) I
	読 55		疫 *1469*		(説) SE-	FŪ	夫 51
	(売) BAI		(没) BO-		TSU		風 134
DON	鈍 *1388*		TSU		(鋭) EI		(嵐) RAN
	(純) JUN		(設) SE-		越 *1021*		封 1124
	曇 *1575*		TSU		謁 *1862*	fuchi	縁 1244

fuda	札 1536	furu(u)	奮 818		外 42		芸 421
fude	筆 69		震 1123		害 450		(伝) DEN
fue	笛 1306	furu(waseru)		(割)	KA-		(雲) UN
fu(eru)	増 693		震 1123		TSU		鯨 1345
or	殖 1396	fusa	房 1116	GAKU	岳 1772		(京) KYŌ
fuji	藤 1975	fuse(gu)	防 680		(丘) KYŪ	GEKI	劇 1078
fū(jiru)	封 1124	fu(seru)	伏 1331		(兵) HEI		撃 997
fuka(i)	深 593	fushi	節 683		学 66		激 1365
fu(kasu)	更 1311	futa	双 1541		(子) SHI	geki(suru)
fu(keru)	老 637	futata(bi)			(栄) EI		激 1365
	更 1311		再 543		(営) EI	GEN	幻 1691
FUKU	復 588	futa(tsu)			(労) RŌ		玄 1113
	複 764		二 2		楽 322		弦 1624
	腹 1010	futo(i)	太 508		額 749		(幼) YŌ
	覆 1699	futokoro	懐 1188		(客) KYA-		(幽) YŪ
	(履) RI	futo(ru)	太 508		KU		(畜) CHI-
	福 629	FUTSU	仏 249		(各) KA-		KU
	副 772		払 904		KU		限 600
	幅 1234		沸 1627	GAN	元 106		眼 674
	(富) FU		(公) KŌ		丸 922		(根) KON
	伏 1331		(私) SHI		(九) KYŪ		(銀) GIN
	(犬) KEN	fu(yasu)	増 693		含 1677		原 202
	服 306	or	殖 1396		(今) KON		源 893
	(報) HŌ	fuyu	冬 165		(吟) GIN		(願) GAN
fu(ku)	吹 1095	fū(zuru)	封 1124		眼 674		元 106
	噴 1239				(根) KON		(完) KAN
fuku(mu)		—G—			(限) GEN		言 43
	含 1677				顔 481		(信) SHIN
fuku(ramu/me-	GA	我 719		(彦) GEN		彦 1931
ru)	膨 1362		餓 1580		願 428		(顔) GAN
fukuro	袋 926		(義) GI		(原) GEN		現 495
fumi	文 71		芽 709		岸 687		(見) KEN
fu(mu)	踏 1186		雅 1211		(干) KAN		減 610
FUN	分 35		(邪) JA		岩 821		(感) KAN
	粉 793		画 477		(石) SEKI		厳 817
	紛 1499		賀 615		巌 1918		(敢) KAN
	(盆) BON		(加) KA		(敢) KAN		験 355
	(貧) HIN	GAI	亥 1916	gara	柄 1168	GETSU	月 13
	噴 1239		該 1504	-gata	形 223	GI	義 244
	憤 1254		劾 1867	GATSU	月 13		議 245
	墳 1461		(核) KA-	GE	下 30		儀 1252
	奮 818		KU		外 42		犠 1811
fune	舟 968		(刻) KO-		解 577		(我) GA
or	船 314		KU		夏 163		疑 752
fu(reru)	触 945		街 1181	GEI	迎 1062		擬 1356
fu(ru)	降 887		涯 1824		(仰) GYŌ		(凝) GYŌ
	振 1612		(圭) KEI		(抑) YO-		技 463
furu(eru)	震 1123		(封) HŌ		KU		(支) SHI
			概 1196				
			慨 1399				

283

(返) HEN	端 1380	(材) ZAI	KI
(仮) KA	hashira 柱 826	HEKI 壁 1369	罷 1870
半 150	hashi(ru)	癖 1702	(能) NŌ
判 497	走 832	(避) HI	(態) TAI
畔 1587	hata 機 415	HEN 編 473	hi 日 5
(伴) BAN	旗 601	偏 1260	火 15
般 1201	畑 699	遍 1279	灯 537
搬 1667	端 1380	片 937	氷 820
(盤) BAN	hatake 畑 699	辺 270	hibi(ki/ku)
犯 771	hatara(ku)	(刀) TŌ	響 1111
範 1067	働 170	返 307	hidari 左 87
凡 1338	ha(tasu) 果 375	(反) HAN	hi(eru) 冷 792
帆 948	hate 果 375	(仮) KA	higashi 東 27
(凡) BON	HATSU 八 10	変 191	hii(deru) 秀 973
班 1804	発 186	(亦) EKI	hika(eru)
(王) ō	(廃) HAI	(恋) REN	控 1658
煩 1859	髪 1224	(蛮) BAN	hikari 光 217
(火) KA	(友) YŪ	he(rasu) 減 610	hika(ru) 光 217
藩 1549	HATSU- 法 213	he(ru) 経 341	HIKI 匹 1120
(番) BAN	hatsu 初 636	減 610	hiki(iru) 率 808
繁 1092	肇 1968	HI 皮 863	hiko 彦 1931
頒 1874	haya(i) 早 117	被 1410	hi(ku) 引 271
(分) BUN	or 速 848	彼 1764	弾 1099
hana 花 328	hayashi 林 57	疲 1798	hiku(i) 低 690
or 華 1409	ha(yasu) 生 67	披 1841	hima 暇 891
鼻 714	hazuka(shime-	非 353	hime 姫 1220
hanaha(da)	ru) 辱 1462	悲 822	hi(meru) 秘 940
甚 1955	hazu(mu)	(俳) HAI	HIN 浜 907
hana(reru)	弾 1099	(罪) ZAI	賓 1732
離 909	hazu(reru/su)	秘 940	(兵) HEI
hanashi 話 180	外 42	泌 1787	品 146
hana(su)	heda(taru/teru)	(必) HI-	(口) KŌ
話 180	隔 1753	TSU	貧 836
放 287	HEI 丙 1782	比 589	(分) BUN
離 909	柄 1168	批 1523	hira(ku) 開 550
hana(tsu)	病 145	卑 1795	hira(tai) 平 136
放 287	(病) BYŌ	碑 1758	hiro 宏 1936
hane 羽 967	幣 1400	妃 1533	弘 1937
ha(neru) 跳 1590	弊 1457	(己) KI	浩 1939
hara 原 202	平 136	否 830	hiro(garu/i/geru/
腹 1010	(評) HYŌ	(不) FU	maru)
hara(u) 払 904	兵 396	肥 724	広 303
ha(re/reru)	(浜) HIN	飛 404	hiroshi 宏 1936
晴 784	並 998	費 608	弘 1937
hari 針 1407	併 1079	(沸) FU-	浩 1939
haru 春 162	陛 873	TSU	hiro(u) 拾 625
ha(ru) 張 681	閉 900	避 1746	hiru 昼 828
hashi 橋 443	(才) SAI	(壁) HE-	hi(ru) 干 1542
			hirugae(ru/su)

	翻 1551	奉 1191	horo(biru/
hisa 尚 1948	俸 1842	bosu) 滅 1228
hisashi 尚 1948	(奏) SŌ	ho(ru) 彫 1167
hisa(shii) 久 704	(棒) BŌ	掘 1265
hiso(mu) 潜 1458	邦 1323	hoshi 星 838
hitai 額 749	宝 981	ho(shii) 欲 535
hita(ru/su)	(玉)GYO-	hoso(i) 細 701
浸 1221	KU	hos(suru)
hito 人 4	(国)KO-	欲 535
hito(ri) 独 618	KU	ho(su) 干 1542
hitoshi 斉 1958	法 213	hotoke 仏 249
hito(shii)	(去)KYO	HATSU 発 186
等 294	朋 1982	HOTSU 法 213
hito(tsu) 一 1	崩 1490	hō(zuru) 奉 1191
HITSU 必 281	封 1124	HYAKU 百 82
泌 1787	(寸) SUN	(白) HA-
(秘) HI	(圭) KEI	KU
匹 1120	(佳) KA	HYŌ 票 774
筆 69	報 295	標 858
(津)SHIN	(服) FU-	漂 1281
(建) KEN	KU	表 308
(健) KEN	豊 624	俵 879
hitsuji 羊 1326	(曲)KYO-	氷 820
hi(yasu) 冷 792	KU	(永) EI
HO 補 744	hodo 程 371	拍 1440
浦 1015	hodoko(su)	評 627
捕 1611	施 1022	(平) HEI
舗 1773	hoga(raka)	兵 396
輔 1981	朗 1610	hyō(suru)
歩 433	hoka 外 42	評 627
(渉) SHŌ	hoko 矛 1813	
保 351	hoko(ri/ru)	**—I—**
ho 帆 948	誇 1202	
穂 1637	HOKU 北 156	I 違 883
HŌ 包 369	(背) HAI	偉 1098
砲 993	homa(re)	緯 1636
飽 1230	誉 1203	(衛) EI
胞 1237	hōmu(ru)	衣 605
抱 1633	葬 1593	依 1135
泡 1904	HON 反 342	(哀) AI
方 26	本 20	尉 1232
芳 1316	(体) TAI	慰 1066
訪 1412	奔 1438	維 1187
放 287	翻 1551	唯 1493
倣 1616	(羽) U	(推) SUI
(防) BŌ		以 221
縫 1235	hone 骨 971	(似) JI
峰 1272	honō 炎 1727	伊 1909
	hori 堀 1837	位 122

(立) RI-	
TSU	
囲 803	
(井) SEI	
(耕) KŌ	
医 440	
(矢) SHI	
委 837	
(女) JO	
易 824	
威 1011	
(滅) ME-	
TSU	
為 977	
(偽) GI	
胃 853	
(田) DEN	
異 581	
(翼) YO-	
KU	
移 607	
(多) TA	
意 225	
(憶) OKU	
遺 656	
(貴) KI	
(遣) KEN	
i 井 916	
亥 1916	
猪 1966	
ICHI 一 1	
壱 708	
ichi 市 119	
ichijiru(shii)	
著 580	
ida(ku) 抱 1633	
ie 家 151	
i(i) 良 586	
ika(ru) 怒 1068	
ike 池 847	
IKI 域 1017	
(惑) WA-	
KU	
iki 息 628	
ikidō(ru)憤 1254	
ikio(i) 勢 299	
iki(ru) 生 67	
ikoi 憩 1710	

IKU	育 *487*	iro	色 241		卑 1795		除 530
	(撒) TE-	irodo(ru)		izumi	泉 915		辞 *594*
	TSU		彩 1660	**—J—**			(舌) ZE-
	(徹) TE-	i(ru)	入 39	JA	邪 *1520*		TSU
	TSU		居 208		(芽) GA	ji	(辛) SHIN
	郁 *1910*		要 262	JAKU	若 *982*	JIKI	路 677
	(有) YŪ		射 989		(右) YŪ		直 304
iku	幾 996		鋳 1423		弱 *595*		食 283
i(ku)	行 24	isagiyo(i)			寂 *1300*	JIKU	軸 *1258*
iku(ra)	幾 996		潔 672		(叔) SHU-		(由) YŪ
ikusa	戦 399	isa(mashii)			KU		(笛) TEKI
iku(tsu)	幾 996		勇 825		(淑) SHU-	JIN	人 *4*
ima	今 94	ishi	石 102		KU		(入) NYŪ
imashi(me/me-		ishizue	礎 1701		着 *403*		刃 *1107*
ru)	戒 1006	iso	磯 1920	JI	寺 *45*		(忍) NIN
imo	芋 1682	isoga(shii)			時 *46*		(認) NIN
imōto	妹 427		忙 890		持 *50*		仁 *829*
i(mu)	忌 1522	iso(gu)	急 330		侍 *1446*		(二) NI
IN	因 *462*	ita	板 468		(詩) SHI		迅 *1871*
	姻 *1159*	itadaki	頂 986		(等) TŌ		尽 *1530*
	(困) KON	itada(ku)			慈 *1194*		甚 *1955*
	陰 *1031*		頂 986		磁 *1288*		(勘) KAN
	蔭 *1908*	ita(meru)			滋 *1395*		(堪) KAN
	員 *374*		傷 1008		爾 *1945*		神 205
	韻 *1294*	ita(mi)	痛 1020		璽 *1866*		陣 *1207*
	(損) SON	ita(mu)	傷 1008		(弥) MI		(車) SHA
	引 *271*		痛 1020		示 575		尋 *1569*
	印 *801*		悼 1771		(奈) NA	ji(suru)	辞 *594*
	音 206	ita(ru)	至 725		地 143		侍 1446
	胤 *1912*	ita(su)	致 1114		(也) YA	JITSU	日 *5*
	院 *237*	ito	糸 113		字 *121*		実 *233*
	(完) KAN	itona(mu)			(子) SHI	JO	除 530
	寅 *1911*		営 780		自 *60*		叙 *1476*
	(演) EN	ITSU	一 *1*		(臭) SHŪ		徐 *1613*
	飲 *489*		壱 708		次 *239*		(余) YO
	(欠) KE-		逸 *1723*		(欠) KE-		女 *62*
	TSU	itsuku(shimu)			TSU		如 1539
	隠 *1374*		慈 1194		(吹) SUI		(安) AN
	(穏) ON	itsu(tsu)	五 *7*		耳 *107*		(妥) DA
ina	否 830	itsuwa(ru)			似 *775*		序 *507*
ine	稲 1293		偽 1157		(以) I		(予) YO
inochi	命 387	i(u)	言 43		児 *782*		助 346
ino(ri/ru)		iwa	岩 821		治 214		(筋) KIN
	祈 1141		or 巌 1918		(始) SHI	JŌ	錠 *1307*
inoshishi	猪 1966	iwa(i)	祝 756		(台) DAI		嬢 *1368*
inu	犬 578	iwao	巌 1918		(胎) TAI		醸 *1547*
i(reru/ri)		iwa(u)	祝 756		事 *73*		壌 *1844*
	入 39	iya	嫌 1901				穣 *1952*
		iya(shii/shimeru)					

成 224	縦 1559	JUTSU 術 447	香 1059
城 886	住 209	述 770	蚊 1119
盛 898	(主) SHU		鹿 1999
丞 1951	(注) CHŪ	**—K—**	kabe 壁 1369
蒸 950	拾 625	KA 可 253	kabu 株 731
定 218	(合) GŌ	何 254	kado 門 105
錠 1745	(給) KYŪ	荷 255	角 273
静 703	(答) TŌ	歌 256	kaeri(miru)
浄 976	柔 1086	河 633	省 408
(争) SŌ	(矛) MU	化 76	顧 1341
乗 312	(木) BO-KU	貨 220	kae(ru) 帰 263
剰 1662	重 161	花 328	ka(eru) 換 957
上 29	(動) DŌ	靴 1907	替 1398
丈 962	(種) SHU	加 787	変 191
冗 1122	渋 1025	架 1085	kae(shi/su)
(机) KI	(止) SHI	嘉 1915	返 307
条 452	獣 1366	(賀) GA	kagami 鏡 647
状 512	(犬) KEN	果 375	kagaya(ku)
(犬) KEN	-JŪ 中 31	課 568	輝 1264
常 199	JUKU 熟 1508	菓 946	kage 影 929
(尚) SHŌ	(熱) NE-TSU	過 368	陰 1031
情 334	juku(suru)	禍 1756	蔭 1908
(青) SEI	熟 1508	渦 1823	kagi(ru) 限 600
場 250	JUN 旬 1327	個 502	KAI 皆 978
(腸) CHŌ	殉 1736	箇 1860	階 436
畳 958	盾 1814	夏 163	介 941
JOKU 辱 1462	循 1707	寡 1855	界 269
(辰) SHIN	准 1743	家 151	会 116
(振) SHIN	準 498	嫁 1223	絵 380
jo(suru) 叙 1476	(集) SHŪ	下 30	戒 1006
JU 受 272	(進) SHIN	火 15	械 474
授 778	巡 905	(灰) HAI	海 99
需 754	(災) SAI	(炎) EN	悔 1166
儒 1579	純 667	仮 696	(毎) MAI
(端) TAN	(鈍) DON	(反) HAN	(悔) BU
寿 1786	淳 1947	(返) HEN	懐 1188
(鋳) CHŪ	(享) KYŌ	瓜 1888	壊 1578
就 759	(郭) KA-KU	(爪) SŌ	回 571
樹 1053	順 506	価 762	(口) KŌ
従 673	(川) SEN	佳 1450	灰 1325
JŪ 十 12	潤 1256	(圭) KEI	(火) KA
汁 1848	遵 1864	(封) HŌ	(炭) TAN
(針) SHIN	(尊) SON	科 385	快 827
充 1319	jun(zuru)	(斗) TO	(決) KE-TSU
銃 1185	殉 1736	(料) RYŌ	改 691
(統) TŌ		華 1409	怪 1176
従 673		暇 891	(軽) KEI
		ka 日 5	

	形	223	kawa(kasu)		渓	1846	(廉)	REN
	型	685		乾 1195	鶏	1548	犬	578
	片	937	kawa(ku)		敬	857	献	1273
	肩	1215		乾 1195	警	902	(伏)	FU-
katachi	形	223		or 渇 1266	(驚)	KYŌ		KU
kata(i)	固	738	ka(wari/waru)		契	1132	(状)	JŌ
or	堅	995		代 85	(喫)	KI-	建	363
or	硬	1598		変 191		TSU	健	364
	難	800	kawa(su)交	86	計	357	券	747
kataki	敵	454	kayo(u)	通 201	(十)	JŪ	圏	1160
katamari	塊	1670	kaza(ri/ru)		(針)	SHIN	(巻)	KAN
kata(maru/me-				飾 1014	恵	1498	県	381
ru)	固	738	kaze	風 134	(穂)	SUI	懸	1283
katamu(keru/			kazo(eru)		啓	1205	堅	995
ku)	傾	938		数 429	(肇)	CHŌ	賢	1072
katana	刀	34	kazu	数 429	掲	1659	(緊)	KIN
kata(ru)語		231	KE	化 76	(渇)	KA-	件	485
katawa(ra)				気 144		TSU	(牛)	GYŪ
	傍	1406		家 151	(謁)ETSU		見	23
katayo(ru)				懸 283	頃	1906	(現)	GEN
	偏	1260		景 509	傾	938	(寛)	KAN
kate	糧	1552		仮 696	携	1666	肩	1215
KATSU	活	198		華 1409	継	894	(戸)	KO
	括	1474	ke	毛 125	断	DAN	研	583
(舌)	ZE-		kega(reru/su)		詣	1885	(刑)	KEI
	TSU			汚 1531	(旨)	SHI	(開)	KAI
(話)	WA		KEI	経 341	(指)	SHI	軒	953
	割	1274		軽 598	境	751	(干)	KAN
	轄	1553		茎 1291	慶	1033	間	174
(害)	GAI			径 1630	憩	1710	絹	658
	合	195		(怪) KAI	(息)	SO-	遣	895
	渇	1266		形 223		KU	(遺)	I
(謁)ETSU				刑 1001	馨	1930	(追)	TSUI
(掲)	KEI			型 685	(香)	KŌ	権	420
	滑	1512		(研) KEN	(声)	SEI	(観)	KAN
(骨)	KO-			(開) KAI	kemono	獣 1366	(歓)	KAN
	TSU			兄 234	kemu(i)	煙 914	憲	622
katsu	且	1865		競 464	kemuri	煙 914	繭	1700
ka(tsu)	勝	266		圭 1928	kemu(ru)		(糸)	SHI
katsu(gu)				桂 1929		煙 914	(虫)	CHŪ
	担	1631		(佳) KA	KEN	験 355	顕	1245
katsura	桂	1929		(街) GAI		険 356	(湿)	SHI-
ka(u)	買	48		系 634		検 785		TSU
	飼	1156		係 426		剣 1436	ke(su)	消 612
kawa	川	41		(糸) SHI		倹 1620	KETSU	欠 713
or	河	633		京 172		兼 669	(次)	JI
	側	538		景 509		謙 1545	(飲)	IN
	革	811		(影) EI		嫌 1901	穴	984
	皮	863						

(八)	HA-CHI	岐	1769	kimo	肝 1516	kiwa(mi) 極 597

控 1658	侯 1479	koba(mu)	koma(kai)
(空) KŪ	候 862	拒 1439	細 701
口 38	荒 1028	koe 声 226	koma(ru)
高 160	慌 1692	肥 724	困 969
向 215	亙 1935	ko(eru) 肥 724	kome 米 112
后 542	恒 1225	越 1021	ko(meru/mi)
拘 1448	(宣) SEN	or 超 1051	込 987
稿 1505	行 24	ko(gasu/geru)	kōmu(ru)
(哀) AI	衡 1358	焦 1606	被 1410
交 86	(衛) EI	kogo(eru)	KON 根 425
校 91	(衝) SHŌ	凍 1435	恨 1227
効 623	孔 1336	koi 恋 1012	(眼) GAN
郊 1030	(礼) REI	鯉 1991	懇 1171
較 1155	(乱) RAN	ko(i) 濃 1503	墾 1576
絞 1394	甲 1082	kokono(tsu)	今 94
(父) FU	(押) Ō	九 11	(含) GAN
公 219	尻 1884	kokoro 心 80	(吟) GIN
広 303	(九) KYŪ	kokoro(miru)	金 18
鉱 532	仰 1534	試 354	困 969
宏 1936	好 882	kokoroyo(i)	(木) MO-KU
弘 1937	(子) SHI	快 827	(因) IN
(拡) KA-KU	亨 1934	kokorozashi	婚 965
(台) DAI	肯 1625	志 757	混 684
(払) FU-TSU	幸 712	kokoroza(su)	紺 1653
構 455	(辛) SHIN	志 757	(甘) KAN
講 702	厚 735	KOKU 告 296	献 1273
購 1353	後 276	酷 1591	魂 1584
考 197	皇 460	(浩) KŌ	(鬼) KI
孝 865	(白) HA-KU	石 102	(塊) KAI
酵 1589	降 887	克 1673	建 363
(拷) GŌ	香 1059	谷 528	kona 粉 793
岡 1889	馨 KEI	(俗) ZO-KU	kono(mu)
綱 1052	浩 1939	刻 1444	好 882
鋼 1509	(告) KO-KU	(亥) GAI	ko(rasu) 懲 1510
(剛) GŌ	耕 812	(核) KA-KU	kore 之 1942
(網) MŌ	(井) SEI	国 111	kōri 郡 480
航 561	(囲) I	(玉) GYO-KU	氷 820
抗 1320	耗 1720	黒 286	koro 頃 1906
坑 1524	康 860	(墨) BO-KU	koro(bu/garu/gasu/geru)
光 217	(逮) TAI	穀 815	転 515
晃 1938	黄 469	(殻) KA-KU	koromo 衣 605
更 1311	(横) Ō	(設) SE-TSU	koro(su) 殺 419
硬 1598	興 338	koma 駒 1927	ko(ru) 凝 1370
(便) BEN	神 205		kō(ru) 凍 1435
洪 1833			koshi 腰 1009
港 337			ko(su) 越 1021
(共) KYŌ			or 超 1051
kō-			

kota(e/eru)			
答	556		
koto 言	43		
事	73		
殊	1019		
琴	1393		
kotobuki			
寿	1786		
koto(naru)			
異	581		
kotowa(ru)			
断	606		
KOTSU 骨	971		
(滑) KA-TSU			
ko(u) 請	1190		
kowa(i) 怖	1784		
kowa(reru/su)			
壊	1578		
ko(yasu) 肥	724		
koyomi 暦	1383		
KU 工	77		
功	467		
紅	1233		
口	38		
句	795		
駒	1927		
区	168		
駆	1271		
(枢) SŪ			
九	11		
久	704		
供	694		
苦	264		
(古) KO			
(居) KYO			
庫	582		
貢	1295		
宮	546		
KŪ 空	184		
(工) KŌ			
ku(chiru) 朽	1683		
kuba(ru) 配	430		
kubi 首	138		
kuchi 口	38		
kuda 管	664		
kuda(ku)			
砕	1467		
kuda(ru) 下	30		

ku(iru) 悔	1166		
kujira 鯨	1345		
kuki 茎	1291		
kuma 熊	1987		
kumi 組	458		
kumo 雲	478		
kumo-			
(ru) 曇	1575		
KUN 勲	1296		
薫	1360		
(重) JŪ			
君	479		
(郡) GUN			
訓	613		
(川) SEN			
kuni 国	111		
kura 倉	732		
or 蔵	779		
or 庫	582		
kura(beru)			
比	589		
kurai 位	122		
kura(i) 暗	576		
ku(rasu) 暮	1140		
ku(rau) 食	283		
ku(re) 暮	1140		
kurenai 紅	1233		
ku(reru) 暮	1140		
kuro(i) 黒	286		
ku(ru) 来	25		
繰	1347		
kuruma 車	54		
kuru(shii)			
苦	264		
kuru(u) 狂	972		
kusa 草	118		
kusa(i) 臭	1308		
kusari 鎖	1698		
kusa(ru) 腐	1378		
kuse 癖	1702		
kus(suru)			
屈	1629		
kusu[noki]			
楠	1978		
kusuri 薬	323		
KUTSU 屈	1629		
掘	1265		
(出) SHU-TSU			

(拙) SE-TSU			
kutsu 靴	1907		
kutsugae(ru/su)			
覆	1699		
ku(u) 食	283		
kuwa 桑	1609		
kuwada(teru)			
企	966		
kuwa(eru)			
加	787		
kuwa(shii)			
詳	896		
ku(yamu)			
悔	1166		
kuzu(reru/su)			
崩	1490		
KYA 脚	1422		
KYAKU 却	1680		
脚	1422		
(去) KYO			
客	434		
(各) KA-KU			
(額) GA-KU			
KYO 巨	1537		
距	1110		
拒	1439		
去	475		
(却)KYA-KU			
(脚)KYA-KU			
拠	1725		
(処) SHO			
居	208		
(古) KO			
(苦) KU			
挙	523		
(手) SHU			
(誉) YO			
虚	1484		
嘘	1905		
(戯) GI			
許	657		
(午) GO			
(御) GO			
KYŌ 兄	234		

況	1267		
競	464		
共	240		
供	694		
恭	1618		
(洪) KŌ			
凶	1337		
胸	1149		
狂	992		
匡	1923		
(王) Ō			
亨	1934		
享	1622		
(郭) KA-KU			
(淳) JUN			
協	572		
脅	1544		
(力)RYO-KU			
峡	1270		
狭	1413		
郷	1165		
響	1111		
(郎) RŌ			
鏡	647		
境	751		
橋	443		
矯	1827		
叫	1685		
(糾) KYŪ			
京	172		
(鯨) GEI			
恐	1163		
強	332		
教	247		
経	341		
興	338		
驚	1061		
(敬) KEI			
(馬) BA			
KYOKU 曲	715		
(豊) HŌ			
局	422		
極	597		
KYŪ 及	888		
吸	1083		
級	228		

Reading	Kanji	No.
miga(ku)	磨	1985
migi	右	88
mijika(i)	短	261
miji(me)	惨	1304
miki	幹	763
mimi	耳	107
MIN	民	246
	眠	1144
mina	皆	978
minami	南	157
minamoto	源	893
minato	港	337
mine	峰	1272
miniku(i)	醜	1703
minoru	穣	1952
	稔	1979
mino(ru)	実	233
mi(ru)	見	23
	診	1081
misao	操	1367
misasagi	陵	1646
mise	店	235
mi(seru)	見	23
mi(suru)	魅	1371
mi(tasu)	満	504
mito(meru)	認	649
MITSU	密	1118
mi(tsu)	三	3
mitsu(gu)	貢	1295
mit(tsu)	三	3
miya	宮	546
miyako	都	173
mizu	水	16
	瑞	1956
mizuka(ra)	自	60
mizuumi	湖	573
MO	茂	1799
	模	1218
	(膜)	MA-KU
	(幕)	MA-KU
mo	喪	1572
MŌ	亡	979
	望	767
	盲	1177
	毛	125
	耗	1720
	(尾)	BI
	網	1282
	(綱)	KŌ
	猛	1420
mochi(iru)	用	110
mō(de/deru)	詣	1885
modo(ru/su)	戻	1850
mo(eru)	燃	541
mogu(ru)	潜	1458
mō(keru)	設	742
MOKU	木	17
	(休)	KYŪ
	(困)	KON
	目	22
	(相)	SŌ
	黙	1581
momo	桃	1428
MON	門	105
	聞	109
	問	175
	(間)	KAN
	(開)	KAI
	(閲)	BA-TSU
	文	71
	紋	1763
monme	匁	1819
mono	者	56
	物	74
moppa(ra)	専	413
mora(u)	貰	1903
mo(reru)	漏	1599
mori	森	152
	守	352
mo(ru)	盛	898
	漏	1599
mo(shiku wa)	若	982
mō(su)	申	204
moto	本	20
or	元	106
	下	30
	基	688
motoi	基	688
moto(meru)	求	584
moto(zuku)	基	688
MOTSU	物	74
mo(tsu)	持	50
motto(mo)	最	291
mo(yasu)	燃	541
moyō(su)	催	1529
MU	矛	1813
	務	491
	霧	1038
	(柔)	JŪ
	武	596
	無	386
	(舞)	BU
	夢	1425
	謀	1054
mugi	麦	816
muka(eru)	迎	1062
mukashi	昔	988
mu(kau)	向	215
muko	婿	1719
mu(ku)	向	215
muku(i/iru)	報	295
mune	旨	1069
	胸	1149
mura	村	154
mura(garu)	群	769
murasaki	紫	1392
mu(reru)	群	769
muro	室	278
mushi	虫	133
mu(su)	蒸	950
musu(bi/bu)	結	359
musume	娘	999
mu(tsu)	六	8
mutsu(majii)	睦	1984
mut(tsu)	六	8
muzuka(shii)	難	800
MYAKU	脈	813
	(派)	HA
MYŌ	名	131
	妙	1321
	(少)	SHŌ
	明	58
	命	387

—N—

Reading	Kanji	No.
NA	奈	1977
	(示)	SHI
	南	157
	納	733
na	名	131
	菜	870
nae	苗	1287
naga(i)	長	155
	永	560
naga(re/reru/su)	流	329
nage(ku)	嘆	1292
na(geru)	投	653
nago(meru/mu/yaka)	和	277
nagu(ru)	殴	1468
nagusa(me/meru/mi)	慰	1066
NAI	乃	1962
	内	132
	(納)	NŌ
na(i)	無	386
	亡	979
naka	中	31
	仲	1332
naka(ba)	半	150
na(ku)	鳴	864
	泣	1049
nama	生	67
nama(keru)	怠	1084
namari	鉛	1109
nami	波	484
	並	998

296

oda(yaka)
穏 1792
odo(kasu)
脅 1544
odo(ri) 踊 1035
odoro(ku)
驚 1061
odo(ru) 踊 1035
躍 1342
odo(su) 脅 1544
o(eru) 終 302
oga(mu) 拝 529
ōgi 扇 1430
ogina(u) 補 744
ogoso(ka)
厳 817
oi 老 637
ō(i) 多 181
ō(i ni) 大 32
o(iru) 老 637
oka 丘 1689
  or 岡 1889
oka(su) 犯 771
  or 侵 1046
冒 1463
oki 沖 1317
ō(kii/ki) 大 32
o(kiru) 起 579
oko(nau)
行 24
oko(ru) 興 338
怒 1068
o(koru/kosu)
起 579
okota(ru)
怠 1084
OKU 億 868
憶 1146
(意) I
屋 251
(握) AKU
(室) SHI-TSU
奥 930
o(ku) 置 345
oku(raseru)
後 276
oku(reru)
後 276

  or 遅 1090
oku(ru) 送 192
贈 1349
omo 主 49
面 321
omo(i) 重 161
omomuki
趣 1047
omomu(ku)
赴 1797
omo 主 49
omote 表 308
面 321
omo(u) 思 95
ON 音 206
(暗) AN
(闇) AN
恩 668
(因) IN
(心) SHIN
温 382
穏 1792
(隠) IN
遠 326
on 御 924
(卸) oro-shi
ona(ji) 同 185
oni 鬼 1226
onna 女 62
ono-ono 各 620
ono(re) 己 676
ori 織 431
折 585
o(riru) 下 30
  or 降 887
oro(ka) 愚 1496
oroshi 卸 1728
oro(su) 下 30
卸 1728
(御) GO, on
o(ru) 折 585
織 431
osa(eru) 押 1632
  or 抑 1318
osa(meru)
治 214
修 563

収 721
  or 納 733
osana(i) 幼 1334
ōse 仰 1534
oshi(eru)教 247
o(shii) 惜 1024
oso(i) 遅 1090
osore 虞 1877
oso(re/reru/ro-
shii) 恐 1163
oso(u) 襲 1094
osu 雄 1387
o(su) 推 877
押 1632
oto 音 206
otoko 男 63
otoro(eru)
衰 1501
oto(ru) 劣 1324
o(tosu) 落 557
otōto 弟 446
otozu(reru)
訪 1412
OTSU 乙 1339
otto 夫 51
o(u) 生 67
負 503
追 746
ō(u) 覆 1699
o(waru) 終 302
oya 親 211
ōyake 公 219
oyo(bi/bu)
及 888
oyo(gu) 泳 562
ō(zuru) 応 718

—R—

RA 裸 1229
(果) KA
RAI 礼 350
来 25
雷 1204
(田) DEN
頼 1172
(束) SO-KU
(速) SO-KU

RAKU 落 557
絡 944
酪 1754
(路) RO
(略)RYA-KU
楽 322
RAN 覧 934
濫 1858
(監) KAN
(艦) KAN
欄 1696
蘭 1990
卵 1527
(卯) BŌ
(貿) BŌ
乱 912
(舌) ZE-TSU
(礼) REI
(札) SA-TSU
嵐 1902
(山) SAN
(風) FŪ
REI 令 496
冷 792
零 1106
齢 1354
鈴 1775
玲 1995
(領) RYŌ
礼 350
(乱) RAN
(孔) KŌ
(札) SA-TSU
励 1495
例 441
(列) RE-TSU
霊 1299
麗 1344
(鹿) RO-KU
隷 1873
(款) KAN
(康) KŌ

REKI
(逮) TAI
曆 1383
歷 839
(麻) MA

REN
練 482
錬 1872
恋 1012
(変) HEN
連 383
(車) SHA
廉 1514
鎌 1996
(兼) KEN
(謙) KEN

RETSU
列 407
烈 1199
裂 1277
(例) REI
劣 1324

RI
里 101
理 104
裏 1076
鯉 1991
(厘) RIN
利 200
痢 1716
吏 1684
(使) SHI
履 1639
(復) FU-KU
離 909

RICHI 律 526
RIKI 力 53
RIKU 陸 193
(睦) BO-KU
RIN 倫 1742
輪 846
林 57
(木) MO-KU
鈴 1775
(令) REI
厘 1820
(里) RI
臨 783
隣 1040

RITSU 立 72
(泣) KYŪ
(粒) RYŪ
(翌) YO-KU
律 526
(筆) HI-TSU
率 808
(卒) SO-TSU
RO 路 677
露 1074
(各) KA-KU
(絡) RA-KU
(略) RYA-KU
呂 1997
(宮) KYŪ
炉 1726
(戸) KO
RŌ 郎 955
浪 1197
廊 1567
朗 1610
(郷) KYŌ
(良) RYŌ
老 637
労 274
(力)RYO-KU
(栄) EI
(営) EI
楼 1744
(数) SŪ
漏 1599
糧 1552
ROKU 録 665
緑 876
禄 1998
六 8
鹿 1999
(麗) REI
RON 論 406
RU 留 412
流 329
RUI 涙 1200

累 1284
(田) DEN
(糸) SHI
塁 1571
類 493
RYAKU 略 678
(各) KA-KU
(路) RO
(絡) RA-KU
RYO 慮 939
虜 1755
旅 335
RYŌ 僚 1752
寮 1459
療 1705
陵 1646
綾 1994
量 743
糧 1552
了 1018
両 859
良 586
(郎) RŌ
亮 1993
料 410
(斗) TO
(科) KA
竜 1992
涼 1268
(京) KYŌ
猟 1655
漁 850
領 849
(令) REI
霊 1299
RYOKU 力 53
(労) RŌ
緑 876
(縁) EN
RYŪ 流 329
硫 1596
留 412
柳 1471
(卯) BŌ
(貿) BŌ
竜 1830

粒 1654
(立) RI-TSU
隆 1193

—S—

SA 左 87
佐 1322
差 662
作 147
詐 1278
砂 1127
(少) SHŌ
査 510
唆 1721
(俊) SHU-N
(酸) SAN
鎖 1698
(肖) SHŌ
再 543
茶 392
saba(ku) 裁 1129
sabi(shii) 寂 1300
sachi 幸 712
sada(meru) 定 218
sa(garu) 下 30
saga(su) 探 1236
 or 捜 1432
sa(geru) 下 30
提 646
sagu(ru) 探 1236
SAI 裁 1129
載 1257
歳 1418
栽 1619
哉 1940
採 710
菜 870
彩 1660
斉 1845
済 536
斎 1269
(剤) ZAI
祭 423
際 424
(察) SA-

TSU	酢 1605	(唆) SA	清 654
才 **574**	搾 1777	賛 841	静 703
財 285	削 1164	(夫) FU	晴 784
(材) ZAI	(肖) SHŌ	(貝) KAI	請 1190
(財) ZAI	(鎖) SA	sara 皿 1891	靖 1957
西 28	冊 956	(血) chi	生 67
切 36	索 1762	sara (ni) 更 1311	性 280
再 543	(糸) SHI	sa(ru) 去 475	星 838
災 788	策 695	sasa(eru) 支 115	姓 1150
(火) KA	(刺) SHI	saso(u) 誘 1222	牲 1812
(巡) JUN	錯 1747	sas(suru) 察 511	(産) SAN
妻 861	(昔) SEKI	sa(su) 差 662	正 123
砕 1467	(借) SHA-	指 729	政 124
(粋) SUI	KU	刺 1139	整 840
宰 1614	(措) SO	sato 里 101	征 1734
(辛) SHIN	sa(ku) 咲 1475	sato(i) 聡 1961	(延) EN
細 701	割 1274	satoshi 聡 1961	(証) SHŌ
(田) DEN	or 裂 1277	satoru 智 1964	(症) SHŌ
最 291	sakura 桜 1050	sato(su) 諭 1357	成 224
(取) SHU	sama 様 309	SATSU 察 511	誠 745
(撮) SA-	sa(masu) 覚 397	擦 1709	盛 898
TSU	冷 792	(祭) SAI	(城) JŌ
債 1515	samata(geru)	冊 956	世 177
(責) SEKI	妨 1674	札 1536	貰 1903
催 1529	sa(meru) 覚 397	(礼) REI	制 635
殺 419	冷 792	(乱) RAN	製 570
saiwa(i) 幸 712	samu(i) 寒 831	(孔) KŌ	井 916
(辛) ka-	samurai 侍 1446	刷 802	(囲) I
ra(i)	SAN 参 514	殺 419	(耕) KŌ
saka 坂 343	惨 1304	撮 1241	西 28
or 阪 1893	三 3	(最) SAI	(酉) YŪ
saka(e/eru)	山 21	SATSU- 早 117	声 226
栄 777	(仙) SEN	sawa 沢 908	(馨) KEI
sakai 境 751	(嵐) RAN	sawa(gu) 騒 1093	斉 1845
saka(n) 盛 898	桟 1834	sawa(ru) 触 945	(済) SAI
sakana 魚 603	(浅) SEN	障 1145	(斎) SAI
saka(rau)	(銭) SEN	sazu(keru)	(剤) ZAI
逆 790	(残) ZAN	授 778	省 408
saka(ri/ru)	蚕 880	SE 世 177	(少) SHŌ
盛 898	(天) TEN	施 1022	(目) MO-
sakazuki 杯 961	(虫) CHŪ	se 背 933	KU
sake 酒 347	産 317	瀬 1037	婿 1719
sake(bu) 叫 1685	(生) SEI	畝 1822	勢 299
sa(keru) 避 1746	散 465	seba(maru/me-	(熱) NE-
saki 先 65	算 720	ru) 狭 1413	TSU
崎 1898	酸 819	SECHI 節 683	歳 1418
SAKU 作 147	(俊) SHU-	SEI 青 331	聖 663
昨 148	N	情 334	誓 1036
		精 457	

	(折)	SE-TSU		浅	722		窃	1641	
sei	背	933		銭	843		殺	419	
SEKI	責	492		践	1802		設	742	
	積	766		(桟)	SAN		(没)	BO-TSU	
	績	805		(残)	ZAN		(役)	YA-KU	
	(債)	SAI		泉	915				
	昔	988		線	389		折	585	
	惜	1024		川	41		(析)	SEKI	
	籍	1343		(訓)	KUN		(誓)	SEI	
	(措)	SO		千	83		抽	1733	
	(錯)	SA-KU		(干)	KAN		(出)	SHU-TSU	
	(借)	SHA-KU		(刊)	KAN		(屈)	KU-TSU	
	夕	734		仙	1959		接	417	
	(多)	TA		(山)	SAN		雪	518	
	石	102		占	985		摂	1665	
	(拓)	TA-KU		(点)	TEN		(耳)	JI	
	(岩)	GAN		(粘)	NEN		節	683	
	斥	1779		宣	569		(即)	SO-KU	
	(訴)	SO		(恒)	KŌ				
	赤	275		専	413		説	216	
	(嚇)	KA-KU		(博)	HA-KU		(悦)	ETSU	
	(赦)	SHA		(縛)	BA-KU		(鋭)	EI	
	析	1634		染	974	SHA	舎	872	
	(折)	SE-TSU		扇	1430		捨	1424	
	席	461		(羽)	U		者	56	
	(度)	DO		旋	1077		煮	1179	
	隻	1153		(施)	SHI		(著)	CHO	
	寂	1300		船	314		(猪)	CHO	
	(叔)	SHU-KU		(沿)	EN		射	989	
	跡	1502		(鉛)	EN		謝	765	
	(亦)	EKI		戦	399		(身)	SHIN	
	(変)	HEN		(単)	TAN		写	494	
	(恋)	REN		(禅)	ZEN		(与)	YO	
seki	関	289		潜	1458		車	54	
sema(i)	狭	1413		選	522		(軍)	GUN	
sema(ru)	迫	1411		遷	1447		(連)	REN	
se(meru)	攻	970		薦	1748		(揮)	KI	
	責	492		鮮	1350		(輝)	KI	
SEN	先	65		(羊)	YŌ		社	203	
	洗	925		(祥)	SHŌ		(土)	TO	
	銑	1588		(詳)	SHŌ		(土)	DO	
				繊	1704		砂	1127	
			se(ri/ru)	競	464		斜	1488	
			ses(suru)	接	417		(斗)	TO	
				節	683		(料)	RYŌ	
			SETSU	切	36				

Right columns:

	(科)	KA			
	(余)	YO			
	赦	1739			
	(赤)	SEKI			
SHAKU	勺	1817			
	酌	1835			
	(約)	YA-KU			
	(的)	TEKI			
	尺	1781			
	釈	660			
	(沢)	TA-KU			
	(訳)	YA-KU			
	(駅)	EKI			
	昔	988			
	借	471			
	(錯)	SA-KU			
	(措)	SO			
	石	102			
	(岩)	GAN			
	赤	275			
	爵	1875			
sha(suru)	謝	765			
SHI	止	552			
	歯	439			
	祉	1803			
	紫	1392			
	雌	1586			
	(渋)	JŪ			
	(武)	BU			
	司	761			
	詞	807			
	飼	1156			
	伺	1315			
	嗣	1671			
	士	59			
	仕	75			
	志	757			
	誌	919			
	次	239			
	姿	1133			
	資	558			
	諮	1558			
	旨	1069			
	指	729			
	脂	1577			

(詣) KEI	施 1022	shime(su)		深 593
支 115	(旋) SEN	示 575		(探) TAN
枝 889	師 547	shi(mi/miru)		進 194
(技) GI	(帥) SUI	染 974		(准) JUN
氏 361	試 354	shimo 下 30		(推) SUI
紙 362	(式) SHI-	霜 1352		(集) SHŪ
(低) TEI	KI	SHIN 申 204		森 152
(抵) TEI	詩 648	神 205		(木) MO-
史 81	(寺) JI	伸 1528		KU
使 210	(時) JI	紳 1645		(林) RIN
(吏) RI	賜 1453	辛 1312		診 1081
市 119	(易) EKI	新 178		(珍) CHI-
姉 120	shiawa(se)	親 211		N
示 575	幸 712	薪 1560		審 1253
視 794	shiba 芝 954	(幸) KŌ		(番) BAN
(禁) KIN	shiba(ru) 縛 1361	(宰) SAI		請 1190
已 1944	shibo(ru)	辰 1954		shina 品 146
(己) KO	絞 1394	震 1123		shino(bu)
子 61	or 搾 1777	娠 1543		忍 1060
(好) KŌ	shibu(i) 渋 1025	振 1612		shi(nu) 死 207
(季) KI	SHICHI 七 9	(辱) JO-		shin(zuru)
之 1942	(叱) SHI-	KU		信 149
四 6	TSU	侵 1046		shio 塩 730
(匹) HIKI	質 325	浸 1221		潮 980
矢 1335	shige 穣 1952	寝 918		shira(beru)
(疾) SHI-	shige(ru) 茂 1799	真 384		調 376
TSU	shii(ru) 強 332	慎 1669		shi(raseru)
(医) I	shiita(geru)	(直)CHO-		知 196
至 725	虐 1248	KU		shiri 尻 1884
(室) CHI-	shika 鹿 1999	(具) GU		shirizo(keru/ku)
TSU	shika(ru)叱 1886	心 80		退 459
自 60	SHIKI 織 431	(応) Ō		shiro 代 85
糸 113	識 486	(恥) CHI		城 886
死 207	(職) SHO-	(思) SHI		shiro(i) 白 79
私 367	KU	臣 435		shiru 汁 1848
(払) FU-	色 241	身 791		shi(ru) 知 196
TSU	式 349	(射) SHA		shirushi 印 801
(仏) BU-	(試) SHI	信 149		shiru(su)記 301
TSU	shi(ku) 敷 1039	(言) GEN		shita 下 30
刺 1139	shima 島 183	津 975		舌 878
(策) SA-	shi(maru)	(筆) HI-		shitaga(u)従 673
KU	閉 900	TSU		shita(shii/shi-
始 545	締 1243	(建) KEN		mu) 親 211
(台) DAI	shime 〆 1880	(健) KEN		shitata(ru)
(治) JI	shi(meru)	晋 1953		滴 1381
(治) CHI	閉 900	(普) FU		shita(u) 慕 1382
思 95	占 985	針 1407		SHITSU 叱 1886
(慮) RYO	締 1243	(十) JŪ		(七) SHI-
	絞 1394			CHI

301

失 238	肖 *1672*	(進) SHIN	(置) CHI
(鉄) TE-TSU	消 *612*	(唯) YUI	織 *431*
(迭) TE-TSU	硝 *1760*	将 *920*	職 *432*
室 278	宵 *1849*	奨 *1519*	(識) SHI-KI
(至) SHI	(鎖) SA	詳 *896*	色 *241*
(屋) OKU	(削) SA-KU	祥 *1562*	(絶) ZE-TSU
疾 *1789*	小 *33*	(羊) YŌ	触 *945*
(矢) SHI	少 *129*	(鮮) SEN	(独) DO-KU
(医) I	省 *408*	上 *29*	(濁) DA-KU
湿 *1402*	抄 *1675*	井 916	嘱 *1297*
(顕) KEN	(砂) SA	匠 *1532*	(属) ZO-KU
執 *1231*	(秒) BYŌ	(斤) KIN	
(幸) KŌ	正 123	声 226	shō(suru)
(丸) GAN	政 124	床 *959*	称 736
漆 *1597*	症 *1563*	(木) MO-KU	SHU 朱 *1681*
質 *325*	証 *697*	承 *854*	殊 *1019*
(斤) KIN	(正) SEI	相 *97*	珠 *1585*
shizu(ka)	(整) SEI	称 736	守 *352*
静 703	生 *67*	(弥) MI	狩 *1023*
shizuku 滴 1381	姓 1150	(爾) JI	取 *108*
shizu(maru/me-ru) 鎮 1348	性 *280*	笑 *1147*	趣 *1047*
shizu(mu)	星 *838*	商 *293*	(最) SAI
沈 1097	尚 *1843*	(適) TEKI	(撮) SA-TSU
SHO 暑 *476*	賞 *621*	渉 *1305*	手 *37*
諸 *617*	掌 *1210*	(歩) HO	(挙) KYO
署 *903*	償 *1355*	勝 *266*	主 *49*
緒 *949*	(党) TŌ	(券) KEN	(住) JŪ
(者) SHA	(常) JŌ	(騰) TŌ	(住) Ō
(都) TO	昌 *1950*	焼 *671*	首 *138*
処 *553*	唱 *814*	(暁) GYŌ	(道) DŌ
(拠) KYO	晶 *1582*	装 *1391*	修 *563*
初 *636*	章 *505*	象 *809*	酒 *347*
(刀) TŌ	彰 *1386*	像 ZŌ	(酉) YŪ
所 *137*	障 *1145*	傷 *1008*	種 *232*
書 *70*	升 *1816*	(場) JŌ	(重) JŪ
庶 *1661*	昇 *1441*	衝 *1117*	SHŪ 州 *445*
(度) DO	庄 *1949*	(重) JŪ	酬 *1774*
SHŌ 召 *1115*	粧 *1595*	鐘 *1695*	周 *187*
昭 *517*	(圧) A-TSU	(童) DŌ	週 *188*
照 *675*	青 331	従 *673*	(調) CHŌ
招 *679*	精 457	SHOKU 食 *283*	秋 *164*
紹 *1130*	清 654	飾 *1014*	愁 *1778*
沼 *1175*	松 *884*	植 *438*	収 *721*
詔 *1213*	訟 *1483*	殖 *1396*	
(超) CHŌ	(公) KŌ	(直)CHO-KU	
	焦 *1606*		
	礁 *1706*		

囚 1538	春 162	(増) ZŌ	速 848
(人) JIN	瞬 1556	双 1541	(勅) CHO-KU
舟 968	SHUTSU 出 40	桑 1609	(疎) SO
秀 973	(拙) SE-TSU	早 117	足 135
(乃) DAI	(屈) KU-TSU	草 118	促 1209
(誘) YŪ	(掘) KU-TSU	倉 732	即 1678
(透) TŌ	SO 組 458	創 789	(節) SE-TSU
宗 248	祖 540	操 1367	息 628
(示) SHI	租 1574	燥 1708	(憩) KEI
(崇) SŪ	粗 1724	爪 1887	so(maru)染 974
拾 625	阻 1767	(瓜) KA	so(meru)染 974
臭 1308	疎 1601	争 311	初 636
(自) JI	(束) SO-KU	(浄) JŌ	somu(keru/ku)
(大) DAI	(速) SO-KU	走 832	背 933
修 563	素 797	(徒) TO	SON 存 405
執 1231	措 1506	宗 248	村 154
習 320	(昔) SEKI	(示) SHI	(寸) SUN
(羽) U	(借) SHA-KU	(崇) SŪ	孫 644
(白) HA-KU	(錯) SA-KU	奏 1643	(系) KEI
終 302	訴 1182	(奉) HŌ	尊 856
(冬) TŌ	(斥) SEKI	(天) TEN	(遵) JUN
衆 651	塑 1791	送 192	損 449
就 759	礎 1701	(朕) CHI-N	(員) IN
集 279	想 324	捜 1432	sona(eru)
(准) JUN	SŌ 壮 1329	掃 947	供 694
(準) JUN	荘 1058	(婦) FU	備 750
(推) SUI	装 1391	(帰) KI	son(jiru)
醜 1703	相 97	巣 1491	損 449
(鬼) KI	想 324	(果) KA	sono 園 327
(塊) KAI	霜 1352	喪 1572	son(suru)
襲 1094	(目) MO-KU	惣 1960	存 405
(竜) RYŪ	総 741	(物) BU-TSU	sora 空 184
(衣) I	窓 1029	葬 1593	so(rasu)反 342
SHUKU 叔 1445	聡 1961	(死) SHI	sōrō 候 862
淑 1487	(公) KŌ	遭 1376	so(ru) 反 342
(寂) JA-KU	(松) SHŌ	騒 1093	soso(gu)注 444
宿 549	(訟) SHŌ	soda(teru)	sosonoka(su)
縮 1142	僧 1007	育 487	唆 1721
祝 756	層 1183	so(eru) 添 1656	sō(suru)奏 1643
(兄) KYŌ	贈 1349	soko 底 590	soto 外 42
粛 1652		soko(nau/neru)	SOTSU 卒 798
(逮) TAI		損 449	率 808
(康) KŌ		SOKU 則 499	so(u) 沿 1013
SHUN 俊 1472		側 538	SU 子 61
(酸) SAN		測 758	主 49
(竣) SA		束 1126	守 352
			州 445

	素 797	(恵) KEI	—T—	(村) SON

305

頭	519	(尚)	SHŌ	to(kasu/keru)		tona(eru)	
闘	1056	納	733	溶	1517	唱	814
痘	1715	(内)	NAI	toki 時	46	tonari 隣	1040
登	559	討	642	toko 常	199	tona(ru) 隣	1040
灯	537	(寸)	SUN	床	959	tono 殿	892
(澄)	CHŌ	(村)	SON	tokoro 所	137	tora 寅	1911
(短)	TAN	島	183	TOKU 匿	1766	虎	1932
騰	1340	(鳥)	CHŌ	(若)	JA-KU	tora(eru) 捕	1611
謄	1554	(山)	SAN	特	411	tori 鳥	182
藤	1975	透	1152	(寺)	JI	酉	1989
(勝)	SHŌ	(秀)	SHŪ	(時)	JI	to(ru) 取	108
到	1041	悼	1771	(待)	TAI	or 採	710
倒	1189	(卓)	TA-KU	得	340	or 執	1231
(至)	SHI	盗	1026	督	1737	or 捕	1611
東	27	(次)	JI	(叔)	SHU-KU	撮	1241
凍	1435	陶	1481	(淑)	SHU-KU	tōru 亨	1934
(練)	REN	湯	844	徳	592	tō(ru) 通	201
(錬)	REN	(場)	JŌ	(聴)	CHŌ	toshi 年	64
逃	1169	(揚)	YŌ	(庁)	CHŌ	稔	1979
桃	1428	(陽)	YŌ	読	55	tō(su) 通	201
(兆)	CHŌ	等	294	篤	1561	tōtō(bu/i)	
唐	1856	(寺)	JI	(馬)	BA	貴	616
糖	1128	(時)	JI	(驚)	KEI	or 尊	856
答	556	(待)	TAI	to(ku) 説	216	totono(eru/u)	
塔	1570	(特)	TO-KU	解	577	調	376
(合)	GŌ	統	521	to(maru) 止	552	or 整	840
筒	1125	(充)	JŪ	泊	1016	TOTSU 凸	1882
桐	1974	(銃)	JŪ	to(meru) 留	412	突	913
(同)	DŌ	稲	1293	or 止	552	(大)	DAI
(銅)	DO	踏	1186	泊	1016	totsu(gu)	
刀	34	道	141	tomi 富	705	嫁	1223
(券)	KEN	読	55	tomo 友	158	to(u) 問	175
(召)	SHŌ	tō 十	12	or 朋	1982	TSU 都	173
冬	165	tobo(shii)		共	240	通	201
(終)	SHŪ	乏	932	供	694	tsu 津	975
当	96	to(bu) 飛	404	呂	1997	TSŪ 通	201
灯	537	跳	1590	tomona(u)		痛	1020
燈	537	todo(keru/ku)		伴	1433	(踊)	YŌ
(丁)	TEI	届	727	to(mu) 富	705	tsubasa 翼	1555
投	653	todokō(ru)		tomura(u)		tsubo 坪	1628
(没)	BO-TSU	滞	1251	弔	1690	tsubu 粒	1654
(設)	SE-TSU	tōge 峠	1473	TON 豚	1738	tsuchi 土	19
(役)	YA-KU	to(geru) 遂	1070	(家)	KA	tsuchika(u)	
党	466	to(gu) 研	583	敦	1976	培	1492
(堂)	DŌ	tō(i) 遠	326	(享)	KYŌ	tsudo(u) 集	279
		to(jiru) 閉	900	団	243	tsu(geru) 告	296
						tsugi 次	239
						tsu(gi) 継	894
						tsu(gu) 次	239

接 417
継 894
tsuguna(u)
償 1355
TSUI 対 370
追 746
(遣) KEN
墜 1240
(隊) TAI
tsui(yasu)
費 608
tsuji 辻 1881
tsuka(eru)
仕 75
tsuka(maeru/
maru) 捕 1611
tsuka(re/reru)
疲 1798
tsuka(u) 使 210
遣 895
tsuka(wasu)
遣 895
tsu(keru)
付 259
tsuki 月 13
tsu(kiru) 尽 1530
tsu(ku) 付 259
着 403
就 759
突 913
tsukue 机 1785
tsukuro(u)
繕 1550
tsuku(ru)
作 147
or 造 551
tsu(kusu)
尽 1530
tsuma 妻 861
tsume 爪 1887
(瓜) uri
tsu(meru)
詰 1507
tsume(tai)
冷 792
tsumi 罪 748
tsu(mori/moru)
積 766
tsumu 錘 1751
tsumu(gu)

紡 1415
tsuna 綱 1052
tsune 常 199
tsuno 角 273
tsuno(ru)
募 1275
tsura 面 321
tsura(naru)
連 383
tsuranu(ku)
貫 1198
tsu(reru) 連 383
tsuri 釣 1836
tsuru 弦 1624
鶴 1917
tsurugi 剣 1436
tsuta 蔦 1969
tsuta(eru/waru)
伝 554
tsuto(me)
務 491
or 勤 726
tsuto(meru)
務 491
or 努 566
or 勤 726
tsutsu 筒 1125
tsutsumi 堤 1404
tsutsu(mi/mu)
包 369
tsutsushi(mu)
慎 1669
or 謹 1151
tsuya 艶 1914
tsuyo 強 332
tsuyo(i) 強 332
tsuyoshi 毅 1919
tsuyu 露 1074
tsuzu(keru/ki/
ku) 続 548
tsuzumi 鼓 1064

— U —
U 右 88
宇 1286
有 267
羽 967
(扇) SEN

(翻) HON
雨 114
u 卯 1983
uba(u) 奪 1603
ubu 産 317
uchi 内 132
ude 腕 1180
ue 上 29
u(eru) 植 438
飢 1717
ugo(ku) 動 169
ui 初 636
u(i) 憂 1518
uji 氏 361
uka(bu) 浮 991
ukaga(u) 伺 1315
u(keru) 受 272
or 請 1190
uketamawa(ru)
承 854
u(ku) 浮 991
uma 馬 142
uma(reru)
生 67
u(maru/meru)
埋 1615
ume 梅 1162
umi 海 99
u(mu) 産 317
UN 運 373
(軍) GUN
(揮) KI
(輝) KI
雲 478
(魂) KON
(芸) GEI
unaga(su)
促 1209
une 畝 1822
uo 魚 603
ura 浦 1015
裏 1076
ura(mi/mu)
恨 1227
urana(u) 占 985
ure(eru) 憂 1518
ure(i) 憂 1518
or 愁 1778
u(reru) 熟 1508

uri 瓜 1888
(爪) tsu-
me
u(ri) 売 47
u(ru) 売 47
得 340
uru(mu) 潤 1256
uruo(i/su/u)
潤 1256
urushi 漆 1597
uruwa(shii)
麗 1344
ushi 牛 534
丑 1965
ushina(u)
失 238
ushi(ro) 後 276
uso 嘘 1905
usu(i) 薄 1091
uta 歌 256
utaga(i/u)
疑 752
utai 謡 1071
uta(u) 歌 256
uto(i/mu)
疎 1601
u(tsu) 討 642
or 打 682
or 撃 997
utsuku(shii)
美 268
utsu(ru/su)
映 910
移 607
utsu(su) 写 494
utsuwa 器 398
utta(eru)訴 1182
uyama(u)
敬 857
uyauya(shii)
恭 1618
uzu 渦 1823

— W —
WA 和 277
(口) KŌ
話 180
(舌) ZE-
TSU

Appendices

Appendix 1

ENGLISH NAMES OF RADICALS

air 84 气
and 126 而
arrow 111 矢
ax 69 斤

bamboo 118 竹 ⺮
barb 6 亅
basket 22 匚 匸
bean 151 豆
bend 5 乙 乚 乚
bent figure 44 尸
big 37 大 ⼤
bird 196 鳥
birth 100 生
bitter 160 辛
black 203 黑 黒
blade 161 辰 辰
blood 143 血 血
blue 174 青 青
boat 137 舟 舟
body 158 身
bone 188 骨
borders 13 冂 冂
both feet 105 癶
bow 57 弓
box 23 匚
branch 65 支 支

capture 171 隶
cart 159 車
child 39 子
city/district 163 邑 阝
clan 83 氏
claw 87 爪 爫 ⺥ ⺤
cliff 27 厂
cloth 50 巾

clothes 145 衣 衤
color 139 色
compare 81 比
cover 14 冖
　　　　146 西 西 襾

dark 95 玄
deer 198 鹿 鹿
devil 194 鬼 鬼
dish 108 皿
disintegrate 78 歹 歺
district 163 邑 阝
divination 25 卜 卜 ⺊
dog 94 犬 犭
do not 80 毋 母
door 63 戸 戸
dot 3 、
dragon 212 龍 竜 竜
drum 207 鼓 鼓

ear 128 耳 耳
earth 32 土 士 圡
earthenware 121 缶
eat 184 食
eight 12 八 ハ ⺍
embroidery 204 黹
enclosure 31 囗
enter 11 入 ⼊
evening 36 夕
eye 109 目
extend 54 廴

father 88 父
field 102 田
fight 191 鬥
fine thread 52 幺

313

fire 86 火 灬
fish 195 魚
flesh 130 肉 肉 月 月
flute 214 龠
fly 183 飛
folded hands 55 廾 廾
foot 157 足
footstep 60 彳
fragrance 186 香
frog 205 黽

gate 169 門
god 113 示 礻
go/do 144 行
grain 115 禾
grass 140 艸 艹

hair 82 毛 毛
hand 64 手 手 扌
head 185 首
head/page 181 頁
heart 61 心 小 忄
hemp 200 麻 麻
herbs 192 鬯
high 189 高
high nose 209 鼻 鼻
hole 116 穴 穴
horn 148 角
horse 187 馬

ice 15 冫
illness 104 疒
insect 142 虫
intertwine 89 爻 爻

jewel 96 玉 王 王

kill 79 殳
kneeling figure 26 卩 巳
knife 18 刀 刂

lame 43 尢
lance 62 戈 戈
lean-to 53 广
leather 178 韋
leek 179 韭
left stroke 4 丿 丿 丿
legs 10 儿
level 210 齊 齐
lid 8 亠 亠

light rays 59 彡
limit 138 艮 艮
literature 67 文
long 168 長 镸
long hair 190 髟

man 9 人 亻 入
melon 97 瓜
metal 167 金
millet 202 黍
minister 131 臣
money 154 貝
moon 74 月
mortar 134 臼
mound 170 阜 阝
mountain 46 山
mouth 30 口

net 122 网 罒
nose 132 自
not 71 无 旡

old 125 老 耂
one 1 一
open mouth 76 欠
oppose 136 舛
ox 93 牛 牜

page 181 頁
pig 152 豕
pig's head 58 彐 ⺕ 彑
plow 127 耒 耒
private 28 厶
proceed 162 辵 辶 辶

rain 173 雨
rawhide 177 革
reach 133 至
receptacle 17 凵
red 155 赤
reptiles 153 豸
rice 119 米
right hand 29 又 又
river 47 川
rod 2 丨
rodent 208 鼠 鼠
roll of cloth 103 疋 疋
roof 40 宀
rule 41 寸
run 156 走

salt 197 鹵
say 73 曰
scholar 33 士
scoop 68 斗
see 147 見
self 49 己 已 巳
separate 165 釆
sheep 123 羊 ⺶ ⺷
shell/money 154 貝
shield 51 干
skin 107 皮
small 42 小 ⺍
small bird 172 隹
sound 180 音
spear 110 矛
split wood (left) 90 爿 丬
split wood (right) 91 片
spoon 21 匕 七
sprout 45 屮 㞢
square 70 方
stake 56 弋
stand 117 立 ⺊
step 35 夂
step down 34 夂 夊 夂
stone 112 石
stop 77 止
strength 19 力
strike 66 攴 攵
sun 72 日
surface 176 面
sweet 99 甘

table 16 几 几

ten 24 十 ⼇ ⼗
thread 120 糸
tiger 141 虍
tile 98 瓦
tongue 135 舌
tooth 211 齒 齒
tortoise 213 龜 龟
tracks 114 禸
tree 75 木
triped 206 鼎
tusk 92 牙 牙
two 7 二 二

urn 193 鬲
use 101 用

valley 150 谷
village 166 里

water 85 水 氵
wheat 199 麥
white 106 白
wind 182 風
wine jug 164 酉
wings 124 羽 羽
woman 38 女
words 149 言
work 48 工
wrap 20 勹
writing 129 聿
wrong 175 非

yellow 201 黃 黃

315

Appendix 2

CHARACTERS ARRANGED BY STROKE COUNT

1 stroke		弓	1419	元	106	止	552	弘	1937
一	1	刃	1107	予	531	支	115	外	42
乙	1339	工	77	冗	1122	木	17	犯	771
		干	1542	父	90	夫	51	卯	1983
2 strokes		千	83	分	35	友	158	幼	1334
八	10	子	61	公	219	井	916	奴	1869
二		士	59	介	941	中	31	礼	350
丁	166	土	19	今	94	午	140	札	1536
又	1851	与	983	犬	578	牛	534	永	560
了	1018	大	32	太	508	升	1816	氷	820
乃	1962	丈	962	丹	1852	夊	1819	示	575
刀	34	才	574	斗	1815	欠	713	写	494
力	53	々	1879	厄	1829	手	37	召	1115
十	12	久	704	区	168	乏	932	矛	1813
九	11	夕	734	凶	1337	毛	125	台	290
七	9	女	62	匂	1895	爪	1887	弁	513
〆	1880	丸	922	日	5	斤	1818	冬	165
人	4	也	1986	円	159			令	496
入	39			月	13	**5 strokes**		穴	984
		4 strokes		尺	1781	必	281	只	1943
3 strokes		心	80	王	310	旧	760	号	227
小	33	火	15	五	7	加	787	旦	1892
川	41	水	16	互	1032	仙	1959	司	761
三	3	切	36	丑	1965	仕	75	可	253
凡	1338	比	589	四	1120	付	259	圧	874
寸	1045	刈	1540	天	78	代	85	石	102
勺	1817	仁	829	弔	1690	他	520	右	88
亡	979	仏	249	及	888	汁	1848	左	87
之	1942	化	76	反	342	以	221	布	737
口	38	引	271	不	130	叱	1886	句	795
山	21	孔	1336	氏	361	功	467	包	369
上	29	収	721	方	26	巧	1363	庁	1034
下	30	双	1541	文	71	刊	604	広	303
万	84	幻	1691	内	132	北	156	平	136
已	1944	六	8	片	937	打	682	半	150
己	676	戸	126	少	129	払	904	囚	1538

母	89	旨	1069	守	352	曲	715	抗
尼	1688	次	239	宅	992	肉	533	投
尻	1884	仰	1534	安	98	成	224	技
処	553	伝	554	芋	1682	年	64	抄
辺	270	仮	696	芝	954	朱	1681	択
辻	1881	伊	1909	各	620	米	112	扱
込	987	任	414	糸	113	血	344	抜
主	49	休	153	至	725	自	60	扶
市	119	仲	1332	早	117	羊	1326	折
立	72	伏	1331	共	240	名	131	防
玄	1113	伐	1535	劣	1324	争	311	阪
玉	103	件	485	丞	1951	色	241	役
正	123	汗	1328	灰	1325	舌	878	狂
巨	1537	江	994	旬	1327	瓜	1888	妨
丙	1782	汚	1531	有	267			妙
占	985	池	847	存	405	**7 strokes**		妊
古	93	羽	967	在	258	児	782	対
去	475	地	143	庄	1949	冷	792	社
世	177	吐	1686	匡	1923	似	775	初
出	40	叫	1685	匠	1532	低	690	助
本	20	帆	948	后	542	但	1853	励
末	565	忙	890	同	185	伺	1315	村
未	626	壮	1329	向	215	佐	1322	材
凸	1882	兆	1687	回	571	位	122	杉
凹	1883	竹	68	団	243	住	209	形
田	52	多	181	因	462	体	176	即
由	297	行	24	尽	1530	伸	1528	却
申	204	妃	1533	危	899	伴	1433	邪
甲	1082	好	882	舟	968	作	147	邦
目	22	如	1539	互	1935	伯	1679	卵
甘	1333	刑	1001	式	349	没	1075	肝
且	1865	列	407	弐	723	汽	490	町
用	110	朴	1828	気	144	沢	908	私
四	6	朽	1683	迅	1871	沖	1317	利
皿	1891	机	1785	巡	905	沈	1097	別
冊	956	肌	1890	亦	1913	決	230	判
民	246	印	801	衣	605	快	827	乱
兄	234	灯	537	充	1319	状	512	豆
史	81	交	86	先	65	岐	1769	言
央	881	毎	92	光	217	吟	1043	亨
皮	863	合	195	当	96	吸	1083	亥
矢	1335	会	116	吏	1684	吹	1095	辛
失	238	全	212	虫	133	改	691	克
自	79	企	966	老	637	坑	1524	声
生	67	吉	990	耳	107	坊	1676	壱
斥	1779	寺	45	百	82	坂	343	売
丘	1689	考	197	死	207	均	869	志
		圭	1928	西	28	批	1523	麦
6 strokes		宇	1286	再	543	抑	1318	条
州	445	字	121	両	859			芸

抗	1320
投	653
技	463
抄	1675
択	1096
扱	1330
抜	1525
扶	1796
折	585
防	680
阪	1893
役	171
狂	972
妨	1674
妙	1321
妊	1314
対	370
社	203
初	636
助	346
励	1495
村	154
材	284
杉	1847
形	223
即	1678
却	1680
邪	1520
邦	1323
卵	1527
肝	1516
町	167
私	367
利	200
別	288
判	497
乱	912
豆	1044
言	43
亨	1934
亥	1916
辛	1312
克	1673
声	226
壱	708
売	47
志	757
麦	816
条	452
芸	421

芳	1316	肖	1672	弧	1729	炉	1726	苗	1287
花	328	臣	435	孤	1768	炊	1626	芽	709
忘	1004	亜	1788	阻	1767	欣	1924	英	377
忌	1522	酉	1989	附	1878	欧	1416	昔	988
忍	1060	辰	1954	味	339	殴	1468	昌	1950
災	788	更	1311	呼	1000	牧	799	昇	1441
妥	1313	里	101	坪	1628	版	689	易	824
系	634	車	54	招	679	放	287	青	331
余	483	束	1126	担	1631	和	277	毒	418
谷	528	来	25	抵	1154	知	196	炎	1727
含	1677	赤	275	拓	1780	的	372	忠	632
吾	1933	孝	865	拘	1448	物	74	典	640
呂	1997	寿	1786	抱	1633	邸	1621	具	400
否	830	角	273	拡	776	卸	1728	奉	1191
告	296	良	586	拠	1725	取	108	学	66
秀	973	身	791	抽	1443	叔	1445	季	641
男	63	我	719	押	1632	到	1041	岳	1772
労	274			拒	1439	刷	802	肯	1625
努	566	**8 strokes**		拙	1733	刺	1139	歩	433
呈	1526	協	572	披	1841	刻	1444	卓	1761
呉	1002	例	441	拍	1440	制	635	育	487
兵	396	侮	1212	拝	529	乳	1216	斉	1845
貝	44	侍	1446	径	1630	享	1622	券	747
完	236	佳	1450	往	875	京	172	受	272
宏	1936	依	1135	彼	1764	参	514	委	837
究	599	供	694	征	1734	奔	1438	妻	861
序	507	価	762	始	545	奈	1977	直	304
床	959	使	210	姉	120	命	387	周	187
応	718	併	1079	妹	427	念	316	岡	1889
局	422	怪	1176	姓	1150	舎	872	画	477
尿	1770	怖	1784	非	353	金	18	国	111
尾	1005	性	280	効	623	盲	1177	固	738
尻	1850	泌	1787	祉	1803	宛	1897	店	235
君	479	泳	562	祈	1141	宗	248	府	260
医	440	沼	1175	明	58	定	218	底	590
困	969	沿	1013	門	105	宝	981	延	706
囲	803	治	214	肪	1806	宜	1042	述	770
図	388	法	213	朋	1982	官	318	迭	1623
何	254	河	633	肥	724	宙	1303	迫	1411
足	135	泥	1840	服	306	実	233	居	208
走	832	泡	1904	枢	1442	空	184	届	727
廷	1417	注	444	板	468	突	913	屈	1629
迎	1062	泣	1049	杯	961	幸	712	肩	1215
返	307	波	484	枝	889	奇	1048	房	1116
近	127	油	298	林	57	岸	687	者	56
希	823	況	1267	枕	1900	岩	821	雨	114
求	584	沸	1627	枚	952	苦	264	武	596
戒	1006	泊	1016	松	884	茎	1291	或	1894
見	23	弦	1624	析	1634	若	982	尚	1843
弟	446	弥	1980	所	137	茂	1799	虎	1932

夜	336	姻	1159	削	1164	音	206	候	862
卒	798	独	618	則	499	香	1059	倍	866
表	308	狭	1413	劾	1867	柔	1086	修	563
事	73	狩	1023	勅	1478	某	1470	俳	1427
東	27	施	1022	帝	906	架	1085	倣	1616
果	375	祝	756	軍	100	染	974	倒	1189
長	155	祐	1988	冠	1170	点	229	借	471
承	854	神	205	勇	825	思	95	倫	1742
並	998	祖	540	盆	1087	急	330	倹	1620
免	931	玲	1995	食	283	怠	1084	俸	1842
垂	1214	珍	1027	品	146	怒	1068	個	502
		昭	517	茶	392	契	1132	値	1414
9 strokes		映	910	荘	1058	美	268	俵	879
胤	1912	昨	148	荒	1028	要	262	涙	1200
信	149	肺	943	草	118	姿	1133	浴	609
便	265	胆	1466	革	811	盾	1814	浸	1221
侯	1479	胎	1477	首	138	厚	735	浜	907
侵	1046	胞	1237	前	139	厘	1820	浩	1939
保	351	柱	826	単	390	風	134	流	329
促	1209	枯	1246	栄	777	度	252	消	612
俗	544	柄	1168	宣	569	幽	1735	浦	1015
俊	1472	相	97	室	278	屋	251	酒	347
係	426	柳	1471	客	434	建	363	浪	1197
洪	1833	牲	1812	窃	1641	逃	1169	浮	991
浅	722	畑	699	炭	842	退	459	峰	1272
津	975	科	385	冒	1463	追	746	悟	1104
海	99	秋	164	是	786	迷	781	悩	1617
派	516	秒	867	星	838	逆	790	悌	1972
洋	305	砂	1127	査	510	送	192	悦	1857
浄	976	砕	1467	昼	828	南	157	将	920
洗	925	研	583	春	162	省	408	孫	644
活	198	既	1309	奏	1643	看	1057	院	237
恒	1225	段	911	発	186	県	381	陣	1207
悔	1166	政	124	皇	460	為	977	除	530
恨	1227	紅	1233	泉	915	疫	1469	陛	873
峠	1473	紀	666	背	933	威	1011	陥	1718
峡	1270	糾	1640	胃	853	虐	1248	唆	1721
限	600	約	451	界	269	哉	1940	埋	1615
降	887	臭	1308	変	191	彦	1931	捜	1432
咲	1475	帥	1741	巻	885	赴	1797	捕	1611
城	886	訂	1134	型	685	面	321	振	1612
挑	1825	叙	1476	専	413	飛	404	徒	834
持	50	計	357	卑	1795	甚	1955	従	673
拷	1642	軌	1465	貞	1238	重	161	徐	1613
指	729	故	707	負	503	乗	312	姫	1220
拾	625	耐	1247	皆	978			娠	1543
括	1474	封	1124	亮	1993	**10 strokes**		娯	1801
待	611	郊	1030	亭	1826	帰	263	娘	999
律	526	郁	1910	哀	1249	凍	1435	祥	1562
後	276	郎	955	衷	1809	准	1743	旅	335

時	46	紋	1763	夏	163	頃	1906	渋	1025
脂	1577	納	733	恭	1618	側	538	渉	1305
胴	1500	紛	1499	烈	1199	停	591	清	654
胸	1149	純	667	笑	1147	偵	1839	混	684
朕	1876	紙	362	挙	523	偶	1112	渇	1266
脈	813	級	228	晋	1953	偉	1098	深	593
班	1804	郡	480	書	70	偏	1260	涯	1824
珠	1585	財	285	骨	971	健	364	淡	1065
残	315	射	989	脅	1544	偽	1157	添	1656
殊	1019	軒	953	恋	1012	張	681	渓	1846
殉	1736	配	430	恵	1498	強	332	婦	313
桃	1428	酌	1835	恩	668	陪	1693	婚	965
梅	1162	訓	613	息	628	陵	1646	術	447
桂	1929	記	301	恐	1163	陸	193	御	924
格	716	託	1408	辱	1462	隆	1193	得	340
校	91	討	642	真	384	険	356	猛	1420
桜	1050	針	1407	哲	1108	陰	1031	猪	1966
核	1608	飢	1717	隻	1153	陶	1481	猟	1655
桐	1974	剣	1436	原	202	陳	1647	族	448
根	425	剖	1805	庫	582	帳	851	旋	1077
桟	1834	剤	1497	唐	1856	唱	814	視	794
株	731	剛	1434	席	461	唯	1493	規	527
被	1410	高	160	座	1089	崎	1898	理	104
弱	595	衰	1501	庭	402	堀	1837	現	495
破	645	桑	1609	匿	1766	培	1492	琢	1963
砲	993	倉	732	展	501	域	1017	球	845
眠	1144	貢	1295	逐	1573	排	1657	豚	1738
畔	1587	員	374	通	201	掛	1143	脚	1422
特	411	荷	255	速	848	接	417	脱	1173
秘	940	華	1409	連	383	探	1236	脳	927
租	1574	宰	1614	透	1152	控	1658	械	474
称	736	宵	1849	途	928	描	1489	略	678
秩	1722	害	450	逓	1863	掃	947	眼	674
畝	1822	宮	546	造	551	措	1506	務	491
蚊	1119	宴	1301	扇	1430	掲	1659	移	607
致	1114	家	151	病	145	授	778	船	314
敏	1429	容	700	症	1563	採	710	舶	1485
師	547	案	500	疲	1798	捨	1424	距	1110
朗	1610	蚕	880	疾	1789	推	877	粒	1654
能	416	晃	1938	栽	1619	据	1831	粘	1644
恥	1431	翁	1594	馬	142	掘	1265	粗	1724
殺	419	索	1762	島	183	悼	1771	経	341
般	1201	素	797	起	579	惜	1024	紹	1130
航	561	竜	1830	差	662	情	334	細	701
耕	812	党	466	勉	852	惨	1304	紳	1645
耗	1720	帯	614	鬼	1226	淳	1947	組	458
粋	1790	泰	1765	兼	669	涼	1268	紺	1653
料	410	益	631			済	536	終	302
粉	793	畜	1740	**11 strokes**		液	659	殻	1832
紡	1415	留	412	頂	986	淑	1487	転	515

軟	1482	菊	1158	傑	1208	暁	1583	飯	768
欲	535	菜	870	弾	1099	晩	901	飲	489
野	128	斎	1269	陽	753	脹	1861	款	1607
販	1650	責	492	階	436	腕	1180	欺	1397
酔	1648	貫	1198	隊	366	勝	266	期	619
断	606	貨	220	随	1712	雄	1387	朝	395
釈	660	貧	836	幅	1234	棺	1730	敦	1976
斜	1488	章	505	帽	1105	植	438	敢	1713
訪	1412	袋	926	喫	1080	棋	1794	散	465
訳	190	異	581	喚	1405	棒	1121	敬	857
設	742	累	1284	堤	1404	検	785	勤	726
許	657	第	360	場	250	焼	671	割	1274
訟	1483	笛	1306	塔	1570	補	744	創	789
敗	670	符	951	堪	1854	裕	1592	尋	1569
赦	1739	翌	1421	揚	1401	硬	1598	喜	564
教	247	習	320	提	646	硫	1596	嵐	1902
救	698	盛	898	揮	1565	硝	1760	富	705
尉	1232	盗	1026	握	1566	疎	1601	寒	831
執	1231	票	774	換	957	短	261	募	1275
乾	1195	祭	423	援	1564	程	371	落	557
彫	1167	望	767	揺	1437	税	488	葬	1593
彩	1660	黒	286	項	1138	粧	1595	葉	179
郭	1793	魚	603	順	506	統	521	棄	1178
部	282	悪	804	慨	1399	絞	1394	歯	439
都	173	患	1206	慌	1692	結	359	森	152
郷	1165	雪	518	惰	1714	絡	944	晶	1582
郵	964	基	688	愉	1276	絶	630	最	291
釣	1836	啓	1205	湖	573	給	348	量	743
副	772	婆	1262	測	758	絵	380	暑	476
剰	1662	麻	1480	港	337	酢	1605	景	509
勘	963	庶	1661	湾	1136	貯	740	畳	958
動	169	庸	1302	湯	844	軽	598	塁	1571
亀	1921	康	860	温	382	軸	1258	登	559
率	808	鹿	1999	湿	1402	跳	1590	童	643
寅	1911	逮	1649	満	504	跡	1502	掌	1210
寂	1300	週	188	減	610	践	1802	営	780
寄	692	逸	1723	渡	897	路	677	覚	397
密	1118	進	194	渦	1823	詠	1161	貴	616
宿	549	虚	1484	滋	1395	註	1896	買	48
窒	1486	鳥	182	街	1181	詔	1213	賀	615
窓	1029	問	175	復	588	評	627	貿	871
常	199	閉	900	循	1707	証	697	費	608
堂	358	産	317	須	1946	詞	807	貫	1903
巣	1491	商	293	猶	1810	詐	1278	貸	472
崩	1490	粛	1652	媒	1403	訴	1182	蛮	1390
崇	1263			婿	1719	診	1081	紫	1392
菌	1651	**12 strokes**		禄	1998	就	759	衆	651
黄	469	博	525	殖	1396	報	295	装	1391
菓	946	傍	1406	雅	1211	鈍	1388	裂	1277
著	580	備	750	晴	784	欽	1925	筋	1137

等	294	象	809	碑	1758	夢	1425	像	524
策	695			腟	1984	蓄	1101	障	1145
筆	69	**13 strokes**		睡	1521	墓	650	際	424
筒	1125	傾	938	稔	1979	幕	1250	隠	1374
答	556	債	1515	稚	1513	愛	456	嘘	1905
番	257	催	1529	踊	1035	歳	1418	鳴	864
雲	478	働	170	辞	594	意	225	境	751
琴	1393	僧	1007	艇	1255	罪	748	増	693
集	279	傷	1008	絹	658	署	903	摘	1600
替	1398	隔	1753	続	548	節	683	慢	1289
智	1964	嘆	1292	継	894	豊	624	慣	442
普	1102	塩	730	群	769	農	394	憎	1217
悲	822	塊	1670	酬	1774	資	558	漸	1184
惣	1960	搬	1667	酪	1754	賃	555	漏	1599
惑	1131	損	449	賄	1776	義	244	漫	1389
煮	1179	摂	1665	賊	1426	盟	739	漂	1281
然	437	搾	1777	較	1155	碁	1757	演	806
無	386	携	1666	触	945	督	1737	滴	1381
焦	1606	慎	1669	解	577	禁	639	漆	1597
善	717	滝	1664	該	1504	雷	1204	漁	850
尊	856	溶	1517	詰	1507	電	222	徳	592
奥	930	滞	1251	詩	648	零	1106	獄	1219
堅	995	漢	401	詣	1885	聖	663	嫡	1385
堕	1511	滑	1512	試	354	楽	322	旗	601
圏	1160	源	893	誠	745	照	675	魂	1584
遇	1285	滅	1228	誇	1202	愚	1496	膜	1379
過	368	微	1668	詳	896	感	333	模	1218
運	373	嫁	1223	話	180	想	324	構	455
遅	1090	嫌	1901	幹	763	愁	1778	様	309
遍	1279	福	629	嗣	1671	慈	1194	磁	1288
達	391	禎	1973	飼	1156	瑶	1519	複	764
遊	587	禍	1756	飾	1014	塗	1759	端	1380
道	141	禅	1063	飽	1230	塑	1791	暢	1967
遂	1070	預	728	鉱	532	準	498	領	849
属	655	瑞	1956	鉛	1109	勢	299	種	232
雇	1604	暇	891	鉄	242	置	345	稲	1293
廊	1567	暗	576	鈴	1775	園	327	聡	1961
廃	1100	暖	917	殿	892	遣	895	雌	1586
痘	1715	腸	810	新	178	違	883	雑	365
痛	1020	腰	1009	鼓	1064	遠	326	精	457
痢	1716	腹	1010	靴	1907	廉	1514	緑	876
喪	1572	概	1196	献	1273	痴	1663	綾	1994
裁	1129	極	597	数	429	載	1257	練	482
幾	996	楠	1978	戦	399	虞	1877	緒	949
着	403	楼	1744	勧	638	虜	1755	網	1282
超	1051	頌	1874	裏	1076	業	292	綱	1052
越	1021	煙	914	誉	1203			綿	539
間	174	煩	1859	寝	918	**14 strokes**		維	1187
開	550	靖	1957	寛	1192	僚	1752	総	741
閑	1280	裸	1229	燕	950	僕	1838		

踏	1186	曆	1383	謁	1862	弊	1457	論	1357
醉	1589	歷	839	請	1190	幣	1400	隸	1873
酸	819	腐	1378	諸	617	履	1639	館	319
酷	1591	層	1183	諾	1452	遷	1447	錄	665
輔	1981	遭	1376	調	376	選	522	鍊	1872
疑	752	適	453	談	378	遺	656	錯	1747
語	231	爾	1945	論	406	遵	1864	錠	1745
認	649	聞	109	養	773	摩	1783	鋼	1509
誤	602	閱	1375	舖	1773	慶	1033	錦	1926
誌	55	閣	1373	鑄	1423	膚	1800	錘	1751
誌	919	關	289	銳	1449	慮	939	融	1359
說	216			餓	1580	趣	1047	親	211
誕	960	**15 strokes**		駒	1927	閱	1261	獸	1366
誘	1222	億	868	駐	1372	魅	1371	憲	622
靜	703	儀	1252	戲	1298			奮	818
銃	1185	噴	1239	歐	652	**16 strokes**		曇	1575
銀	379	囑	1297	毅	1919	凝	1370	罷	1870
銅	855	鄰	1040	敵	454	儒	1579	篤	1561
錢	843	墳	1461	敷	1039	壇	1711	薦	1748
銘	1731	撮	1241	影	929	壤	1844	薄	1091
銑	1588	撲	1464	劇	1078	壞	1578	築	711
歌	256	撤	1456	藏	779	擁	1750	薬	323
穀	815	徹	1638	質	1732	操	1367	薪	1560
驅	1271	衛	686	寮	1459	懷	1188	薰	1360
驛	189	衝	1117	審	1253	憶	1146	賢	1072
彰	1386	慎	1254	暴	833	憾	1694	繁	1092
豪	1915	潮	980	賞	621	激	1365	整	840
嘉	1377	潔	672	窯	1821	濁	1749	憩	1710
奪	1603	潛	1458	窮	1259	濃	1503	壁	1369
寡	1855	澄	1455	器	398	獲	1364	墾	1576
察	511	潤	1256	範	1067	嬢	1368	興	338
寧	1602	標	858	箱	935	衡	1358	磨	1985
暮	1140	橫	470	輩	1451	膨	1362	避	1746
慕	1382	權	420	靈	1299	燃	541	還	1557
蔫	1969	確	661	震	1123	樹	1053		
蔭	1908	稿	1505	贊	841	橋	1922	**17 strokes**	
罰	936	穗	1637	質	325	橘	443	優	1148
鼻	714	蝶	1970	緊	1088	機	415	償	1355
管	664	輝	1264	監	1460	積	766	嚇	1868
算	720	緣	1244	盤	1290	穩	1792	擬	1356
箇	1860	編	473	暫	1242	糖	1128	擦	1709
誓	1036	締	1243	憂	1518	縛	1361	犧	1811
需	754	緯	1636	擊	997	縱	1559	環	1568
舞	1003	線	389	慰	1066	縫	1235	騰	1554
肇	1968	緩	1454	默	1581	頭	519	燥	1708
製	570	輪	846	熟	1508	頼	1172	磯	1920
髮	1224	賜	1453	熱	300	輸	409	瞬	1556
熊	1987	賠	1808	勳	1296	謀	1054	矯	1827
態	835	賦	1635	墜	1240	諮	1558	聰	1055
墨	1494	課	568	導	755	謠	1071	纖	1704

績	805	**18 strokes**		離	909	譜	1346	護	796
縮	1142	濫	1858	難	800	鶏	1548	議	245
醜	1703	曜	14	観	567	鏡	647	鐘	1695
購	1353	礎	1701	鯉	1991	韻	1294	競	464
轄	1553	穣	1952	翻	1551	髄	1697	巌	1918
謹	1151	穫	1807	繭	1700	願	428	籍	1343
謝	765	糧	1552	藤	1975	鯛	1971	露	1074
講	702	職	432	藩	1549	鯨	1345	響	1111
謙	1545	織	431	覆	1699	艶	1914	馨	1930
鍛	1351	繕	1550	懲	1510	蘭	1990	懸	1283
鮮	1350	臨	783	闘	1056	薄	1073		
齢	1354	贈	1349	簡	1103	霧	1038	**21 strokes**	
爵	1875	鎮	1348	題	393	麗	1344	魔	1546
翼	1555	鎖	1698	癖	1702	警	902	艦	942
霜	1352	鎌	1996	暦	2000	璽	1866	鶴	1917
覧	934	額	749					顧	1341
礁	1706	顔	481	**19 strokes**		**20 strokes**			
懇	1171	顕	1245	瀬	1037	騰	1340	**22 strokes**	
療	1705	類	493	臓	921	欄	1696	襲	1094
厳	817	騒	1093	爆	923	醸	1547	驚	1061
闇	1899	騎	1174	繰	1347	躍	1342		
		験	355	識	486	譲	1307	**23 strokes**	
								鑑	1310

The "weathermark" identifies this book as having been designed and produced at the Tokyo offices of John Weatherhill, Inc. Typography and book design by Meredith Weatherby. Composition by Samhwa Printing Company, Seoul. Printed by Kinmei Printing Company, Tokyo. Bound at the Makoto Binderies, Tokyo. The type faces used are Monotype Times New Roman and, for the Japanese, handset Mincho.